GAMBLING
DEBT

GAMBLING
DEBT

ICELAND'S RISE AND FALL
IN THE GLOBAL ECONOMY

EDITED BY **E. PAUL DURRENBERGER** AND **GISLI PALSSON**

UNIVERSITY PRESS OF COLORADO
Boulder

Published by University Press of Colorado
5589 Arapahoe Avenue, Suite 206C
Boulder, Colorado 80303

 The University Press of Colorado is a proud member of
The Association of American University Presses.

The University Press of Colorado is a cooperative publishing enterprise supported, in part,
by Adams State University, Colorado State University, Fort Lewis College, Metropolitan
State University of Denver, Regis University, University of Colorado, University of Northern
Colorado, Utah State University, and Western State Colorado University.

∞ This paper meets the requirements of the ANSI/NISO Z39.48-1992 (Permanence of Paper).

Publication supported in part by the US National Science Foundation.

ISBN: 978-1-60732-334-1 (paperback)
ISBN: 978-1-60732-335-8 (ebook)

Library of Congress Cataloging-in-Publication Data

Gambling debt : Iceland's rise and fall in the global economy / ed. by E. Paul Durrenberger
and Gisli Palsson.
    pages cm
  ISBN 978-1-60732-334-1 (paperback) — ISBN 978-1-60732-335-8 (ebook)
  1. Iceland—Economic conditions—21st century. 2. Financial crises—Iceland—History—21st
century. 3. Global Financial Crisis, 2008–2009. 4. Debts, External—Iceland—21st century. I.
Durrenberger, E. Paul, 1943– II. Gísli Pálsson, 1949–
  HC360.5.G36 2014
  336.3'4094912—dc23
                            2014012194

Photo credit: Public protest in front of Parliament House in Reykjavík, Iceland, after the
financial meltdown. Photograph © goddur.

Publication supported by the National Science Foundation under award numbers 1209045 and
1430286. The opinions expressed in this work are those of the authors and do not represent the
positions or policies of the National Science Foundation.

A dark slumber cloaked the land. Not only had the sense of crisis passed without any serious attempts to rectify the flaws that had nearly caused the economy to grind to a halt, but unaccountably, the political right had emerged from the tumult stronger, unapologetic, and even less restrained in its rapacity and credulity than prior to the crash.

Philip Mirowski, *Never Let a Serious Crisis Go to Waste*

If we want to reduce the savage inequalities and insecurities that are now undermining our economy and democracy, we shouldn't be deterred by the myth of the "free market."

Robert Reich, "Political Uses of the 'Free Market' Myth"

Contents

Summing Up

At an August 2012 workshop at the University of Iowa, an unusual collection of scholars and students presented papers on the 2008 Icelandic financial meltdown. They were from anthropology, business, education, history, linguistics, literature, philosophy, and sociology, although anthropologists made up the majority of the group. Participants were encouraged to draft their papers and read each other's work posted online before the conference. Then once they assembled in Iowa City, they spent considerable time discussing and critiquing the work in person. The chapters in this book represent the initial thinking that went into the drafts, the collegial critique at the conference, and the final honing of the papers, accomplished with the support of a generous grant from the National Science Foundation (NSF).[1]

It seemed to us that discussion of the meltdown, both in Iceland and elsewhere, tended to be narrowly limited to economic issues, even though an increasing number of academic disciplines were weighing in on the various causes and implications of the financial crashes. We believed that the meltdown itself and its complex implications demanded both ethnographic description and some kind of comparison, and that an anthropological perspective, combined with perspectives from these other disciplines, could significantly raise the level of that debate.

The Iowa event turned out to be memorable and successful, with a set of original papers and lively discussion of many relevant issues. We thank all the people who attended the workshop, especially the presenters and discussants, for their contributions and the amicable company they provided. We also thank Anna Kerttula at the NSF for her support and enthusiasm in funding and arranging the event itself and for the publication of this book. Thanks likewise go to Jo Dickens and her colleagues at the University of Iowa Center for Conferences for their highly skilful handling of travel and logistics, which ensured the smooth running of meetings and related events despite the unexpected interference of nasty storms and inefficient airline companies. Finally, we thank Suzan Erem for her extensive help throughout. Not only did she skillfully attend to important details at the workshop to make things flow smoothly, she also carried out extensive editorial work, writing biographical notes for the chapters, preparing the final version of the articles to make them accessible to a broad readership, and helping us structure the overall volume.

E. Paul Durrenberger and Gisli Palsson
Iowa City and Reykjavík, 2013

NOTE

1. "The Icelandic Meltdown: A Workshop on the Causes, Implications, and Consequences of the Collapse of the Icelandic Economy," August 11–14, 2012, Iowa City, Iowa.

GISLI PALSSON AND
E. PAUL DURRENBERGER

Gisli Palsson is a professor of anthropology at the University of Iceland and visiting professor at King's College, London. E. Paul Durrenberger is emeritvus professor of anthropology from the University of Iowa and the Pennsylvania State University.

• • • • • • • • • • • • • • • • • • • •

The late twentieth century is widely heralded as the time that proved the inadequacies of communism and socialism and the triumph of the free market. Free trade interlinking an increasingly globalized economy would make war among nations unthinkable. Resources that previously supported governments were freed for private use. The liberated and self-regulating market would insure efficiencies unknown to centralized planners, remove the need for most regulations, and usher in an age of unknown plenty and prosperity for all. The foundation of the successful free market would be the unfettered individual. This ideology, known as "neoliberalism," would have tragic consequences for millions as its proponents such as the Chicago School economists and their political allies implemented its tenets around the world (Klein 2007; Mirowski 2014).

Iceland was not immune. Icelandic economists, ideologues, and politicians enacted their own version of neoliberalism centered on the instantaneous creation of wealth through the privatization of the resources of the sea—fish (Bergmann 2014). As it had done around the world, neoliberalism eventually concentrated wealth in a few hands. Although most of the world is accustomed to skewed distributions of wealth to aristocrats or successful capitalists, Iceland was not.

Since its independence from Denmark in 1944, Iceland had been positioned along with the other Scandinavian countries toward the egalitarian extreme of the scale, with everyone more or less in the same boat, as they say. As neoliberals won political victories in the United States, its Gini coefficient—economists' measure of wealth distribution—moved quickly toward a concentration of income and wealth in fewer hands and increasing levels of poverty for many. This was a pattern shared around the world even as proponents insisted that a rising tide lifts all boats.

For all of the ideological talk that neoliberalism promotes political democracy, there has been no evidence of such an association. On the contrary, persuasive evidence suggests that neoliberalism can only be held in place by undemocratic means. Iceland is by many measures a democratic land. Therefore, when neoliberal policies resulted in a meltdown of the national economy, which at best instantly doubled daily expenses and levels of debt for cars and houses, Icelanders took to the streets. The protests resembled those in Egypt or Libya rather than Scandinavia. But the government did not respond with violence. Rather, it changed.

The chapters in this book tell the story of how that meltdown happened, how it affected ordinary Icelanders, and what happened in its wake. Iceland was the canary in the global coal mine, a warning of danger. One of the side effects of the ideology of individualism and markets was the liberalization of gambling policies in the United States, where many states now have their own lotteries or licensed casino gambling. While these do raise revenues for the states, some have criticized it as a tax on the poor, because those least able to bear the cost fall deeply into debt when they compulsively gamble their earnings. Critics and apologists alike agree that the one sure thing about gambling is that, in the end, the house wins. But in the meantime, individuals entertain the fantasy that they can beat the odds with one more play, based on the illusion that they are somehow special, that the laws of chance do not apply to them. So we adopt the metaphor to describe what happened in Iceland when a few individuals came to see themselves as special, exempt from the rules of international finance, and thrust the whole country deeply into debt. Hence our title, *Gambling Debt*. The title is descriptive in another sense because these "Business Vikings" used the debts of their fellow Icelanders as collateral for their international gambling spree until the rest of the world called in the debt and the fantasies collapsed into a vision of a grim new reality.

Our story starts with a hapless Icelandic anthropologist on the way home from France on October 9, 2008.

"WELCOME TO THE BANK RUINS!"

While Gisli was in transit at Copenhagen's Kastrup Airport, it became evident that something spectacular was brewing. The TV screens throughout the terminal were running almost continuous live news about Icelandic banks and the national economy on the international networks, mainly CNN and Sky. One after another, the big banks of Iceland whose scale and profits had grown exponentially in just a few years were collapsing.

A couple of Icelandic businessmen were waiting with Gisli. Visibly drunk and disturbed by the news flashing on the TV screens, one was speaking loudly into several cell phones. He appeared to be one of the "Business Vikings" (*Útrásarvíkingar*, "outvading" Vikings) in the rhetoric of the time—a modern media version of the fabled medieval Vikings who heroically pillaged distant lands. The Icelandic term connotes the violence of an invasion (*innrás*), but in the opposite direction (*útrás*) (see Jóhannesson, this volume). Gisli was not on duty as an anthropologist. This was life itself, demanding, complicated, and messy, not the detached ethnographic observation of anthropological fieldwork. But the memory of the event would stay. There was panic in the air, and the atmosphere during the flight on Icelandair was gloomy.

Often, when Icelandic planes touch down on the airstrip at Keflavík, a stewardess warmly addresses passengers with "Velkomin heim!" ("Welcome home!") over the plane's loudspeakers, and people clap enthusiastically at the conclusion of another safe flight. This time, a man's voice came over the system and, in a deep cynical tone, said: "Velkomin í bankarústirnar!" ("Welcome to the bank ruins!"). There was a strange, hesitant, and somewhat neurotic applause.

The aim of this book is to discuss the meltdown rather broadly, emphasizing both a comparative perspective and propinquity to the relevant events, through a series of descriptions of the complex developments that led to the meltdown and their larger social and cultural implications and consequences. These chapters benefit from a certain distance in time—away from most of the heat that the meltdown generated—with a sense of hindsight.

THE MELTDOWN

"Life is saltfish" goes an old Icelandic saying. Fishing has been central to the Icelandic economy since the settlement when it provided food from one year to the next. At the beginning of the twentieth century, fishing became mechanized when fishermen put motors on their boats. With overfishing, the government of Iceland began various systems of quotas to manage the fisheries (Durrenberger and Pálsson 1989). That government action culminated in the Individual Transferrable Quota (ITQ). Market fundamentalists championed ITQs because they privatized access to the resources of the sea that had been an "open access" resource available to anyone who could retrieve and make use of it.

Now each boat received a quota based on its history of catches. Those who received quotas could buy, sell, or lease them (see Pinkerton, this volume). Quotas were a new form of property. Now anyone with a quota could use it as collateral for a loan. In spite of empirical evidence that the system was having deleterious effects, free market proponents defended it. Even as Iceland teetered on the brink of collapse, economist Ragnar Árnason (2008) wrote about the system in glowing terms because it created new wealth. He compared fish stocks to oil. The chief difference, he argued, was that fish stocks are renewable and oil is not. Thus profits from the exploitation of fisheries must also be sustainable. He blamed open access for all the ills of fisheries. There could be no profit in a system that a government subsidizes just to supply food or to keep people employed. The solution was privatization. Furthermore, he argued, quotas themselves come to have value when people can buy, sell, and trade them. The right to fish is a commodity akin to an oil lease.

The value of quotas depends on how much profit people expect them to produce. The total value of the Icelandic fishery, thus computed, increased as each new species came under this system (Helgason and Pálsson 1997). By 2002, the ITQ values came to equal more than 40 percent of the annual GDP of Iceland. Financial firms and banks began to build on the ITQs, and their value increased.

People sold their quotas and moved their winnings into the financial—or virtual—sector of the economy. Meanwhile, Iceland's consecutive neoliberal governments were reducing taxes, dropping regulations on banks, and privatizing the telephone system, the energy system, and, in 2000, the banks. Until that time, Iceland's government defined rights such as full employment, housing, health care, education, and retirement. Now corruption was endemic, and bending the rules became the order of the day as political parties handed out entire institutions, notably the banks, to powerful supporters while relaxing regulations on everything, including the banks and the environment. The situation spun out of control.

Níels Einarsson (this volume) discusses how the Icelandic ITQ policy allocated collective wealth unfairly to individuals and violated basic principles of human rights. Evelyn Pinkerton (this volume) sets those ITQs in comparative perspective, pointing out the significance of fisheries for economic modeling and differences in ITQ systems. James Maguire (this volume) indicates how ITQs moved fish from the smelly reality of real wealth into the equally malodorous virtual realms of finance.

Politicians lifted regulations so their banker friends could borrow heavily from foreign lenders and depositors. Soon Icelanders had spent up to 213 percent of their income per household (Holmes and McArdle 2008). The average paper wealth—stocks and other financial instruments—of households grew by about half.

Without regulation, banks kept only small cash reserves and borrowed heavily to finance the purchase of stocks across Europe. From 2001 to 2007 the value of the Icelandic stock market rose an average of 44 percent per year in what became a bubble that simply had to burst. As interest rates on the Icelandic currency, the krona, increased, Icelanders borrowed foreign currencies—euros, dollars, and francs—from foreign banks with lower interest rates. Meanwhile, Icelanders' salaries were paid in kronur, and Icelanders had to use kronur to repay foreign loans.

The 2008 financial crisis in the United States alerted foreigners that banks in Iceland were deeply in debt, that they had no cash reserves to repay the money they had borrowed, and that their debts were so big relative to the whole Icelandic economy that there was no chance of a government bailout. The three largest banks owed as much as all of Iceland could produce in ten years. Lenders stopped lending to Icelandic banks, and investors began to bet against the Icelandic economy. Beginning in 2008, the krona crashed and by October had fallen 43 percent relative to the dollar, which was also crashing against other currencies. In 2005 a dollar would buy about 60 kronur; by the end of 2008 it would buy about 125 kronur, and in 2009 it bought 148. The money Icelanders were being paid in wages had lost more than half of its value on international markets.

The price of virtually all products, including gasoline, doubled overnight because most consumer products, except for dairy, fish, and lamb, are imported. Icelanders had to pay off foreign currency debts with their greatly devalued Icelandic currency, so the price of debt multiplied as well. People who were in debt for twice their annual income were now facing repayments of four times their annual income.

To Icelanders who had usually felt relatively secure in the social contract with their government, this was a major dislocation. No longer was their economy secure, and it was certainly not in the hands of the super-smart supermen of the media stories. Instead, it had just collapsed and those noble Vikings were beginning to look like criminals. The collapse of US banks rewarded their financiers with great fortunes instead of jail time. Taking a leaf from that book, Icelandic bandit-financiers were jetting from one pied-à-terre to another and lording it over the whole world, annoying their egalitarian-minded Icelandic compatriots all the more.

While developments in Icelandic fisheries provided the superhighway into neoliberalism and collapse, marine science played an important role as well. Motivated by "sustainability" and "carrying capacity," marine science established a ceiling in catches through a political process characterized by the formation of a regulatory alliance of big capital (boat owners) and biology. This regulatory alliance, or capture, and the dispossession it involved (Harvey 2007) removed small-scale players from the game and set the financial machine in motion.

Also, there were other roads beside fisheries that took the country in the same direction. One of them was a new fusion of biomedicine, banking, politics, and international commerce through the activities of deCODE genetics. The early projects of deCODE, its patient studies, and its plan for the Icelandic Health Sector Database were launched to advance medicine by assembling and linking medical records, genetic characteristics, family histories, and other datasets pertaining to the Icelandic population (Pálsson 2007). Investors welcomed this plan to hunt genes among the genetically unique Icelanders, living descendants of Vikings.

During the financial boom, the rhetoric of the genetically superior Viking became increasingly common. Thus, the so-called Business Vikings were likened to figures of the saga age. Implicit was the assumption that the financial boom was the result of the peculiar nature of (male) Icelanders, shaped by a combination of the "noble" origins of Icelanders and their engagement with Icelandic nature over the centuries—in sum, of "Icelandic genes" (ibid.).

IN THE EYE OF THE STORM

In late 2008 the Icelandic government shut down the stock market and nationalized the banks. The United Kingdom invoked anti-terrorism laws to freeze Iceland's assets in British banks because so many British citizens and agencies had deposited money in Icelandic banks (the notorious high-interest IceSave accounts of Landsbanki) to get high rates of interest. The Icelandic government began to search for a large loan and finally had to accept $2 billion from the International Monetary Fund. This put Iceland in the same situation as Third World countries and Greece, countries facing structural readjustment and the abolishment of the social contract and therefore any security for citizens. This heightened the sense of insecurity of Icelanders, who were familiar with the negative impact of the IMF on other countries.

On October 6, 2008, three days before our hapless anthropologist boarded his plane full of nervous businessmen, Prime Minister Geir H. Haarde addressed the nation on television. Having outlined the apparently insurmountable problems of Icelandic banks and the rough road ahead, he concluded with a sentence that has become iconic for surrender and meltdown: "God bless Iceland!" ("*Guð blessi Ísland!*").

No Icelandic political leader had ever invoked God in such a way. For Icelanders this signified complete loss and total abandonment, a deep sense of the country being out of touch with all reality and beyond any reason or governance. This benediction seemed to abandon all possibilities to some unknowable higher power. To ever-pragmatic Icelanders it was like a skipper navigating a ship by praying to find his location instead of using his instruments.

If the prime minister himself had been reduced to a prophet and a clown, there was no hope in sight. Anarchy seemed to prevail, and the so-called Pots and Pans Revolution that followed was a logical response. This protest movement reached its unprecedented apex at the beginning of 2009 as downtown Reykjavík became a battleground of antigovernment demonstrations. The protestors enjoyed such high levels of public support that the entire government resigned in six days. Jón Gunnar Bernburg's (this volume) survey data indicate that the shared experience of economic loss coupled with outrage over political corruption, growing neoliberalism, and the necessity for reform fueled the protests. Hulda Proppé (this volume) discusses another form of public protest highlighting public disillusion with the resilient four-party structure of Icelandic politics. It takes the form of the Best Party, with its surreal politics and carnival playfulness (see Boyer 2013).

The traditional four-party system of Icelandic electoral politics entails a complicit mixing of business and governance, the dangerous conflation of public and private interests, and the tendency to allocate public offices more on the grounds of nepotism than on merit. The position of the director of the Central Bank, a key player in the advent of the meltdown, is a case in point (Johnsen 2014). Party allegiance and membership not only superseded any skill or training such a position might require, but the close affiliation of the director with the ruling party at the time undermined the independence of the institution and the public trust associated with it.

In October of 2008 the conservative Independence Party held twenty-five of the sixty-three seats in the Icelandic Parliament (Alþingi) and formed a coalition with the Social Democrats. But the rest of the Parliament and the public demonstrations forced the neoliberal prime minister to call a new election in May 2009 and then resign. The president then called on the head of the Social Democrats to form a coalition with the Left-Green movement until the election. She, in turn, appointed the ministers of the government.

As a new class, the superwealthy came into existence in Iceland, and the middle class was reduced to paupers. In the words of Einar Már Guð-mundsson (2009, n.p.), "All sense of values was thrown out of kilter. Ordinary vocations, like that of teaching, were considered déclassé. No one took the bus anymore. Everyone jumped into a new car, even cars people didn't own but bought on installment, from the tires up." Guðmundsson blames the development of the bubble on postmodern relativity, which renders politics, reality, and history irrelevant, echoing James Carrier's argument (this volume) that postmodernism in anthropology is itself a variant of neoliberalism, focused on a narrow understanding of individual freedom and autonomy. Thus, neoliberals can have free rein in politics and commerce as well as the media, where they put on airs. Guðmundsson (ibid.) observed: "As a consequence we are not only dealing with a financial depression which is rattling the homes of this country and all the foundations of society, but a profound spiritual depression which makes it even more difficult to face the financial one."

VIRTUAL ECONOMIES

For some analysts, "virtualism" represented a new political economy that brought together the domains of economy, society, and the community of economists modeling the market: "Perceiving a virtual reality becomes virtualism when people take this virtual reality to be not just a parsimonious description of what is really happening, but prescriptive of what the world ought to be: when, that is, they seek to make the world conform to their virtual vision" (Carrier 1998, 2). For Polanyi ([1944] 1968), true commodities are those produced through labor for exchange and use, while fictitious commodities—such as "financial instruments"—are not produced but bought and sold *as if* they were real. Because so much of the global economy is virtual, it is important for anthropologists and others to develop theoretical understandings of the transformation of capitalism to virtualism and the global and local implications of this transformation for culture and society.

Some anthropologists offered early warnings, based on their ethnographic work. Gillian Tett (2009), whose studies in central Asia sensitized her to the power of ethnography when she joined the *Financial Times* as journalist, played the role of the canary in her warnings. She not only predicted the crisis, but offered a sketch map of the financial world rhetoric, which was not represented in the media. Karen Ho's (2009) ethnography of bankers was also prophetic.

In 2007 Paul Durrenberger and Suzan Erem published an introductory anthropology textbook subtitled *A Field Guide to the 21st Century*. In their discussion of global economic processes, they asked, "How could a bunch of highly educated economists with Ph.D.s screw up the world's economy? By looking after the interests of corporations and the ruling class instead of the people of the planet" (Durrenberger and Erem 2007, 228). They suggested that money was akin to magic and the financiers were akin to shamans, and pointed out that their mistakes, far from being punished by the invisible hand of the market, are well rewarded. Finally, they showed that the corporate world supports a vast propaganda machine to make these ideas seem not only feasible but natural and inevitable.

No one who had thoughtfully analyzed the major components of the global system was surprised by the meltdown in the United States or in Iceland or subsequent events. In the second edition of the book, Durrenberger and Erem (2010) were able to show just how the Icelandic meltdown was part of this global pattern and why it was not a surprise.

NEOLIBERALISM AND ITS CHEERLEADERS

Often seen as one of the chief architects of neoliberal politics in Iceland, in 2001 political scientist Hannes Hólmsteinn Gissurarson published a book that emphasized the opportunities of neoliberalism in Iceland, speculating that by advancing privatization on every front, Iceland could become the richest country in the world. In an article published three years later, entitled "Miracle on Iceland" (Gissurarson 2004, n.p.), he argued, "Now, after a radical and comprehensive course of liberalization that mirrors similar reforms in Thatcher's Britain, New Zealand and Chile, Iceland has emerged as one of the world's most prosperous countries." Gissurarson (ibid.) wonders why Iceland turned in this direction: "The international trend toward economic liberalization played a role. Free-market economists like Friedrich von Hayek, Milton Friedman and James M. Buchanan all visited the country in the 1980s, influencing not only [Prime Minister] Mr. Oddsson but many of his generation. In the battle of ideas here, the right won." This was the beginning of what Einar Már Guðmundsson (2009) calls a web of deceit.

Tryggvi Thor Herbertsson, then director of the Economics Institute of the University of Iceland, collaborated with Frederic Mishkin, professor of economics at Columbia University, to produce a report (Mishkin and Herbertsson 2006) for the Iceland Chamber of Commerce on the state of the banks in 2006, at a critical moment in the inflation of the bubble. They concluded that the banks were solid, on track, and that severe criticism from foreign institutions, including Danske Bank, was unfounded and misplaced. Mishkin was paid US$135,000 for his work, while Herbertsson, who later became a member of Parliament for the conservative Independence Party, received ISK 3 million (Árnason, Nordal, and Ástgeirsdóttir 2010, 214n949, and this volume).

Another report, also commissioned by the Chamber of Commerce in 2006, written by Friðrik Már Baldursson, professor of economics at the semiprivate Reykjavík University, and Richard Portes, professor at London Business School, similarly drew a rosy picture of Icelandic banks, concluding a couple of years before complete meltdown that there were no serious problems ahead (Portes and Baldursson 2007). Again, the authors were generously paid for their work (Árnason, Nordal, and Ástgeirsdóttir 2010, 215n953). Overall, the two universities in the capital city operated as vanguards of the neoliberal turn, privileging the role of the market and silencing critique (Gíslason 2014). Both the media and the Office of the President docilely followed, giving voice to the cheerleaders and ignoring opposition. There was negligible space for canaries in this coal mine. All of this is documented in volume 8 of the parliamentary report on the meltdown (Árnason, Nordal, and Ástgeirsdóttir 2010).

Staff members at the two universities in Reykjavík also engaged in intensive ideological work that highlighted the uniqueness of the Business Vikings of Iceland. Thus, Svafa Grönfeldt, rector of Reykjavík University, suggested that the historic "battle with the forces of nature, weather, storms, volcanic eruptions, and isolation had fashioned individuals determined to survive whatever occurred"; this was reflected, she argued, "in the life of Icelanders through difficult times as well as now lately in the outvading turn of Icelandic companies . . ." (Grönfeldt 2007, 8). "We are just about beginning," she added.

Specific research projects at the University of Iceland were designed to explore, draw upon, and advance the unique characteristics of the Business Vikings, of *Homo oeconomicus islandicus*. In the fall of 2006, Snjólfur Ólafsson and colleagues in the Business Department launched a project "to explain the excellent success achieved by the outvading companies of Iceland" (Ólafsson 2007, 2), focusing on the personal characteristics of the business people and their organizational culture. The Business Vikings worked fast, took big risks, and operated within a strong organizational, entrepreneurial culture, leading the researchers to conclude that "the times ahead are exciting, both for the outvading companies and those studying them, as the outvasion [*útrásin*] seems on full course" (Ólafsson, Aðalsteinsson, and Guðlaugsson 2007, 9). "Everything indicates," Ólafsson and colleagues emphasized that "the out-vading of Icelandic businesses will remain strong in the coming years, pre-senting an occasion for various kinds of research and the publishing of results both domestically and abroad" (ibid., 4). The project was supported finan-cially by some of the banks and companies heavily implicated in the melt-down, including Actavis, Eyri Invest, Glitnir, Kaupthing, and Landsbanki. While the evangelical faith of the researchers and their close financial ties to the bankers drew some critique both from within and outside the universities, opposing voices were either weak or without a platform. The media paid no attention.

The financiers of Iceland were brash newcomers on the global financial scene. Even as they brandished large sums of money they had accessed via unsecured loans they knew they were outsiders, a kind of nouveau riche breaking down the doors of the European good ol' boys' sanctum. They developed and worked with the Icelandic media to promote the image of the genetically superior Scandinavian celebrated in Icelandic medieval literature. They disregarded the fact that while this image was celebrated by nineteenth and early twentieth century European nationalist ideologies, it had been largely discredited after the fall of the German version during World War II.

Media attention to the sagas was very selective. Not only did the imagery neglect the points of views of most of the women of the period, as well as of all the victims of Viking raids, those peasants who worked to produce the goods the Vikings pillaged and who considered them the scourge of a wrath-ful god, but also the Icelandic slaves, concubines, and bondsmen whose labor produced the wherewithal for the raiders' daily lives. They also neglected the archetypical biography of the saga hero. Part and parcel of that biography is to die young in glorious combat. Those young warriors who lived to be old are treated as tragic because they had been denied that necessary warrior's end. Intoxicated by their financial greed, their economic creed, their easy access to money via their political connections to make new rules, and the creation of new forms of wealth from nothing, these were more akin to the medieval model of the berserker. These new berserkers set out to conquer the financial world, much like the earlier ones, inebriated by their "berserk" mushrooms—and with predictable consequences.

Media echoed public relations efforts of the financial sector to portray the seemingly miraculous creation of wealth from nothing as the result not of some bankers' Midas touch but of their ruthlessness and cunning individuality rooted in Iceland's Viking past. Guðni Th. Jóhannesson (this volume) explores the genesis and history of the notion of "Viking spirit" and its relation to the earlier hype associated with the golden age of saga times (Pálsson and Guðbjörnsson 2011). The bankers became the new Vikings. As Kristín Loftsdóttir (this volume) shows, this ideology quickly overwhelmed popular images and stories, emphasizing the importance of individualism.

Schools perpetuated these nationalist images in textbooks and classes. Such ingrained ideas of Viking individualism fit the neoliberal mode and allowed little room for critique from inside or outside.

Neoliberal apologists in government and elsewhere were quick to try to co-opt artists with the logic that they, like the new Business Vikings, were also profoundly predisposed to novelty, risk, and untrammeled individuality (Grétarsdóttir, Ásmundsson, and Lárusson, this volume).

In the production discourse of the peasant era roughly between the end of the Commonwealth and independence from Denmark, the chief hero was the independent peasant, a character scrutinized and satirized in Nobel Prize–winning Halldór Laxness's novel *Independent People* (Laxness 1946). Later on, with competitive industrial fishing, the skipper (*skipstjóri*) replaced the fishing foreman (*formaður*) of earlier centuries to become the central character of production discourse (Pálsson and Durrenberger 1983). Following ITQs in fisheries and the financial bubble, fishing skippers became relegated to the sidelines as well. The Business Vikings now took their place.

Örn D. Jónsson and Rögnvaldur J. Sæmundsson (this volume) examine developments that generated the phenomenon of these new characters at the center of Iceland's latest mythology of Business Vikings, seeking to explain how a small group of entrepreneurs with limited capital and even less training managed to overthrow the national economy. As a former young banker himself, Már Wolfgang Mixa (this volume) explains how more conservative, older bankers were disregarded and even how younger bankers were disregarded when they suggested more attention to basics.

Always a perceptive observer, Laxness made acute and cynical remarks on the excessive bravery of fishing skippers. His descriptions seem to capture the new berserkers just as well. Drawing attention to frequent accidents at sea, he pointed out that they were caused not only by storms and high seas but also by irresponsible behavior: "An investigation . . . should be carried out to establish which skippers are seaworthy. At the same time, some ethical concept associated with seafaring might be re-evaluated, including the concept of the hero of the sea . . ." (Laxness [1944] 1985, 39). Discussing the case of a skipper who allegedly lost several crew members during unnecessary drama, Laxness continued: "What a primeval hero! What a Viking!" While, occasionally a reckless skipper might risk his crew, financial berserkers were risking the entire fabric of the community and economy. What Vikings!

If we had to seek a modern analog for the medieval Vikings, it would come close to the negative stereotypes of the murderous, violent, psychopathic motorcycle gang. McCloskey famously characterized neoclassical economists as "a motorcycle gang among economists, strutting about the camp with clattering matrices and rigorously fixed points, sheathed in leather, repelling affection" (McCloskey 1993, 76). The metaphor of the motorcycle gang usefully drew attention to the gender issue of neoclassical economics in somewhat humorous terms, pointing out the failure of neoclassical economics—and other schools in economics, for that matter—to meaningfully address the issue of solidarity, except within the patriarchal family and the corporation: "No wonder. *Vir economicus* sporting around the marketplace is stereotypically male: rule driven, simplemindedly selfish, uninterested in building relations for their own sake. A cross between Rambo and an investment banker, our *vir economicus* has certain boyish charms, but a feminine solidarity is not one of them" (ibid., 79).

After the Enron scandal, the financial meltdowns of 2008 and associated events, the metaphor of the motorcycle gang seems impotent and obsolete. In particular, it misses much of the hype involved, the fierceness in "going berserk," a condition echoed in Emily Martin's (2009) take on the "bipolar expeditions" of American culture. Perhaps an allusion to monster-truck or bulldozer gangs would be more appropriate, but even these seem weak and small-scale.

ANTHROPOLOGIES OF TROUBLE

Neoliberal politicians and policy makers drew upon professional economists who emphasized the "laws" of the market and the "natural" being of *Homo economicus* (McCloskey 1998). As Margaret Schabas points out in her analysis of the conceptual roots of economic thought, social as well as natural scientists "have implicitly agreed to divide the world into two parts. When physicists today think of the world they investigate, it is one with all the social institutions stripped away. . . . Economists, in parallel fashion, have come to adopt a domain of discourse that is similarly segregated" (Schabas 2005, 12). Yet, ironically, economists, business experts, and political scientists were often thoroughly imbedded in the social world upon which they were reflecting.

Neoliberalism remains a contested comparative term, witnessed by a recent lively discussion in anthropology (see, e.g., Gudeman 2009; Hart 2012; Kalb 2012). While it has been difficult to pin down and recent definitions vary depending on their emphases (see, e.g., Collier 2012), it seems to be a term sufficiently robust to address recent events in the global economy and community. Undoubtedly, the political forces we associate with neoliberalism are partly responsible for massive financial turmoil of recent years, along with several other developments, including the virtual economy, Internet technology, and globalization. But it is also true that the language of equilibria emphasized in the past needs to be tempered by respect for chaos, becoming, and contingency.

The meltdown resulted in immense social unrest, unemployment on an unprecedented scale, a threat to the contract between government and people, and massive loss of property—problems that still remain largely unresolved. There has been massive and costly research by the Parliament and state prosecutors on what exactly happened before and during the meltdown, personal responsibility, wrongdoings, and legal violations.

The coalition of the Social Democrats and the Left-Green Party that was established after the financial crash had an ambitious agenda—to revise the constitution in order to avoid similar crashes in the future and to make legal, social, and financial amendments for dealing with the immediate problems of families and companies. While it was successful in many respects, it failed in others. As events showed, the policies of ITQs were not easily reversed. Even the left-leaning government, less enthralled by neoliberal ideology than the earlier one, did not overturn the very quota system upon which the financial bubble was based. Many people feel that the process of getting back on track and bringing the relevant politicians, bankers, and Business Vikings to justice was painfully slow and inefficient (see, e.g., Higgins 2013) and that too much effort has been spent on attending to the demands of the IMF and the needs of banks and companies. The superrich are surviving, if not thriving, while the public is enmeshed in debt and collapses.

This partly explains the somewhat surprising return to power in 2013 of the parties that primarily were responsible for the neoliberal turn and the financial crash, the Independence Party and the Progressive Party. The success of their election campaigns and the formation of their coalition government testifies to the continued seductive appeal of neoliberal politics. The failures of the past were presented as the result of foreign developments independent of Icelandic politics and momentary problems unrelated to neoliberalism itself. Overnight, it scrapped the measures taken by the previous government to ensure greater returns to the community from the fisheries in order to provide necessary social services. The distracted market, it argued, would bring things back on course once it reverted to "normal" mode.

While bribery may not be widespread in Iceland, the massive contributions of financial firms to politicians amount to one form of corruption of democratic processes. Another form of corruption is the translation of political power into private and corporate wealth through privatization, as seen in the case of banks in Iceland in the advent of meltdown. Cris Shore and Dieter Haller argue (Shore and Haller 2005) that the financial scandals and crises of recent years pose a comparative challenge for anthropology to explore both the *meaning* of corruption from the "native" point of view and the different forms and implications in different contexts. This means moving beyond the rigid Western-biased Transparency International's (TI) Corruption Perceptions Index to "interrogate the *idea* of corruption as a category of thought and organizing principle, and to examine its political and cultural implications" (ibid., 2). Interestingly, while before the crash Iceland ranked low in corruption comparison, the parliamentary investigations that followed demonstrated extensive corruption.

While the grassroots movement that overthrew the government after the crash remains disillusioned and disappointed, its impact should not be underestimated. One important development in its wake, and an important emerging theme for further research, is a series of experiments with direct democracy and social media. Soon after the crash, a crowd-sourcing company drew upon social media to prepare for a National Meeting (*Þjóðfundur*) of 1,000 participants for outlining a new constitution. While the end result of this work remains unclear, and much depends on the formal, indirect democracy of the Parliament, it seems safe to say that the public has been sensitized to new avenues for democracy and alerted to potential signs of corruption.

The National Meeting emphasized that the key "values" of the past needed to be replaced by new ones (including morality, human rights, justice, well-being, and equality) upon which a new constitution had to be based. The language of old and new values may violate modern social theory, which has rejected norms and values as explanatory variables, insisting on flows and process, but perhaps sudden crises necessitate a social theory of value replacement. William Connolly outlines some of the challenges involved when "a surprising turn occurs, that is, when a period of intense disequilibrium issues in a new plateau that scrambles the old sense of progress and regress in this or that way" (Connolly 2011, 150).

The chapters in this volume paint a portrait of the meltdown from many points of view—from bankers to schoolchildren, from fishers in coastal villages to the urban poor and immigrants, from artists to philosophers and other intellectuals. Unnur Dís Skaptadóttir (this volume) discusses the impact of the meltdown on immigration and immigrants from Asia and Eastern Europe who had come to Iceland for its favorable wages, which they could use to support families at home. In the wake of the meltdown, social services for immigrants decreased as unemployment increased. Pamela Joan Innes (this volume) shows this trend in increased sensitivity to the issue of foreigners, in particular in the context of courses to teach the Icelandic language for foreigners, in terms of lack of funding.

Neoliberalism relies on private charities to take up the slack between need and government programs, as in George H. W. Bush's "Thousand Points of Light." James G. Rice (this volume) discusses his experience with one of Iceland's major charities and how it functions not to redress poverty but to reinforce the system that creates the problems. The meltdown has also affected rural and urban communities differently. Guðný S. Guðbjörnsdóttir and Sigurlína Davíðsdóttir (this volume) emphasize differences among the consequences for different school districts and communities. Margaret Willson and Birna Gunnlaugsdóttir (this volume) explore the implications of the meltdown for a rural fishing community.

Vilhjálmur Árnason is an Icelandic philosopher who was requested by the Parliament to join others in investigating the reasons for the financial crisis. He suggests (this volume) that one of the main reasons is an orientation at the heart of neoclassical economics and its political manifestation in neoliberalism—methodological individualism, the assumption that collective consequences flow from individual decisions.

Hannah Arendt suggested that Adolf Eichmann's participation in the Third Reich was an example of a wider phenomenon she called the banality of evil, that when people act consistently with a set of coherent cultural assumptions that inexorably lead to evil actions, the actions seem normal and acceptable because they are culturally consistent and validated (Arendt 1963). Several famous psychological experiments in the United States (Milgram 1974; Zimbardo 2007) came to similar conclusions. Yet Eichmann and his likes were not just following orders; they passionately believed in the cause and the system for which they worked. Neoliberalism is just as banal. We argue that the ideology of neoliberalism, with its powerful cultural revolution that started in the United States (Doukas 2003) and culminated in the Shock Doctrine (Klein 2007), its intense and incessant propaganda machine (Durrenberger and Erem 2010), and the ascent of the Chicago School economists and the formulation of neoliberalism as a coherent doctrine, is a historical parallel: It seems normal, no one seems responsible, and everyone is simply obeying orders. Neoliberalism has the justification of the "science" of economics; yet it has resulted in untold violence and misery around the planet. From the victims' point of view, this is indeed analogous to the Viking pillagers. The enactment of this ideology and the widespread acceptance of it, whether on the small scale or large, is a prime example of the banality of evil.

In Iceland the mine has exploded and the canaries are dead. Iceland was the first to fall. The most dramatic. The warning to others. The people have survived to learn that neoliberal meltdowns have nothing to do with genetics and everything to do with neoliberal economics and the political cronies who promote corruption, engineer multinational corporate cooptation of governments, and orchestrate massive propaganda assaults on news, on literature, and, most insidiously, on common sense. It is up to the rest of the world hear Iceland's story, to see the dying canaries in their own countries, and respond.

Prologue
Some Poetic Thoughts
Concerning Meltdowns

Einar Már Guðmundsson is Iceland's premier novelist. In this chapter, a collage of earlier writings, he weaves poetry and satire into a caustic review of the opportunists behind the boom and bust.

· · · · · · · · · · · · · · · · · · · ·

REALITY IS ALWAYS CATCHING REALISM BY SURPRISE

One rainy afternoon,
on a ship from a much-travelled dream,
Homer the singer of tales arrived in Reykjavík.
He walked from the quayside
and took a cab that drove him
along rain-grey streets
where sorry houses passed by.

———————

At the crossroads Homer the singer of tales turned
to the driver and said:
"How can it be imagined
that here in this rain-grey
monotony lives a nation of storytellers?"
"That's exactly why," answered the cab driver,
"you never want to hear
a good tale as much as when the drops
beat on the windows."

In the summer of 1990, Iceland and Albania played
a soccer game.[1] It was a momentous event. This was

DOI: 10.5876/9781607323358.c000

a qualifying game for the European Cup and one of the first portents that Albania intended to join the community of nations in its work and play. The country had been isolated for decades and hardly visited except by a handful of admirers of its dictator, Enver Hoxa. The players can be expected to have found it quite a novelty to venture beyond their country's borders.

Nothing was known about the Albanian national team until they arrived at Heathrow Airport in London where they made a stopover on their way to Iceland. It was a sunny Sunday afternoon in June when news reports reached Iceland that the Albanian team had been taken into custody at Scotland Yard. The players were suspected of shoplifting duty-free goods by the armful. During questioning, the Albanians referred to the "duty-free" signs that where hung up everywhere in the terminal. In their country various goods, for example beer, were free in their country on Sundays. For all they knew, this was the custom in other countries as well.

Though the Albanians escaped the clutches of Scotland Yard, their dealings with the eagle-eyed authorities were far from over. Upon the Albanian team's arrival in Iceland, an extensive customs search was made through their luggage, and the team was kept almost under house arrest until the time for the soccer game came around. So the Albanians' weak attempt to break their isolation with the rest of the world took on a very peculiar form.

Nonetheless, the soccer game began. The teams entered the field and lined up to hear their national anthems being played. But no sooner had the stadium brass band played a few notes than a naked Icelander, male, came running out from the spectators' stand and started hopping around in front of the Albanian team.

At once, six brawny policemen appeared on the scene. They rushed the naked man, rugby-tackled him, and piled on top of him in a heap. But the naked man was slippery as an eel and slipped out of their clutches. He ran past the Albanian team, waving his genitals at them. At that point the police managed to overpower him. They were last seen carrying him away.

Then everything went wild. The brass band stopped playing, and one of the stadium groundsmen switched on the microphone and began reciting an impromptu verse in celebration of the incident.

I have often wondered what it would have been like if an Albanian writer had been sitting in the capital city Tirana, a year or two before the game, imagining it taking place and describing everything that actually happened. He would have smashed every rule known to socialist realism and imposed by the Albanian Writers' Union on its members, because reality often outdoes fiction, and nothing is so poetic that reality has no place in it.

This Albanian writer has suddenly become very real.

As I visualize him, his predicament demonstrates two things. Firstly, how ridiculous it is to subject mental activity to rules, or rather, to social goals; and, secondly, how unrealistic it is to intend to be realistic, in particular when a predetermined definition of reality is used as a yardstick for truth.

Reality is always catching realism by surprise.

THE GHETTOS INSIDE US

We rose to the occasion and showed our homes.
The guest thought to himself: You live well.
Your ghettoes are inside you.

This is the poetry of the Swedish Nobel Prize–winning poet Tomas Tranströmer, and you could say that in these lines the truth of the poem manifests itself, the living core of that which is covered by no other layer.[2] No one knows what makes the poem the recipient of that which cannot be put into words by other means. Not philosophy, not theology, not rhetoric, much less politics, can tell the truth that the poem seems to catch on the rebound. There the magic and the magic of the language manifest themselves. Its magic is drawn from the thought, but a poem comes into being when a thought and emotion are enjoined.

"It is difficult to get the news from poems, yet men die miserably every day for lack of what is found there," wrote another poet, William Carlos Williams, who was also a medical doctor and knew exactly what he was talking about. That so few seek out poetry says more about modern times than about poetry. Poetry does not enjoy a huge following in the polls and has long been unemployed in the society of superficiality. But that's only part of it, because poetry springs forth under the most amazing circumstances and finds its voice, not in a dissimilar fashion to public protest. Poetry is a struggle against the void and a search to find substance in life. The economic boom which has just passed, the period of an empty chase after the void. Thus its epitaph.

So, I can go on knitting, but what about the ghettoes? Do they live within us? How do we measure such a trade balance? Is there much inflation in pain? What is the stock index of joy? But should we rather ask: What happened to caring amongst all these riches? Did the economic system of liberalism, which is now coming to pass, lead us away from compassion and solidarity? How tasty was the big cake, which was much discussed and digested by the high priest of neoliberalism, Professor Hannes Hólmsteinn Gissurarson, and who is meant to clean up after all the dyspepsia it has caused? Other people of other nationalities came in and did the work. How did we regard these people? How did we receive them? Did anyone say, "These are just foreigners. We'll get rid of them once the job is done." Did we never hear those sentiments expressed? How have the asylum seekers been received, our brothers in need? Has the Reverend Pálmi Matthíasson told the police and the judiciary to be kind to them? How about the bishop telling the Icelandic directorate of immigration to hug a few fugitives? Does the president have a mind to invite them to dinner at his residence at Bessastaðir, like Martha Stewart and the financial grandees?

There is a cannibal joke that goes something like this.[3] A cannibal is flying first class. The stewardess comes along with a menu, a spiffy one with a vast selection. The cannibal is as polite as can be, as is a cannibal's wont, supposedly, at first encounter. The cannibal peruses the menu and then says to the stewardess, "I don't see anything I fancy on the menu. Would you please bring me the passenger list?"

I'm not going to compare Iceland's billionaires, who, in cahoots with the government, have left us in the lurch, to cannibals. Not literally. But after having been handed over virtually everything on a silver platter, banks and state-owned companies seem to have said to the government and inspection agencies, "There is nothing we fancy on the menu. Would you be so kind as to hand us the national registry."[4]

WORLD LIGHT

In Halldór Laxness's *World Light*, first published in English in 1969, two characters discuss the state of the financial system[5]:

> "Friend," said the Second Gentleman, and embraced the poet. "The Bank's been closed. The English have closed the Bank."
>
> . . . .
>
> "And why have the English closed the bank?" asked the Second Gentleman. "It's because there's no money left in the Bank anymore. Juel has cleaned out the Bank. Juel has squandered all the money the English lent this ill-starred nation out of the goodness of their hearts. Juel has sunk all the English money in the depths of the ocean. That's why the Bank's been closed." (Laxness 1969, 464)

If caring was scant among the riches, how will it be in times of deprivation, which now loom over us? Now that Juel has emptied the banks?[6] The boom passed some by. We witnessed pensioners languishing in garrets, vagrants without a roof over their heads. The low wages were preposterous; the average wage hardly covered debts; and families were barely able to scrape by even without plasma TVs, campers, or salmon fishing. There was no mistaking it, people with the lowest salaries were not spending the money that streamed in from the high-interest, foreign-invested IceSave accounts. I do not intend to plead innocent, but I had never heard of these IceSave accounts until the terrorist act was passed against me.[7]

But speaking of solidarity: There were people who said the Bónus discount stores were the best wage supplement possible, and considered Jóhannes, the owner of the Bónus stores, a sort of Robin Hood of the people. Some whispered of dodgy business practices, but others said that the unions should just be dismantled because Bónus would take care of things; and to some this seemed to have been the case. At any rate we are now saddled with feeble unions that instead of fighting for workers' rights have considered the business world their forum and gambled with peoples' pensions, often with utter lack of responsibility. But it's not just that: We are also saddled with the Bónus tycoons and all the other Juels who have pauperized the country but lie in wait to snatch it up again.

The world of commerce seems about to get its way, and people are left asking, what hold does this lot have on the political parties? The tycoons are completely indifferent to the fact that their presence is not requested. They force their way through the door and raid the store. We, our children, and our grandchildren are in turn saddled with their debts. People speak of thousands of billions from the Baugur Empire,[8] and then there are the IceSave accounts of Landsbanki.

Again, Halldór Laxness comes to the fore, but this time with a description from *The Great Weaver from Kashmír*:

> At the end of a bad year one can always be certain that an ingratiating lanky fellow with a golden tongue slinks in through the back doors of the banks: this is Örnólfur Elliðason. He makes suggestions, using carefully chosen blandishments, concerning whether it might not be more prudent for the banks to empty their vaults into his companies' hands than for the state to go bankrupt. He asks, with deepest respect for the public, whether he might not be allowed

to reach into the pocketbook of every man, woman, and child in the country, and filch a third of the value of every króna so Ylfíngur could continue to speculate. (Laxness 2008, 192–93)

Should we compare the IceSave accounts to plagiarism? If an Icelandic author plagiarized the work of, let's say, an English or Dutch writer, the book would become so popular that the Icelander would make money hand over fist, although not by the standards of the Icelandic jet set, just everyday standards. If he were found out, a trial would ensue and the author, but not his nation, would be called to account. This should apply to the IceSave accounts. The responsibility should rest with the Landsbankinn and those who ran it. It is as clear as day that the tycoons are not going to shoulder any responsibility because they don't see themselves as bearing any. They understand the word responsibility only in a legal sense. They don't say anything except: "I did nothing illegal." In their world the word "responsibility" has no social or moral meaning. Such is the world of commerce. The attendant greed seems to breed a disease of the soul, a psychopathic state. It is said such people believe their own lies. Now, I'm not psychoanalyzing tycoons, but this rhymes with their excuses for the bank collapse and their denial of all responsibility. Still, economists must warn of such diagnoses, that the collapse should be viewed as an example of human frailty. The economic principles are the core, but the shadowy sides of the avarice are the manifestation. Did the society of libertarianism care about any rules? If we look at this in light of *Hávamál*, which can be called the moral manifesto of our cultural heritage, the question resounds: Could the men who were turned into monkeys by money have been tamed? That was the role the politicians should have played, but instead it seems that the monkeys tamed *them*. How did they do it?

In an article published in the cultural journal *Skírnir*, Icelandic economist Þorvaldur Gylfason states: "Many warned of the danger inherent in placing the banks in the hands of inexperienced individuals, both within the banks and outside them, but no heed was paid to these warnings" (Gylfason 2008, 491–92). Yes, what hold did the tycoons exercise over the political parties? Gylfason writes in the same article:

This course of events was initiated a quarter of a century ago with the establishment of the quota system for the community fishery sector, when the politicians agreed on granting the leading magnates of the sector free access to a communal resource of the nation. The unjust decision for which all the parties in Parliament bore a communal and heedless responsibility, inured the moral consciousness of the politicians to such an extent that it would not be long before other even more drastic measures of the same nature were taken. Why should men who had no compunction about creating a new class of affluent men with the free surrender of fishing quotas into the hands of the happy few hesitate to behave in a similar fashion when it came to the privatization of the banks and other government companies? The way things turned out was a forgone conclusion. (ibid., 495)

We can wind this down with a third Halldór Laxness quotation, this time from *Christianity at Glacier*. The question is asked, "What's a quick-freezing plant?" And the answer is:

> It's an Icelandic enterprise. Jokers build them with a subsidy from the State, then they get a subsidy from the State to run them, next they get the State to pay all the debts but finally go bankrupt and get the State to shoulder the bankruptcy. If by some accident some money even happens to come into the till, then these jokers go out and have a party. (Laxness 1972, 245)

BANKS AND VOLCANOES

"Icelanders can neither control their banks nor their volcanoes," said the British comedian John Cleese when he had to take a taxi from Oslo to Brussels.[9] According to media reports, the cab ride cost 650,000 crowns [US$5,100]. It is likely the comedian's hosts or those who were expecting him in Brussels paid the entire fare. Someone as indispensible as John Cleese does not pay his own cab fare. But no further story follows, and it remains to be said whether he planned to meet Mr. Brussels, the European Union itself. Then again, paying a single cab fare should not make much of a difference to John Cleese considering all the advertisements he appeared in for Kaupthing Bank.[10] He was the face of Kaupthing for some time and thus plays his part in the deregulation and collapse of the banks.

John Cleese was like a cheerleader on the sidelines, in some ways similar to a court jester and yet not quite ensconced in the traditional role of the jester. His function was to embellish a situation which was actually criminal, and as such he helped preserve faith in the bubble economy of the Icelandic financial princes, and in their casino capitalism. He sold himself for the benefit of their world. I do not know whether the sum John Cleese was paid for his role in the Kaupthing advertisements appears in the Alþingi's investigative report on the collapse of the banks, but Kaupthing's Resolution Committee should be able to find the figure among the accounts of the failed bank. His job was to praise Kaupthing and the executive board's dreams of world domination; and expenses were not spared for Kaupthing's cronies. As a case in point, the bank's directors lent a British pub owner the equivalent of the entire state budget. They lent each other and their friends huge capital, and sure enough the company's bankruptcy ranks as one of the largest in world history. The bank's directors earned 100,000 crowns [US$750] an hour. The highest monthly salaries were equal to the Nobel Prize award money. Accounting experts have calculated that payment of their wages would have begun long before Christ had they been earning an average salary.

One bank director, Sigurður Einarsson, was wanted by Interpol for some time. Another bank director, Hreiðar Már Sigurðsson, sat in custody for a few days. In pictures they look like Laurel and Hardy. Although it is not possible to call them comedians, bank director Einarsson made light of opening 200,000 crown [US$1,500] bottles of red wine, one after the other, according to Davíð Oddsson, the former director of the Central Bank. This appears in the report of the Alþingi's Special Investigation Commission. Although Oddsson waged his own war against the directors of Kaupthing and made a public show of closing his savings account with the bank in protest of the bank directors' salary policy, he nonetheless lent them immense amounts of money in the final stages. It appears Sigurður alleges Davíð had been rude to him at parties, not unlike Lenin complaining in a telegram to Stalin that he had been impolite to his wife on the phone.

Regardless of Sigurður Einarsson, Hreiðar Már Sigurðsson, Lenin, Stalin and Davíð Oddsson, I hope that John Cleese enjoyed his trip from Oslo to Brussels and laughed a lot on the way, both at the volcanoes and the banks as well as the incredible connections linking the two. As to the cab fare, 650,000 crowns is peanuts in comparison with the money our government will squander on trips from Reykjavík to Brussels in order to get us accepted into the European Union so that jackalackeys and their sweethearts in power suits can walk the halls over there and marvel at how much progress has been made since the four freedoms of the Common Market were discovered, not to mention all the menus in Brussels and the beer, the marble, the glass, and the steel. On the other hand, few people mention Grímur Thomsen, a nineteenth-century poet and public servant. He worked in foreign affairs for the Danish king and was one of the first scholars to discover the works of Hans Christian Andersen. He wrote a long essay about the latter and another essay on Lord Byron, but while staying in Brussels, Grímur wrote a letter to a friend saying he found the city so uninspiring that he was unable to get an erection.

Such is life in these years of our Lord: The world slows down and that may be a good thing. Airplanes come to a halt in the air or they cannot take off. Airlines count their losses from volcanoes, but the volcanoes have no concern for airlines. Air transport is paralyzed all across Europe because of ash coming from Eyjafjallajökull. Airports close in the British Isles, in the Nordic countries, and in Belgium. John Cleese has to take a taxi from Oslo to Brussels. Television reporters around the world compete to pronounce the name of the volcano. It fares rather badly, but this is precisely what the advertisements with John Cleese were about, the pronunciation of the word "Kaupþing." But we Icelanders do not think it strange to pronounce the names of such mountains as Kilimanjaro or Himmelbjerget. No, the English comedian cannot fly on the wings of his wit or send himself with the devil as magicians did in the Middle Ages.

It is not more complicated than that, but British blogs announce: "First they steal our money with collapsing banks and then they spew ash over us. These Vikings—next they will steal our women!" *Cash* rhymes with *ash* and *ash* with *cash*. "We asked for cash, not ash!" exclaim the British. Thus can dramatic events bring out people's sense of humor, but humor is sometimes the flip side of despair. I suppose it will end with the British government making Icelanders responsible for all the airline tickets sold in Europe, and our government will grant a state guarantee on them. Our politicians will say that it is only polite to pay for the airline tickets as it will serve us well in the international community, even if we bear no legal obligation to pay, for surely we have the means. And this is to say nothing of negotiating a payment postponement and the fact that the payment could save the global air transport industry. But the Briton who is afraid for the women can take comfort because that deed is done. There exists a theory which attributes the lack of pretty women in England to the fact that they were kidnapped by the Vikings and brought here to the northerly seas so they could keep us warm and multiply.

A good example of this is recounted in *Laxdæla saga*. Melkorka, daughter of the Irish king, was purchased by Höskuldur Dala-Kollsson, a famous figure in both Norway and Iceland, from Gilli the Russian at a gathering on the island of Brännö. Höskuldur believed her to be mute for she refused to speak in protest of her captivity. She raised Höskuldur's son, and he spoke both her Celtic tongue as well as his father's Nordic tongue. This is a story of great importance. I do not know whether it is possible to trace Prime Minister Gordon Brown's anger towards Icelanders back to these ancient disputes over women, but the above-mentioned quotation testifies to a similar fear. However, it is not at all certain whether the British correspondent or Gordon Brown or his successors fully understand this fear, for it resides in the subconscious.

On the other hand, there is solid ground on which to argue that there are Britons who went broke because Icelandic barons took over their savings and lent them to their friends who squandered the money on empty foolishness, on all kinds of toys, jets, yachts, ski hills, and luxury apartments. They held banquets where they allowed politicians to play and bankers to amuse themselves in no small measure, if the bills from escort services are to be trusted along with other rumors that have circulated since everything collapsed. Even so, none of them ever came home with an Irish princess like Höskuldur Dala-Kollsson, but of course there is no longer a king in Ireland. Some of these barons live in London, where they worked with their money, so it ought to be easy for the British authorities to collect from them. But they are more interested in collecting from the Icelandic public, and we are only waiting for the day that they hold us accountable for the volcanic eruption as well and invoke terrorist laws against volcanoes.

WAR CRY FROM THE NORTH

We must ask: At the end of the day, what brought our society success?[11] It is not the smug ignorance that has taken so much from society without giving anything back. It was the struggle of the working class, the class struggle, that brought us success. It was the last century's class struggle which brought us a robust welfare system, a school system, a health system, telephone lines, swimming pools, pension funds, and the list goes on. The so-called boom consisted of privatizing the yields of the class struggle, the communal assets of the people, and then turning them into a product. What was communal property before—the fish, telephone lines, and banks, for example—was brought to private parties on a silver platter and consequently squandered. Neoliberal spokesman Hannes Hólmsteinn Gissurarson said himself that the boom consisted of invigorating the so-called "dead capital," i.e., the communal assets of the people. The trafficking with this capital created a turnover in society, a boom, but now this traffic has come to a stop. It could in fact be said that there has been a traffic accident. The assets of the people have been squandered on useless junk, glass palaces, and shindigs, and little remains to be sold. Even if a large part of the boom consisted of an economic bubble grounded on pipe dreams, one must not forget that the basis of all this was the real assets of the people: the fish, the pension funds, and the state companies. The pension funds have been sucked dry in collusion with utterly corrupt governments, while the privatization of the banks enabled the billionaires to acquire firms and companies and pay themselves dividends without creating anything of value. The communal assets of the people, the "dead capital," was squandered. It is our role to retrieve it.

Therefore we must fight, protest, and stay alert, establish a new economy where the resources belong to the people, and where whatever is theirs is made so by constitutional right: the right to exploit natural resources and the fish in the sea. The special privileges of the wealthy must be abolished, legal ones as well as tax privileges, and all privatization must be approached with caution. At the moment, emergency measures to aid families and companies are called for. We must break free of the curse of corruption and write our own constitution, and we must not use the depression as an excuse to shirk our responsibility to uphold civil projects, education, and culture for those in need, the poor, immigrants, and refugees. Having said that, I leave you here so you can go on and add what you wish to change, but I finish my piece with the poem "War Cry from the North":

> You who live with an island in your heart
> and the vastness of space
> a sidewalk beneath your soles.
>
> Hand me the Northern Lights!
> I shall dance with the youngster
> who is holding the stars.
>
> We peel the skin from the darkness
> and cut the head off misery.

The author would like to thank translators Bernard Scudder, Jónas Knútsson, and Alda Kravec for their work on this chapter.

NOTES

1. The poem, titled "Sagnaþulurinn Hómer," and the passages in this section were originally published as part of the essay "Um raunsæi" in *Kannski er pósturinn svangur* (Reykjavík: Mál og menning, 2001), 13–16; translated by Bernard Scudder.

2. This essay is a version of "Kapítalismi undir Jökli" in *Hvíta bókin* (Reykjavík: Mál og menning, 2009), 59–60; translated by Jónas Knútsson.

3. The following passages were first published in "Má ekk bjóða yður þjóðskrána?" in *Hvíta bókin*, 21–22; translated by Jónas Knútsson.

4. The national registry (Þjóðskrá Íslands) is the census that keeps track of every Icelander born on the island.

5. The passages in this section appeared in slightly different form as part of "Kapítalismi undir Jökli" in *Hvíta bókin*, 60–61, 62–64, 65; translated by Jónas Knútsson.

6. Juel J. Juel, one of the characters in the novel, is a fishing entrepreneur.

7. After the crash Great Britain used its Anti-Terrorism, Crime and Security Act of 2001 to impound the (falsely) high-interest IceSave accounts that held British funds.

8. Baugur was a major investment firm that failed in the crash.

9. This section was originally published as "Bankar og eldfjöll" in *Bankastræti núll* 2011 (Reykjavík: Mál og menning, 2011), 38–44; translated by Alda Kravec.

10. Kaupthing Bank is one of a handful of entities that made a killing off the boom at the expense of Iceland's citizens.

11. This section was part of a speech delivered on August 13, 2009, at a protest rally. The concluding poem, "War Cry from the North," was originally published as "Herhvöt úr norðri" in the poetry collection *Í auga óreiðunnar* (Reykjavík: Mál of menning, 1995), 11.

GAMBLING DEBT

*Before the
Beginning*

I

Vikings Invade Present-Day Iceland

Kristín Loftsdóttir is a feminist anthropologist who takes on the use of the "Business Viking" image to promote the neoliberal agenda, showing how twentieth-century schoolbooks helped set the stage and then promulgate the sexist and otherwise inaccurate historical memory of a country.

• • • • • • • • • • • • • • • • • • •

It is August 2007, a year before the economic meltdown. Muscular and half-naked with weapons in their hands and helmets on their heads, Iceland's three main business tycoons, Björgólfur Guðmundsson, Jón Ásgeir Jóhannesson, and Hreiðar Már Sigurðsson flicker across my television screen, photoshopped as Vikings. I'm somewhat astonished because these images are airing in the context of an interview I gave earlier in the day. I had given a talk at my university about the similarity between the current icon of the successful Icelandic businessman—or "Business Viking"—and textbook portrayals of Icelanders from the early twentieth century touting the uniqueness of Icelanders. I had noticed this similarity when collecting data on two entirely different projects—one on Icelandic music performance, the other on images of Africa in schoolbooks. The interview decorated with the doctored images was supposed to be about this comparison I had presented at my university earlier that day. The images doctored by the news staff intensify the entertainment value of my results, which, after all, is what the news is about these days. The narrator proclaims: "Image and reality don't always go together, as this comparison was

DOI: 10.5876/9781607323358.c001

3

only done for entertainment value."[1] I'm puzzled. Which comparison is the narrator calling entertaining—the one I made in my interview or their visual illustration of it?

I start with this story because it vividly reflects the hegemonic authority of the Business Viking narrative in Iceland prior to the economic crash. The power and pervasiveness of that narrative made it absurd to locate the present-day nationalistic image of the Business Viking within a historical frame of nationalism and masculinity. It must be stressed that these news reporters still wanted to create a space for my critical analysis within the context of news that mainly glorified these men and their business adventures. Perhaps it was difficult to do so at that time without placing it as the last story, reflecting how critical analysis was at the margins of society.

In this chapter I outline this similarity between the early twentieth-century textbook portrayal of the settlement of Iceland and the mid-2000s celebration of the Business Vikings in Iceland. I assert that ideas about Iceland's recent economic expansion were deeply shaped by nationalistic symbols that carry a strong gendered component and touch upon longstanding anxieties regarding Iceland's historical position in the world. In turn, these symbolic self-perceptions were part of intensified neoliberalism in Iceland.

The Icelandic "economic miracle," as it was called at the time, began in the mid-1990s when Iceland adopted strong neoliberal economic policies that promoted the gradual liberalization of banks and capital flows and emphasized global integration as demonstrated by the adoption of the EES [European Economic Space, later changed to European Economic Area—ed.] treaty in 1994 (Ólafsson 2008; Sigurjónsson and Mixa 2011). The October 2008 crash, when the government bailed out three major commercial banks, created a paradigm shift in which this narrative lost its power almost overnight. As if we were in the fairytale by Hans Christian Andersen in which a child suddenly declares, "The emperor has no clothes," the aftermath of the crash caused some Icelanders to suggest that the Business Vikings who had been so celebrated before the crash now could be guilty of treason (Jóhannesson 2009a).

My theoretical perspective is influenced by postcolonial theorists who focus on the interrelationship between past and present (Dirks 1992) and by feminist critical thinkers who emphasize the creation of gender-specific perspectives in the context of nationalism (Yuval-Davis 1997). My work is also influenced by classic anthropology's holistic perspective, which holds that no aspect of human society can be understood without considering its relationship to other aspects, and the importance of investigating phenomena cross-culturally (Durrenberger and Erem 2007, 6). When applied to the Icelandic economic crash, anthropology teaches us the importance of investigating the global and historical context of the crash, and the need to look at economic aspects in relation to other spheres of Icelandic society (Loftsdóttir 2010, 190). In other words, the economics have to be analyzed in the context of larger social and cultural questions (Schwegler 2009) and as integrated into wider webs of meaning and selfhood.

THEORETICAL OVERVIEW

Intensified global processes have led to new questions regarding national identity. When scholars first started to address the effects of globalization, some predicted it would undermine nationalism (Appadurai 1996). Nations, however, seem to remain one of the most important everyday settings in which people imagine themselves (Ginsburg, Abu-Lughod, and Larkin 2002, 11). Furthermore, "culture," once a term used only in the social sciences, has become a global commodity. Globalization has simplified and packaged cultural stereotypes, allowing "culture" to gain wide currency with the increased neoliberalization of the global economy (Lavie and Swedenburg 1996, 6). Branding nations the same way a company trademarks a product also relies on the idea of culture. The prevalence of nationalism in the age of globalization and neoliberalism makes it important to analyze how neoliberalism and nationalism have reconciled with one another. I assert that the strongly nationalistic idea of the Business Viking is in concert with the neoliberal emphasis on flexibility and individualism. Neoliberalism, as scholars have increasingly stressed, is not only about specific policies but also about a particular rationale that is negotiated on a political and uneven field (Schwegler 2008, 686).

Feminist scholars have demonstrated that nationalism is deeply gendered, for example, in Mary Louise Pratt's (1990) criticism of Benedict Anderson's (1983) nation as an imagined community. Pratt (1990, 50) asserts that concepts such as fraternity and camaraderie reflect the nation as a community of males. Her point reflects the ongoing criticism of how theories of nationalism have tended to ignore gender and articulate ideas of women and men differently according to the ideas of the nation (see also Yuval-Davis 1997). In Iceland, as elsewhere, nationalistic identities have certainly been constructed through deeply gendered ideas. This is clearly demonstrated by Sigríður Matthíasdóttir's (2004) research showing that at the turn of the nineteenth century, when important Icelandic nationalistic ideas were being formed, crucial symbols of "Icelandicness" such as logic, courage, and honor were primarily assigned to males. This notion of maleness constituting crucial Icelandic characteristics is also apparent in Icelandic texts about non-European people (Loftsdóttir 2009; 2010).

Furthermore, this treatment of culture engages with older ideas and creates new forms of subjectivity. Nationalism involves a particular remembering and reconfiguration of the past and has not decreased in the present, as underlined by Andreas Huyssen's (2001) work. The successful marketing of memory creates a framework for understanding the present. In a sense, the past becomes a resource used by different actors in different contexts for understanding the present and making it meaningful.

As postcolonial theories claim, colonialism and imperialism helped shape European identities (Dirks 1992; Gilroy 1993). My research shows how Icelandic identity has been affected by its position as both a dependency of Denmark and as a country that, while not a colonizer itself, has participated in the racist and imperialistic attitudes of other colonizing powers (Loftsdóttir 2009; 2012a). While Iceland was not colonized brutally like many other countries were, it was still a subjugated country. Therefore, analysis of Icelandic identity must be enriched by how Icelanders saw their relationship to Denmark as a Danish dependency within the context of other colonized people (Loftsdóttir 2012a). As I have discussed in other publications, the acceptance of the images and actions of the Business Viking in Icelandic society in the 2000s can be linked to Icelandic anxieties of being classified with the "wrong crowd," a fear dating back to the period when Iceland was forming its consciousness as an independent nation state while still a Danish dependency (ibid.; Loftsdóttir 2012b). Images of the Business Viking were thus made meaningful through a particular social memory of times when Icelanders were under foreign rule, indicating a search for recognition as a legitimate nation deserving independence.

ICELANDIC IDENTITY AND SCHOOLBOOKS

In 1262 Iceland became a subject of Norwegian rule. In 1536, when the Norwegian and Danish kingdoms were unified, Iceland became a part of the Danish kingdom. It remained so until 1944. Throughout this period Icelanders maintained a separate identity (Karlsson 1995), and their strong pride in Icelandic culture created a fertile environment for nationalistic ideas (Hálfdanarson 2000, 90).

By the mid-nineteenth century, Iceland was one of Europe's poorest countries. In spite of being a financial burden on Denmark, it had struggled for independence for a century (Karlsson 1995). The final struggle started in the mid-nineteenth century under the influence of Icelandic students in Copenhagen who were affected by nationalism in Europe (Hálfdanarson 2000). During this time medieval Icelandic literature (the sagas) and the Icelandic language became the most important factors in the creation of an Icelandic national identity. They served as a basis for demanding the nation's independence (Pálsson and Durrenberger 1992) and created continuity between the Icelandic commonwealth's glorious past and the present.

Icelanders' ideas of how they thought others perceived them contributed to Icelanders' developing identity. Denmark may have been reluctant to let go of Iceland because it saw Iceland as preserving the old Nordic culture (Karlsson 1995). Although this belief glorified Icelandic culture, it also presented Iceland as pre-modern (Oslund 2002, 328), a more troubling idea to Icelanders. As Paul Durrenberger and Gisli Palsson have shown, Icelanders have struggled since the Middle Ages to correct what they believe to be misconceptions that foreigners have about their country (Durrenberger and Pálsson 1989b). In 1593 Arngrímur Jónsson published the book *Brevis Commentarius de Islandia*, and in 1597 Oddur Einarsson published a description of Iceland titled *Qualiscunque descriptio Islandiae*, both intended to defend against foreigners' misconceptions about Iceland (Benediktsson 1971).

In 1915 two textbooks were published under the title *Íslandssaga* (Iceland's History). One was intended for young children and written by Jónas Jónsson, usually identified by his origin at the farm Hrifla in northern Iceland. The other was by Jón Jónsson Aðils and was intended for older students. Both of these men were extremely influential in Iceland's history. Both were authors of many books. Jónas from Hrifla was also a member of the Icelandic Parliament, while Jón Aðils is sometimes identified as one of the most important people to shape Icelandic nationalistic sentiments (Matthísardóttir 2004). The book by Jónas from Hrifla was used for the next seventy to eighty years and Jón Aðils' book for half a century, indicating their striking influence over several generations of Icelanders (Þorsteinn Helgason 2008).

Jón Aðils proclaims in his text that 84 percent of Icelandic settlers came from excellent stock (*úrvalsættum*) (Jónsson Aðils [1915] 1946, 22). In his widely read book *Íslenskt þjóðerni* (Jónsson Aðils 1903), he had already elaborated on this idea by emphasizing that Icelanders possessed a mixture of Celtic intelligence and the inner strength of Norwegians, which gave birth to "national culture which is hardly similar to anything in history" (ibid., 22–23). He claims furthermore in his educational text that during the Viking period, many good men and rich chiefs had been unable to tolerate the ruling of the Norwegian kings and thus sought to settle elsewhere (ibid., 22–23, 7). Jónas from Hrifla presents a similar narrative in his book, that of Icelandic history as a story of hardworking men who built the country. He mentions women occasionally. When discussing the settlement of Iceland, Jónas states that those who settled Iceland were the best part of the Norwegian population but also the most stubborn (*óbilgjarnastur*) and most difficult to control (Jónsson [1915–16] 1966, 15).

Even though these two schoolbooks would be used for decades to come, other books were also published that perpetuated a similar view of Icelandic nationality. Stefán Jónsson's *Eitt er landið* (The Country Is One), published several decades later in 1967, claims that Icelanders originated from the best Norwegian stock and that the country itself has shaped Icelandic nationality. This fact, the author claims, makes Icelandic nationality different from the "nationality of related nations" (Jónsson 1967, 76). For Jónsson, the courage required to settle Iceland became ingrained in Icelandic heritage and serves as a light shining on the lives of future generations (ibid., 4). This idea of Icelandic nationality being shaped by hardship was not new. It can be seen, for example, nearly seventy years earlier in the book *Lýsing Íslands* (Description of Iceland), published in 1900, which states that the nature of the landscape shaped Icelandic nationalism as well as the physical body of Icelanders (Thoroddsen 1900, 76).

It is interesting to compare these views of the Icelandic nation to world history textbooks of the early twentieth century. Instead of emphasizing the unique origin of Icelanders, the world history books include Icelanders as part of other civilized Europeans and thus as a part of the inevitable progress of European males. Usually these texts do not address Iceland in particular but more indirectly refer to the collective "us" in which Iceland is woven into the birth of the modernity story. In this story colonized peoples are not seen generally as deserving much attention or sympathy but rather are characterized as natural subjects of European control (see Loftsdóttir 2009). Men and masculine qualities are highlighted, just as in books about Iceland's history, by positioning world explorers as the key players of history (ibid.), for example. This viewpoint is similar to that of other writings in Iceland at that time. For example, in the annual journal *Skírnir*, Icelandic men are invited to imagine themselves as part of progressive, civilized Europeans exploring and subjecting the rest of the world to their power. An issue of *Skírnir* from 1890, for example, focuses on the famous explorer Henry Morton Stanley and describes one of his most controversial trips to Africa. Stanley is presented as a heroic figure, masculine and resilient (Stefánsson 1890; see discussion in Loftsdóttir 2009). Icelandic authors seem not to have been primarily interested in constructing images of Africans and other colonized people but in positioning Icelanders as part of civilized Europe (Loftsdóttir 2009).

THE BUSINESS VIKINGS (ALMOST) TAKE OVER THE WORLD

In the early 2000s, Iceland became much more visible globally with Icelandic businessmen buying up companies in other parts of the world as well as extending the operations of their companies internationally. Banks collaborated with firms in their international expansion both by lending them money and by investing their equity in their customers' projects (Sigurjónsson and Mixa 2011, 210). A part of this global integration included increased immigration to Iceland (Skaptadóttir 2010a) and intensification of transnational activities. For example, the Icelandic government developed a heightened interest in participating in various international operations. This aim was often explained using the same rhetoric as the business venture (Loftsdóttir 2010).

Of particular interest is how the economic expansion was interpreted in highly nationalistic terms by the media and leading politicians and became incorporated into Icelandic social discourses. Across diverse social contexts, the economic boom was attributed to the special characteristics of Icelanders. For example, the success of the Icelandic entrepreneur overseas is expressed in terms such as *útrás* (outward expansion) and *útrásarvíkingur* (Business Viking). When economic success was attributed to individual qualities in the entrepreneurs, the populace nevertheless claimed them as *Icelandic entrepreneurs*, and as such their success reflected on the character of Icelanders as a whole.[2] The intensified nationalistic discourse of the time focused on the Business Viking and showed similarities with older conceptions of Icelanders evident in the textbooks discussed earlier, but these ideas were still articulated differently in this new global environment. I have used the term "individualistic nationalism" to attempt to capture how older national symbols of Icelandic identity were negotiated in a highly globalized context, where individualism and market orientation were also strongly emphasized (Loftsdóttir 2007).

A speech from 2006 by the Icelandic president, Ólafur Ragnar Grímsson, shows clearly how the Business Viking concept works by anchoring it in the past. The president stated that the "Age of Settlement was the beginning of this whole process," referring to the economic miracle (Grímsson 2006, 2). He explained that one of the leading causes of Icelandic success internationally was that Icelandic entrepreneurs inherited a tradition rooted in the origin of Icelandic settlement. Thus he claimed that the settlement of

Iceland and the Viking era had given contemporary Icelanders a particular role model. Hannes Smárason, former CEO of FL Group, one of the leading companies at that time, made similar claims when he said in 2007 that Iceland's foreign acquisitions may be traced to the energy of the Viking spirit (Schram 2007).

A statement made by Iceland's former minister of trade, Björgvin G. Sigurðsson, is another example of how Icelandic national culture was evoked in relation to the economic expansion: "Power, guts, and good knowledge of the Icelandic Business Vikings has given more results faster in regard to Icelandic investments overseas than could be speculated, and the Viking has gained a lot of attention internationally" ("Útrás og árangur bankanna" 2007, 19). An influential report on Iceland's international image, developed by a committee established by the prime minister in 2007, strongly emphasized the settlement heritage of Iceland, also without any kind of critical analysis or discussion (Forsætisráðuneytið 2008).

Masculine imagery was invoked in the fall of 2007 when Sigurðsson told a crowd of investors and business owners in Denmark that the Icelandic economic expansion overseas (*útrás*) was like a volcano: it began with earthquakes and then, at the turn of the millennium, ended with a volcanic eruption (Erlingsdóttir 2007). A report by the Iceland Chamber of Commerce about the extension of Icelandic business to London uncritically used concepts like "Vikings" and "pillage," both of which highlight masculinity (Sigfússon and Þorgeirsson 2005, 21). Both of these examples illustrate how males were primarily credited with the so-called economic miracle, as did discussions about the Viking settler in the early twentieth century.

These social narratives were not scattered statements by leading politicians or occasional comments in reports but were reinforced by the changing social fabric of daily life. As economic inequality grew (Oddsson 2010, 8), so too did the Icelandic tabloid media, which to some extent emerged during these years. Tabloids reported glowingly on the conspicuous lifestyles of the Business Vikings (Mixa 2009) and gave regular updates on the intermingling of prominent Icelanders with international superstars. Such idolization of the rich and famous was unknown prior to the economic boom and ran contrary to the common belief that equality was a basic characteristic of Icelanders (Durrenberger 1996; Pálsson 1989). The concept *útrás* was also used for the growing success of Icelandic novelists overseas, which the media also reported actively on. When I along with many other Icelanders visited Copenhagen in 2006, a window display in a big bookstore highlighted Icelandic novels, thus underlying the success of Iceland internationally. Finally, the social narratives of Icelandic success abroad mirrored the experience of people at home who were playing and winning big in the Icelandic stock market.

Together these different social discourses created an environment saturated with success stories and connected powerfully to the historical memory of Icelanders as different from everyone else. Ideology has to be in sync with the experiences of individuals (Eagleton 1991, 14–15), and this "common sense" feeling that Antonio Gramsci's work refers to indicates how particular ideas gain strong hegemony within society at particular times (Gramsci 1971, 210–11). A 2008 children's song is a vivid example of the saturation of these narratives at the most basic level of Icelandic society.[3] Likely referring to an old children's song about two kids fighting over which one has the strongest dad, this song is a dialogue of two children fighting over who has the richest dad. One dad has bought Eden and redesigned it, while the other has an Egyptian pharaoh in the freezer. The text is meant to be funny, of course, but it becomes particularly so in the context of Iceland's economic boom. Certain words used in the song, such as "derivative contracts," could *almost* be used by children in the social atmosphere of the time.

The term "the Manic Millennium years," which was used critically over the boom period (Mixa 2009), captures the pervasive idea that the turn of the century would be a new turning point for Iceland. As such, this period reflects the old anxiety of Icelanders that foreigners have a misconception of them and don't see their uniqueness or specialness. Anne Brydon (2006, 236) notes that Icelanders often find foreigners oblivious of Iceland's "full modernity on a par with that of Europe and the United States," and Palsson and Durrenberger found that when Icelanders talk among themselves, the "primary scholarly task was not so much to understand others but to be understood *by* them" (Pálsson and Durrenberger 1992, 313; emphasis in the original). Therefore the exuberance expressed in the boom years can be understood as self-affirmation, as if finally Icelanders could show their worth on the international stage. The optimism and sense of a new bright future, as Mixa points out, resembles the Roaring Twenties in the United States in many ways (Mixa 2009). My analysis of two business newspapers in 2006 and 2007 reveals that in addition to celebrating their international success, Icelanders also demonstrated a desire to disinherit their lowly status of the past. In 2006 Danske Bank issued a warning about the way Icelandic banks were operating, which Icelanders interpreted as Danish jealousy toward their economic miracle. Often this perceived jealousy is so evident to the writers that they don't bother to mention it directly. In the business newspaper *Viðskiptablaðið*, for example, Gísli Reynisson, the CEO and main owner of the investment firm Nordic Partners, proclaimed that "in spite of that certain press [in Denmark] getting pleasure from and enjoying bullying Icelanders, that has not been the case with all the Danes" ("Nordic Partners kaupa sögufræg hótel" 2007, 1). One of the bluntest expressions of this kind was uttered by the acting minster for foreign affairs when she stated that there was something "unnatural about the criticism that Danske Bank issued." She claimed that this was due to "scratches in the Danish self-image in relation to Iceland" after "Icelanders started to invest a great deal in Denmark" ("Sjálfsímynd Dana farin að rispast" 2006, 12–13).

NEOLIBERALISM AND NATIONALISM

The idea of the Business Viking and the economic boom relied strongly on a familiar theme—dating from Icelandic independence—about the unique characteristics of Icelanders due to their Viking or settler background, which was shaped by the roughness of the land itself throughout the centuries. As in earlier times, these ideas primarily focused on men, portraying Icelandic nationality as masculine. To intensify the association with the past, parallel discourses about Danes as enemies of Icelandic prosperity seemed to engage with this historical memory. It is important to locate this strong association with past discourses of Icelandic nationalism within the global perspective, where scholars have shown increased reification of "culture." It is probably no coincidence that we see intensification of nationalism at times when Iceland is becoming more globally integrated. During the Manic Millennium years, we see almost a reinvention of Icelandic nationalism that articulates older ideas in concert with those of individualism and neoliberal ideology (Loftsdóttir 2007). Nationalism during the Manic Millennium years thus emphasized local nationalistic symbols as well as their creative application for a wider marketplace where individual success was celebrated.

Also, how did the changing working environment in Iceland during this time interact within this "reinvention" of Icelandic nationalism? As Elizabeth Dunn has pointed out in her brilliant ethnography of neoliberalism in Poland, neoliberalization involves changes in labor practices such as audits and quality control. These are used to shape people into "flexible, agile, self-regulating workers," who presumably then assist their companies in adapting to shifting conditions in the global markets (Dunn 2004, 7). This emphasis on flexibility often means that workers must tolerate risk and insecurities on the job market, embedded within the rhetoric that they should be "self-directed, self-activating [and] self-monitoring" (ibid., 19–20). In Iceland we see an increase of audit and surveillance techniques in the workplace, where it is the worker, rather than his or her work, that is being monitored (Rafnsdóttir et al. 2005).

The Business Viking narrative of flexibility and individualism as inherited Icelandic characteristics overlaps in an interesting way with these wider ideas of neoliberalism. It is tempting to ask to what extent did those who wanted certain Icelandic businessmen to take control of Icelandic banks and companies manipulate these nationalistic ideas? Clearly the businessmen encouraged comparisons of themselves with Iceland's first settlers, evident, for example, in Jón Ásgeir Jóhannesson's naming of his yacht *Viking* and displaying statues of Leifur Eiríksson, Iceland's first settler, in the lobby of his London headquarters (Elíasson 2009). These ideas were applied not only to the takeover of companies but to other Icelandic successes, and as such notions of inherently Icelandic characteristics appeared in many spheres of society and fed off of each other, making it extremely difficult to contradict them prior to the crash.

FINAL COMMENTS

The Icelandic economic expansion gained strong acceptance in Iceland due to its association with Icelandic nationalistic symbols that had a strong gendered component. These symbols were reconceptualized within a global environment, building on the historical image of Icelanders as unique individuals by adding neoliberal ideas of flexibility and individualism. As Henrietta Moore (2004, 74) has pointed out, the "global" has become a part of most people's imagined worlds, reflecting how notions of globalization are in various ways embedded with questions of identity and selfhood. As such, the economic expansion signaled an intense conversation with the present globalized world with identity becoming meaningful by anchoring it in past national symbols and discussions.

With the economic collapse, Iceland was the prime object of global media attention—labeled by some international media as the canary in the coal mine. It wasn't the kind of attention Iceland had hoped for since seeking independence. Stefán Jónsson's comment in his textbook for children reflects this desire to be recognized the right way. Reformulated in somewhat naïve arrogance, he states, "[I]t is a pleasure for a small nation to best larger nations" (Jónsson 1967, 4).[4] During the economic boom, Icelanders certainly seemed to be relishing their moment in the spotlight, which perhaps explains why there was so little critical discussion around what was happening to Iceland's economy until it was too late.

NOTES

1. Translated by the author from Icelandic: "Ímynd og sönn mynd fara ekki alltaf saman enda var þessi samanburður bara til gamans gerður." A film clip from the interview can be seen at http://www.visir.is/islenskir-utrasarvikingar-i-aldanna-ras/article /200770819044#.

2. Older schoolbooks primarily refer to the first Icelanders as settlers (*landnáms-menn*) rather than Vikings, the Viking period being considered more a prelude to the settlement of Iceland.

3. The song was written prior the crash ("Pabbi minn er ríkari en pabbi þinn" 2008).

4. Translated by the author from Icelandic: "Ánægjulegt er það fyrir litla þjóð að skara fram úr öðrum þjóðum."

2

Exploiting Icelandic History

2000–2008

Guðni Th. Jóhannesson is a historian who takes his own discipline to task in this occasionally sardonic critique of the role that historians have and haven't played in the lead-up to the crash. He urges them to tell their stories to the people, or others will fill in the void with whatever version of history is politically expedient at the moment.

•••••••••••••••••••••

Chronological turning points can create artificial watersheds. Still, the start of the new millennium seemed to herald new and exciting times within the historical profession in Iceland. Icelandic historiography in the postwar period had generally been marked by caution, empiricism, and conservatism (Ingvarsdóttir 1996) with only sporadic individual cases of revisionism, radicalism, and challenging conclusions. Furthermore, historical writings on the whole had been nationalistic, a trend that began in the mid-nineteenth century when Icelandic intellectuals and political representatives started to call for increased rights within the Danish kingdom (Hálfdanarson 1995, 66–67).

At the risk of oversimplification, the history of Iceland can be divided into three periods of rise, decline, and rise again. First there was the "glorious age" when the island was settled in the ninth century by Norse farmers and Vikings who had acquired fame and fortune through raids and pillage. Fleeing tyranny in Norway, they founded a free republic, discovered new lands farther westward, and later composed the sagas, that world-renowned literary treasure. Alas, civil strife

DOI: 10.5876/9781607323358.c002

in the thirteenth century led to the loss of independence. Centuries of decline and misery followed under Norwegian and, later, Danish oppression. Only in the nineteenth century did the nation "wake up," led by the national hero Jón Sigurðsson and other brilliant individuals. The struggle for independence had begun, culminating in full independence on June 17, 1944, Sigurðsson's birthdate.

NEW MILLENNIUM, NEW BEGINNINGS?

By the last two decades of the twentieth century, this version of the past had definitely changed. New directions in the history profession of the Western world found their way into the community of Icelandic historians. First, social history became more popular at the expense of political history and its focus on "great men." Thus, the poor masses of tenants and laborers emerged from the shadow of prominent settlers, chieftains, clergy, and officials. Later on, postmodern, gender, and other progressive approaches to history reached Iceland. New recruits joined the history department at the University of Iceland. The Reykjavík Academy, founded in 1997, gave shelter and strength to a growing number of independent young researchers. More public conferences and lectures began to receive media attention, in particular a popular series of biweekly lunchtime events organized by the Association of Icelandic Historians (Magnússon 2007, 52–53).

Most notably, a thorough revision of the nationalistic version of Icelandic history seemed complete. "The struggle for Iceland's independence is over," University of Iceland–based historian Guðmundur Hálfdanarson said in 1995, paraphrasing François Furet's famous comment from 1978 that the French Revolution had long since ended (Hálfdanarson 1995, 67). To progressive historians, this revision was a positive development. It represented diversity, theoretical strength, international influences, and critical approaches.

As a graduate student of history at the University of Iceland, I remember reading Hálfdanarson's statement with fascination. In 1997 I completed my master's thesis. Shortly afterward, I took part in the inaugural History Congress in Iceland and noticed the spirit of revision and enthusiasm for new research. In his opening speech, President Ólafur Ragnar Grímsson, a former professor of political science at the university, praised the nearly one hundred participants—including the large majority of professional and active historians in the country—for this new approach. Half-jokingly, he recalled how a teacher had "corrected" an essay of his in high school on Hannes Hafstein, Iceland's first minister, who took office in 1904, by turning the word *goðmenni* (idol) into *góðmenni* (kind man). Thankfully, such an uncritical and nationalistic understanding of history was now a thing of the past, Grímsson (1997, 16) claimed at the time.

ASSAULT

The turn of the millennium also seemed to mark a watershed in fields other than history. In 1991 a new center-right coalition, led by Davíð Oddsson, chairman of the conservative Independence Party, began a large-scale campaign of economic liberalization and privatization. The process culminated in the privatization of state-run banks that almost immediately ballooned in size, opening branches or subsidiaries in various European countries.

Those international endeavors were part of a greater, rapid internationalization of the Icelandic economy. Icelandic companies soon made international headlines. Most prominent were entrepreneurs like Jón Ásgeir Jóhannesson and Björgólfur Thor Björgólfsson, the first Icelander to appear on *Forbes* magazine's list of the world's wealthiest people (Jóhannesson 2009b, 70, 203).

Why did Iceland ascend so quickly on the international scene? Why were Icelanders blessed with an "economic miracle" in the opening years of the new millennium? Naturally, the proponents of public policy offered political and economic explanations, but history seemed to provide an unequivocal answer as well. By the late 1990s, the growing internationalization of the economy had been given the label *útrás*, a word denoting a sudden assault that resonated with the Viking era (Helgason 2006). The modern English interpretation of this term is best translated as "expansion," but one that implies assault. The entrepreneurs were often called *útrásarvíkingar*—Venture Vikings, also translated as Business Vikings—and they attempted to live up to this image of the brave, fearless, and adventurous voyagers and warriors (Loftsdóttir 2009, 127–131).

The growing tourist industry in Iceland was even more eager to highlight the "Viking past" and the literary treasure of the sagas (Kjartansdóttir 2011, 466–471). But historians were more hesitant and increasingly unhappy. "The question is rarely asked whether they [the Vikings] were not simply the terrorists of their time," medieval specialist Helgi Þorláksson pointed out at the third History Congress in 2006 (Þorláksson 2007, 323). Likewise, archeologists and other academics shook their heads over the tourist-oriented "Saga Centers" (Stefánsdóttir and Sigurðardóttir 2007).

Political and business leaders were constructing a particularly positive view of history despite the spirit of revisionism in the historians' ranks. And if the

"Viking nonsense" was not enough, to quote an apocryphal historian in the first years of the new millennium, memories of "great men" like Jón Sigurðsson and Hannes Hafstein were very much alive in the minds of the political elite. Apparently, the struggle for Iceland's independence was not over at all.

THE "DISCOVERY OF AMERICA"

Arguably, the main battles over the uses of Iceland's history occurred on four separate occasions—in 2000, 2004, 2006, and 2008. In 2000 a replica of a Viking ship set sail from Iceland to New York to celebrate the Norse discovery of North America. In Washington the Smithsonian Institution opened an exhibition and published a book on Viking voyages (Fitzhugh and Ward 2000), which justly portrayed the Norse journeys as true feats of navigation, individual resilience, and courage. Meanwhile, in Los Angeles, at an Icelandic American Chamber of Commerce luncheon, President Grímsson made his own connections with the past. Delivering a perfect example of the nationalistic history he had criticized at the History Congress three years before, the president described how Icelanders should strive to "excel like our ancestors, poets and pioneers, dreamers and discoverers, and bring our entrepreneurial spirit to explore the world" (Grímsson 2000, 6).

More than a decade later, I learned that a scholar in the president's entourage was heard saying, "I did not write this, I did not write this." Some historians were certainly dismayed at the uncritical tone of the speech (Magnússon 2007, 129). More generally, they complained about what they considered the hype and exaggeration that marked the celebrations (Björnsdóttir 2001).

In 2000 Iceland also celebrated the 1,000th anniversary of the adoption of Christianity. Again, critically minded historians lamented the commemorative speeches. On the other hand, the academic community had been crucial in producing a four-volume history of Christianity in Iceland. Yet as one of the contributors later opined, the extensive and expensive tomes were barely promoted, so "nobody knew about it" (Valdimarsdóttir 2013, 64).

Finally, in 2000 the National Centre for Cultural Heritage opened in Reykjavík. Aimed at locals and tourists alike, the center displayed the sagas and other medieval manuscripts prominently and dedicated separate rooms to Hannes Hafstein and Jón Sigurðsson, the nation's two founding leaders, as Prime Minister Oddsson described them at the opening ceremonies (Oddsson 2000). Again, historians were quick to find fault with the state-run commemoration, an allegedly outdated version of history no credible historian could countenance (Rastrick 2000).

"GREAT MEN" RETURN

In February 2004 Iceland commemorated the century since it had gained home rule from Denmark and Hannes Hafstein had assumed his role as the first minister. As part of the festivities, an editorial committee sought contributors among academics, journalists, and others to compile a tome on all of Iceland's prime ministers to date. Most controversially, Prime Minister Oddsson, an admirer, composed a flattering piece on Hannes Hafstein (Oddsson 2004). The prime minister was no friend of the most prominent Venture Vikings and never alluded to any bond between them and the past. Instead, he raised historians' ire with his old-fashioned admiration of leaders like Hafstein, whom he labeled the driving force for progress and prosperity. I also gladly accepted an offer to contribute a piece about a prime minister who had figured largely in my thesis. By this time, I had completed my archive-based examination of fishing disputes in the North Atlantic after World War II. It was less patriotic and one-sided than many accounts of these conflicts.

I had secured a postdoctoral position at the University of Iceland and became head of the Association of Icelandic Historians. Our group held a symposium, hoping to gain media attention for the book. At the event a couple of history students with strong links to the Reykjavík Academy, by then a bastion of progressive thought in the history community, condemned the work for its archaic idolization of "great men" and pitiful attempts to produce a glorified version of the recent past (Pétursson 2004). In an equally fiery response, the editor defended the book, saying the aim had been to produce an entertaining work in which readers could find basic information about the nation's past leaders; there could be nothing sinister about that (Guðnason 2004).

Caught in the crossfire, I tried to sympathize with both, arguing that while the work was definitely old-fashioned, historians must not forget to distribute the fruits of their research and write in a lively style for the general reader. Furthermore, I argued that, if anything, academic historians could be censured for having avoided the project since it included not a single member of the University of Iceland's department of history. The book sold well and met with generally positive reviews outside of academic circles (Guðni Jóhannesson 2004).

"ICELANDIC VENTURES"

By 2006 the economic success story was still running at full tilt. Icelanders disregarded warnings from abroad about excess, hazard, and overheating as envy or the foreigners' failure to understand the daring mentality of these descendants of Vikings and voyagers (Sigurjónsson, Schwartzkopf, and Arnardóttir 2011, 167–79).

In the first half of the year, expansion or *útrás* was the theme of the still-popular Association of Icelandic Historians lunchtime lectures. When President Grímsson accepted my request to deliver the opening address, it guaranteed public attention to the entire series. Confident and optimistic, Grímsson attributed the unquestionable success of Icelandic entrepreneurs to "the Icelandic character" and the joint heritage of individualism, strong leaders, solidarity, daring, trust, honor, and poetic skills. "The achievers of our own day are frequently judged by these standards, and we look upon them as the heirs to a tradition that goes all the way back to the time of the first pioneer settlers in Iceland" (Grímsson 2006, 7).

This was the classic, nationalistic Grímsson, and a far cry from the more progressive speaker I had heard at the first Historical Congress in 1997. My colleagues in the audience were aghast. Indeed, in just a few hours Sigurður Gylfi Magnússon, a driving force behind the founding of the Reykjavík Academy, published an online riposte mocking the notion that Iceland's "neo-capitalistic entrepreneurs" shared some admirable traits with glorified Vikings, voyagers, and poets of the past (Magnússon 2006, n.p.).

Here we had another clash between a statesperson and historians. The differences are personified in President Grímsson and Prime Minister Oddsson, who may have been bitter political enemies but who shared the vision that history was meant to unite the nation and highlight the past achievements of "great men." Historians were not of one mind, and those years were marked by heated theoretical debates. Still, one overriding issue united them: history should *not* be used this way.

"THIS IS WHAT THE PEOPLE THINK"

In early 2007 I obtained a nontenured position at Reykjavík University, a small private institution that was thriving in these years of economic expansion. A year later, an official task force delivered a detailed report, under the leadership of Reykjavík University rector Svafa Grönfeldt, to enhance the image of Iceland abroad. The task force based its findings on responses from a number of 100-strong focus groups, concluding that Icelanders envisaged themselves as proud, courageous, resilient, smart, unpredictable, undisciplined, independent, and free. Moreover, they believed that the original settlers had shared these characteristics, which had then been carried from one generation to another, through struggles with nature and foreign oppressors, until Icelanders managed to build one of the most successful states on earth (Forsætisráðuneytið 2008).

Apparently, the "Viking spirit" still permeated the self-image of average Icelanders. Again, historians rose up in protest. The Association of Icelandic Historians, under new leadership, asserted that the mythical presentation of Iceland's past reflected long-outdated views (Huijbens 2011, 569). At Reykjavík University I was on the receiving end of some friendly banter as the sole professional historian. "But this is simply what the people think," Grönfeldt said. While I tried to maintain that no academic historian would portray the past this way, I could hardly refute that statement. Other academics later concurred that, among the general public, the traditional outlook prevailed (Ágústsson 2010, 91–96).

By 2008 it seemed clear that historians had lost the history wars. Tellingly, President Grímsson had never been so popular. Despite signs of impending economic danger, in August he was still busy explaining to the outside world how Icelanders had managed to construct one of the most prosperous societies on earth (Jóhannesson 2012). History remained an important part of that. But just a few weeks later, the whole thing collapsed.

POST-CRASH LESSONS

In the spring of 2009, a few months after the banking collapse, a new government report on Iceland's standing in the world suggested that, while Iceland had to rectify the damage to its image, people should avoid previous allusions to Icelandic inherent superiority (Utanríkisráðuneytið 2009). A Working Group on Ethics that coordinated with a Parliament-appointed Special Investigation Committee to investigate the collapse of the Icelandic banks reached similar conclusions (Árnason, Nordal, and Ástgeirsdóttir 2010, 170–174). So did I, in early 2009 in a popular work that narrated the stunning events of the previous months in Iceland (Jóhannesson 2009b). Incidentally, it turned out to be my last published book during my stint at Reykjavík University. I became the victim of necessary cutbacks in the wake of new economic realities.

Pride comes before the fall. The hyped history of Iceland had not only been embarrassing in hindsight, it had been harmful at the time. In the words of historian Sumarliði Ísleifsson, "[t]he imagined superiority of Icelandic financiers in international business and ideas about the cultural significance of the nation proved to be influential in the way Icelandic businessmen conducted their affairs" (Ísleifsson 2011, 6).

Why had this happened? It would be easy to blame the Venture Vikings, statespersons, and the gullible public. Even so, historians should take a critical look at their own approach. It simply was not enough to find fault time and again with an outdated, glorified, nationalistic version of the past. Historians should have provided an enticing, readable, and entertaining alternative. In this they failed. They did not produce popular works on the Vikings, the settlement, or even the sagas, and when they did, they were not sufficiently promoted.

Likewise, the history of the collapse, its causes and consequences, must not be analyzed only in learned conference papers later published in little-known compilations. Vital as that effort is, the work must not end there. To be fair, we must consider limited funding and scarcity of professional posts. The academic system with its undue emphasis on publications in scholarly journals may also discourage staff to produce works for the general public. Nonetheless, in Iceland as elsewhere in the Western world, too many historians have turned inward and lost touch with the outside world. They have ignored the need to provide a receptive public with stories, with narrative. "Let's avoid thinking so much about how to do things that we do not have time to do anything," I wrote to my colleagues in 2005, adding the conviction that history was beautifully simple: "the art of telling stories." Their response was overwhelmingly negative. They deemed theoretical debates vital and described history as a complex, academic field of study, so much more than simple narrative (Jóhannesson 2005, n.p.).

That is true, but not enough. The means are nothing without the end. "History is a branch of storytelling," British historian David Starkey recently insisted (quoted in Mandler, Lang, and Vallance 2011, 26). "We need to remember the roots of discipline and *keep telling stories*," said William Cronon, president of the American Historical Association (Walsh 2013, n.p.).

I could not agree more, just like I heartily applauded the assertion back in 1995 that the struggle for Iceland's independence was over. That did not turn out to be true, partly because the historians only said so to each other. If they do not use their standing in the community to tell stories to people, others will dominate the stage. The results can be even more regrettable than the collapse of banks in Iceland in October 2008.

3

Free Market Ideology,
Crony Capitalism, and
Social Resilience

Örn D. Jónsson is a professor in the School of Business at
the University of Iceland; Rögnvaldur J. Sæmundsson
is an associate professor in the Department of Industrial
Engineering at the University of Iceland. In this chapter
they apply three well-established theories of entrepreneur-
ship to an analysis of the Icelandic meltdown.

. . . .

> Iceland is, of course, one of the great economic
> disaster stories of all time. An economy that
> produced a decent standard of living for its
> people was in effect hijacked by a combination
> of free-market ideology and crony capitalism.
>
> PAUL KRUGMAN, "THE ICELANDIC
> POST-CRISIS MIRACLE"

At the beginning of the twenty-first century, the
Icelandic economy was characterized by openness, a
highly educated workforce, diverse international connections, and abundant access to foreign capital. Less
than ten years later, its banking system had collapsed
and many of the country's largest companies were facing bankruptcy.

In this chapter we use theories of entrepreneurship
put forward by Schumpeter, Kirzner, and Baumol to
analyze how improved innovation capacity, the opening of foreign markets, and privatization connect a
prosperous microstate to the international economy
with unforeseen consequences, and how and why
the nation could cope with the crisis despite gloomy

DOI: 10.5876/9781607323358.c003

projections. We ask if the favorable conditions at the beginning of the century can be restored based on the resilience the country has shown since the crash. We argue that this is possible by providing a favorable environment for the development of the specialized innovation companies that survived the crisis.

ENTREPRENEURS, INNOVATION, AND RENT-SEEKING

Schumpeter (1934), Kirzner (1973), and Baumol (1990) have all made significant contributions to our understanding of the role of the entrepreneur in socioeconomic development. In their theories the concept of the entrepreneur refers to an economic actor who performs the entrepreneurial function in the economy, rather than to specific individuals and their part in the course of events.[1]

According to Schumpeter (1934; [1942] 1976), the entrepreneur's role is to drive innovation in the economy. Innovation is the introduction of new combinations in the market—for example, the use of new technology, the opening up of new markets, or changes in industrial organization. Innovations disrupt the equilibrium in the economy and are the precondition for new value creation and profit. Through innovation, entrepreneurs compete in a manner that is difficult for incumbent companies to match, as innovation is directed at the very nature of their products and processes and simply reducing the price is not an effective response. After an innovation, the market becomes flooded by imitators, moving the economy back toward equilibrium and thereby diminishing profits. Controlling companies and even industries, which have often secured their position in a cartel-like manner, are unable to respond. As a result, industries rise and fall in a process Schumpeter ([1942] 1976) termed "creative destruction." Even though the short-term effects can be problematic for less competitive companies, the overall results are positive for the economy and a necessary precondition for renewal and long-term economic development and growth.[2]

Although entrepreneurs drive innovation, they do not do so in isolation or in a straightforward way, that is, by the application of new scientific knowledge. Innovation is a chain-linked and path-dependent process involving a large number of actors and shaped by institutional context and historical circumstances (Kline, and Rosenberg 1986; Nelson 1992).

Entrepreneurs aiming for novel innovations have a difficult time finding financing due to the high level of uncertainty of outcomes. However, in the wake of innovations—for example, major technological changes—there is less uncertainty and profit expectations may rise, making it easier for imitators to fund their activities. Numerous imitators take advantage of these opportunities, increasing the capital in circulation and the expectations of future profits, resulting in overinvestment and inflation. The result is a bubble economy that is based on expectations that cannot be met in the real economy and must eventually be corrected (Perez 2002).

Kirzner (1973; 1997) gives the entrepreneur a different but similarly important role in the development of the economy and the prosperity of society. To Kirzner, the entrepreneur is an alert person who is willing to exploit opportunities that arise due to disequilibrium in the economy. For a variety of reasons, such as its participants' different knowledge and access to different information, the economy is constantly moved out of the balance predicted by economic theory. Because of the imbalance, those things that contribute to the cost of production, or production factors, are not priced according to their value, creating an opportunity for profit (Baumol, Robert, and Schramm 2007). However, through his activities, the entrepreneur sends out information about the value of those production factors, and as a result the economy moves toward equilibrium, leading to better utilization of resources and improved welfare. Kirzner's analysis is somewhat consistent with Schumpeter's ideas about the entrepreneur as a change agent but ignores the importance Schumpeter assigns to radical change brought about by innovation and the role of investors. While Schumpeter emphasizes the role of entrepreneurs in creating imbalance in the economy, Kirzner emphasizes their role in establishing balance.

According to Baumol (1990), the entrepreneur performs both the role of the innovative agent who promotes change and disequilibrium in the economy and the one who is alert to changes and, through entrepreneurial action, drives the economy toward equilibrium. Thus, Baumol combines, to some extent, the views of both Schumpeter and Kirzner. However, unlike Schumpeter and Kirzner, Baumol does not regard the entrepreneur's impact on economic development as always positive. Baumol (ibid.) argues that entrepreneurship at any point in time depends on the structure of payoffs in the economy. In general, profit motive leads to innovation and prosperity, but in some cases entrepreneurial activity can become destructive.

He mentions, for example, rent-seeking, an effort to gain by changing the rules, whether that be creating a license for a service like cutting hair or giving financial advice or privatizing fishing quotas, where the entrepreneur benefits without a corresponding benefit returning to the society. This is not necessarily through illegal activities, such as drug dealing or blackmail, but rather through lawful activities, such as a company buying out a shareholder who has threatened a takeover or big investment funds manipulating the markets by legal maneuvers.

The government both directly and indirectly influences the structure of economic payoffs, through legislation, policies, and administrative rules and actions, but it is also dependent on the prevailing culture in society that broadly defines right and wrong. Thus, according to Baumol, the institutional setup determines whether or not overinvestment following radical innovation is economically productive. Although such overinvestment does not profit the entrepreneur and investors directly, as a whole the economy may benefit from the activity, for instance, through increased technical knowledge and "sectoral" networks. This can hardly be said of innovative rent-seeking, both because it does not lead to prosperity and because it can be made less attractive or impossible through changes in the law.

DEVELOPMENT OF THE ICELANDIC ECONOMY

In the twentieth century Iceland evolved from one of the poorest countries in Europe into one of the richest (Jónsson 2002). As we have discussed before (Jónsson and Sæmundsson 2006), this development occurred over several periods of initiative and development with government participation.

Throughout most of the twentieth century, there was a worldwide conviction that a gradual move toward modern society could be navigated through socioeconomic planning. Despite recurring fluctuations and economic downturns, the major players in Icelandic politics more or less agreed with this view. The Icelandic version was that, as latecomers, Icelanders could learn from the mistakes of those who had gone before. Although the "rules of the game" are significantly similar in an ever more globalized world, historical determinants (North 1990), structural and organizational settings, and new "social technologies" are difficult to transfer abruptly from one economy to another (Eggertsson 2005).

In Iceland the fishing industry was operating under several specific conditions: its geographical embeddedness (fishing communities were located close to the most productive fishing banks); Iceland's relatively strong civil society, based on positive freedom ("freedom to" rather than "freedom from" [Berlin 1969]); and the cartelized organization of the fisheries sector.

The basic idea, until World War II, was that Icelanders should "work themselves into prosperity" in their own time and under their own terms. The driving force should be the household—farmers, fishermen, and wage laborers. In Karl Polanyi's terms, the system should be based on reciprocity. Icelanders enforced this through an emphasis on local community and local initiatives achieved through the absence of outside capital and several protectionist measures, including limiting the number of players allowed to import goods (Polanyi [1944] 1968). Icelanders regarded the savings as collective earnings to be either redistributed internally or used to pay for collective goods.

The result was an entrepreneurial economy based on a trial-and-error approach to innovation, wherein the basic actor was the "practical man" or "collective entrepreneur" rather than the "optimizing capitalist" (Hansen and Serin 1997). In addition to the rationality of the system, policies sought to extend the workday and encourage a wide-ranging participation in wage work rather than household provisioning. The country's industry was predominantly a cottage industry, with commerce dominated by craft-based corner shops operating, more often than not, from coastal fishing villages.

World War II fundamentally changed this situation. The occupying Allies built basic infrastructure with Icelandic labor, and a consequent influx of money via widespread wage work led to the long-awaited monetization of the economy. In the postwar era of the early fifties, the government emphasized the creation of a mixed economy built on the Nordic model and the promotion of main structures and organizations necessary for a successful welfare system.

Innovation was defined as a political initiative with an emphasis on adopting foreign technology and practices. Private funding for entrepreneurs was locally induced through incremental initiatives. The need for change and nation-building was obvious and visible; the challenge was to prioritize. The government took on the role of the innovative entrepreneur by way of its investments in infrastructure and efficient production processes in the fisheries—investments made possible through savings accumulated during the war and development aid from friendly allies.

The organizational principles of the Icelandic economy's two main sectors, fisheries and, later, aviation, were not capital-intensive after the initial start-up phase. The two fundamental technological innovations, the jet engine in aviation and the move from side trawlers to stern trawlers in fisheries, were financed by soft loans from the state banks, which meant that, in general, only working capital was required in the industries themselves. The nation's two largest business conglomerates were both at their core mercantile but relied heavily on political redistribution of the return from ever-increasing fisheries efforts, on a local as well as state level. The larger of the two clusters, aviation, adhered to capitalistic optimization; while the other was a diversified grouping of fisheries co-ops.

Both business clusters were based on rapidly increasing pension funds and trade, transport, insurance, and the importation of oil. Their networks abroad were, for the most part, confined to the sphere of imports and relied more on pension funds as their central source of capital.

Iceland's economy developed into a comprehensive, more or less closed system driven largely by political governance in which market forces had only a marginal influence. The two reigning business groups were small in scale, confined to Iceland, and unable to reap the benefits of the liberalization they themselves designed. Their governance was grounded in organic growth protected by a favorable regulatory system. Financial capital played an insignificant role. In Kirzner's sense, the Schumpeterian disruptions were leveled out via informal contractual relationships between the two businesses.

In the early 1970s the pioneers in export tied to the fisheries sector saw the opportunity to exploit rapid technological developments, like the introduction of microprocessors and the increased expertise in materials technology. In Schumpeter's (1934) sense, they were innovative in that they developed new ways around the obstacles that had slowed productivity. Along with other changes, including the introduction of a new fisheries management system, they created the foundation for a revolution in the industry by changing work methods and making associated changes in the power structure within the industry.

It soon became apparent that the innovations in fish processing could also be applied to other types of food processing and markets outside Iceland. Efficient fish-processing methods and equipment were used for chicken production. The insulated containers used to preserve fresh fish were useful in hot countries, and product development initially aimed at fresh seafood became useful in the market for high-quality convenience food. At the same time, internationally competitive innovation, such as prosthetics and generic pharmaceuticals, appeared in other industries.

Despite the emergence of internationally competitive innovation and free trade treaties, such as the EFTA agreement, the activities of Icelandic entrepreneurs were still limited to the seafood industry for several reasons. First, seafood trades, which were about 90 percent of total exports, were controlled by two industry groups. Second, expertise, skills, and networks were difficult to transfer from the fishing industry to other industries, even in related fields.[3] Third, the economy was relatively closed, and there was limited access to funding. For example, there were severe limitations on currency exchanges; there was no stock market; and the major banks were run by the government and historically tied to the industry, farming, and fisheries sectors. Furthermore, each sector had its own funding structure and numerous local "Savings and Loans" located around the country.

Attempts had been made to create a public stock market in Iceland, but such a market did not become firmly established until 1990 when the first shares were listed on the Icelandic Stock Exchange (Kauphöll Íslands). The Icelandic stock market grew slowly at first. In the beginning, one-third of the companies listed on the exchange belonged to the fishing industry, and in 1997 their relative value reached its peak of 40 percent (Kristinsdóttir 2009). These companies, which previously raised funds with the help of political relationships within the state-owned banking system, were able to take advantage of market mechanisms to grow. Innovative companies related to fisheries were also able to finance their growth with expansion into foreign markets and other industries, such as meat processing. Lack of raw materials, however, limited the growth of industries associated with agriculture.

Despite the emergence of capital markets, reduction of tariffs, and further opening of foreign markets through membership of the European Economic Area (EEA) in 1993 and GATT in 1995, these factors as a whole did not have much impact on the diversification of exports, at least initially. Exports of products, as opposed to exports of raw material being processed abroad, increased steadily in the 1980s as a result of advances in fisheries management and fish-processing equipment.

THE ADVENT OF CRISIS

The privatization of the banking system (between 1998 and 2003) created more opportunities for Icelandic entrepreneurs. Access to domestic and, later, foreign capital investment improved, and the investment capability of the economy multiplied. Following the privatization, three banks emerged, all of which grew very rapidly through increased activity abroad. They became related to the boom-bust cycle, which proved to have a logic very different from that of the import-export model that liberalization was expected to facilitate.

Expansion and the size of the banks had a major impact on the Icelandic economy. The market value of the companies listed on the Icelandic Stock Exchange grew from ISK 100 million in 1996 to ISK 2.5 billion in 2006, and banks and financial institutions dominated the market.[4] More and more companies had become investment companies, or even hedge funds, without changing their names. Most manufacturing companies in the fishing industry had been taken off the stock exchange, and few businesses that practiced international innovation had been added. Registered profit from the banks had become several times greater than the value obtained from seafood exports.

The factors behind the underlying crisis were inexperience in banking; political favoritism when the banks were privatized; and strong ties between economy and politics (Danielsson and Zoega 2009). Transforming the three major banks from saving banks into investment banks transformed savings into investment capital, and, to the surprise of almost everyone, new players or outsiders took hold in a matter of two to three years.

The development can be characterized as a three-step move:

1. a successful diversification and strengthening of exports along with an overall liberalization of trade,
2. the shift of governance from the Reykjavík stock exchange to the City in London, and
3. the systematic and opportunistic exploitation of Icelandic ties by newly cre-ated business groups operating in London.

New business groups, which had existed in 2002 only in embryonic form, took on the role of the risk-takers on the stock exchange in London and, to a lesser extent, in the Nordic markets. The Icelandic "entrepreneurs" in the City became alliances of three to four groups deriving their mandates from the Icelandic banks.

The meltdown had much to do with leveraged takeovers by the clustered Icelandic groups that financed themselves with foreign funds that were rela-tively easy to obtain at the time. Icelanders were attempting to become players in the world of the superrich—high yield and risk on a massive scale. A bunch of amateurs were able to seize opportunities in the wake of the privatization of the Icelandic banks. In the process, they indulged in conspicuous consump-tion on an unprecedented scale, buying an English football club, a Formula One racing team, a yacht formerly owned by Armani, and England's most prestigious bank, Singer & Friedlander.

In order to create such vast, complex, and conflated webs, these groups needed international accounting firms (such as KMPG and PricewaterhouseCoopers). This design was deliberately opaque in order to avoid accountability, which was one of the main characteristics of the bubble internationally. In less than five years, a simple, enclosed, and transparent economic universe had been transformed into an infinitely complex and fuzzy one.

Instead of strengthening the economy, the privatization and expansion of the banks had the opposite effect. Increased opportunities for investment were used only to a limited extent to strengthen economic sectors already in place, such as fisheries, or for international innovation in Schumpeter's and Kirzner's sense. Instead, conditions and strong incentives were created for rent-seeking and asset price inflation (Rannsóknarnefnd Alþingis 2010, 1:31–47). The size and type of business agreements were not in accordance with former practices or the size of the Icelandic economy, which formed the basis of the credit ratings of the Icelandic banks. Despite their radical innovation, the pioneers became the destructive force that Baumol warns against.

The "real economy" based on the four main economic sectors—fisheries, energy-intensive production, tourism, and high-tech innovative companies—has reemerged following the collapse of the banking system and the associated meltdown of the economy. These sectors have regained their significance, characterized by stable fisheries and growing utilization of hydro- and geothermal power.

Fisheries, energy production, and tourism are all examples of industries that utilize limited resources for value creation. Since return on the investments themselves is limited in the long term (because they all depend on finite natural resources), it is necessary to build in the capacity for future innovation. The focus on fisheries, energy production, and tourism is likely to be at the expense of knowledge-based businesses.

CONCLUSION

In the 1980s Icelanders were in a very favorable position: they had built up a Nordic welfare model and ruled over the fishing grounds surrounding the country. Growing technical skills increased both productivity and product quality in fisheries, but the turning point came when it was possible to transform knowledge of fish processing into knowledge to develop and produce fish-processing equipment. When it was later discovered that the solutions developed within fishing were applicable to many other industries, new possibilities opened up. It was not the increase in the value of the catch that was decisive but the more extensive usage of manufacturing technology and the organization that had been developed for the fishing industry.

Innovative entrepreneurs had created new opportunities for expansion into foreign markets, and one can say that this was a natural extension of knowledge, skills, and international networks that had been accumulating for some time. Privatization and improved access to foreign markets increased these opportunities but also created opportunities for rent-seeking of unknown proportions more appropriately scaled to London than Iceland.

The Icelandic financial crash was first and foremost the result of neoliberal economic policies and unscrupulous investment backed by foreign banks and funds. The Icelandic banks were allowed to go bankrupt, making some people millionaires and others debtors. A simple and transparent economic universe had been transformed into a vastly more complex and inscrutable one.

Following the crash, the "real economy" has reappeared. Companies have again become the foundation for the economic well-being of the country. In addition, a new generation of knowledge-intensive companies has been created. These companies may provide a potential backbone for future development, given the opportunity to prosper. Unlike before, when innovation was localized and focused on adopting technology and practices from abroad, knowledge-intensive companies are likely to create work for the primary sector and not vice versa. Therefore, it is appropriate that policy makers reduce the weight of support for basic sectors and focus on strengthening the innovation capacity of the nation. It is important that the future backbone is not sacrificed for short-term solutions based on the further utilization of almost fully used resources, no matter how tempting it may be.

NOTES

1. Here no distinction is made between entrepreneurship involving the creation of new businesses, entrepreneurship in existing businesses, and the entrepreneurship of individuals and groups.

2. Schumpeter's ideas about creative destruction referred primarily to great technological change, such as the steam engine, railroads, and electricity. It can be argued that the term is often misapplied to events that do not have so extensive an impact on society. Nevertheless, Schumpeter's basic idea is that the competition between companies is based not only on price and costs for similar products but also on innovation that cannot be addressed with changes in prices and costs of existing products. If companies or industries are unable to meet such competition, it can be said that they will be victims of creative destruction.

3. The market for frozen fish was based on raw-material, but the market for freezing containers in the supermarkets was monopolized by a few big companies like Unilever. In the United States the main focus was on large institutional purchases and restaurant chains. In both cases there was no identification of the origin of the product or other distinction.

4. This information is based on data from Kauphöll Íslands (the Icelandic Stock Exchange).

4

---

*A Day in the Life of
an Icelandic Banker*

*Már Wolfgang Mixa was one of those reviled Icelandic
bankers, but unlike most of his colleagues, he worked from
the inside trying to warn against the insanity. Now he's fin-
ishing his PhD in cultural finance. In the course of writing
this chapter, he was appointed to the Special Investigative
Committee to study the fall of the savings banks. Here he
offers a unique perspective, from interviews with insiders
and from the inside himself, on what went wrong and how.*

• • • • • • • • • • • • • • • • • • •

The Icelandic banking system, which had no history in
investment banking, engulfed Icelandic society during a
period I refer to as the Manic Millennium (Mixa 2009).[1]
Its seeds were sown during the mid-1980s, took root in
1994, and reached full bloom from 2003 to 2008. In the
midst of a transformation in ideologies and a revolution
in communication technologies, the distinction between
investment banker and Icelander was sometimes blurred;
the qualities of investment bankers at times reflected on
Icelanders as a whole (Loftsdóttir 2009).

The financial community thus began defining the
behavior and perception of what an Icelander was.
Conversely, Icelanders increasingly saw themselves as
risk-takers, a view that was reinforced, at least for a
few years, by the market. But few Icelanders, including
bankers, had any idea how high the risk was or how far
prices had diverged from their intrinsic value.

In this chapter I examine the environment in which
Icelandic banks and bankers developed their business ideas and practices during the boom years. I also

DOI: 10.5876/9781607323358.c004

discuss how national and international factors concealed what should have been obvious to anyone with a minimum of financial savvy, namely that Icelandic bankers in general were dangerously inexperienced in the rapidly growing international investment market, and how this oversight lead to the demise of the Icelandic banking system, one of the biggest financial disasters in history, dwarfing well-publicized debacles such as Enron and WorldCom.

A BANKER'S LIFE

My Icelandic banking career began in early 1997. My first job was in a new department that had recently been created and that would become a blend of brokerage and investment banking. There were hardly any employees, but we had many desks and chairs side by side and twice as many computer screens on the desks, an unusual sight in 1997. There was a real difference between the people working there and other bankers I had worked with.[2] Our attire was international business suits, not the old-fashioned dress code for men or the bank uniforms worn by almost all women. The meeting rooms were simple in setting yet private, in stark contrast to either the customer service areas people were used to when discussing banking services or the formal bank manager offices where people tried to provide loans (bearing negative interest rates) within a restrictive and localized banking environment. While most of the workers had university business degrees, most had no investment banking experience. Financial terms were most often English slang, both because it sounded more modern and because Icelandic hadn't yet developed a special language around financial markets.

With this limited experience, there was little training. The previous year, when working at Dean Witter,[3] I had to take a three-month course and complete a nationwide exam before selling securities to customers. In Iceland I received a one-day training limited mostly to how the trading system worked before being set up in front of a computer to trade on behalf of customers and the bank without any written limits.

RISKY EXISTA

During the economic boom of 2003 to 2008, no one in Iceland, neither the general public nor most bankers and investment managers, fully realized the risks associated with fast, exponential growth. The investment company Exista illustrates how sociological factors blinded even the most financially savvy people.

Exista was formed by Kaupthing Bank in cooperation with Iceland's savings banks, which owned Kaupthing before its shares were spun off. In 2003 the brothers Ágúst and Lýður Guðmundsson (known as the Bakkavör brothers) became Exista's largest shareholders, and by the end of 2007, they owned 45.2 percent of its shares via their holding company (Exista 2007). Savings banks were the second-largest shareholder, with a combined 16.2 percent ownership via direct holdings and its Kista holding company.[4] Exista was by no means small, with total assets at year end 2007 amounting to 8 billion euros; about half of Iceland's annual GDP using the currency rate of the time.

Exista invested the bulk of its capital in very few companies and mostly in its largest shareholder's own company, the food producer Bakkavör, and their main associate, Kaupthing Bank. The largest holding was, however, the insurance company Sampo Group, which was rumored to be a take-over target of Kaupthing. The combined book value of Kaupthing and Sampo was 4.7 billion euros, nearly 60 percent of Exista's total assets. Bakkavör accounted for approximately 7 percent of total assets; hence two-thirds of Exista's capital was sitting in three companies, all listed on public stock exchanges.

Exista was a big shareholder in those three companies, holding 39.6 percent of Bakkavör's stock, 23.7 percent of Kaupthing's stock, and 19.98 percent of Sampo's stock (20 percent was the threshold regarding obligations related to the control of the company). Essentially, Exista had almost no exit route if markets took a nosedive.[5]

The leverage and thus risk of Exista was alarming. Judging by the book value, the equity ratio at year end 2007 was 29.5 percent,[6] down from 43.2 percent the prior year. In a report in the business newspaper *Viðskiptablaðið* regarding Icelandic holding companies, Sigurður Jónsson (2009) points out that those equity ratios may be normal for companies that actually produce goods, especially consumer staples yielding relatively constant revenues, but not for investment companies that are wiped out in the next downturn in stock markets. For some perspective, the lowest equity ratio since the first quarter of 2003 of Sweden's main investment holding company, Investor AB, is 77 percent.[7] Warren Buffett's investment holding company,[8] Berkshire Hathaway, generally has an equity ratio around 100 percent, meaning that it has no net liabilities (Buffett and Clark 1997; Hagstrom 2005).

The report refers to an interview in *Viðskiptablaðið* in early 2006 in which Lýður Guðmundsson (then the current owner) said that Exista aimed at investing in companies through leveraged buyouts. A research report titled *Exista hf.: Right Place, Waiting for the Right Time* (Ögmundsdóttir and Pétursson 2007) confirms this. The report is the only detailed one regarding

Exista that was publicly distributed and, not surprisingly, since its analysts were employed by Kaupthing, contained a recommendation to buy. It shows that while Exista's assets swelled in size, growing fourfold in a span of two years, its liabilities multiplied even more; they were fivefold during the same period. With an immensely leveraged balance sheet, the meager profits of the underlying investments actually appeared as substantial profits, pleasing the shareholders who seemed oblivious of the associated risks. However, given the historical volatility of stock markets, where valuations fall every now and then more than 40 percent (which has already happened twice this century), it is difficult to see how this strategy would not have ended by crashing and burning.

Despite the obvious risk associated with Exista, no one in the public or banking sectors at home or abroad seemed to notice. More alarming was that its stock was a huge base of equity of many savings banks in Iceland and its rise in market value the major source, in most cases the sole source, of temporary profits during the peak of the Manic Millennium. A case in point is the Savings Bank of Keflavík (Sparisjóður Keflavíkur 2007), which had three-quarters of its shareholder equity directly and indirectly in Exista. From year-end 2002 to year-end 2006 it had more than doubled its balance sheet.[9] Other savings banks had similar stories, recklessly lending money from extremely fragile balance sheets.[10]

Financially the Manic Millennium resembled the Roaring 1920s in the United States in many ways (Mixa 2009). During both periods, there was an explosion in the formation of investment trusts (Fridson 1998), many of which leveraged themselves, frequently buying shares of the issuing companies or their affiliates at prices as much as double their intrinsic market value (Galbraith 1997). Kaupthing's research report, paradoxically, shows that the price-to-book ratio was 1.5 at the time of writing.[11] Put another way, people were paying at least 1.5 times the amount of money for a few stocks generally available on the open market because of the company's representation of success built upon reckless risk. In the end equity investors lost everything, and bondholders lost a sizable percentage of their lending, since Exista's crash was also the single biggest company bond loss among Icelandic pension funds (Landssamtök Lífeyrissjóða 2012).

SETTING THE STAGE FOR THE MANIC MILLENNIUM

So what kind of environment creates and promotes the likes of Exista? It has been said that the four most expensive words in the English language are

"This time is different."[12] Those words certainly applied to Iceland during the buildup of the bubble that Exista thrived in. Iceland is special because it had no real history of commercial banking and absolutely none of investment banking. For a long time it was relatively isolated from other Nordic nations and Europe, with its population spread in rural areas and its banking localized. After the Bank of Iceland (Íslandsbanki) went bankrupt during the Great Depression, it became a highly regulated system similar to those of Nordic nations, with political connections and governmental policies dictating which industries should receive preferential treatment (Sigurjónsson and Mixa 2011; Jonung 2008; Englund 1999). Foreign currency restrictions became the norm in Iceland, and Icelanders traveling abroad, for example, had to specifically apply for currency for their travel expenses. Real interest rates were often negative, meaning that access to money was an asset in itself, with demand constantly higher than supply. Specific interest groups thus began creating "their" banks during the next decades, their names reflecting the groups they mainly served and lent to rather than promoting any specialization in lending (Sigurður Jóhannesson 2004). Some of these include the Bank of Industry (Iðnaðarbankinn), formed in 1953; the Icelandic Bank of Commerce (Verzlunarbanki Íslands), formed in 1963; and the People's Bank of Iceland (Alþýðubanki Íslands), formed in 1971 by the labor unions (Ásgeir Jónsson 2009).

This restrictive environment began to change very slowly during the mid-1980s. Domestic bank rates were fully liberalized in 1986 and restriction on capital movements fully abolished in 1995. A year earlier, Iceland had joined the European Economic Area (EEA), which also liberalized foreign direct investment within parameters of the EEA agreement (Mixa and Sigurjónsson 2010), breaking down the currency restrictions and connecting the country's economy globally. This development marked two watershed moments: it opened the door to the internationalization of financial markets, and it set up the same kind of financial liberalization that had befallen the Bank of Iceland in 1930. These innovations were aimed at making efficient a banking system that had been bloated and inefficient for years. In Iceland this was further amplified with its 1994 EEA membership.

The trend in international banking was to combine traditional banking and investment banking. Traditional banking revolves mainly around basic lending procedures, and banks make money from traditional banking services, such as ATM services, checking accounts, and lending. The interest rate differential—lending, say, at an interest rate of 6 percent but paying on average 3 percent for saving accounts—is usually the prime source of profits of such banking. Investment banking, however, is focused on raising money for companies, an act that often involves investing in other companies. For a long time, such companies were owned by owners, who, like in-law firms, guarded their interests with great care since their own money was on the line (Lewis 2010).

Unlike traditional banks, investment banks do not raise money from the public via deposits but, instead, almost entirely through what is known as long-term investments.[13] The traditional banking that Icelanders were accustomed to was more like the grease for the economy, with short-term funding the norm. There is, however, the inherent danger that depositors may demand their money back. That's what deposit insurance is made for. By providing such programs, which became universal following the Great Depression, governments placed restrictions on banking practices to dampen the kind of speculative behavior that was rampant during the 1920s (Galbraith 1997; Sobel 1968; Bruner and Carr 2007), justified by the fact that taxpayers' money would fund depositors' losses. While walls between US investment and commercial banking had been in place for decades,[14] there had never been a need to set them up in Iceland because no investment banking existed. Thus, Icelandic banking entered the international arena with adrenalized risk-taking and no restrictive shackles in place, with the chance to act like investment bankers yet funded with deposit money backed by the government.

PRIVATIZATION—A WORLD OF EFFICIENCY

The privatization that had begun in 1992 was going full bore by 2002. Two of Iceland's main banks had been partially privatized in 1998, just a year after my Icelandic banking career began. The large number of shareholders made it look like the banks were still owned by the people of Iceland. Just four years later, though, individuals and groups that had little if any banking experience but excellent political connections were allowed to buy a controlling stake in each bank. This new dynamic changed the mission of the banks from service to growth. The banks' new goal was to expand their balance sheets and become big players (Sigurjónsson and Mixa 2011). One CEO remarked to one of the board members that he wanted to duplicate Merrill Lynch, which he had recently visited.[15] The main investor of the Central Bank of Iceland, who also became chairman of the board, declared in a television interview shortly after the privatization that he was determined to make his bank the biggest one of the three.

As Icelandic bankers went on acquisition sprees across Europe, the media, increasingly owned by the same bankers (Áskelsdóttir 2010), began reporting on them as Vikings pillaging on foreign shores, dubbing the bankers "Business Vikings." Despite having banking roots that were localized and regulated like Nordic banks, Icelandic bankers (at least the ones deemed successful during the boom years) were described in the media as having greater financial expertise and working more quickly than bankers in most other nations (Loftsdóttir 2009). The public believed this, despite the fact that modern banking in Iceland was only a few years old. I was considered one of the most experienced investment bankers in the country, yet had been a novice just a few years earlier.

DOMESTIC AND FOREIGN PERCEPTION

Public awe of the "brilliance" of its bankers is a common phenomenon during the buildup to financial crashes (Englund 1999; Gleeson 1999; Chancellor 2000). Galbraith (1997) states that the mood is far more important than the interest rate during a boom. He adds that the prerequisite of a boom is trust in leaders and in the benevolence of others to create some sort of conviction that ordinary people should be rich. In Iceland the media became a central player in creating such trust. The Icelandic tabloid *Séð og heyrt* focused on businessmen and politicians, the latter becoming ever less relevant during the Manic Millennium. In an article published barely half a year before the collapse, pictures taken at the Business Conference 2008 show politicians mingling with businessmen at the conference. The article quotes one CEO saying, "It was enjoyable seeing all the politicians there. It is good that such a good relationship exists between politicians and the business community" (Jónsson 2008, 19).

The country was engulfed in the developments of financial markets, and owners of the banks promoted their interests via the media they largely owned. A reinforcing cycle developed in which those who sought the most risk became media heroes. The perception of Icelandic bankers being the best and fastest was promoted inside as well as outside the banks. An internal video at Kaupthing, entitled *"What Is Kaupthinking?"* (Kaupþing, n.d.), emphasized the values of acting quickly. It starts with images from the United States, such as Martin Luther King Jr. demonstrating in Washington, Bill Gates, and a launch to the moon and juxtaposes them to scenes from Tiananmen Square and the fall of the Berlin Wall, coupled with the written and spoken words "We can." The narrator then says; "We thought we could double in size and we did, every year for eight years," and a few seconds later in a reference of winning out over the authority of a rigid state, the narrator says, "We think we can grow by outwitting bureaucracy, by moving faster, by being flexible . . . " The message was clear: growth mattered.

The Financial Supervisory Authority had big problems catching up with the new environment. Simple regulations separating the bank's proprietary investments from investments on behalf of their clients, for example, had just been enacted in 2002 (Fjármálaeftirlitið 2002), with more separation between the operation of banks and mutual funds coming in 2003 (Fjármálaeftirlitið 2003). The staff of the supervisory agency did not grow in nearly the same proportion as the ranks of the financial industry. It was common knowledge in the industry that the best workers were snatched up by the banks when they began learning how to question the banks' operations.

Thus bankers learned slowly but surely that making deals quickly counted the most. A former Icelandic banker who headed one of the big three banks told me that when he first arrived in 2003, he had lots of ideas about how to improve the bank's operations and efficiency. By 2007, he was amazed at how focused his coworkers had become on simply getting deals together with little due diligence. Within a few years he had gone from being considered an aggressive banker to being viewed as a "fuddy-duddy."[16]

This was not a phenomenon exclusive to Iceland. An international banker I interviewed in London gave an example of a prudent banker working the numbers to reach a decision. The banker across the street decided to skip the number-crunching and focus instead on getting the deal done quickly and simply trusting *the market*. Bankers' confidence in the market price blinded them to research done by ratings agencies, such as Moody's, Standard & Poor's, and Fitch (Lewis 2010). Another international banker told me that finance professionals all over the world lost sight of their role in an industry that rewarded short-term personal greed and punished long-term value. Worldwide, central figures in the finance industry, such as bankers, were able to claim just enough knowledge to keep their power by getting deals done (as opposed to putting thought into them) but not enough knowledge to take responsibility (Davies and McGoey 2012), something that became apparent after the crash.

GOOD AND BAD BANKERS

In his 1989 exposé, *Liar's Poker*, Michael Lewis describes the person who makes the most money as a "Big Swinging Dick." No matter what happened, he ruled. One experienced banker I interviewed felt the same about what happened in Icelandic banking at the time: Inexperienced bankers powered manic growth while making easy money. Meanwhile prudent, more experienced bankers were sent to the sidelines. At Icebank's trading desk, where I worked in 2008, the combined banking experience of the twelve to fourteen employees there was barely fifteen years, with no one having worked in banking for more than two years. They were handling interbank loans amounting to 20 percent of Iceland's GDP and lost almost all of it during the 2008 meltdown. Without the anchor of experience, it was easy to be convinced that all was well. Most of the experienced bankers I interviewed agreed that young people could be easily molded. One Icelandic banker quoted another as saying that twenty-five was old for a bank employee.

This inexperience may also explain how stratification within the banks developed easily, with the top layer keeping information from the rest. Only a very few people knew the dire state of the banks for the longest time. When I expressed concerns to an Icebank employee in April 2008, I had to backpedal quickly when I saw how shocked my coworker was at what I considered a casual remark. After that, I made sure that I expressed my concerns only to persons who had some knowledge of the precarious state of the bank. Little by little, a small group would meet regularly in a specific room to make sure that our talks were limited to a small circle.

These small, highly stratified layers made the deals of the primary owners and bank associates a priority over the banks' normal operations. Many loans were made to holding companies with close ties to the owners of the banks and their cronies. As Figure 4.1 demonstrates, between 2005 and 2008 the robust increase of household loans looks tame compared with the frenzied rise in loans to holding companies.[17]

In one glaring example, bankers lent the equivalent of well over $100 million to holding companies for the sole purpose of buying a controlling stake in a savings bank. The owners of the holding companies were business partners of the biggest shareholder (another savings bank) of the bank in question and the top management team of the savings bank being bought. With the exception of one buyer, the people involved only had to lay out costs connected with the creation of the holding companies, an amount estimated to total $100,000. Practically the entire purchase price was lent by other savings banks, and shares in the bank were the sole collateral. This meant that if the bank remained successful (as it had been in previous years), the buyers would become millionaires. Since the bank went bankrupt shortly afterward, each of the new owners (with one exception) lost what amounted to approximately $10,000.[18]

Suspicions of such cronyism entered my mind when I was asked in early 2008 to write a memo about whether it was prudent to lend money to a holding company whose only purpose was investing in stocks, which was also their

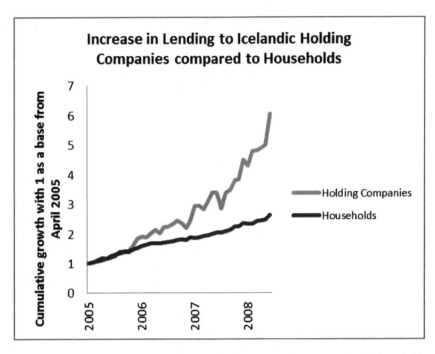

FIGURE 4.1. *Increase in lending to Icelandic holding companies compared with households, 2005–2008. Data based on Central Bank of Iceland 2009.*

only collateral. I asked why the bank didn't simply buy shares in the companies themselves, reaping the rewards if the stocks rose in value. Wouldn't this be more valuable than getting the loan back with some interest? But of course the bank stood to lose money if the stock value decreased, I explained. I was never asked to write such a memo again.

Many people I interviewed, as well as coworkers, expressed bitterness at having fought to keep the banks afloat for what they then considered a just cause, only to find out that they were actually fighting for the interests of small groups. It was amazing how so many bankers were kept in the dark.

Interviews with other mid-level foreign bankers about their Icelandic counterparts have been rather positive. One banker specifically said that the myth of Icelandic bankers moving so quickly on deals did have some substance, explaining that the Icelanders were willing to do what it took to get business going and were in general "not out to get me." Another Nordic banker said that, in his experience, business in Iceland was not materially different from business in other Nordic countries with the exception of the relative lack of experience and the strong appetite for risk. This view does not, however, apply to the top level of bankers. One foreign banker called them crooks, while another one talked at length about how they lied to maintain business relationships. Tony Shearer, CEO of Singer & Friedlander when Kaupthing bought the company, described Icelandic top-level bankers with whom he worked as being very confident of themselves and their capabilities (personal communication, January 27, 2012). Despite Shearer's decades of international banking experience, the Icelanders who bought his company *never* asked his advice on any matter.

"BAD" BANKERS WITHIN A UTOPIAN ECONOMY

Iceland was like its farmers' cows freed in the spring after being locked inside the barn all winter, full of life but not necessarily managing freedom very well. Icelanders embraced the free market mantra that they believed entailed harmony and stability, something Cassidy (2009) argues was built on an illusion. Neoliberalism was initially built upon the concept of freedom, the argument that governments could not decide what was best for their citizens, and slowly the argument evolved until the efficiency of the market was in the front seat (Davies and McGoey 2012). Icelanders justified the privatization of banks not only because it increased efficiency but also because of the implied declaration of nationalistic freedom. As Cassidy (2009) puts it, by privatizing the banks the way they did, neoliberal proponents created free markets that contained incentives for individuals and groups to act in ways that were individually rational but in the end damaging to themselves and others. It is also no secret that the main owners of the new banks had political ties. It became general knowledge that being associated with the Independence Party enhanced one's chances of being hired at the Central Bank of Iceland, as was the case with a former director of the Independence Party becoming one of the bank's board members.

Forces in the top levels of Icelandic business and politics thus had great incentives to embrace the neoliberal movement by handing the banking sector and many national treasures over to their cronies. It was essential that the public followed suit. By increasing bank profits, improving efficiency, and abandoning the shackles of a restrictive past, the public was willing to go along.

These developments opened certain doors to liberating the financial system. What was different about the liberalization process in Iceland, judging from the behavior of Icelanders and citizens of other Nordic countries, can be partially explained by the fact that the Nordic countries didn't throw those doors wide open. In addition to having learned their lessons from the financial crisis of the early 1990s, the Nordic countries did not have as much to prove to the world as Iceland, which desperately wanted to be a player on the international stage (Loftsdóttir 2010; 2012b). The Icelandic banking system was opened to corruption without the necessary accountability. Like the general public, most bankers were simply part of a process that enabled those at the top with ties to politicians (Vaiman, Sigurjonsson, and Davídsson 2011) to concentrate on their self-interests while sacrificing the long-term interests of the nation.

THE MOMENT OF TRUTH

Chronic nationalism and the feeling of prosperity made Iceland particularly vulnerable to the economic boom and bust, but it is not the only country to have suffered this tragedy. Following the breakdown of the Iron Curtain in 1990 and the subsequent fall of communism, a belief in the superiority of capitalism reigned worldwide (Steger and Roy 2010). Keynesian economics, which was crafted after the Great Depression and gave governmental controls their place, gave way to free market views, which had been gathering steam since the 1970s (Fox 2009). The collapse of communism shifted the ideological balance, giving neoclassical ideologies—free markets govern themselves best—a strong foothold. The new ideology was amplified in Iceland in 1994 when it gained EEA membership, making it more globalized and simultaneously susceptible to international trends. International phone communications during that time became much less expensive, and the rise of the Internet transformed Iceland from a country in isolation to one in constant touch with the world. The domination of capitalism and increased communication potential set the stage for the irrational optimism that Shiller (2001) lists as a precipitating factor of a financial bubble. When such a trend persists, a representation of the past amplifies the general view of future trends (Kahneman and Tversky 1982). This is consistent with the insights of Soros (2003): financial markets operate with a prevailing bias, a dynamic that validates this bias by influencing not only market prices but also the assumed fundamentals that market prices should reflect (and that may actually transform toward the prevailing bias). This is amplified until the moment of truth, when people stop believing the hype but may still participate in the madness until they swiftly come to their senses.

Reports after the crash indicate that most politicians were in the dark about the situation until early 2008. The light flickered on following an internal conference at the Central Bank of Iceland in February 2008, when grim warning signs of the impending crisis were announced.[19] The day after the meeting, a Central Bank of Iceland internal memo was circulated, expressing shock over the negative views that foreign senior bankers had expressed during a recent visit. The memo states, for example, that the foreigners said Glitnir bankers were both desperate and inexperienced and Kaupthing bankers were not to be trusted.[20] When Prime Minister Geir Haarde announced a state of emergency at the height of the crash on October 6, 2008, and declared "God Bless Iceland!" my fellow Icebank employees stared at the television screen in utter disbelief. It was the beginning of the end.

NOTES

1. The combined balance sheets of the banking system was approximately the same as the amount of Iceland's gross domestic product (GDP) in a single year around the millennium, but had grown to around seven to eight times that figure in 2007 (Halldorsson and Zoega 2010).

2. I had worked at various positions at Landsbanki Íslands from 1986 to 1987 and as a summer employee from 1988 to 1992.

3. Dean Witter bought Morgan Stanley two years later and became among the biggest investment houses in the world.

4. This information was derived from Exista's 2007 annual report (Exista 2007) and other annual reports from smaller savings banks, which have limited general availability.

5. Holding such a large percentage of the outstanding stock meant that attempts to liquidate the assets would drive the market price quickly down unless a buyer could be found for a huge share. Such a buyer would likely be acutely aware of this and demand a discount unless other interests were also involved.

6. The equity ratio is a financial ratio indicating the relative proportion of equity used to finance a company's assets. The less it is, the more risk is associated with the financing of the company. If total assets are, for example, $100, of which $60 is financed with bonds and loans, then the equity ratio is 40 percent. If merely $30 is financed with bonds and loans, the equity ratio has gone up to 70 percent, meaning the company is less reliant on the "understanding" of lenders if losses begin piling up.

7. Investor AB, "Investor in Figures: Key Figures," 2009 (spreadsheets), author's files.

8. Warren Buffett is arguably the world's most famous investor, becoming one of the richest people in the world through shrewd investments.

9. Its balance sheet was ISK 18.9 billion at year end 2002 and ISK 48 billion four years later. Its growth in real terms was, however, slightly more than double since the combined inflation during that period was 19 percent.

10. This was also done via issuances of subordinated debt, which can be used to conceal the fragility of balance sheets.

11. A ratio that shows the market price of a stock compared to the book value of the owner's equity.

12. Also the title of a book by Reinhart and Rogoff (2009) concentrating on financial data as warning signs of financial crashes.

13. Some people argue about the state of investment banking prior to the crash in 2008, which at that point relied to a great degree on short-term lending funds, but that was not the traditional way of investment bank funding.

14. The Glass-Steagall Act, enacted by the US Congress in 1933, separated investment banking and commercial banking following the failures of some banks that had invested heavily in the stock market; it was repealed in 1999.

15. This is from a confidential source. The CEO's name and company will remain anonymous.

16. This person will remain anonymous.

17. Figures are available only from early 2005.

18. At the time of writing, this information was confidential but is expected to become public at a future date.

19. For an analysis in English of reactions to the precarious financial standing of Iceland's banks, see "Causes of the Collapse of the Icelandic Banks—Responsibility, Mistakes and Negligence," sec. 21.5.4.2, in Rannsóknarnefnd Alþingis 2010; available at http://www.rna.is/media/skjol/RNAvefurKafli21Enska.pdf.

20. The memo, stamped "Trúnaðarmál" (Confidential) and dated February 12, 2008, is available at http://eyjan.pressan.is/frettir/wp-content/uploads/2009/03/minnisblad -si-feb-2008.PDF.

5

*Something Rotten in
the State of Iceland*

*"The Production of Truth"
about the Icelandic Banks*

*Vilhjálmur Árnason is professor of philosophy and chair
of the Centre for Ethics at the University of Iceland. He
chaired a parliamentary Working Group on Ethics that
studied the meltdown and its causes. He offers an insider's view of the deliberations of this important committee, which had little patience for any meltdown theories
that echoed the rationale that caused it. By analyzing four
sectors of Icelandic society, Árnason skewers "methodological individualism"—a companion of neoliberalism that
blames individual bad behavior instead of a system of
policies—for its failure to adequately explain the causes of
the financial collapse.*

••••••••••••••••••••

Unfortunately, the diagnosis and cure share
a basic misconception: that professional and
corporate misconduct are problems caused
by some few weak, uninformed, or misguided
individuals making poor choices.

SUSAN S. SILBEY, "ROTTEN
APPLES OR A ROTTING BARREL"

The Working Group on Ethics (WGE) worked in
close cooperation with the Special Investigation Commission (SIC) of the Icelandic Parliament, which was
charged with finding out the truth about the events
that led to the financial crisis. The WGE addressed
the question: Could the collapse of the banks and
related financial setbacks to some extent be explained

DOI: 10.5876/9781607323358.c005

by morality and work practices? In this chapter, I try to shed light on how the WGE approached this complex task through a discussion of the example of the success story of the banks. I chose this example because it demonstrates the complex interconnection of agents and events at various levels of society. In order to discern the network of forces at work in "the production of truth" or the dynamics of image-making in Icelandic society and the lack of resistance to it, the analysis of this example draws upon Foucault's notion of horizontal power. This approach rejects methodological individualism as an inadequate and distorting way to deal with complex social phenomena. Ethical analysis must not be restricted to individual actions and character traits, as is prevalent in the quasi-moral discourse about the causes of the financial collapse and the concomitant social and political crisis in Iceland.

There are many who want to tell the story differently. When Davíð Oddsson, former prime minister of Iceland and former chairman of the board of the Central Bank of Iceland, was asked about the financial collapse, he said, "Perhaps it can be said that in many ways we were very unlucky with the crew that came aboard these banks. They are competent men in every regard but they were seized by enthusiasm [. . .] for an enormous profit" (quoted in Árnason, Nordal, and Ásgeirsdóttir 2010, 189). In this statement, two things are especially striking. First, that a handful of individuals, the bankers, are the main culprits in the collapse of the Icelandic banks. Second, that they were overtaken by greed, one of the seven deadly sins and a cardinal vice in Western thought. This is a clear example of a half-truth. Oddsson has much at stake in diverting attention from his own political legacy and neoliberal ideology to the bad behavior of bankers who betrayed the trust invested in them. But this is not my concern here. What interests me is the methodological individualism this kind of explanation demonstrates and how it covers up important explanatory factors.

The president of the Icelandic Parliament stated in the letter of ordinance to the WGE that the inquiry was not to be restricted to morality and working practices within the Icelandic financial sector; other sectors might come under scrutiny as well. This was of crucial importance for the WGE's analysis. Group members realized early on that they could not explain the actions in the financial sector and their impact without examining them in a wider context. So they attempted to assess morality and work practice in three main sectors or social spheres and their interrelations: the business and financial sector, the administrative and political sector, and the social and cultural sector.

I will demonstrate this approach by showing how the various threads of the social discourse about the banks that developed in Icelandic society in the years before the financial crisis were interwoven in a complex net of social relations. Success stories of the Icelandic bankers were conspicuous in the period preceding the financial collapse in 2008. These stories originated from within financial institutions where highly ranked public relations officers had direct access to their CEOs. During the course of the investigation, it became clear that much of the narrative about success was built on shaky ground, was at times largely fabricated, and was part of an image-making machine needed to perpetuate the process. And who should have resisted these processes? Anyone with a direct or indirect obligation to guard the public interest: professionals; politicians; media reporters; experts (e.g., in universities); and the general public.

PROFESSIONAL RESISTANCE

The WGE's report argues that professionals never work exclusively in the interests of a company or institution that pays for their services but must also take the public interest into account. This is evident from most professional codes of ethics where the public responsibility of professionals is described by principles like the following, on honesty: "We adhere to the highest standards of accuracy and truth in advancing the interests of those we represent and in communicating with the public" (PRSA 2012, n.p.). A public relations officer who distorts facts about a company and hinders media access to truthful information undermines the structures of the democratic state (Weaver, Motion, and Roper 2006). The WGE analysis showed that, as a rule, professionals such as lawyers, accountants, and public relations people did not take their public responsibility seriously. Instead, they uncritically facilitated the dynamics of the financial companies.

To be sure, PR people and other professionals were acting in accordance with a corporate culture promulgated by the banks. An experienced and well-respected foreign compliance officer who worked in one of the Icelandic banks for a short period in 2007 described the atmosphere in the bank as "cultish." There was considerable pressure for everyone to think alike. One way this was achieved was through generational change. Managers with traditional banking experience were replaced by young (mostly) males who had what was considered the appropriate mentality for investment banking. As one of the bank directors of Kaupthing Bank said, "It is very hard to change a culture without changing employees" ("Eftir höfðinu dansa limirnir" 2006). This new organizational culture was characterized by a lack of professional detachment and a strong devotion to the institution. Growth became more important than following the rules (Árnason 2010).

In this way, the organizational setting and culture of the banks provided both the motivation and opportunities for misconduct as well as the thoughtlessness that enables it. Certainly, individuals make bad decisions and are guilty of wrongful action, but they do so within an environment that breeds it. By the same token, environmental conditions can also provide moral incentives that constrain bad actions. A major lesson to learn from the Icelandic banking experiment is that it was unrealistic of the Icelandic financial regulators to place trust in bankers who had no roots in a trustworthy banking culture and, in fact, undermined the industry's traditional foundations by an excessively risky business model. Instead of trying to build a manageable banking system for a small nation that had no experience in international investment banking, Icelandic politicians let young bankers loose to build a banking sector that became almost nine times larger than the national economy with drastic effects on all sectors of society.

THE RESPONSIBILITY OF POLITICIANS

The primary responsibility of politicians is to work in the public interest and to promote the common good. The WGE analysis demonstrated how many Icelandic politicians failed to exercise this responsibility by siding unconditionally with the bankers. For example, politicians typically backed bankers' characterization of criticism in foreign reports and media abroad as malicious attacks by competitors envious of Icelandic banking success. Key ministers participated in road shows meant to strengthen the image of the banks. In so doing, they also made it manifest that the Icelandic state was behind the banks, lending them credibility.

Uncritical support of the banks was also predominant among members of Parliament, for which the WGE report blames an immature political culture. The partisan bickering and strategic rhetoric that dominates political discussion is an obstacle in the way of dealing objectively with information and identifying the true state of affairs. The primary emphasis is on winning the political game, making the origin of the statement more important than its validity. Politicians tend to behave like the polemicist who "possesses rights authorizing him to wage war and making that struggle a just undertaking; the person he confronts is not a partner in the search for the truth, but an adversary, an enemy who is wrong . . ." (Foucault 1984a, 382).

The WGE inquired about the direct financial connection between the political sector and the financial companies. It turned out that with the exception of the Left-Green Party, all political parties and many individual politicians had received donations from financial companies. While the US financial industry donated $180 million to political campaigns in 2010, or 60 cents per person, "the roughly comparable Icelandic figure, according to the SIC report, was $8 per person in 2006, or 14 times as much" (Gylfason 2012, 9). Moreover, ten members of Parliament were in considerable debt to the banks, an average of €9 million (US$12 million) per person (Rannsóknarnefnd Alþingis 2010, 2:200), or, in current exchange rates, €5.4 million (US$7.3 million) per person. For decades, until 2007, Icelandic politicians—especially members of the largest party, the Independence Party—resisted setting rules about financial donations to politicians.

Iceland has always scored very high on international monitoring of corruption, largely because one of the key measures is bribery of public officials. Such corruption hardly existed in Iceland, but the relationship between the financial and political sectors has always been close, if not "incestuous," as one professor of economics put it (Gylfason 2012). Privatization of the banks was meant to be the remedy, but contrary to the principles established for the process, it ended as a political deal between the two main parties, the Independence Party and the Progressive Party. The banks were sold to relatively young and inexperienced bankers, favored by key politicians.

These are a few of the reasons why politicians were not motivated to resist the message of Icelandic banking success. They had themselves invested in their success, both politically and financially, and were unlikely to undertake a critical analysis of the banks, as would have been consistent with their primary responsibility of protecting the public interest. A parliamentary proposal to investigate power and democracy in Icelandic society, as some other Nordic countries had done (Togeby et al. 2003), was sent to a committee for consideration but never implemented. The Nordic countries had launched such an investigation because power had been gradually moving from elected representatives to financial corporations in the private sector.

Nowhere in the Nordic countries had this development been as drastic as in Iceland. The same authorities who had purposefully facilitated the growth of the banks by various political decisions related to the liberalization of the financial environment later stood paralyzed in front of their own creature. This is well analyzed in the executive summary, provided in English, of the Special Investigation Commission (2010, 17):

> The powerlessness of the government and the authorities, when it came to
> reducing the size of the financial system in time before a financial shock hit,
> is evident when looking at the history . . . It is also clear that when the size

of the financial system of a country is, for instance, threefold its gross domestic product, the competent authorities of the country have, in general, the potential to set rules for the financial system to comply with and to ensure compliance with such rules. However, when the size of the financial system of a country is nine times its gross domestic product the roles are reversed. This was the case in Iceland. It appears that both the parliament and the government lacked both the power and the courage to set reasonable limits to the financial system. All the energy seems to have been directed at keeping the financial system going. It had grown so large, that it was impossible to risk that even one part of it would collapse.

THE ROLE OF THE MEDIA

The role of the media in a democracy is to keep citizens informed about what is happening in society (Preston 2008). The WGE prepared a special report (Guðmundsson et al. 2010) on the media in the years preceding the collapse. It concluded that the Icelandic media had failed badly in this regard. Media reporting about the financial sector was largely built on press releases issued by the companies, framed in such a way that it served their interests (Árnason, Nordal, and Ástgeirsdóttir 2010, 265). Independent, critical professional analysis was minimal. All the main media were owned by the financial corporations except the state-owned radio and television. Editors of Icelandic media reported to the WGE interesting anecdotes about the interaction between the media and the financial sector. For example, in some cases business reporters had befriended spokespeople of the company and formed such a "cozy relationship" that they lost all credibility as reporters.

This is characteristic of the change in the workings of power in Iceland during these years. Consider the following remark from the news director of the Icelandic National Broadcasting Service (RÚV), appointed after the meltdown:

> It could be said that our main energy in the last few years has been spent on making us independent of the political power. For example, I happen to be the first director of RÚV who is hired without direct political interference, without being selected by a politically appointed council. In other words, I think that we have become experts in defending ourselves against politicians, but this big change in society regarding increased power of the business sector may have escaped us and we had no proper experts in analyzing the business life. And those who became close to being knowledgeable were simply bought out by the banks (quoted in ibid., 199).

The descending, intervening power from above in the form of orders, backed by a threat or a sanction, had changed to a horizontal power that never threatens but invites and befriends. Moreover, this power "is not that which makes the difference between those who exclusively possess and retain it, and those who do not have it and submit to it" (Foucault 1980, 98). The phenomenon of self-censorship repeatedly came up in the interviews with the editors. In a small society with a small media circle, there is self-imposed pressure to avoid a reputation for being difficult. Or in the words of an editor of an Icelandic newspaper: "There were here a few corporations that dominated everything and if people wanted to work with certain trades they didn't have many options. If they came into opposition with one or two men even, they would literally not have any job opportunities. I think that this is at least part of the explanation, that people were afraid of losing their very subsistence" (quoted in Árnason, Nordal, and Ástgeirsdóttir 2010, 206).

It proved unusually difficult for journalists to get information from the financial system for the same reason. The editor observed, "It was bit scary when we were looking for information how the collusion in the system was pervasive." According to the editor, this was not because there was some systematic silencing terror going on. "People simply kept silent because they did not dare to speak or did not want to speak. They had perhaps some knowledge about something they found suspicious in the system, but they all had a good salary or took part in lucrative projects etc." (quoted in ibid., 205).

Judging from this description, the reason why the success story of the banks met with so little resistance in Icelandic society can be put in terms of the subtle workings of horizontal power, which normalizes behavior in much more effective ways than traditional forms of subjugation and domination. This is because the individuals who are subject to the power are employing it at the same time: "Power is employed and exercised through a net-like organization. And not only do individuals circulate between its threads; they are always in the position of simultaneously undergoing and exercising this power. They are not only its inert or consenting target; they are always also the elements of its articulation. In other words, individuals are the vehicles of power, not its point of application" (Foucault 1980, 98).

ACADEMIC EXPERTS

The editors interviewed by the WGE criticized experts in Icelandic universities for being unwilling to take part in the public discussion about the state of the Icelandic banks and the financial sector in general. In a small country where the media are both financially and professionally weak, it is important that journalists can seek the assistance of academics in analyzing facts and assessing complex situations such as those which frequently arose in the years preceding the financial collapse. Complex financial products, such as financial derivative instruments, as well as multiple cross-lending and cross-ownership relationships, characterized the period and made the situation opaque and difficult for the media to discern and interpret. In 2008 a Danish business editor said that it was unusually difficult to obtain information about the ownership and operation of the Icelandic financial companies ("Segja danska fjölmiðla ósanngjarna" 2008).

Do academics have an obligation to take part in public debate or contribute to public literacy, for example, in financial matters? Should they have provided resistance to the narrative about the success of the Icelandic bankers? Often academics alone have the knowledge that is necessary to analyze the issues, place them in a sensible context, and reveal distorting statements. According to Foucault, this has implications for the role of the intellectual in contemporary society: "The role of the specific intellectual must become more and more important in proportion to the political responsibilities which he is obliged willy-nilly to accept, as a nuclear scientist, computer expert, pharmacologist, etc." (Foucault 1984b, 72).

This relates to the role of the university and the civic obligations of academics. The primary responsibility of academics is to teach and perform research, for which they are granted academic freedom. This is fleshed out in the third principle of the *Magna Charta Universitatum*: "Freedom in research and training is the fundamental principle of university life, and governments and universities . . . must ensure respect for this fundamental requirement" (Magna Charta Observatory 1988, n.p.). It is important to take both an internal and external perspective on the conditions for this principle. Internally, this relates to the culture and practices of universities, while externally it concerns the social and cultural atmosphere in which a university either thrives or doesn't. One of the major preconditions of fruitful academic work is that it is carried out in a tolerant democratic environment that fosters informed public opinion. "This means," a commentator on the principles of the Magna Charta declaration writes, "exercising a critical part—well informed, constructive and relatively free from those special interests most people are affected by. The third Magna Charta principle thus implies that academics, because of their professional standing and capacity for critical thinking, have also the obligation to take up issues that they know to be ignored by others, due to various pressures" (Jónasson 2008, 62–63).

Foucault writes that the intellectual is obligated whether he or she likes it or not. That implies that every intellectual or academic accepts or neglects this responsibility by the way he or she acts. It is crucial, however, to see the task as one not of separating the truth from the effects of power and ideology "(which would be a chimera, for truth is already power), but of detaching the power from the forms of hegemony, social, economic, and cultural, within which it operates at the present time" (Foucault 1984b, 74–75). The hegemony, or over-whelming presence and power of the financial discourse in "the production of truth" or image-making in Icelandic society, required critical resistance from academics, who were in a unique position to analyze it.

Some Icelandic intellectuals tried, but the soil for receiving their criticism was not fertile. There were also striking examples of the reverse, of academics going uncritically into the service of the "financial regime of the production of truth," to use Foucault-inspired terminology. In 2006 the Danish Central Bank issued a report that proffered a negative prognosis of the financial situation and exposed many weaknesses of Icelandic banks (Danske Bank 2006). In response, the Iceland Chamber of Commerce commissioned its own report, authored by Frederick S. Mishkin, professor of economics at the Columbia Business School, and Dr. Tryggvi Thor Herbertsson, director of the Economic Institute at the University of Iceland (Mishkin and Herbertsson 2006). That report played a major role in assuring both Icelandic politicians and the international community at a critical time in the period leading up to the financial collapse.

The Iceland Chamber of Commerce was instrumental in shaping the political ideology and atmosphere in the years preceding the financial collapse. A very clear statement of the chamber's social vision is to be found in another report, entitled *Ísland 2015* (Viðskiptaráð Íslands 2006). Its message is that the state, not the banks, needs to downsize. Solutions are to be sought in privatizing many government functions. It explicitly states that Iceland should no longer compare itself with other Nordic countries because it had already exceeded them in most important economic aspects (i.e., indicators of competitiveness).

This report was a product of a committee on the future of Icelandic society, Framtíðarhópur Viðskiptaráðs Íslands, set up by the Chamber of Commerce and chaired by the rector of the semiprivate Reykjavík University, owned in part by the Chamber of Commerce. The rector of the Icelandic Academy of the Arts was also a member of the committee, as was the chair of the Association of Icelandic Artists, the director of the National Theater, representatives of two of the biggest banks and investment firms, the chairman of a major pension fund, the director of one of the largest audit companies, and representatives of several other leading Icelandic companies. The composition of this committee clearly shows how the prevailing ideology saturated many levels of society in the period before the collapse and how the various sectors of society cooperated in creating and conveying the message.

In 2007 the Chamber of Commerce published yet another report in the same spirit, with ninety suggestions for Iceland to improve its competitiveness. The common thread throughout is laissez-faire economics with a minimal state, emphasizing self-regulation of the financial institutions: "It would be much more sensible to let players on the market set their own rules and implement them rather than rely on public regulation which is burdensome and costly" (Viðskiptaráð Íslands 2007, 19). This was also the tone set by the government and the policy implemented by the Icelandic regulatory agencies. The Iceland Chamber of Commerce clearly functioned as an ideological think tank that strongly influenced the politics in the years before the financial collapse.

The chamber commissioned another report on the Icelandic financial sector, published in late 2007, written by academics Richard Portes, professor of economics at London Business School, and Friðrik M. Baldursson, professor of economics at Reykjavík University (Portes and Baldursson 2007). That report was less influential than the one by Mishkin and Herbertsson, but the chamber and its allies used both reports strategically in "the production of truth" about the Icelandic financial sector. In May 2006, soon after the publication of his report, Mishkin participated in a meeting set up by the Iceland Chamber of Commerce in New York with Icelandic prime minister Geir H. Haarde. The meeting was entitled "Financial Crisis or Economic Opportunity: The Real Story about Iceland." The press announcement described Mishkin as "a leading world authority on financial stability" (Consulate General of Iceland 2006).

A week later the Icelandic newspaper *Morgunblaðið* published an interview with the chief financial analyst at Landsbankinn. She said, "The report by Herbertsson and Mishkin about the state of economy has already had impact on the markets. It is crucial that such a well-known economist as Mishkin contributed to the report. This shows as well that it matters who speaks about these issues" ("Miklu skiptir að Mishkin tók þátt" 2006, n.p.). Portes took part in a business conference held in Copenhagen in March 2008, along with the Icelandic prime minister and the chairman of Kaupthing Bank. Judging from Icelandic media reports, Portes heroically defended Icelandic businessmen from foreign criticism. On March 25, 2008, he appeared on the US television network CNBC to say that Icelandic banks were well-run, sound corporations ("Icelandic Crown Rallies" 2008). The director of the Iceland Chamber of Commerce commented that it was "very positive to see a turn of the tide in the reports in the foreign media. . . . This also shows that a joint effort of all stakeholders to convey correct information has now succeeded" ("Við nýjan tón" 2008).

This joint effort of politicians, academics, and businessmen in defending the image of the banks is a testimony to the pervasive collusion in "the production of truth" about the financial regime in Iceland. It should be noted that the Iceland Chamber of Commerce paid Mishkin US$124,000 for coauthoring his report, and Portes received £58,000 (US$76,000). Robert Wade, professor of political economy at the London School of Economics, and Silla Sigurgeirsdóttir, lecturer in public policy at the University of Iceland, reflect on this: "It is not clear to what extent their willingness to assert the 'highly professional' quality of Iceland's financial regulator and the basic stability of the banks was influenced by the size of their fees from an organization which had a strong vested interest in securing their favorable 'expert' opinion; and to what extent their willingness reflects the wider epistemology of economics, which since the neoclassical ascendancy has given little weight to meticulous observation of people and organizations . . ." (Wade and Sigurgeirsdóttir 2012, n.p.).

THE ICELANDIC PUBLIC

There were honest attempts among Icelandic academics and intellectuals to raise critical voices about the standing of the Icelandic banks, but, as I stated above, the soil was not fertile for their criticism. This leads us to the role of the Icelandic public, which embraced the message with enthusiasm and almost no resistance, contributing to and maintaining the atmosphere for the success message of the banks. Clearly, the common Icelander had neither the incentive nor the means to be critical of this social development. The times during the economic boom were characterized by an excessive consumerism; many used ample opportunities for access to loans as well as unprecedented ways of saving with high interest. Icelanders could also free themselves from the lowest-paid jobs in the service sector, leaving those to foreigners. Traveling abroad became relatively cheap, largely due to changes in international air travel but also to the strong standing of the national currency.

The highly consumerized Icelandic public was neither motivated to act as citizens nor provided with favorable conditions in which do so. It is questionable whether a public sphere "in which critical public discussion of matters of general interest was institutionally guaranteed" (McCarthy 1991, xi) has ever really existed in Iceland. But clearly the elements sustaining it, such as the media, were largely colonized by the financial sector. Moreover, the media in Iceland are very open to articles from the public that give the impression that they are serving their democratic function well. As a consequence, however, the media are full of opinions on matters of public interest, but short of objective and critical scrutiny of the issues. Lacking both in financial strength and professional competence, the media have not been able to provide objective reporting based on research in order to provide the conditions optimal for informed public opinion and social debate. This is a major reason why the Icelandic public had no resources to draw upon in order to resist the success narrative flowing from the banks.

It is also true that financial institutions used their corporate social responsibility programs to create goodwill among members of the Icelandic public. Supporting charity, sports, education, and cultural programs, the financial moguls created their image as public benefactors while simultaneously feeding into the attitude that these contributions were indispensable for thriving cultural institutions. Again, the workings of power come through generous invitation and support, not through order and domination. The docile citizenry went willingly into the service of the financial regime that at the same time was threatening the very economic structure of society through the high-risk policies of the bankers.

The WGE commissioned a report from a social psychologist about how general group dynamics as well as the characteristics of a small nation contributed to the course of events that led to the financial collapse. The report used a vivid metaphor to illustrate that individualistic explanations are not useful: "In relation to the collapse of the Icelandic banks, explanations of social psychology are primarily aimed at exploring whether the barrel was rotten and therefore many apples rotted. The emphasis is not on finding a few rotten apples which caused the entire barrel to rot" (Þórisdóttir 2010, 297).

The report charges that people have a strong tendency to receive and interpret information in accordance with their system of aims and beliefs. The Icelandic public had strong incentives to believe that the economy was going well and the financial sector was successful and thriving. As consumers, they gained from this state of affairs, and as citizens of a small nation they took pride in it. Almost everything in their surroundings reinforced their belief, and they were likely to reject or deem invalid information that contradicted it. This approach provides an important corrective to the simplistic moral demand that people should think more critically and be more vigilant citizens (even though these are important guidelines for citizenship education in a democratic society).

I have used the story of the success of the Icelandic banks as an example to demonstrate the need for a multidimensional analysis of the financial collapse. The creation and maintenance of the image of the banks required interplay between professionals in the banks, actors in the political sphere, the media, experts, and the general public. I have argued that methodological individualism is gravely misleading and inadequate to deal with such a complex net of relations as that which existed during the events preceding the meltdown. In addition to analyzing the interplay between the social actors, we must factor in the enabling background conditions, structural processes, institutional culture, and social norms that contributed to the event. The problem was not isolated to a few rotten apples—a handful of greedy, risk-taking bankers—but was rooted in a lack of resistance at all levels of Icelandic society.

After the Crash

6

Overthrowing the Government

A Case Study in Protest

Jón Gunnar Bernburg is a professor of sociology on the faculty of the social and human sciences at the University of Iceland. Based on a representative survey conducted months after the events, he argues that a perfect storm of relative deprivation, message framing, and political opportunity led to the success of protests that overthrew the Icelandic government after the crash. He also makes a specific call for more research on the subject.

....

Although political protest has been on the rise in democratic societies in recent decades (Norris, Walgrave, and Van Aelst 2005), mobilization in protests rarely gains enough momentum to pose a real challenge to the political establishment of such societies. Recent exceptions have occurred in the aftermath of the global financial crisis that started in 2008. The crisis has triggered mass protests, demonstrations, and riots in several European countries, including Greece, Iceland, and Spain, all of which were hit hard by the crisis. In some cases these protests have put serious pressure on their respective political establishments. These cases offer opportunities to study how mass protest can occur in contemporary democracies.

The series of mass protests, demonstrations, and riots that occurred in Iceland between the fall of 2008 and January 2009 provide a case in point. After the sudden financial collapse in Iceland in October 2008, an antigovernment social movement emerged and gained widespread support among the Icelandic public. In

DOI: 10.5876/9781607323358.c006

the weeks and months following the bank crisis, public protests and citizens' meetings became regular events in the nation's capital of Reykjavík. Hundreds and sometimes thousands of individuals began to attend weekly Saturday meetings at Austurvöllur, a small symbolic 8,000 m² square in front of the Alþingi, the Icelandic Parliament. Protesters carried signs with antigovernment slogans, and nationally known artists, critics, writers, and intellectuals gave speeches. Claiming that the economic crisis had revealed flaws in Icelandic government and politics, as well as in the policies of the government, spokespeople of the movement called for democratic reform. The protesters demanded that the ruling government along with selected government officials, including the chairman of the Central Bank, take responsibility for the crisis by resigning from power. Government leaders refused to do so, instead blaming the banks and the financial elite and emphasizing that the crisis had been caused by external (global) market forces.

Eventually, on January 20, 2009, after weeks of constant protest meetings, downtown Reykjavík became a battlefield of large-scale antigovernment demonstrations, an unprecedented development in Iceland's peaceful contemporary history. The large-scale public mobilization created an atmosphere of public disorder and threat against the political establishment. Most protesters were nonviolent, confining their activity to beating pots and pans, but a sizable minority of frontline protesters engaged in acts of symbolic threat, vandalism, and confrontation with riot police who formed a protective lineup right in front of the Alþingi. On occasion, police used clubs and tear gas to prevent groups of aggressive protesters from damaging property and bursting into state buildings, including the Alþingi, the Central Bank, and the police headquarters. The demonstrations created strong pressure on the government to meet the key demand of the movement, that is, to step down from power, and on Monday, January 26, six days after the demonstrations started, the government resigned. A new coalition government was formed and announced new elections to be held in the spring. The mass protest ended as soon as it had brought down the government, and institutionalized politics ruled again in Iceland.

Economic crises, even severe ones, usually do not cause large-scale antigovernment demonstrations. Sometimes they do, as in Argentina in 2001 (Borland and Sutton 2005), but often they do not, for example, in the Faroe Islands and Finland in the early 1990s. If efforts to generalize about the societal conditions triggering large-scale protests and revolts constitute a major topic in social movement research (Andrews and Biggs 2006; Davies 1962; McAdam, McCarthy, and Zald 1996; Opp and Gern 1993), the protests in

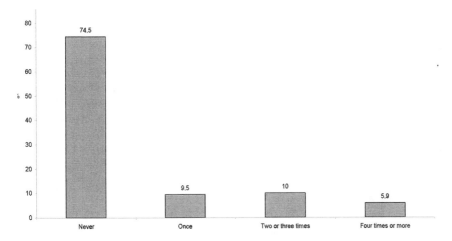

Figure 6.1. *Rate of public participation in the January demonstrations*

Iceland provide an opportunity to study what happens when an economic crisis triggers large-scale public protest, contributing to the limited empirical work on crisis-evoked mass revolt in affluent democratic societies.

I examine the level of mobilization in the antigovernment protests and explore selected processes to explain how the economic crisis triggered the protests. In addition to relying on descriptive accounts (Benediktsdóttir, Daníelsson, and Zoega 2011; Matthíasson 2008; Jóhannesson 2009b), I use two original sources. First, I use a representative survey of 610 adults living in the Reykjavík metropolitan area to estimate the level of participation in and support for the protests, as well as to examine hypotheses about individual support and participation.[1] Second, I explore issues of framing and political opportunity by examining the speeches held at the protests as well as articles and blogs by those who spoke on behalf of the social movement during this period.[2]

LEVEL OF PUBLIC PARTICIPATION AND SUPPORT

If the forces of mass mobilization in collective behavior constitute an important topic in social movement theory, an important feature of the January demonstrations is the high level of public participation. The survey results in Figure 6.1 show that about 25.5 percent of the 610 respondents indicated attending the January protests at some point and that about 16 percent said that they attended repeatedly. Given a 95 percent confidence level (25.5 + 3.5

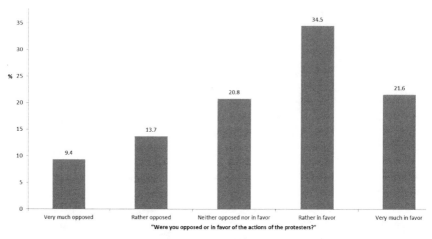

FIGURE 6.2. *Rate of public support for the protesters' activities*

percent) and given a total adult population of the Reykjavík metropolitan area of about 151,000,[3] the findings indicate that between 33,200 and 43,800 individuals attended the January protests.[4] Moreover, Figure 6.2 shows that about 56 percent of the respondents were in favor of the protesters' activities, while a little less than one-quarter of the respondents were opposed to the actions of the protestors.

FORCES OF MOBILIZATION AFTER THE ECONOMIC MELTDOWN

Having confirmed the high level of public mobilization and support for the protests, we can now ask how the financial crash caused so much social movement activity. In particular, what forces influenced the decisions of individuals to participate in it? I explore three processes: relative deprivation, framing, and political opportunity.

RELATIVE ECONOMIC DEPRIVATION

The concept of relative deprivation refers to the perception of unfair disadvantage compared with a reference point that is salient to the individual—for example, compared with others in society or with one's own situation at another point in time (Ragnarsdóttir, Bernburg, and Ólafsdóttir 2013; Crosby 1976; Runciman 1966). While the concept is used mostly to focus on emotional and health problems (Smith et al. 2012; Bernburg, Thorlindsson, and Sigfusdottir 2009), scholars have argued that relative deprivation can create a fertile ground for revolt. Davies (1962) argues that public revolts often occur after a large-scale backlash, such as an economic crisis, that has put a prolonged period of rising prosperity to a sudden end. Proposing a social-psychological explanation for this pattern, Davies argues that in long periods of prosperity (economic or political) people's expectations and goals rise, and thus when a severe crisis suddenly ends the prosperity period, many individuals experience shattered expectations and blocked goals, resulting in widespread frustration and a sense of injustice, creating a fertile ground for public revolt.

The Icelandic protests occurred in such a "daviesian" historical circumstance. From 1993 up to the bank crash, the Icelandic economy was characterized by growth and huge increases in the standard of living (see Palsson and Durrenberger, this volume). Public opinion polls from 2007, the year preceding the crisis, show a historical peak in economic expectations among Icelanders (see Ragnarsdóttir, Bernburg, and Ólafsdóttir 2013). The high expectations were shattered by the sudden bankruptcy of the Icelandic banks in October 2008 (Benediktsdóttir, Daníelsson, and Zoega 2011; Matthíasson 2008). Suddenly the Icelandic public faced a severe economic downturn. In a matter of hours, the Icelandic Stock Exchange was wiped out, with huge losses for most investors, businesses, and owners of capital. Homeowners saw the value of their homes depreciate, while at the same time mortgages rose due to inflation. Many businesses suddenly faced the threat of bankruptcy, leading to group layoffs and widespread salary reductions. The Icelandic currency fell more than 95 percent against the dollar, and Iceland became the first developed country to require assistance from the International Monetary Fund in thirty years. Economic expectations reached a historical low point in opinion polls (Ragnarsdóttir, Bernburg, and Ólafsdóttir 2013).

Although the historical context triggering the Reykjavík protests rings true to Davies's thesis, a historical account cannot suffice in demonstrating the mobilizing role of relative deprivation. We know that economic crises often create emotional problems for individuals (Tausig and Fenwick 1999). Ragnarsdóttir, Bernburg, and Ólafsdóttir (2013) found that Icelanders who experienced a reduced standard of living due to the crisis experienced more emotional distress and were also more likely to perceive their social status as unjust. But even if subjective financial deprivation due to a crisis creates emotional distress, it may or may not make individuals rebellious, or, more specifically, it may or may not have motivated people to participate in the Reykjavík protests. Davies did not use individual data in his comparative research, and in fact the theory has rarely been tested with systematic individual-level data collected in the appropriate historical circumstance.

The Icelandic meltdown provides an opportunity to examine Davies's theory. The theory implies that individuals who either had experienced or thought they were about to experience a reduction in their standard of living prior to the Reykjavík demonstrations should be more likely to participate in and support the protests. My survey data can be used to explore this hypothesis, although the data are not ideal for this purpose. The survey respondents were asked if they believed that their economic standard of living was better, the same, or worse than it had been prior to the economic crisis of October 2008. Since the survey was conducted several months after the demonstrations (November 2009 through May 2010), it does not tackle the individual's experience of economic loss prior to the demonstrations but rather several months later. This is a strength in that the question then tackles experienced as well as anticipated deprivation at the time of the protests (both of which should motivate revolt, according to Davies's theory). But it is also a weakness since some individuals experiencing a reduction in their standard of living at the time of the survey may not have anticipated it at the time of the demonstrations, a random measurement error leading to an underestimation of the "true" effect of this measure.

Despite this limitation, the data support the hypothesis. Figure 6.3 shows protest support and participation by level of subjective reduction in the standard of living at the time of the survey. A positive association appears between subjective economic deprivation on the one hand and protest participation and support on the other hand. Individuals who have experienced a reduction in their economic standard of living are significantly more likely to have participated in the demonstrations ($p < .05$), and they are significantly more likely to have been in favor of them ($p < .05$). But, these effects are modest. Thus, the participation rate among those who indicated that their standard of living was no worse than it was before the crisis is about 21 percent, while it is 31 percent among those experiencing a high degree of reduction in their standard of living. Comparable percentages for protest support are 48 and 62 percent, respectively.

Thus, while the widely shared experience of economic loss appears to have been a mobilizing force in the protests, the weakness of the effect suggests that other forces also played important roles. Indeed, as Zagorin (1973, 44) argues, "a very long distance separates discontent from revolution." To understand how personal discontent can lead to revolt, we need to consider the interplay of individual discontent and the broader social context of "conflicts and changes

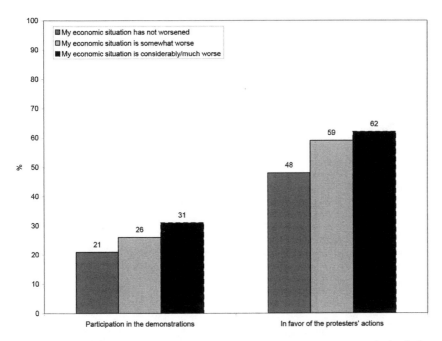

Figure 6.3. *Rate of participation in/support for the January demonstrations by level of subjective reduction in economic standard of living during the economic crisis (p < .05)*

in the political system, the emergence of ideologies, and the like." In what follows, I attend to such processes.

FRAMING PROCESSES

The framing approach emphasizes the role of interpretive orientations or "frames" in mobilizing individuals in participating in collective action (Snow et al. 1986; Zald 1996). Individuals participate in collective action only if they share a set of definitions that motivate and legitimate such activity, and hence a key to explaining mobilization is to study processes of framing (e.g., Oberschall 1996). This approach implies that even widespread grievances caused by relative deprivation due to a crisis will not trigger collective action against the authorities unless these experiences are framed in a way that motivates such action.

The framing approach focuses our attention to what Snow et al. (1986) refer to as "frame alignment processes," that is, strategies that social movement agents use to influence individuals' frames to gain their support and participation (see McAdam 1996). For example, they may use "frame bridging"; that is, they may appeal to values and beliefs that already exist in the society, claiming to provide a way to realize these values and beliefs. They may also use "frame amplification"; that is, they may amplify existing values or beliefs by clarifying or invigorating "an interpretative frame that bears on a particular issue, problem, or set of events" (Snow et al. 1986, 467), for example, by amplifying belief in the seriousness of a particular problem or in the efficacy or timeliness of collective action.

Examining the framing efforts of those who spoke on the part of the antigovernment movement may help to explain how the crisis ended up triggering mass protests. An examination of the speeches held at the protest meetings in the fall of 2008 and early January 2009, as well as articles and blogs written by the movement spokespeople during this period, shows attempts to frame the economic crisis as a "moral shock" (Jasper and Poulsen 1995). Specifically, the crisis was said to have revealed (1) the problem of political corruption in Iceland, (2) the problems of unfettered neoliberalism, and (3) the necessity, timeliness, and feasibility of antigovernment collective action demanding democratic reform. I will briefly discuss each of these themes.

Contrary to statements made by government leaders that factors external to the government (i.e., global market forces and the reckless behavior of business leaders and bankers) were to blame for the economic crisis and its effects on the Icelandic public, spokespeople of the protest movement framed the crisis as a problem caused by local factors, namely, failures in Icelandic politics. Specifically, they emphasized two flaws. First, they argued that Icelandic politics were corrupt and plagued by political nepotism that had created widespread incompetence in government and public administration. Moreover, they argued that strong connections between politics and business gave much power to "special interests" and "the rich." A known government critic and public intellectual stated in a speech a few weeks after the financial collapse:

> Politics and business is an unhealthy mixture. Icelandic business life was for a
> long time infiltrated by politics. The privatization of banks and state organizations was meant to change that structure and clarify the difference between
> politics and business . . . The government failed in this task. It gave the state
> banks to men with party connections but no experience with running banks. In
> their hands the banks grew immensely and secretly cast a heavy responsibility
> on the nation. The Central Bank, the government, and the Financial Affairs did
> nothing—until the dam broke.[5]

Thus corruption in Icelandic politics had undermined democratic principles, leading to decisions and policies that went against public interests and resulting in the extreme effects of the global economic crisis in Iceland.

The majority of movement spokespeople expressed a strongly "left-wing" political stance. They framed the economic crisis as proof that the "invisible hand" policy of free market liberalism was wrong for the country and needed to be replaced by something else. Many movement spokespeople blamed the Independence Party–led government (a large right-wing party that had led Icelandic governments since the early 1990s) for the severity of the economic crisis. By deregulating the market and implementing free market and neoliberalist policies, the government had allowed the financial sector to run wild in the years leading up to the crisis. Although the new policies created rapid economic progress, they also greatly destabilized the Icelandic economy and made it extremely vulnerable during the crash. According to movement spokespeople, the government's neoliberalist policies had been proven wrong, and therefore the ruling government needed to step down from power.

Finally, movement spokespeople emphasized the moral necessity, timeliness, and effectiveness of antigovernment collective action. Due to the widespread system failure, a new society could now be built on "democratic" principles (as opposed to corruption and neoliberalism). These voices became more radicalized in the weeks following the bank crash, especially as it became clear that the government leaders were not going to step down from power. Movement leaders urged collective action, claiming that only through public protests would the political leaders be held accountable for their actions and be forced to resign. New elections and democratic reform could happen only if new people took over.

Did these framing efforts motivate Icelanders to support and participate in the protests? Again, my survey data can be used to examine hypotheses about protest support and participation. First, to measure perceived political corruption, survey respondents were asked about their belief in the importance of having "political connections" to "get ahead in Icelandic society." The results in Figure 6.4 show that the perception of political corruption is significantly associated with both protest support ($p < .05$) and participation ($p < .05$). Those who strongly believed that political connections are needed to get ahead in society were more than twice as likely to participate in the demonstrations than those who did not have this belief, and they were somewhat more likely to support the protests. Thus, framing the crisis as a consequence of political corruption seems to have motivated many of those aligned with

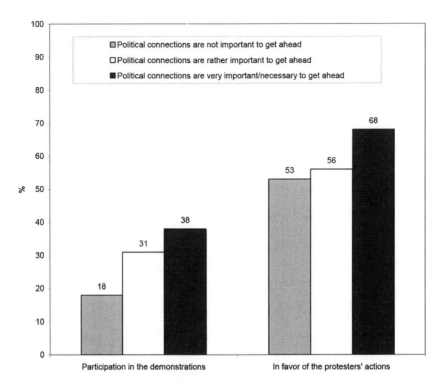

FIGURE 6.4. *Rate of participation in/support for the January demonstrations by level of perceived political corruption (p < .05)*

such framing to support and participate in the demonstrations. Other surveys have also found dissatisfaction with Icelandic politics to play a role in the protests (Önnudóttir 2011).

Second, Figure 6.5 shows a strong association between political orientation on the one hand and protest support ($p < .05$) and participation on the other hand ($p < .05$). Individuals who had a left-wing political orientation were about 2.4 times more likely to participate in the protests than those with a right-wing orientation, and they were almost twice as likely than right-wingers to support the demonstrations. The antigovernment protests seem to have gained momentum in part because movement agents successfully framed the crisis as revealing the failure of neoliberalism, thus mobilizing the large numbers of individuals who had a left-wing political orientation to participate in and support the demonstrations.

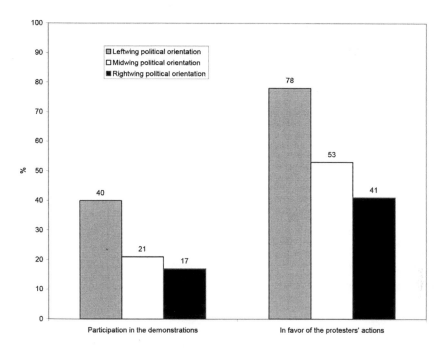

FIGURE 6.5. *Rate of participation in/support for the January demonstrations by political orientation (p < .05)*

POLITICAL OPPORTUNITY

I finally explore how the financial crisis in Iceland inspired and facilitated the framing efforts, making them so effective in mobilization. The political opportunity perspective emphasizes that changes in some aspects of the political system, such as power relations, elite alliances, shifts in public opinion, and so on, can create opportunities for collective action. But, as McAdam, McCarthy, and Zald (1996, 8) have argued, whether or not such openings actually lead to collective action is dependent on other factors, including framing processes: "Most political movements and revolutions are set in motion by social changes that render the established political order more vulnerable or receptive to challenge ... [But] such changes only become an 'opportunity' when defined as such by a group of actors sufficiently well organized to act on this shared definition of the situation." Thus, political or social changes trigger mobilization "not only through the 'objective' effects they have on power relations, but by setting in motion framing processes that further undermine the legitimacy of the system or its perceived mutability."

The economic crisis created opportunities for the successful antigovernment framing due to the historical convergence of several factors. First of all, the way in which the economic crisis struck Iceland created a collectively shared national disaster. On October 6, 2008, six days after a sudden government takeover of Glitnir Bank, the first of the three largest banks in Iceland to go bankrupt, Landsbankinn, the second bank to fail, went bankrupt. On that day, in a dramatic and highly unusual special national broadcast, Prime Minister Geir Haarde declared a state of national emergency, informing the nation about the necessity of placing special emergency laws making the state responsible for the public's money in the failing banks. He ended the broadcast on the now famous words "God bless Iceland!" Suddenly the general public in one of the most affluent democracies in the world was in a state of panic, fear, and desperation about its economic future. That night Icelanders went to bed not knowing if they would be able to withdraw money from the banks the following morning. Later that week the third and largest bank, Kaupthing Bank, went bankrupt. About 85 percent of the Icelandic banking system had gone bankrupt in a period of ten days.

The emotionally charged and collectively shared focus of the public on the economic crisis provided a fertile ground for collective action. At the outset the financial crisis was particularly harmful to the middle and upper classes, society's "mainstream," who lost a lot when the banks failed. For several weeks and months following the bank crash, the unfolding economic crisis had the full attention of the Icelandic media as well as the public. If media attention is essential to mass mobilization (Andrews and Biggs 2006; Klandermans and Goslinga 1996; McCarthy, Smith, and Zald 1996), the Icelandic media paved the way for the protest movement by constantly delivering news and analyses about the alleged local causes of the crisis as well as the country's bleak economic future. The shared national focus on the financial collapse, along with the public's confusion, anxiety, and disappointment, gave public speakers who interpreted the events a tremendous amount of publicity in the media as well as widespread public attention and enthusiasm.

Associated with this shared traumatic experience were particular issues or "scandals" that surfaced and were particularly conducive for framing the crisis as a consequence of government failure (for details of these scandals, see Benediktsdóttir et al. 2011). The Icelandic public learned at the onset of the crisis that the three largest banks in Iceland, all former state banks that had been privatized a few years earlier, had been allowed to grow immensely, becoming more than ten times the size of Iceland's GDP, while at the same time the Icelandic state continued to be liable for large parts of the banks' actual and anticipated losses. From the public's perspective, the government, under the leadership of the conservative right-wing party that had been in power since the early 1990s, seemed to have made serious mistakes by failing to regulate and control the financial sector, for which it was ultimately liable. Moreover, at this point Iceland's economy appeared to have been hit much harder by the global financial crisis than any other country, giving much leverage to a "local problem" framing. From the point of view of public opinion, the ruling government was in an extremely vulnerable position.

The two key features of the financial crisis—the shared, emotionally charged focus on the economic crisis, along with the revelations about the state's liability of the overgrown banks—created leverage for dissidents to influence public opinion by amplifying well-established themes of social and political critique of ruling political powers. Dissidents and critics of the ruling political powers successfully framed the crisis as a "moral shock" (Jasper and Poulsen 1995), mobilizing large number of individuals who were receptive to these views.

DISCUSSION AND CONCLUSION

The current analysis is a first step toward a comprehensive understanding of the forces behind the Icelandic protests. Further research should explore other factors that likely influenced the mobilization process. The actions and reactions of government leaders influence the occurrence of revolt (Skocpol 1979), and the reactions of the government leaders in Iceland likely played an important role in the creation of political opportunity. Their refusal to accept responsibility for the crisis and their refusal to step down gave the protest movement a goal resonating well with the public's notions of the democratic process, namely, to demand new elections. Indeed, the momentum of mass mobilization vanished immediately after the ruling government resigned, despite the willingness of frontline protesters and movement leaders to continue the protests and demand democratic reform.

Also, the role of organized activists and radical groups in the mobilization efforts and in amplifying the protests themselves needs to be explored. As part of a global phenomenon (see Nash 2005), an activist tradition rooted in an ideology of discontent and opposition to neoliberalist developments had been emerging in Iceland during the decade leading up to the crisis. Activist groups already had experience with organizing small-scale protests against big (transnational) industry in Iceland's wilderness. Like other dissidents of the ruling political establishment, these groups saw the economic crisis as an opportunity for mass mobilization against neoliberalism, and it is clear from historical accounts that young radicals played a highly visible role at the protests. Radical groups may also have played a key role in providing an organizational base for the protest events. Further research needs to be done to determine the role of such groups.

The pivotal role of the media in Iceland in creating political opportunity needs to be explored. The media played a key role not only in focusing the nation on the crisis as well as on the protests and citizen's meetings taking place in the fall of 2008 and in January 2009 but also in reporting on the scandals associated with the crisis, which in turn became the raw material for the framing of the crisis as a moral shock revealing the need for democratic reform. Future research should examine how social movement agents gained media attention for their framing efforts (McAdam 1996).

In conclusion, the widespread public support for and participation in the Icelandic protests underscore that in times of crisis collective action can become a serious challenge to the political establishment, even in a contemporary democratic society, just as it has been at various critical points in the history of modernizing societies. The protests demonstrate how economic crisis can produce fertile ground for collective action by creating not only widespread economic grievances but also political opportunities for successful collective action framing.

The preparation of this chapter was aided by grants from the Icelandic Centre for Research, EDDA—Center of Excellence, and the University of Iceland Research Fund. The author thanks Linda Björk Pálmadóttir for her assistance in obtaining historical material.

NOTES

1. Standardized (face-to-face) interviews were conducted on a sample of adults living in the Reykjavík metropolitan area between October 2009 and July 2010. A random sample of 968 individuals was drawn from a complete list of individuals eighteen years or older living in the Reykjavík metropolitan area. A total of 610 interviews were completed by interviewers who visited all participants in their own homes, a final response rate of 63 percent (for details about survey data and procedures, see Ragnarsdóttir, Bernburg, and Ólafsdóttir 2013).

2. I obtained transcripts of more than half of the speeches delivered at the protest meetings in the fall of 2008 and January 2009 along with about fifty articles by prominent spokespeople of the protest movement.

3. This figure is based on calculations using Statistics Iceland, "Population by Municipalities, Sex and Age, 1 January 1998–2014—Current Municipalities," http://www.statice.is/?PageID=1172&src=https://rannsokn.hagstofa.is/pxen/Dialog/varval.asp?ma=MAN02001%26ti=Population+by+municipalities%2C+sex+and+age+1+January+1998-2014+-+Current+municipalities%26path=../Database/mannfjoldi/sveitarfelog/%26lang=1%26unit.

4. Other surveys confirm the high levels of protest participation and support. Önnudóttir (2011) found that the participation rate in the protests was about 24 percent for the period between October 2008 and January 2009, and she found a support rate of 70 percent.

5. Þorvaldur Gylfason, speech delivered at a public meeting, Háskólabíó, Reykjavík, November 24, 2008; http://www.youtube.com/watch?v=Pey_M_6ocDU.

7

"Welcome to the Revolution!"

*Voting in the
Anarcho-Surrealists*

Hulda Proppé is an anthropologist at the Icelandic Centre for Research and a PhD student in social anthropology at the University of Cambridge. She offers an insider's perspective with an anthropologist's eye to the ascendance of the Best Party. Describing itself as both anarchist and surreal, the Best Party effectively took over Reykjavík's local government after the meltdown, holding the mayor's post longer than anyone has in a decade.

• • • • • • • • • • • • • • • • • •

In October 2008 Prime Minister Geir Haarde appeared on Icelandic national television and delivered his "God Bless Iceland!" speech. The following weeks found the nation in a state of shock. A state of uncertainty had emerged, a state that four years later had turned into the new normal.

As the shock wore off and people began to feel the effects of the economic crash, crowds gathered outside the Parliament building with greater intensity. In January 2009 a violent undertone emerged, and on January 21 the demonstrations took a new twist. That night in my home, only a five-minute walk from the city center, I heard the drumming of pots, pans, and drums and saw the sky glowing blood red from the light of a torched Christmas tree. For the first time in sixty years, the Reykjavík police used tear gas to move demonstrators away from the building in order to gain control of the situation.

These demonstrations forced the conservative/ social democrat government out of power. A new temporary left-wing/social democrat government took

DOI: 10.5876/9781607323358.c007

over and was then elected in May 2009, led for the first time in the nation's history by a woman, Prime Minister Jóhanna Sigurðardóttir, who is also the first openly gay prime minister in the world. Politics in Iceland had shifted significantly.

During the spring of 2010 there was a parallel political shift in the capital city of Reykjavík as well. This was reflected most notably in the establishment of the Best Party: a loosely allied group of friends and collaborators, mostly artists, musicians, and performers, who decided to form a slate under the name of the Best Party and run for election to the Reykjavík city council in 2010 on a platform that they described as "anarcho-surrealist."

To everyone's surprise (not the least, their own) the Best Party won a resounding victory. In May 2010 the newly established party secured 34.7 percent of votes for the city council and captured six of the fifteen seats on the council. Best Party leader Jón Gnarr had said during his campaign that he would not enter into coalition discussions with anyone who had not seen the American TV show *The Wire*. After the election, Jón Gnarr launched his coalition by giving Dagur B. Eggertsson, the leader of the social democrats on the city council, a DVD set of the show.

Similar election results were seen in other communities. The Next Best Party ran for town council in nearby Kópavogur on similar seemingly nonpolitical grounds and won 13.8 percent of the votes. It participated in a majority coalition that then broke up after a year in office. In Akureyri the L-List, a new party, garnered more than 43 percent of the votes. It has a pure majority, with six out of eleven members on the town council, while all other parties only have one member each. In Hafnarfjörður an unheard-of 45 percent of voters either did not vote or did not vote for any of the political parties up for election (no new party ran for election in the municipality). Nearly 14 percent of the ballots were returned empty.

Reykjavík, Kópavogur, Akureyri, and Hafnarfjörður are the four most populated districts of Iceland. The results of the municipal elections indicated that there was a strong desire for both political and cultural change. When the Best Party victory was announced, mayor-elect Jón Gnarr met with his fellow group members and supporters and gave a victory speech that ended with the words, "Welcome to the revolution!" But what is the revolution the Best Party stands for? What is the situation this group is constructing, and what is the process of acting out their message? Or is there even a message?

Leading up to the elections, many people, particularly members of other political parties, considered the Best Party campaign a joke. They were taken by surprise by the party's popularity and especially by the messages the Best

Party was, or was not, relaying. Jón Gnarr, now the longest-sitting mayor of Reykjavík since 2003, is well known in Iceland as a stand-up comedian and producer of comic radio programs and comic series for television and movies. His candidacy caught people off guard. The public and the media were sure the Best Party would withdraw and announce that the campaign was just one big joke. It was such a widely held belief that Jón Gnarr announced in one debate that the campaign had been hard on him, indeed a bit boring, and that he had decided to withdraw from the elections. After a moment of silence he looked up and said, "JOKE!" and then said he would rise up like "the bird Felix"—knowing well that he was referring to the rising Phoenix. Gnarr was creating utter confusion among the public. Was he in or out of the game? Was he so stupid he thought the Phoenix really was called Felix? Was he a genius? A clown? A moron? By playing the part of the slippery trickster, he could play the political game by not playing it—and, in that way, control it.

The composition of the Best Party is no coincidence. In one way or another, group members' paths have crossed, be it gathering at rock concerts, hanging out at the same coffeehouses, or going to the same high school. The members also share an unconventional background quite different from that of the participants in other political parties who, for the most part, started their political careers participating in university politics and in the youth leagues of those parties.

In contrast, Best Party members have been independent entrepreneurs working on popular projects. A large number of Best Party members have been public figures; one has even had some international fame as a member of the pop group Sugarcubes with Björk. So the public already knew them by the time they started campaigning. They stood for a particular type of difference, a particular cultural scene. People who had attended one of their concerts, plays, or movies were able to feel a personal connection to the group. It is perhaps this factor that makes the Best Party a social movement of the avant-garde, a movement of people who are living on the cultural and political margin. The "angry votes" are perhaps not just votes about the economic crash but votes indicating an empathy with the avant-garde. This unique group continues to prove its relevance, earning almost 35 percent of the vote in Reykjavík in the last municipal elections. Although there are a number of examples of public personalities being voted into office—Clint Eastwood, Arnold Schwarzenegger, and Jesse Ventura, for example—it seems the public personalities elected in Reykjavík in May 2010 are part of a movement for cultural change on more than simply a political level.

My path has crossed with most people in the group at some time or other. One Best Party city council member is my brother; another lived a couple of doors down the street where I grew up, and we went to college together. In my teen years I used to watch cult movies with yet another one, and another has a child in the same class as one of my sons. Because of Iceland's small size, it would be difficult to find a group of people one does not already have some connection to, but I've known the majority of Best Party members for the past twenty-five to forty years. We share a preexisting trust. Gaining access to the innermost circles of political parties is no easy task, which in part explains the lack of anthropological research about political parties, particularly in the Western world, or explains why analysis from inside political parties is often based on life histories of the anthropologist herself and her participation (see, e.g., Kristmundsdóttir 1997).

IS A JOKE EVER JUST A JOKE?

But the popularity of Jón Gnarr and others in the Best Party does not, in itself, explain the popularity of the party, its methods, or its message. The joke is much more than a local prank, reflected in part by the fact that the elected people have taken their responsibilities seriously and put their careers as musicians, actors, businesspeople, producers, and architects on hold in order to serve their city and carry forth their message. Behind what at first glance looks like foolishness lies biting criticism.

Jón Gnarr and other members of the Best Party used satire and parody to convey their message during the election campaign. Boyer (2005; 2011; 2013) has observed the increased use of a "particular mode of parody on the margins of western politics" (2011, 2). Also known as *stiob* in Russian slang, the parody is a form of political cultural critique in which the actors take on the language and culture of mainstream politics to such an extent that it is difficult to tell if the actor is being sincere or critical. This tactic was evident in the Best Party platform. It states: "The Best Party's platform is based on the best of all other platforms. We mostly base it on platforms that have been the base of Nordic and North-European welfare societies. That has a very good ring to it at this moment in history" (Besti Flokkurinn 2010, n.p.).[1] In other words, the Best Party will build its platform based on what is popular at the time. Implied is a critique of populist and mainstream politics during election campaigns: handing out empty promises.

The rest of the text is also ambiguous, combing mainstream political discourse like "transparency" into meaningless slogans such as "sustainable transparency" (*sjálfbært gagnsæi*), shedding light on the fact that the discourse is indeed meaningless. Before listing the thirteen points of their "ten-point" platform, the group promises: "We are going to attend all meetings and always be cheerful and fun, but also, speculative, responsible, and diligent." This is a straightforward critique of mainstream politicians who are known for the opposite traits.

This has been one modus operandi of party members since they came into power. They have focused "on getting things done as best as we can through 'besting' and not getting stuck in political dialogues and name-calling that is only hurtful to people and to the society and that, in their view, does not solve any issues." Weekly meetings of Best Party council members and supporters emphasize the importance of keeping true to their original sense of naiveté in the political realm. They do this through hugging and kissing, for example, and by focusing on humility and vulnerability. I have seen people at these meetings with tears in their eyes, even crying, when the political pressure boiled over. Jón Gnarr has said that he cried publicly at a meeting when he felt the pressure was too much ("Jón Gnarr grét á fjölmennum fundi" 2012). Best Party meetings are an attempt to create a "safe place" where people can speak openly and seek support.

Members of the Best Party have said publicly that they did not see themselves as politicians. Best Party council member Óttarr Proppé has been active in the music scene in Iceland. He plays in a punk band named Rass with Sigurður Björn Blöndal, the mayor's advisor. One song on their album, "Burt með kvótann," became popular and could be heard in schoolyards and other public spaces. The lyrics offer a sharp critique of Icelandic fishing policy, access to the natural resources, and the neoliberalization of the fishing industry. Another song on the same album criticizes politicians and people who supported the construction of the biggest dam in Iceland, Kárahnjúkar, during which a large portion of land was flooded. People from all over the world came to protest the dam, not least because it was built to provide electricity for new aluminum plants. A rock group called Dr. Spock, of which Óttarr is also a member, recorded a song about Condoleezza Rice that criticizes US foreign policy and global capitalism. So these Best Party leaders are not politicians in the traditional sense but people engaging in highly politicized acts.

The medium is the message, and it is a message that people who voted for the party are hearing. Voters from all across the political spectrum supported the Best Party, which offered no plan of action. Instead it promised to break all of its promises, make corruption more visible, and advocate for "sustainable transparency" in addition to calling for a drug-free Parliament by 2020. Although the message is barely comprehensible, people were able to relate to it and vote for it.

TIME FOR A (NEW) PARTY

The Best Party election results can be explained in part by the social and economic crash in Iceland in 2008 and the so-called Pots and Pans Revolution of January 2009. The municipal elections took place just after the publication of the best-selling nine-volume report of the Special Investigation Commission on the economic crash and its causes (Rannsóknarnefnd Alþingis 2010). Although the election results could be explained by people not wanting to vote for the old political parties that had been in power before the crash, that explanation gets us only so far. There seems to be something behind the recent shift that is different from the odd election of so-called "populist parties" or famous individuals. There seems to be something new and different going on here.

Shortly before Christmas 2010, I attended a brunch with members of the Best Party. As I stood in the hallway talking to Jón Gnarr, I realized I had lost his attention. He had spotted a child's Darth Vader mask sitting on a shelf next to us. He later sent out a Christmas greeting from the Mayor of Reykjavík on his Facebook site wearing a Darth Vader mask and a Santa Claus hat, standing in front of a Christmas tree.[2] Jón Gnarr regularly uses social media to communicate with the citizens and was named NEXPO's "web hero of the year" in early 2013. The jury said that Jón Gnarr had presented a unique example regarding the use of social media and had revolutionized the conceptual thinking of a whole nation through his Facebook page ("Jón Gnarr vefhetja ársins á NEXPO" 2013).

The Darth Vader Christmas message is an example of how Jón Gnarr uses symbols of popular culture and the media to send an ambiguous message. In this example, he took on the role of father and protector while simultaneously referring to a surrealistic fantasy world whose famous antagonist contradicts the archetypal father figure. Meanwhile, he constantly communicates through humor and the absurd, reflecting the surrealistic anarchist political vision he stands for.

In an interview on November 8, 2010, on Icelandic national television's current affairs program, *Kastljós*, Jón Gnarr described himself as the Predator in local politics and referred to himself as Whoopi Goldberg in the movie *Ghost*.[3] People understand these references to pop culture. He doesn't use the usual political jargon. He is also unafraid to stop in mid-interview to ask his assistant for information about something he needs to confirm, an act almost unheard of in Icelandic political media where politicians usually answer questions by not answering them and comment on issues of which they have little or no knowledge.

In another example, Jón Gnarr opened the Reykjavík Fashion Festival in 2011. He started out by reading from a biography of a former soldier who described what it had been like to walk through the cities of Germany after the end of World War II, with people dying unnoticed on the side of the road and seeing a woman washing herself with water where the body of a dead child floated nearby. Looking around while he spoke, I sensed uneasiness. The audience was there to see high fashion and sip blue vodka cocktails. At first a few people laughed nervously. Whispers went through the crowd. "What is he talking about?" "Why is he lecturing us?" He continued reading the description by the author of how shocked he was when he and other soldiers opened up a crate of goods sent to German war survivors. It contained only red lipstick! But the soldier described how he watched a woman with eyes that did not reflect the will to survive reach out for a lipstick and in putting it on, in the act of decorating herself, she came back to life and felt human again. What had appeared to be a criticism of people engaged in such trivial pursuits as fashion was in fact a commentary on how fashion can be an important part of being human.

The speech reflected some of the Best Party's priorities as well. Although leaders must make budget cuts, they must also set aside some funds for supporting humanity and peace. Although there isn't enough money for a new nursery school, the party has encouraged artists to paint murals on city walls, changed the main street into a pedestrian-only area during part of the summer, encouraged bicycling and environmentally friendly acts, and brought out tables and chairs to create a space for people to gather together and be human. The mayor has joined the group Mayors for Peace, and the emphasis of the Best Party is humanity, nature, culture, and peace (*mannúð, náttúra, menning og friður*). True to this vision, Jón Gnarr has refused to greet a captain of a German battleship that came to the Reykjavík harbor, has discussed human rights with Chinese representatives, and has openly spoken on behalf of refugees.

THE "BEST" CURE FOR SICK POLITICS

Taking over a city after an economic crash does not provide much space for going beyond the essentials. After the Best Party came into office, it learned that the financial situation of the city was even worse than expected. Orkuveita Reykjavíkur, the utility company in which the city has majority ownership, was in serious debt, one equivalent to four years of city tax revenues. The scale was on par with the financial blow the national government suffered with the fall of the banks. In addition, cuts to the city budget had been delayed by draining the utility company. If the company weren't cleaned up and refinanced, the city would go bankrupt. With such high stakes, utility workers were laid off and utility costs went up. City staff were laid off, and the city closed down or combined nursery schools, elementary schools, and more, cutting back services of all kinds. These actions were not popular. Teachers and parents, the elderly, and many other interest groups demanded meetings with members of the city council. Each group lobbied for their issues to be put first on the city's priority list.

The Best Party suffered from the fallout. Best Party council member Einar Örn Benediktsson said that since they were not trying to get reelected, they were not afraid to make difficult and unpopular decisions. This differentiated the Best Party from previous ruling parties. By refusing to deal with the city's financial chaos as it was developing, these parties made things worse in the long run. Jón Gnarr addressed the "sick" culture of politics that had prevailed in the city when introducing budget cuts for the year 2011. In his speech he compared the city to an alcoholic father who holds his family captive with his drinking. (In fact, Jón Gnarr has described the Best Party as more of a self-help organization than a political party [Gnarr 2010].) The sickness creates tension in the family, and the family manages the tension by supporting the sick authority figure and ignoring the needs of each member. The codependency of other family members then gives the authority figure power to manipulate the situation and feed his own disease. At a conference in the spring of 2012, Jón Gnarr said that even though he had worked in mental asylums, a Volvo manufacturing company in Sweden, as a taxi driver, in the media and in theater, he had never encountered such a *sick* culture as that of politics.

The Best Party issued a video during the campaign in which a party member sang an Icelandic version of Tina Turner's song "Simply the Best." It featured Jón Gnarr and other party members walking around the city, kissing babies, and smiling to people. The places that were chosen have deep meaning for the citizens of Reykjavík—for instance, Hljómskálagarðurinn (the city center park) and Perlan (a building and restaurant built over hot water tanks constructed during the era of Davíð Oddsson as mayor). Oddsson is also the former prime minister and was a national bank manager during the economic crash. The construction of Perlan was highly criticized and represents the "old Iceland" and the policies that led to the economic crash. The video was a big hit during the election campaign and has been viewed more than 300,000 times on YouTube.[4]

GROWING UP ON THE OUTSIDE

During the election campaign, the Best Party had a slogan, "*Áfram allskonar*," meaning "ahead for all kinds," or "ahead for everything" or "all kinds of everything." The use of the word *allskonar* again reflects the party's use of words that mean everything and simultaneously nothing. The slogan reflects the type of anarchism that Jón Gnarr and other Best Party members support.

Jón Gnarr's book *Indíáninn* (The Indian [Gnarr 2006]), the first in his trilogy of fictional biographies, focuses on his childhood years. The second book in the trilogy, *Sjóræninginn* (The Pirate [Gnarr 2012]) focuses on his early teenage years. He writes about isolation from his family and society and the bullying he encountered during these years. He tells the story of how mainstream ideas of being and acting were limiting and in particular how they limited understanding of diversity, how teachers were blind to the violence in front of them, how adults gave up on him and teachers wouldn't even report that he wasn't at school most of the time because of the bullying he was enduring, how the system allowed him and others to fall through the cracks as a cost society is willing to pay to maintain order. In the books, particularly in *The Pirate,* he writes about how punk came into his life "like a liberating angel," how he got interested in anarchism, and how it is a humane political approach that allows space for diversity, the individual, and society. Speaking through his own personal experience, he explores how the personal extends into the political.

These books are another example of how Jón Gnarr and the Best Party have focused on "de-powering" mainstream ideas and how, through his actions, Jón Gnarr has changed the image of political power that focuses on maintaining the divide between the people and authority figures. Jón Gnarr has moved the image of the mayor of Reykjavík from being "one of them" to being "one of us." After these books came out, I heard a number of people of all ages start a discussion with the words, "You know, I have never been a fan of Jón Gnarr and didn't vote for the Best Party, but . . ."—and then they would talk about how important it was for them personally that an authority figure came forward and talked about his feelings and admitted his faults. They talk about how he works on creating an environment where he can function. Following the discussion, people then would talk about their own experiences and admit how they sometimes feel out of control of their lives, actions, and circumstances. In an interview of February 20, 2013, on *Kastljós,* Jón Gnarr discussed openly his problems with ADHD (attention deficit hyperactivity disorder) and how it has affected his life, schooling, and work. Many people posted the interview on their Facebook page, and a flood of discussion echoed the discussions I had heard after the books came out.

One of Jón Gnarr's first acts as the mayor of Reykjavík was to open the Gay Pride festival in 2010. Instead of a speech full of politically correct words, he showed up as Fröken Reykjavík, or Miss Reykjavík, who is "a girl like no one else" (*stúlka engum örðum lík*). The name, again, refers to a popular song by the music group Ríó Tríó, which most Icelanders know and can identify with. The act combines comic performance with a strong political message.

In August 2012 Jón Gnarr again attended the Gay Pride festival in Reykjavík, this time in drag as a member of the Russian activist group Pussy Riot. In October 2012 the members of Pussy Riot were awarded the LennonOno Grant for Peace in Reykjavík alongside Lady GaGa, the late Christopher Higgins, John Perkins, author of the book *Economic Hit Man,* and activist Rachel Corrie, who was killed in Gaza in 2003. Jón Gnarr attended the ceremony in his Obi Wan Kenobi robe. In his speech he once again articulated his vision of world peace and his belief "that empathy is the very core of humanity."[5]

Óttarr Proppé, head of the Reykjavík board of education, also participated in the Gay Pride parade in drag. Óttarr is known for crossing boundaries, being the lead singer of nationally famous hard rock bands that draw crowds of mostly young men. Yet in his role as one of the lead singers of the group Dr. Spock, he is famous for wearing costumes and clothes that are on the margins of mainstream gender roles, such as high-heeled platform shoes. And in his role as lead man in a group called HAM, he performs the hit song "Ingimar" about the love of two men.[6] Neither Jón Gnarr nor Óttarr is gay, but they support diversity and everyone's right to be as they are.

Both Jón Gnarr and the rest of the Best Party do not categorize themselves politically, although they have aligned themselves with anarchist parties such as the Pirate Party in Germany. The Best Party describes its political line as "anarcho-surrealism." In a spring 2012 interview Jón Gnarr stirred up his political opponents when he said that since taking over as mayor and seeing up close what the extreme neoliberal economic politics have done to the city and country, he now considers himself more of a socialist, an anarcho-surrealistic socialist. Since Jón Gnarr and the Best Party came into existence, a new concept has taken root—Gnarrism—which reflects how both lucid and ambiguous the message is. Dominic Boyer (2013) has said that Gnarrism reflects fun and the joy of life. In my view it also reflects a deep political vision that strives to be nonpolitical but contains the basic values of humanitarianism, peace, nature, culture, respect, and humility. The language and actions that party members use to convey these values is then surreal and ambiguous, risking misunderstanding or even ridicule.

During the election campaign the Best Party was criticized for not being democratic because it did not hold primary elections within the party. The party was criticized for being composed mostly of old male friends, all the same age, coming from similar backgrounds. Much of this criticism is true and echoes criticism of most political parties, even radical ones such as the African National Congress. But has the lack of diversity among party members resulted in an agenda that seeks to limit political participation? I suggest not. During the election campaign the Best Party bonded closely with Betri Reykjavík (Better Reykjavík), a company founded by computer scientist Gunnar Grímsson to facilitate citizen participation in the local political process. This cooperation continued after the election and resulted in the first democratic opportunity for citizens to vote online regarding the city's spending. Called participant budgeting, voters could go to the Better Reykjavík website and offer ideas about how to spend public funds. To participate in the election, voters signed into Better Reykjavík via a secure system and chose where they wanted to apply their vote—for either new projects or maintenance. They then prioritized what they wanted done. They could "like" the proposed budget, as in the Facebook model, or vote for other ideas. The results were then considered and either forwarded to the appropriate governing bodies or recycled for further voting. The final budgetary decisions resulted in ISK 300 million in public funding going to 180 projects in all ten neighborhoods of the city. In the report *Northern Lights: Nordic Cities of Opportunity* (PricewaterhouseCoopers 2012), Reykjavík is the only city to receive a high score for its political environment. The report credits the city for giving citizens a voice through participant budgeting.

Although the Best Party has indicated that it abides by an anarchist-surreal conceptual model, members have not wanted to define themselves any further. The party does not adhere to any kind of "high theory" or school of thought named after a great thinker (Graeber 2004, 4). The meaning seems to lie in action and the transformative nature of anarchism, a nature that aims at creating space for a world where people are free to govern themselves, though not the way neoliberals or capitalists would define it. The party operates on an underlying belief that there are many possible roads to any end and that the institutions we are accustomed to can—and should be—broken up, reconstructed, and rethought. At "best," the Best Party seems to have come to a consensus about what is "Best," and how to "Best" things and issues through actions of "Besting."

Because of the nature of anarchist politics and movements, the analytical models most often used to study social movements or political parties are not sufficient to understand the Best Party as a cultural and political phenomenon. I found it helpful to look beyond mainstream anthropological studies toward cultural and media studies research on subcultures and music (see Hall 1992; Hebdige 1979) as well as research on punk movements (see Davies 1996; 1997; Phillipov 2006; Sabin 1999). Although I relied heavily on ethnographic research and data, performance-based approaches provide a built-in model for studying politics and power.

In studying the Best Party, one can use performance-based approaches to illustrate negotiable processes and symbolism at work, looking at both visual performance and narrative as a way of speaking and communicating (Bauman 1975; 1986). Since performance is reflective in nature, it provides a space for the creation, storage, and transmission of both identity and culture, a space where behavior is performed and goes through a process of reflexivity (Fine and Speer 1992, 8).

Although the Best Party does not define the anarchism its members adhere to, one can see a thread leading back to anarchist and surrealist movements of the twentieth century, such as the Situationists, who paved the way for the student uprisings in Paris in the late 1960s. There also seems to be a strong connection to the art and literary culture of punk and the cultural movement around the RE/Search archive and oral history project, established in San Francisco in the late 1970s.[7] Both of these movements encourage the creation of situations in which a particular performance whose aim is to produce cultural and political awareness, if not change, is made possible. This goes back to André Breton's surrealist manifestoes, which call for the exploration of the irrational shadow of official culture with the aim of altering conceptions of reality, common sense, and what is considered natural and unchangeable.

Political anthropology has a long history as a field within social and cultural anthropology, moving slowly from studies of nonstate societies to state societies and the interaction of groups with the state (see Aretxaga 1997; 2005; Gledhill 1994; Lazar 2007; 2008; 2010; Navaro-Yashin 2002; 2003; Vincent 2002). Nonetheless the focus has mostly been on groups that stand outside of political power, perhaps partly because of problems of access to those in power. Anthropological research models have been developed for the analysis of various kinds of political groups, traditional political parties, single-issue mass movements, and separatist groups, religious or political. The Best Party does not fit well into any of these categories. It is not built on a single issue, as we see in many of the social movements described in anthropological texts, for example, women's rights (see Reddy 2005; Kristmundsdóttir 1997; 2004; Simonian 2005; Stephen 2005), HIV (Susser 2005), land and water rights

(Sylvian 2005), globalization (Albro 2005; Doane 2005; Grimes 2005), and peace (Rutherford 2005; Bond 2005). The group has no history in politics and does not seek to ally itself with any particular social grouping or sector, as many separatist movements do. By using classic models of analysis, focusing on single-issue social movements, or political philosophy or classical political science, I believe it is impossible to grasp this sense of being and acting, to understand the wide, creative, lifestyle politics behind the Best Party and its version of anarchism. A new model of study and analysis is called for in order to provide a new mode of identifying political formations.

NOTES

1. "Stefna Besta Flokksins er byggð á því besta úr öllum öðrum stefnum. Við byggjum mest á stefnum sem lagt hafa grunninn að velferðarsamfélögum Norðurlandanna og Norður Evrópu. Það hljómar mjög vel núna" (English translation in text is mine).

2. See "Dagbók borgarstjóra," December 24, 2010, Facebook, https://www.facebook .com/video/video.php?v=1778910238524.

3. For transcribed excerpts from the interview, see "Úttekt: Jón Gnarr á mannamáli,' Vísir, November 9, 2010, http://www.visir.is/uttekt--jon-gnarr-a-mannamali/article /2010515332792. A lengthy discussion of the interview can be found on the web forum Málefnin.com under "Brynja Þorgeirsdóttir og Jón Gnarr," http://www.malefnin.com /ib/index.php?showtopic=124543.

4. The original YouTube video (http://www.youtube.com/watch?v=xxBW4m Pzv6E) is no longer available in the United States. At this writing, it can be seen, with English subtitles, at "Besti Flokkurinn–Simply the Best video," *The Telegraph*, May 26, 2010, http://www.telegraph.co.uk/news/newsvideo/7768742/Besti-Flokkurinn-Simply -the-Best-video.html.

5. Jón Gnarr's speech at the October 9, 2012, ceremony was delivered in English and can be viewed at http://visir.is/section/MEDIA99&fileid=CLP14226.

6. The audio track is available at http://www.youtube.com/watch?v=4uJtJ3-WE_I.

7. More information about the project can be found on the RE/Search website: http://www.researchpubs.com/about/history/.

8

Creativity and Crisis

In this chapter, anthropologist Tinna Grétarsdóttir and her artist colleagues Ásmundur Ásmundsson and Hannes Lárusson look into the neoliberalization of culture and nation branding. They build on previous research each of them had carried out individually and collaboratively—research that eventually brought them together curating the exhibition Koddu, *or* Come Along, *exhibiting more than forty artists at the Living Art Museum and the Alliance House.*

••••••••••••••••••••

Political changes occurring in Iceland since the 1990s have sailed in on a tidal wave of market rationality, neo-liberal enterprise culture, and shifting fields of governing and social engineering.[1] The small island nation turned into a veritable microcosm of the ethos of privatization that has become dominant over the last two decades in Euro-American societies. Iceland had high hopes of becoming more visible in the global competition for power, influence, investment, export, and tourism.

Other chapters in this volume have discussed the toolbox of Viking metaphors that neoliberalists used to promote their ideas. Based on the Icelandic term *útrás*, both the state and private sectors used words such as "incursion," "go Viking," and "occupation" to create a new national narrative and impose "new representations of the world" (Fairclough 2000, 147) on Icelanders, as evoked by the image in Figure 8.1.

The neoliberal shift in ethics and values that demanded a new mind-set of creative enterprise, entrepreneurial

DOI: 10.5876/9781607323358.c008

FIGURE 8.1. The Viking Ship Arrives, *by Einar Falur Ingólfsson. From Ásmundsson, Lárusson, and Grétarsdóttir 2011a, 101. Reprinted with permission.*

endeavors, and risk-taking were presented in Iceland not as breaks from tradition, as would be the case in many Asian nations (see Ong 2006), but as in line with the society's historical, cultural, and natural heritage. Creativity and innovation were repetitive themes in public discourse during the acceleration of neoliberal enterprise culture and are cherished in the production of various images, such as that of Icelanders as free-spirited, innovative Vikings and entrepreneurs bursting with creativity in every sector—from art to business. Images of creativity based on so-called Icelandic heritage and, not least, on Iceland's untamed nature were central to reinventing national narratives to manage the nation, harmonize the national with the international, and represent difference in the phase of forming a globalized, neoliberal nation-state. Language, images, and iconography were central not only to engineering and redefining the nation-project but also to making and presenting the Icelandic brand, which was given higher priority than ever before. The process of nation-branding and highly coordinated public- and private-sector image-making has become not only an instrument of power but also an "institution" of government, reworking people's agency and their practices.

In this chapter we address the range of discourses, images, and technology used to regulate and shape individual activities (including artistic production) and to reform and direct the population to be enterprising and creative as appropriate to the neoliberal project and to "corporate nationalism" (Mackey 2002, 123). One of the conclusions in the report of the Special Investigating Commission established by the Icelandic Parliament in the wake of the economic meltdown was that Icelanders should be encouraged to develop more "realistic, responsible, and moderate identit[ies]" and to engage in critical thinking and media literacy in order to resist the hollow propaganda of marketing and branding masters (Árnason, Nordal, and Ástgeirsdóttir 2010, 195).

Icelandic society has become an interesting "laboratory," bubbling with a combination of neoliberal rationality, economic meltdown, and societal transitions. We address drastic transformations in the field of cultural politics in Iceland, both prior to and after the economic meltdown, as we look at the neoliberalization of culture, including the arts, and reflect upon its subtle methods of governing.

Contemporary Iceland has seen a blurring of the boundaries between public, private, aesthetic, and entrepreneurial spheres that has given rise "to a new way to channel conduct and enable action" (Yúdice 1999, 18) and generated shifting values, ethics, and norms. This restructuring of government's role and channeling of conduct "require new legitimation narratives for the arts and culture" (ibid.). David Harvey (2007) states that the acceleration of neoliberal reforms has been a form of "creative destruction," modifying and even debilitating social institutions. These neoliberal transformations have affected the Icelandic art world. The Icelandic art world has attempted to legitimize itself using increasingly pragmatic, utilitarian descriptions of its outcomes, such as revenues, employment strategies, international networking, enhanced corporate image, nation-branding, and corporate and economic growth, to name but a few.

Art has always been involved with powerful agents of the state and the capitalist market, but it is the realignment of the public-private partnership in the neoliberal regime that has redefined the scope of, and discourse on, contemporary art (Wu 2002). Scholars have argued that this restructured/reframed space shaped by neoliberal rationality and values not only affects the content of artworks and the ways in which institutions operate within the art world, but also influences the "different meanings art takes on in the social milieu" (ibid., 269; see also Sholette 2011). Discourses of creativity and innovation are central to the neoliberal regime, reflected in its emphasis on the creative industries and creative class (see Hesmondhalgh and Baker 2011). Advocates bid on investment in such creativity and the rising creative class to point out "solutions" for the current economic crisis; yet loss of autonomy has become a concern in terms of artwork and cultural policies, causing scholars to talk about "the end of cultural democracy" (Jacquermin 2005, 52), and a "contemporary crisis of voice" (Couldry 2010, 1). Artists have not only become prototypical icons of creativity in the neoliberal project; they have also become the prototype of immaterial labor—the role model in the Post-Fordian work environment (Hardt and Negri 2004; Gielen 2010). Moreover, as Pascal Gielen (2009, 12–13) argues, immaterial labor "does not mean that the material—in this case the work of art—simply vanished, but it became staged within a performance of ideas." Reflecting upon the booming number of people identifying themselves as artists (also referred to as cultural workers) in the neoliberal moment, Gregory Sholette (2011, 117) suggests that artists have acquired increased social legitimacy within the neoliberal economic reforms as the "enterprise culture has so de-radicalized" them, that they have come to stand as a compromise, a kind of détente. Thus, instead of the "longstanding role of artist as a force of independent social criticism" (ibid.), artists are more like a part of the managerial class suited to solving sociocultural problems, soft versions of the technocrat and the bureaucrat.

INSPIRED BY ICELAND

Sociopolitical changes brought on by the rise of neoliberal enterprise culture have affected the arts, as they have affected other sectors of Icelandic society. In the process of entering the world stage (*komast á kortið*) and in creating reimagined, national narratives in accordance with the neoliberal project, Iceland saw a highly coordinated image-making and nation-branding campaign take shape in the late 1990s and early 2000s, whereby creativity became a mantra in motivating and representing Icelanders, Icelandic culture, economics, and nature.[2] Artists and the image of untamed creativity have gained improved social status in this new order. Moreover, catchphrases in the language of the branding have increasingly been applied to artworks and artists: "Nordic Miracle" was used in the late 1990s to spotlight the creativity of the Nordic "periphery" and the rise of international interest in Nordic art (Ekroth 2007).

In collaboration with governing bodies, such as the state and marketing agents, administrators, entrepreneurs, artists, and other representatives of the creative industries have become an indispensable catalyst for redefining Icelandic culture as adventurous and innovative in accordance with marketing strategies carried out under the logo of the Icelandic brand. Artists and other representatives from the creative industries might be described as Iceland's new "beauty queens"—icons of free spirit, originality, and innovation, all of which is in line with the branding of the all-inspiring, creative, and market-friendly Iceland. The synchronized, consistent, and coherent "Iceland" brand—projected internationally—provides the nation with a symbolic system of national paradigms, peculiarities, aesthetic distinctions, and taste. The brand thus becomes a kind of disciplinary institution, dictating the development, management, and streamlining of the Icelandic image as it is directed both outwardly at the larger world and inwardly at Icelanders themselves. Such dual focus is perhaps best reflected in *Ímynd Íslands* (The Image of Iceland), a report officially compiled by the Public Image Committee and directed by Svafa Grönfeldt, then a rector of Reykjavík University. Grönfeldt assembled the report for the Icelandic Prime Minister's Office in 2008 to strengthen Iceland's brand, image, and reputation. The findings of the published report are quite peculiar in that the Public Image Committee explains the process of branding with a model of an erupting hot spring. In other words, the Icelandic brand arises from "natural" Icelandic characteristics: a bubbling, erupting core that can be defined by the slogan "Power, Freedom, Peace." The report states:

> Powerful economic innovation, freedom of speech, security and freedom to act characterize the governmental system, the society and the economy. The untamed forces of nature are analogues to Icelanders' wild and often bold and unpredictable behavior. Yet, these characteristics should not be intimidating, as they have been central to the life-struggle of the nation; they should be celebrated and used. (Forsætisráðuneytið 2008, 5)

The report thus echoes the illusions and the self-congratulatory discourse that was asserted with certainty in Iceland during the *útrás*. One could hear maxims such as "Iceland, best in the world" even used by the director of the Iceland Chamber of Commerce at its business convention in February of 2007.[3] In addition to ministers and business people, one of the main members introduced at the convention was an expert and international advisor to various governments and cities in identity management and branding.

Efforts such as the "Image of Iceland" report, designed to pinpoint Icelandic strengths, relied on harnessing Icelandic confidence and projecting that confidence abroad. Any disconnect between Iceland's self-image and its international reputation was meant to be properly remedied via marketing Iceland as a strong, coherent brand. By design, this brand, as it was presented in the report, was supposedly mapped out with public input. The Public Image Committee asserted that it was the result of focus groups and roundtable discussions.

Such reliance on public input was meant to lend the report authenticity. The report states that successful branding rests on the "true" identity of the nation and of Icelanders, "which are true or 'authentic' and have deep roots" (Forsætisráðuneytið 2008, 24). Yet the process demonstrates the manipulation of the "participating public" in brand-making. The report is characterized by endless clichés and myths about Iceland, which, as ever, are described by creativity, freedom, power, adaptability, and endurance, qualities that support the belief that the nation can "perform the impossible" (ibid., 5).

All of these pre-crisis assurances of Iceland's superiority show how Iceland's self-image was based on illusion, which ironically rendered Iceland unable to fully apprehend the unbridgeable gap between image and reality. Yet nation-branding did not slow down after the meltdown; instead, it was rolled into a politics of crisis—not just economic but environmental—due to the eruption of the volcano Eyjafjallajökull. Again, Icelanders were encouraged to participate directly in creating the brand by becoming involved in the promotion of Iceland and by disseminating Icelandic imagery to friends and business partners abroad through greetings and an invitation to Iceland. A central example of such marketing strategies is the recent *Inspired by Iceland* video—part of "The nation invites you home" campaign—which was made for Promote Iceland (Íslandsstofa), an institution run jointly by the government and the private sector in order to promote Iceland abroad as a destination for tourism and investors.[4] The minister of finance urged Icelanders to circulate the video across Iceland's borders and advocated that directors and managers give their employees leeway to circulate the video at work ("Þjóðarátakið 'Þjóðin býður heim'" 2010). Telecommunications did not charge for overseas phone calls during one whole weekend so that the nation could call their friends and clients overseas and "invite them home." The campaign also produced videos of Icelanders volunteering to provide tourists with a personal experience by opening their homes and playing music, talking to them about knitting, cooking pancakes for them, etc.

The marketing effort seems to be one of the few things that created a sense of solidarity among the nation in the wake of the collapse and volcanic eruption. Icelanders have adopted the inseparable interests of the state and the market as their own with what appears to be spontaneous enthusiasm, and these interests have become an integral part of their own identities, as evidenced by the volume of web traffic to the video *Inspired by Iceland*. Those who refuse to protect the brand are often attacked from within—accused of undermining a small nation's reasonable options for self-reliance and self-sufficiency. As it turns out, Icelanders have proven themselves quite receptive to this virtual reality. Perhaps in times of uncertainty and diffusion, the iconic image of Iceland gives them a break from their sobering and painful resentment after the party ended and the bubble popped (see also Ellenberger 2010).

In accordance with these marketing strategies, artists have become central catalysts for redefining and remodeling the culture of Iceland as one of adventure and innovation. The arts are subordinated to rational, technocratic management techniques that arguably serve the select interests of the powers that be. Artists are addressed as suitable agents expected to create, perform, and promote appropriate "success stories" of Icelanders on the global stage. Such possibilities are advocated in the "Image of Iceland" report, which shows how contemporary Icelandic artists, as representatives of the creative industry, can be useful in the business of branding, design, and image enhancement.

The instrumentalization of artists and art for an economic purpose is the theme of an article by Halldór J. Kristjánsson, the director of Landsbankinn (which was a key patron of Icelandic culture); he elaborated on the fusion of branding, art, and enterprise culture in the following statement:

> . . . culture can, as everyone knows, be a pure source for business with its inspired thinking and innovation . . . With increased globalization of the workforce, the promotion of Icelandic culture becomes a more important factor in strengthening business relations. For a company that builds on trust and security, cultural issues are one of the best marketing venues available. (Kristjánsson 2005, 8)

In the early 2000s, the expansion of private sponsorship was welcomed by the government and had a significant effect on policy regarding the funding of art and culture. The presence of executives from corporations and financial institutions, referred to as Vikings of enterprise, became pervasive in the cultural milieu. This "partnership" of art and corporate culture, generally addressed as corporate social responsibility (CSR), did not, in general, result in the establishment of autonomous nonprofit, art-supporting organizations run with professional independent boards. Instead, it took a pragmatic direction by making the private funds established to support contemporary art in Iceland more or less controlled by their donors, the banks and corporations.

Another example of the co-option of artists by enterprise culture can be found in the motives of the Future Group of the Iceland Chamber of Commerce (Framtíðarhópur Viðskiptaráðs Íslands). The chamber invited the visual artist Þorvaldur Þorsteinsson to a lunch meeting where Iceland's future was on the agenda. Subsequently, to his surprise, both his name and his portrait appeared prominently in the report *Ísland 2015* (Viðskiptaráð Íslands 2006). He was featured alongside other business leaders and representatives from the creative industry as a member of the Future Group and as one of the authors of the report. Þorvaldur Þorsteinsson rejected being an author of the report.

ICELAND = NATURE = CREATIVITY = ART

During marketing campaigns abroad, artists have been invited by the public and private partnership to participate in "lobby exhibitions," as one artist has put it, to promote the nation's characteristics, spicing up Iceland's idiosyncrasies in order to promote a distinction based on nationality. Promoting national stereotypes has indeed been a part of the national project at home, a necessary "pep talk" in a small nation's alleged fight for independence. During these campaigns, artists are used as mules to pull the marketing wagon, to enter communities across borders and catch foreign attention at critical moments in international politics and business. Often their work is sought by government and business in a desperate measure to bolster the "Iceland" brand.

One such exhibition created turmoil within the art community—the panoramic exhibition *From Another Shore: Recent Icelandic Art* at the Scandinavia House in New York in 2008. The exhibition, featuring a selection of the National Gallery of Iceland's permanent collection, is often referred to as an example of a partnership of art, international politics, and business. The exhibition was sponsored by Alcoa's community fund (as explicitly stated on Alcoa's website) and by the Icelandic government,[5] and was held in connection with Iceland's campaign for a seat on the UN Security Council. It was very much in sync with the aforementioned "Image of Iceland" report. The exhibition highlighted the unique qualities of Icelandic art—and thus "Icelandicness" in general. Specifically, the exhibition tapped into the clichéd equation: Iceland = nature. What differentiates Icelandic artists and their work from others, as stated by the director of the National Gallery of Iceland in the exhibition press release, "is the[ir] attitude . . . to nature, which is the basis of their art whether it is conspicuous or not" (Scandinavia House 2008, n.p.). This cliché fits perfectly with Iceland's branding campaign in which Icelandic originality and entrepreneurship are not only comparable to the forces of nature but can also be traced back to nature, taking root in the natural world and finding expression in the individual Icelander.

The concept of nature in Iceland has become a master narrative in Icelandic contemporary cultural politics. While nature has always had a prominent place in the eighteenth-century romantic nationalist movement in Europe, influenced by the German philosophers Johann Gottfried Herder and Johann

Gottlieb Fichte, it seems like nature has replaced the Icelandic language as the fundamental symbol of national pride, unity, and difference (Hálfdanarson 1999, 328). Central to the narratives of nature found in the contemporary cultural politics is the conflation of art, nature, and ethnicity that dominates discussions and presentations on Icelandic art. Whether we speak of it as a serious factor in the development of Iceland as a nation, or tongue in cheek, nature is considered a major player in the shaping of not only the Icelandic physique but also the Icelandic character. Nature is seen as fueling Icelanders' creativity, which contains a primal energy that correlates to human qualities such as wildness, honesty, innocence, and so forth. These qualities lie at the heart of Christian Schön's description of Icelandic art. According to Schön, a former director of the Icelandic Art Center, "Icelandic art has kept a bit of its creative virginity, which most other European societies had already lost centuries ago. That is my explanation of what makes Icelandic art so special" (quoted in Canarezza and Coro 2010, 182).

According to one master of Iceland's branding program, Iceland Naturally, the program has been quite successful because people are increasingly perceiving Iceland and Icelandic products in line with the slogan "Pure, natural, and unspoiled." On the side of the arts, Icelandic music is seen to be distinctive on the world stage. At Iceland's pavilion website at Expo 2010 in Shanghai, China, for example, Icelandic musicians were presented as inspired by nature, and Icelandic music was presented as pure and profound. Ironically, while Icelanders are promoting the "pure" and "unspoiled" nature of the island, they are simultaneously turning it into one of the world's greatest aluminum smelting sites.

Meanwhile, many Icelandic artists find themselves tied down, or even haunted, by this reduction of Icelandic art to the simplistic conflation of art with ethnicity and the land/nature. This reduction is so prevalent that it has even become a recurrent feature of foreign analyses [6]

A "WIN-WIN" SITUATION?

Many artists criticize that when funds are invested in promoting art abroad, as in so-called lobby exhibitions jointly organized by the public and private sectors such as Promote Iceland (Íslandsstofa), these projects are often propped up far removed from the aesthetic and critical context of the art world. In Promote Iceland's case, such exhibitions are evaluated based on its potential to strengthen Iceland's good image and reputation, promote tourism, investment, and trade, and create other synergistic opportunities. For example, Promote

Iceland criticized an ambitious exhibition at Fargfabriken Norr in Östersund, Sweden, titled *The Nordic Third World Country? Icelandic Art in Times of Crisis* (Engqvist and Englund 2010), because it did not portray the "right" image of Iceland. In a personal communication with one of the authors of this chapter, the director of Promote Iceland shared his antipathy toward the exhibition title and detailed his frustrations with the exhibition catalogue, which included critical texts on Iceland. He said Promote Iceland would never have supported it had he known the context of the exhibition. As it turned out, the exhibition had received some dried fish for the opening from Promote Iceland.

As the artist Ásmundsson once put it, both public and private interests will valorize artwork that "in the right context [can] transform into a volcano, declaration of support, an advertisement or something else" (Ásmundsson 2008, 8). The result of such contractual partnerships and anticipated results have little to do with artistic values and strategies, cultivating dialogue, or critical assessments. When it comes to measuring the profit of the partnership, significant achievements are measured quantitatively in terms of marketing value.

The partnerships are presented as "win-win" situations in which everyone benefits, a mantra often repeated in the art world. The morality of the system is reflected in the trickle-down effects of the pyramid, which is "enterprise culture's version of 'egalitarianism'" (Heelas and Morris 1992, 21). Artists are generally closer to the bottom of the pyramid, often seen as "cheap labor." While the creative industries are supposedly a growing sector, artists work in an insecure environment. They are and have to be constantly flexible—a flexibility reflected in their physical and mental mobility; irregular working hours; ability to adjust to multiple jobs, and limited job protection. They often inhabit a space of uncertainty, without access to benefits, and are accustomed to taking on less creative, temporary jobs to fund their own creative projects and unpaid hours (Hesmondhalgh and Baker 2011; Lorey 2011).

In the neoliberal moment, this description of artists' flexibility and precariousness is becoming the norm for many workers. Isabell Lorey (2006) suggests that the normalization of precarious conditions, such as those that artists usually endure, is a neoliberal instrument of governance. Or, as Lorey further argues,

> creative workers . . . are subjects so easily exploited; they seem able to tolerate their living and working conditions with infinite patience because of the belief in their own freedoms and autonomies, and because of the fantasies of self-realization. In a neoliberal context, they are so exploitable that, now, it is no

longer just the state that presents them as role models for new modes of living and working. (Lorey 2011, 87)

Post-Fordist work ethics and the instability of artists' working conditions have contributed to the silencing of labor exploitation by neoliberal administrative bodies. Thus focusing on "the politics of the field of art as a place of work" (Steyerl 2012, 93) as well as systemic exploitation and self-exploitation is essential when discussing the precarious conditions of artists, their anticipated conformity, the marginalization of critical cultural production, and what modes of subjectification arise in these times of economic uncertainty.

In times of austerity, post-2008 Iceland has witnessed intensification of the valorization of art as predominantly an instrumental labor; an economic stimulant where all types of artistic productions are systematically united under the rubric of the "industry" and associated first and foremost with generating places for tourism, competitions, revenues, spin-offs, and measureable quantities. It is evident that the discourse of creative industries (which penetrates at regional and supranational levels of cultural policies), has been rigidly adopted at governmental level in Iceland. In accord with the government and Promote Iceland, a collaborative platform of the arts was established in 2009 and transformed, in 2011, into the Association of the Creative Industries. One outcome of this structure is the publication "Towards Creative Iceland: building local, going global" which maps the economic scale of those "creative industries" (Sigurðardóttir and Young 2011). The report provides Icelandic artists the ability to point out in a scientific, standardized, and acceptable language, the viability of the cultural sector. It endows them with a set of numbers, graphs and charts, that they can use when members of Parliament or the public voice frustration at endowments given to the arts sector by the state. Interestingly, after the publication of the aforementioned economic report Iceland's minister of industry, energy and tourism was so thrilled that she proclaimed in a speech, "We are finally starting to understand the importance and the possibilities of the creative industries" (Júlíusdóttir 2011). Shifts toward the development of the creative industries in Iceland have taken place almost uncritically. Legitimating narratives that link art with aesthetic strategies, critical creativity, humanist values, and social dissent seem to be considered odd, disruptive, or irrelevant in the present discourse. Post-economic meltdown, art as part of the creative industry is now subject to performance-oriented, statistically measureable, pragmatic results—results that render its successes indisputably valid.

Yet a few are beginning to speak up. Incorporating nonprofit sectors (such as alternative artist-led spaces) and commercial sectors (such as video gaming, music, etc.) within the framework of the creative industries, despite their different needs and intended agency, runs the risk of uneven developments and declines to consider the benefits of the nonprofit sector as marketing forces become too powerful (Hesmondhalgh 2012). The obvious risk surfacing is that the development of creative industries fails to recognize the value of artistic productions that are "difficult," ones that do not support the demands of the market, profit, or the promotion of the *good* image.

CONCLUSION

In Iceland we are seeing a boom in the number of people identifying themselves as artists or, if you will, "cultural workers," in the neoliberal moment. The artist, the adaptable and mobile entrepreneur, is indeed celebrated as the agent of creative solutions and dynamic nation branding. In the wake of neoliberal restructuring in Iceland, we have witnessed the neoliberalization of art and culture, which is increasingly associated with competitiveness and insecurity among creative workers, as well as with performance-oriented, statistically measureable results. In the meantime, the increased integration of cultural policy with economic wealth in art/culture legitimation narratives in the system has become a concern to many artists. While this is the reality within the Icelandic art scene, it remains unspoken as utilitarian expressions of legitimation have become so pervasive that "even 'progressives' have found a way of making peace with it" (Yúdice 1999, 17).

Raising questions regarding "the destiny of the power of creation" (Rolnik 2011, 23), we enter into a space where we can critique creativity and at the same time begin to address the disquieting issue of alternative, subversive and dissident creative practices and from where they can arise. Perhaps it is more important now then ever to dwell on how it is possible to creatively develop spaces where one is not at work in the neoliberal labor system—in the structured, channeled, and supervised relations and "communication" of branding—and how it is possible to dismantle spaces that prevent one from being active citizens.

NOTES

1. The following discussion is largely based on writings that we published in the catalogue *Koddu* (Ásmundsson, Lárusson, and Grétarsdóttir 2011a) and the paper "The Cultural Worker," presented at the conference Þjóðarspegill on October 28, 2011, at the University of Iceland in Reykjavík (Ásmundsson, Lárusson, and Grétarsdóttir 2011b) We want to thank EDDA—Center of Excellence for supporting our research.

2. One of the first nation-branding programs, Iceland Naturally, was established in 1999 to promote Iceland in North America. The slogan "Pure, Natural, Unspoiled," created with the assistance of the US public relations firm FleishmanHillard, has been used to describe the main qualities of the Icelandic "brand."

3. For a summary of the presentation by Halla Tómasdóttir, director of the Iceland Chamber of Commerce, see "Hvernig verður Ísland best í heimi?" http://vi.is/malef nastarf/frettir/536/. A link to her slide show, "Ísland, Best í Heimi!" (Iceland, Best in the World!), appears at the bottom of the web page.

4. The video used in the campaign is accompanied by the song "Jungle Drum" by Emilína Torrini. *Inspired by Iceland* is available at http://vimeo.com/12236680.

5. The exhibition was supported mainly by the Alcoa Foundation and the Icelandic government. Additional support was provided by Baugur Group; Icelandair Cargo; Blue Lagoon; Iceland Naturally; and the Icelandic Cultural Fund of The American-Scandinavian Foundation (see Alcoa website http://www.alcoa.com/iceland/en/news/whats_new/2008/2008_05_scandinavian.asp).

6. A *New York Times* review of two Icelandic exhibitions held in New York, *From Another Shore: Recent Icelandic Art* and *It's Not Your Fault: Art from Iceland*, was entitled "Inspired by Vikings and Volcanoes." Reviewer Karen Rosenberg identified a "friction between global contemporary art and an island nation's folk traditions, between urban hives and otherworldly landscapes. . . ." She goes on to ask, "What, then, makes their work recognizably Icelandic? In some cases, a yearning for the volcanic and glacial landscape of home; in others, an interest in local folklore" (Rosenberg 2008). Echoing Rosenberg's review, Gregory Volk also sees nature as central to Icelandic art. In an article published in *Art in America*, Volk states that "eventually the country itself comes to figure in their work: as a physical locus, as a trove of images and materials, or—more mysteriously for outsiders—as comprehensive forces with which one is perpetually in dialogue" (Volk 2000, 40).

The Magic of
"Virtual" Fish

9

The Icelandic government's decision to implement Individual Transferable Quotas (ITQs) in the country's crucial fishing industry played a central part in the economic meltdown. But Iceland is not alone in being ravaged by such a system. Evelyn Pinkerton is a fisheries expert in the School of Resource and Environmental Management at Simon Fraser University in British Columbia, Canada. Here she offers a primer and a global perspective on ITQs and their effects.

• • • • • • • • • • • • • • • • • • • •

WHAT IS AN ITQ?

Individual Transferable Quotas (ITQs) are permits allowing their holders to catch or transfer the privilege of catching a share of the total allowable catch (TAC) of a fish species. The TAC is usually set by government or independent scientists who study the productivity of the *stock* of fish in order to determine the annual *flow* from that stock that can be sustainably harvested (Loucks 2005). Stocks of fish along with the marine habitat and food web that support them are usually owned by a national or regional government. *Thus it is only the annual sustainable flow or yield from that stock that fishermen can have permits to catch or transfer.* This point is crucial, as it exemplifies the problem a nation creates if it decides to consider ITQs completely private rights. The nation still must concern itself with the health of the stock and its surrounding ecosystem, public uses of them, and competing uses of marine space. To adequately protect these public goods and diverse

DOI: 10.5876/9781607323358.c009

uses, the nation cannot be under political pressure from powerful private groups that have much narrower interests. As discussed below, ITQs inevitably create more powerful and consolidated fishing interest groups.

ITQs are not fishing licenses. Fishermen normally buy annual fishing licenses, which are permits to try their luck at catching whatever quantity they can during the time a fishery is "open" or permitted by the state. The state stops fishing activity when it deems that the maximum sustainable yield or total allowable catch has been taken. After that, no one can fish that species until the next season. With an ITQ, three things change:

1. The quantity of fish a quota holder is permitted to catch is specified before the season starts. The fishery is managed by the state so that the quota holder has enough opportunity to catch his permitted amount, or quota. This condition reduces his costs because he does not have to invest in engines, gear, or boats to compete as much in time and space with other fishermen for fishing opportunity.

2. The permit becomes quite valuable, since it is practically a guarantee of catching a certain quantity of fish at less cost. Therefore the state is in a strong position to require the first generation of ITQ holders, who are given the permit gratis, to take on a substantial portion of the management costs.

3. The permit becomes a tradable commodity like stock on a stock market, with few or no limits on who can buy it. Like any other stock, it attracts investors who have access to capital and can buy up the permits and lease them out to fishermen who cannot afford to buy them.

Although ITQs can be sold, many countries (including the United States and Canada) have defined them as a privilege that can be revoked or diminished by the state, according to new policies or changes in stock condition (Bromley 2009). In Canada, for example, a percentage of the Pacific halibut TAC has been reallocated away from the commercial fishery to the sport fishery without compensation to the commercial fishery. In other countries, such as the Faroe Islands and the Netherlands, ITQs have been either revoked or their value reduced by changes in state fisheries policy, without compensation to ITQ holders or fishermen. These changes were caused by the need for greater state and local regulation, because the ITQ systems were not meeting management objectives. For example, in the Netherlands, which adopted ITQs in 1976, state regulations were later added requiring that fishermen lease parts of their quota only to other members of their regional group and sell quotas only at a registered auction. Accountability to their group provided scrutiny of their accounts and direct controls on landings, plus peer pressure from other quota holders. Often greater state regulation was accompanied by greater local involvement in implementation of the regulations (Symes et al. 2003; van Hoof 2010).

Since their initial adoption by Iceland, New Zealand, and Canada in the mid-1980s to early 1990s, ITQs have received widespread positive evaluations from numerous resource economists and fisheries managers and have been widely adopted and accepted as a way of dealing with problems in fisheries management (National Research Council 1999; Costello et al. 2008). At the same time, problems with this approach have been identified by numerous researchers from various fields, including but not limited to economists (Armstrong and Sumaila 2001; Schott 2004; Bromley 2009), political scientists (Agrawal 2002), anthropologists (McCay et al. 1995; Pinkerton and Edwards 2009), and geographers (Bradshaw 2004; St. Martin 2007).

ESCALATING CLAIMS ABOUT THE BENEFITS OF ITQS

Alongside growing critiques and identification of problems with ITQs has been an extension of claims about their benefits, claims that began with economic efficiency but then expanded into quite different territory. These claims are summarized below.

ITQs ARE ECONOMICALLY EFFICIENT

ITQ advocates held that these "efficient" ITQ permit holders yield the greatest public benefit because they have the lowest fishing costs and thus their operations result in the least dissipation of wealth for society in general (Munro 2001). According to this reasoning, fishing costs are low because with an almost guaranteed catch, permit holders do not have to invest in more competitive gear and boats to wastefully race for the fish. In addition, ITQ advocates posited that if ITQs are transferable via the market, they will automatically gravitate to the vessels and operators with the lowest fishing costs, by definition the most efficient (Scott 1989). Thus small operators will automatically sell out to larger operators, who enjoy economies of scale. But economies of scale are not a factor in all fisheries, and ITQ advocates did not consider that those able to fish with the lowest costs may not be able to outbid investors with access to significant capital. In other words, ITQs can gravitate toward those with the most capital, not necessarily those who are most efficient.

ITQs PROMOTE CONSERVATION

Ecologists (Costello et al. 2008) compared fisheries managed as ITQs and those that were not to claim that ITQs promote conservation. These authors failed to note that the choice of fisheries where an ITQ system had been introduced significantly skews their sample, since governments and managers attempt to introduce ITQs in the most profitable and well-managed fisheries first. Comparing ITQed and non-ITQed fisheries for conservation success is thus not a revealing comparison. In fact, the Organisation for Economic Co-operation and Development (OECD 1997: 82) found that twenty-four out of thirty-seven ITQed fisheries it examined had at least some temporary declines in stocks due largely to inadequate information and illegal fishing. Of these, twenty needed additional regulations such as closed areas, size restrictions, trip limits, and vessel restrictions, demonstrating what has become common practice: ITQs have to be supplemented by the extra regulations they were intended to replace.

Initially, ITQ advocates told the people of Iceland and New Zealand that ITQs would help with the declining abundance of fish stocks in their fisheries because they would promote conservation. This was also why the Faroe Islands briefly experimented with ITQs during a cod collapse in 1993. However, the way those governments addressed conservation had nothing to do with ITQs. They simply lowered the TAC and gave fishermen ITQs that were much lower than their previous annual catches, thus forcing many small fishermen out because their annual allowed catch was no longer sufficient to support their operation (Stewart et al. 2006).

Economists have adopted the claim that ITQs promote stewardship (Grafton et al. 2006), even though there are many examples of private acquisition of common pool resources such as forests leading to the liquidation of the good (Acheson 2006). Private actors unattached to particular landscapes, communities, or regions are more likely to respond to the current interest rate, or how much they could earn by liquidating the resource, than to issues of stewardship. They will liquidate the resource if interest rates make this a more attractive option than harvesting at a sustainable rate (Sumaila 2010). Globalization and the decoupling of active fishermen from ITQ owners make this outcome more and more likely (Gibbs 2009).

ITQs WILL LOWER MONITORING AND ENFORCEMENT COSTS

An extension of the claim that ITQs promote stewardship was the claim that ITQs would lower monitoring and enforcement costs because individual owners would have incentives to maintain their privileged access and therefore monitor themselves (Munro 2001). Yet the major processing companies' drastic overfishing of the Newfoundland northern cod, closed since 1992, offers a striking example of the failure of ITQ holders to monitor, enforce, or fish sustainably (Bavington 2010). The companies there held the equivalent of ITQs (called "enterprise allocations"). In the British Columbia halibut fishery, self-monitoring under ITQs improved very little, and eventually all fishermen were required to pay for expensive on-board cameras and dockside monitors, which substantially raised monitoring costs (Pinkerton 2013).

Ecologists Gibbs (2009; 2010) and Ban and colleagues (2008) are skeptical about the extent of the claim that ITQs contribute to conservation and stewardship and emphasize the tendency of ITQ advocates to ignore the incompatibility between ITQs and ecosystem-based management (which requires attention and adjustment to ecosystem concerns). This is unsurprising, as ITQs are narrowly focused market instruments directed toward achieving the efficient allocation of catch shares within a biologically meaningful, prescribed harvest cap. More recently, ITQ advocates have begun to grapple with this issue, acknowledging that ITQs are not a panacea or appropriate for all fisheries. I argue, however, that ITQs benefit a very few at the expense of the overall public welfare and also provide questionable solutions to fisheries problems.

PROBLEMS NOW IDENTIFIED IN ITQ SYSTEMS WORLDWIDE

What the aforementioned economists, managers, biologists, and ecologists have insufficiently considered is the question that should override all others: is the nation that institutes ITQs better off as a whole than one that does not? What needs to be considered in a full-cost accounting of the impacts of ITQs?

We must consider, for example, the impact of the radical transformation of a large segment of the population that has lost access to fishing. Then we must consider the effect of abolishing the social contract between the state and fishing-dependent coastal communities, a social contract that has been in place for centuries in many European countries. Formerly, communities and regions in many countries had the power to control the conditions under which fishing licenses left the community or region as well as most individual fishermen's right of access and the conditions under which their crews fished. According to Danish anthropologists Andresen and Hojrup (2008, 33), when ITQs were created in Denmark, one of the biggest gifts in Danish history has been given away. A small majority in the Danish Parliament gave away ownership of national fish resources valued at EUR 2,500,000,000 to 1,500 boat owners. Most of the owners have sold out, bringing in EUR 500,000–1,000,000 for their boat and the allotted quota. Thus, . . . [crew and fishermen lacking quotas] are left with nothing and have no official voice to defend their cause.

There are two major elements in this radical transformation: (1) the loss of traditional livelihoods and (2) the loss of the political power to defend traditional rights of access to this opportunity.

In her study of the privatization of large segments of the economies of Chile, Argentina, and Bolivia, Naomi Klein considered the enormous loss of assets by the majority of the population to be a form of theft (Klein 2007). In addition, she documents the dramatic rise in unemployment, poverty, and economic crisis suffered by those countries undergoing major privatization of national assets. Researchers in the Department of Management and International Business at the University of Auckland in New Zealand consider the large players who benefited from this transfer of assets in New Zealand to be "little more than an organized crime syndicate" (Stringer et al. 2014). In Scandinavian countries, known for the highest levels of economic equality in the developed world, the new inequality created by ITQs will undoubtedly have a substantial psychological impact at many levels (Wilkinson and Pickett 2007).

However one characterizes this transformation, the state is left bearing new costs, including increased unemployment by a previously self-supporting population, increased health and welfare costs, and reduced well-being of its citizens from the loss of power, livelihoods, and security. The analysis of these costs has not been done because the issue has been treated as a fisheries management problem or a gross domestic product issue involving only part of fish production, not a problem of how entire communities have been removed from their traditional livelihoods, usually with no alternatives. In the case of aboriginal communities in Canada, geographic mobility is often not possible, even if there were jobs for them elsewhere. Until this full-cost accounting occurs, the benefits allocated to the first generation of quota holders and investors who enjoy soaring profits will be the focus of analysis. The following list of problems with ITQs should be seen as dimensions of the costs imposed on the majority of the population (at least in cases where fishing was a major component of the national economy) and also on the state at large.

1. *Inequity of initial allocation raises the cost of entry for future generations.* The first generation of quota holders is usually given the quota on the grounds

that it is "politically expedient to allocate a substantial part of the economic rent to existing users as the price of securing their support for moving to ITQs" (Tietenberg 2002, 217). However, since the market is considered the most efficient method for transferring ITQs, all subsequent owners pay a very high price for what is now a valuable commodity. Concentration of more quotas is usually required of the second generation to achieve economies of scale, having paid for the now very expensive quota. All future generations who must buy the permit from the first generation incur substantial debt. The first generation may alternatively become permanent landlords who lease out their ITQs for substantial fees and will the ITQ to their children, who may have never fished, unless there is an explicit and enforceable "owner-operator" requirement that prevents leasing.

2. *Concentration of quota ownership or control creates market power.* There is a high level of agreement that ITQs inevitably lead to concentration of ownership, and a number of scholars have documented that processing companies thereby acquire market power, either through direct ownership of ITQs or through leasing arrangements. Processors do not need to own ITQs in order to control leasing and have market power. They merely have to lease substantial quotas early in the season and then sublease them to fishermen, usually with the understanding that they will receive all the fish, giving them some leverage over price (Eythorsson 1996; Copes and Charles 2004; Pinkerton and Edwards 2009, Stewart and Callagher 2011).

3. *Crew share is greatly reduced.* In most jurisdictions, crewmen were formerly allocated a share of the value of the catch as "co-venturers" who shared both the risks and the benefits of fishing. Crew and rental skippers have been radically downgraded to low-wage earners under ITQs. In Denmark "share fishermen [who do not own a boat or share of a boat], a system that has dominated in Scandinavia and in old west European sea powers as Great Britain, the Netherlands, France, Spain and Portugal for a very long period, are disappearing" (Andresen and Hojrup 2008, 32). In the British Columbia halibut fishery, crew members who formerly earned 10 to 20 percent of the catch value now earn 1 to 5 percent (Butler 2004; Pinkerton, and Edwards 2009).

4. *Leasing arrangements, where allowed, create inequity.* Those with the most access to capital can buy quotas and lease them out, so investors buying quotas as an investment with high returns quickly become new players. Leasing fees are increasingly becoming a larger and larger percentage of the value of the catch (Pinkerton and Edwards 2009, van Putten and Gardner 2010).

5. *Inequity of free transferability of quota out of communities, out of regions, even out of countries.* The social contract concerning what the fishery is for, who should benefit from it, and what control they should have over it has been violated unless there are rules limiting transferability. When Denmark went to ITQs it took only two years for the biggest harbors to lose their fishermen (Andresen and Hojrup 2008). In New Zealand, crew wages have become so low that New Zealanders will no longer take them, so New Zealand quota holders now take over 60 percent of the offshore quota via Foreign Chartered Vessels (McCurdy 2012). In 2011, a scandal erupted when researchers at the University of Auckland learned that the largely Indonesian crews on these 27 Chinese or Korean vessels were being held in slave-like conditions on the boats and had not been paid. This finding led to a public outcry and a Ministerial Inquiry, which in 2013 declared that all fishing vessels must be reflagged as New Zealand vessels by 2016 and thus come under New Zealand jurisdiction. However, the fish on these boats is still processed in China, so processing jobs are not even retained in New Zealand (ibid.; Stringer et al. 2014). This is because the quota holders, now largely investors and large processing companies, are leasing quota where they can make the largest profits, which is where labor is cheapest. The original economists' prediction that ITQs would enhance public welfare because it would "reduce the dissipation of rent" has shown itself to be far from the mark when transferability is not restricted. ITQs enhance the welfare of the quota owners at the expense of not only the rental skippers and crews but the national economy as well. The nation is left with the cost of protecting the health of the stock, while the quota holders benefit from the flow and send jobs offshore.

6. *Quotas are overcapitalized instead of boats.* The economists claimed that ITQs would reduce overcapitalization of vessels and thus avoid undesirable competition, which reduces fishermen's profits. Instead the quotas themselves have become highly capitalized (Edwards et al. 2006), increasing in value by 600 percent over ten years in British Columbia's halibut fishery (Pinkerton 2013). In Denmark the boat and quota value together increased by 500 percent in one year (Andresen and Hojrup 2008). This puts quotas out of the reach of most fishermen who did not receive the initial gift.

7. *Safety is not always improved.* Iceland and New Zealand have an unimpressive accident and fatality record under ITQs (Windle et al. 2008). ITQs were predicted to increase safety because they would end the race for fish. However, it is likely that these countries suffer the same situation

as the British Columbia halibut fishery, where the portion of the fleet that leases under exploitive prices goes out in worse weather and takes more risks because they are desperate (Pinkerton and Edwards 2009; Emery et al., forthcoming).

8. *Small boats are forced out.* Small boats have disproportionately left the fishery in New Zealand, Iceland, and British Columbia. In British Columbia small boats cannot afford the fixed costs of monitoring, which have become far more expensive under ITQs (Pinkerton 2013). Iceland at an early stage (Bogason 2007) and New Zealand later (Stewart and Callagher 2011) have made some efforts to protect some small fishermen but have still lost a substantial number of smaller operators (Pálsson and Helgason 1995). In many fisheries small boats are more efficient than large ones and contribute more to social welfare because they employ more people per fish sold, supporting numerous small-scale livelihoods (Nikoloyuk and Adler 2013; Sabau 2013), and they have a more beneficial ratio of input to output than larger boats (Pinkerton 1987). Ban and colleagues (2008) point out that ITQ "success stories" poorly represent the artisanal (small-scale) fleets that take 28–58 percent of the global catch and employ 99 percent of the world's approximately 51 million fishermen.

9. *Monitoring costs rise under ITQs.* Contrary to claims that ITQs would be self-monitoring because the incentives would protect private property, greater monitoring became necessary because, as Copes (1986) predicted, in fisheries where larger fish fetch higher prices, a fisherman with a fixed quota has incentives to discard smaller fish, thereby "high-grading" to get the greatest possible value out of the same number of fish taken. The Faroe Islands passed a ban on discarding fish in 1994, but the state could not prevent it under the ITQ system (Gezelius 2008). Discarding and misreporting was 18 percent in 1995. The Faroe Islands dropped ITQs in 1996 due primarily to the advantages of regulating fishing effort directly.

10. *ITQs are not compatible with the precautionary approach and not easily adjusted in response to problems.* ITQs are more difficult to reverse than other systems. In the mid-1990s the Royal Society of Canada asked a team of ecologists, economists, and other social scientists to examine the performance of Canadian marine fisheries. They concluded that ITQs are not compatible with the precautionary approach needed to deal with the complexity and uncertainty of the marine environment today. Instead, management systems need flexibility and adaptability (de Young et al. 1999). Faith in ITQs was shaken throughout the North Atlantic by 1994, but since many countries have adjusted their entire administrative system

to ITQs and share stocks with other EU countries, it is very difficult for them to get out of the system (Andresen and Hojrup 2008).

11. *ITQs alone are not effective and need to be accompanied by input controls and adequate enforcement* (Symes et al. 2003; van Hoof 2010; Emery et al. 2012). Many countries have learned that, instead of being a substitute for input controls such as gear, area, and time regulations, ITQs (output controls) require input controls to work, and many countries have had to add them over time. The Netherlands adopted ITQs in 1976, but as they added more and more input controls over time, ITQs eventually became an obstacle rather than an asset (Symes et al. 2003).

WHY DO SOME GOVERNMENTS SUPPORT ITQ SYSTEMS?

So why do governments embrace ITQs and, in some cases, force them onto fishermen despite substantial opposition? There are both ideological and pragmatic reasons. Ideologically, neoliberal economists and politicians who believe that the market should be the major regulator and that state expenditures should be drastically reduced influence policy. Klein (2007) documented the major influence of neoliberal economists in nations that decided to privatize public goods.

However, government agencies that are forced to make budget cuts may move to ITQs as a mechanism to recover costs from fishermen, whether or not they embrace the neoliberal agenda. In considering the British Columbia halibut fishery, Pinkerton (2013) notes that ITQs provide cash-strapped government departments an opportunity to download onto fishermen the costs of monitoring and the costs of "co-managing," which together were 102 times the fishermen's costs paid to government before ITQs. Citing James Scott's concepts of "cadastralization" and "legibility" (Scott 1998), she also notes that government regulators tend to prefer the simplicity of a few large actors to many small actors, who are assumed to be less predictable, overly diverse and contentious, and more difficult to manage.

In Europe a more specific version of this logic is apparent. Andresen and Hojrup (2008) hold that the Danish government believed that the Danish fishing fleet had to be able to compete more efficiently with other large European fishing fleets and to capture future "historical rights" to fish stocks still unregulated by quotas in deep EU fishing waters. According to them, economists at the Danish Institute of Fishing Economy and the Ministry of Food, Agriculture, and Fisheries operate according to an economic model that calculates that the largest fishing boats yield the most profits, so therefore the Danish fishing fleet is better off catching the total national quota of fish with a few large trawlers. Their assumption is that Denmark is able to increase profit from the national quota by forcing out the large, "expensive" fleet of smaller, fisherman-owned and share-organized boats that employ "too many" people. From the conceptual world of these civil servants, ITQs will mean a diminishing need for the extensive administration of inspections and regulations. The government will no longer have to finance an "old-fashioned" and unprofitable fleet. In short, ITQs are seen as much more beneficial for the national GDP. The visionary plan of the civil servants at the Danish Ministry of Food, Agriculture, and Fisheries was to suspend and confiscate the old national fishing licenses and permits from the large population of share fishermen who did not have part ownership in a boat. Through this powerful move, all remaining boats were given "their own" part of the confiscated quota, enabling them "to plan their fishery. . . . Instead of artificial financial support, the industry was meant to henceforth attract venture capital from private investors" (Andresen and Hojrup 2008, 34). This bureaucratic logic is a good example of one department focusing narrowly on its own costs and not considering the costs imposed on other government departments that have to deal with the consequences of its actions.

It is worth noting that moving to ITQs was not the only way to get fishermen to pay some reasonable royalty to contribute to administrative costs. Less draconian ways of achieving this objective include scaling royalties to the ability of fleets to pay, as is the case in some jurisdictions (Edwards et al. 2006; Lam 2012).

WHAT ARE THE ALTERNATIVES TO ITQS FOR SOLVING "THE RACE FOR FISH"?

There is reasonably widespread agreement that participating in the "race for fish" is undesirable because it encourages fishermen to spend money on faster engines and gear in order to be competitive, both of which would be unnecessary without the race. However, there are many well-documented ways to solve this problem other than ITQs. Maritime anthropologists, economists, political scientists, and others have documented local community-based fisheries that create, monitor, and enforce rules regulating space, time, and gear that reduce or eliminate the race for fish (Schlager and Ostrom 1993; Wilson et al. 1994; Pinkerton and Weinstein 1995; Wilson, Nielsen, and Degnbol 2003; Armitage, Berkes, and Doubleday 2007). Agrawal (2002, 43) notes that these management methods "help allocate resources equitably, over long time periods, with minimal efficiency losses." Some of these fisheries are simple trap fisheries for lobster or inshore cod, which operate locally, while other major offshore ground fisheries operate on a regional scale. For example, eighteen fishermen's associations in the Pacific Northwest worked together to space out the timing of their halibut fishery to avoid the race and crowding on the grounds (Pinkerton 2013). In addition, there is a substantial ethnographic record of partnerships of varying scope and scale between regional fishermen's organizations, industry, and governments and the conditions under which these arrangements are successful and effective (Pinkerton 2009a; 2009b). Many of these fisheries management systems are desirable because they cost governments nothing. Fishermen's organizations have taken on the work of designing and enforcing the regulations themselves. Ironically, neoliberal ideology seeking to diminish the role of government often favors devolution of rule-making to more local organizations. ITQ advocates would probably consider many of the successful mechanisms used locally—such as community quotas, license banks, pooling cooperatives, and locally designed trip limits—to be desirable, so it is ironic that when local fishermen ask senior government officials to institute gear regulations for the protection of stocks (Brewer 2011), these same advocates reject them as undesirable because they can create "inefficiency." Such a position loses sight of the fact that a fishery has to be effectively pursued before efficiency can be considered and that fishermen often have the most practical ideas for preventing undesirable outcomes.

CONCLUSION

ITQs are far from being the best and only solution to the race for fish and are far from predictably promoting a profitable fishery that contributes to overall social welfare. Problems with ITQs have been understated and their presumed solutions overstated. Policy makers have not fully considered alternatives. Currently, countries are adopting ITQs under the sway of a neoliberal economic paradigm without properly analyzing their costs and risks. This chapter has outlined eleven problems with ITQs identified in the literature, problems that impose costs and risks on the nations adopting ITQs. The overarching problem is that ITQs constitute the privatization of a public good that profoundly alters the social contract between fishing communities and the state, a contract that has been in place for centuries in many European countries. The subsequent societal transformation is very costly to the state and its citizens in the long term and remains largely unexamined in the literature.

10

Virtual Fish Stink, Too

*James Maguire is enrolled at the IT University of Copen-
hagen as a PhD Fellow. He did his fieldwork among fisheries scientists and fishermen in an Icelandic village, docu-
menting the effects of turning fish into a scientific, legal and
economic abstraction. In this chapter he describes how ITQs
affected rural Iceland. He introduces the term "virtual fish,"
echoed by a later contributor as "paper fish," or those that
are not made of flesh but are still quite real. He describes
how a process billed as one that would create abundance
instead caused scarcity, just one contradiction among many
he illustrates here.*

•••••••••••••••••••••

> We activated capital that was dead before. . . . The
> fish stocks did not have a price tag, they were non-
> transferable and could not be used as collateral—non-
> tradable. Then the quotas were allocated, which creates
> capital. . . . Here in Iceland, capital was handed over to
> private owners, and then it became alive.
>
> HANNES HÓLMSTEINN
> GISSURARSON, *ÍSLAND Í DAG*

Historically, fish have been both an economic funda-
ment and a source of sociopolitical tension in Iceland,
and the recent crisis has only exacerbated these ten-
dencies. Fish have played a central role in the development of regional communities over the last one hundred years as coastal towns have come and gone relative
to the presence or absence of such marine resources.

DOI: 10.5876/9781607323358.c010

This traditional relationship has seen a subtle transformation over the last two decades. Instead of following fleshy fish swimming in nearby seas, people have increasingly been following virtual fish; ones that have been taken out of the sea and brought to life in exchanges and electronic marketplaces and upon which extraordinary sums of money can be and have been made. Thus during the pre-crisis period in Iceland, the fishing industry became bound up within a constellation of neoliberal policies and practices in which the rush to privatization became the dominant motif.

Based on ethnographic fieldwork carried out in the West Fjords of Iceland in 2010, this chapter shows how the virtual fish emerged at a particular conjuncture in the life of the Icelandic nation, one in which the processes and practices of a new "financial economy" were under way. While the emergence of such fish cannot be pinned down to a specific causal trajectory, I assert that the practices of fisheries science, fisheries legislation, and finance capital intersected with, or were enfolded into, one another in such a way as to enable the virtual fish to sustain themselves. In leaving the seas, the virtual fish entered the lives of Icelanders on a spatiotemporal scale very different from that of the ordinary fleshy fish. Although neither type of fish (virtual or fleshy) makes a greater ontological claim, they both have different "modes of existence." I further suggest that the financial crisis opened up a "generative moment" in which more fundamental questions about fish were posed. I argue that the paradox at the heart of fisheries legislation, in which fish are considered both common and individual property, can be constructively reconfigured. Rather than postulating that such a contradiction is the work of political machinations, I will instead argue that it is in fact the multiplicity of fish that enables such a paradox to continue in abeyance.

THE NEW (VIRTUAL) FISH IN TOWN

"Fish bring life to towns," Palli commented to me late one evening as we sailed back to the harbor after a satisfying day's catch. This remark is far from an overstatement; the relationship between people and fish has been the driving force behind the development of coastal towns all around Iceland since the mid-1500s. Fishing towns did not, however, begin to flourish fully until after the abolition of the Danish trade monopoly in 1782 (Pálsson 1991). The nascent Icelandic independence movement saw fishing as a way to assert economic independence from the crown. By the time the restrictive land tenure laws were removed in the mid-1800s, technological developments and an increased labor supply had established fishing as a viable way of life.

In this regard, people here have always been following fish; small remote villages have nestled themselves in the winding arms of the West Fjords, their raison d'être being proximity to rich fishing grounds. Historically, such areas have had their share of turbulent times. One notable example is the collapse of the herring stock in the fifties, which resulted in the near decimation of Djúpavík, a small town in the West Fjords. However, the situation today is subtly different; despite the presence of fleshy fish in nearby waters,[1] the very existence of these fishing towns is still being threatened because the new virtual fish have moved away.

At this juncture, it is important to unpack my use of the term "virtual," which is usually employed to refer to virtual reality; computer-simulated environments that have taken on the connotation of the not-real. This is not the understanding I wish to convey. As Slavoj Zizek quips, "What is important is not virtual reality but the reality of the virtual."[2] Gilles Deleuze, drawing on Marcel Proust, sets out a more philosophical approach to the term, defining it as "real without being actual, ideal without being abstract" (Shields 2003, 2). In essence, the virtual is something that is real even though not concrete or actual and is mainly known through its effects. For example, dreams or memories, though not actual because they do not have a tangible or concretized form, are still nonetheless real and are felt through their effects.

Recent strains of political economy also use the term virtual to address the ever-increasing tendency toward the nonmaterial in the global economy (complex financial instruments such as derivatives, being but one example). Such theorizing of the drive toward the nonmaterial in economic processes is premised on Karl Polanyi's notion of a disembedded economy in which economic activities become removed from their social relationships and, ever increasingly, their productive material bases (Polyani [1944] 1968). Authors such as J. G. Carrier and D. Miller have characterized this as a somewhat inexorable process whereby the empirical world has begun to conform to the structures of the conceptual, mainly via abstract economic models and concepts; something they term "virtualism" (Carrier and Miller 1998, 3). However, this approach problematically collates the virtual with the abstract,[3] and not unlike other political economy accounts, it leaves the employment of the term "nonmaterial" underdetermined, whereby it usually becomes shorthand for everything that is not a traditional tangible commercial product. So in these accounts we are left with material products on the one hand and abstract-conceptual models on the other, with the latter increasingly inflecting the former, while the ontological complexity of the new economy is given short shrift.

My use of the term "virtual fish" is not entirely abstract. While it takes on ideal dimensions, it is not entirely nonmaterial since it is traded in electronic markets, and although such markets may be called "de-territorialized" it is difficult to call them dematerialized. As the epigraph at the opening of the chapter tantalizingly suggests, "capital was handed over and then it became alive." Such virtual fish do come alive, but differently from fleshy fish. Emerging at a distinct spatiotemporal scale at the intersection of scientific, financial, and legal practices is what allows these fish to reenter the lives of Icelanders in a fashion that has serious effects and consequences, and it is this impact on human lives that makes the reality of the virtual all the more palpable.

SCIENTIFIC PRACTICES AND THE EMERGENCE OF VIRTUAL FISH

A portion of my fieldwork in 2010 took place among fisheries scientists, in particular those working at the Marine Research Institute (MRI). Fish do not reside in the world or in the scientific imagination. Rather, fisheries scientists create them as scientific objects through their practices in which fish ultimately *emerge* as virtual. Scientists are particularly keen to distinguish themselves from fishermen, who hunt, while scientists transform fish from samples to indexes for populations to stocks to virtual entities.

During the biannual trawler rally that occurs in and around the Icelandic continental shelf, a selected sample of fish is taken from the catch and separated out by species.[4] Each fish is weighed and measured, the stomach gutted, and the contents examined and noted. The liver is also weighed, the scales are measured, and the otoliths are counted. Fish are numbers, statistics; they are *done* very carefully, and through consistent measurements and techniques they are transformed into being. These fish are not representations, however; they are indexes, indexes that point to a fish stock. The individual fish that is caught at a specific time and place becomes in practice an index that points to a generalized stock.[5] So what is this stock? Defining what a stock is, and distinguishing one from another, is a complex practice-based activity. Mostly, the definition of a stock is interchangeable with a species. As Roepstorff puts it with a nice hint of sarcasm: "One simply has to determine the species, or subsets of it, that move around within more or less spatial-temporal borders, ideally without mixing with neighbouring subsets, and voilà, one has identified a stock" (Roepstorff 2000, 171).

Things are of course not so simple in practice. Genetic mixing tends to take place in fisheries more so than in other biological habitats because of a high degree of larval drift due to constant current flows and temperature changes. So not only is there not one distinctive biological marker by which an individual fish can genetically be said to belong to one stock,[6] but different scientists define stocks very differently. Given the tremendous degree of complexity and variation in all of this, determining a stock is a very definitive type of practice. Complicating things further is the fact that scientific data are not the only or even primary consideration in ascertaining what a stock is. For management purposes a stock is not only its genetics or migration pattern, it is usually a semi-discrete group of fish with some definable attributes of interest to administrators. A stock is the conjunction of the biological, the ecological, the historical, the political, and the administrative (Secor 1999, Law and Lien 2013). It is an active *doing* of genetics, fish reproductive and feeding behavior (biology), and environment (ecological), along with considerations of management requirements (the political) and its catchability and accessibility (historical). Rather than a representation of a given biological entity "out there," or purely a product of scientific and administrative discourse, the stock is, in the idiom of Karen Barad (2007), meaningful matter, both concept and thing. Finally, a last switch from stock to biomass is the practice through which the stock is transformed into tons and kilos. Biomass, fish in tons and kilos, is what allows differing regimes of practice to align and provides the link between scientific, juridical, and financial practices in which fleshy fish move out of the sea and enter into the everyday lives of Icelanders as virtual.

LEGAL AND FINANCIAL PRACTICES

As recounted earlier, Iceland went through a series of neoliberal reforms during the 1980s and 1990s that radically altered the economic landscape in a relatively short time. The fishing industry was swept up in a rush to privatization that started with the introduction of the quota management system in 1984. This system was the first step in a series of measures that enfolded biomass—fish in tons and kilos—within a complex set of legal and financial practices and relations, ultimately giving rise to the age of virtual fish.

Established in the early 1980s as a temporary measure to avoid what at that time was considered to be the impending collapse of the cod stock,[7] the quota system originally garnered a wide degree of support among the various stakeholder groups in Iceland (Eythorsson 2003). Such consensus, however, quickly evaporated after a series of legislative adjustments in the 1990s that resulted in supplanting the primary tenet of ecological sustainability with economic efficiency. In 1991 an ITQ system was adopted, effectively allowing virtual fish to be bought, sold, and rented on the market. In 1996 the introduction of a collateral law (the details of which I will examine later) paved the way for fish to be used as a type of mortgage in the raising of capital.[8]

It is hard to overstate the degree of change that the ITQ system imposed on the lives of the fishermen and inhabitants of small coastal towns. From this point forward, access to fishing grounds was predicated not on the availability of fleshy fish in local waters and all that implied,[9] but on the accessibility of virtual fish. The basic premise of the ITQ system is therefore a mixture of both scientific and economic goals: to manage the stocks by adopting a fishing effort to the point where maximum *economic* yield occurs or where maximum *sustainable* yield results. In essence, this means that the quota system has always held out the promise of not only preserving the fish stocks but also increasing them over the long term. In fact, one of the reasons why the original adoption of the quota system generated such cross stakeholder support was this very promise of increased future stocks and hence more profits for quota holders over time. Therefore, it would appear to be a primary logic of the system that more fish will lead to more money, and while this may still be true for ordinary fleshy fish, the reverse is the case for virtual fish: curiously, fewer fish have come to mean more money.

Despite intensive management of the stocks over the last thirty years, the cod quota has continued to decline, from a peak of close to 500,000 tons in the early eighties (Íslandsbanki Seafood Team 2010) to 160,000 tons for the fishing year 2010–2011 (Hafrannsóknastofnun 2010). The MRI rationalizes this by arguing that, despite the technical management of the stocks over the last three decades, it is only since the mid-nineties that the fishing industry has been following their scientific advice to the letter. Interestingly, criticism of the apparent failure of the MRI's program generally comes from renegade scientists and small communities rather than from the large boat owners association, Landssamband íslenskra útvegsmanna (LÍU),[10] as one would expect. In what can be described as a classic Foucauldian knowledge-power axis, LÍU supports the MRI's metrics, arguing that long-term preservation of the stocks is in the entire industry's interest, even if it results in smaller catches for its members in the short term. While it is hard to argue against the ecological logic of this position, it is more than a little ironic that the lower the quota goes—and technically the less fish these companies can catch—the more money they earn. Since the virtual fish can be rented out on a yearly basis, sold for life, or mortgaged to raise finance, lower stock levels equate to higher quota demand and hence increased rental, sale, and mortgage values. The effects of virtualization on the fishing industry in general and on smaller communities and small-scale fishermen in particular have been extensive.

The escalating price of virtual fish becomes both a barrier to entry into the fishing industry for new fishermen who cannot afford the sums required to buy into the system as well as a seductive point of exit for current small-scale holders who can sell out for vast sums of money. This is still a highly contentious issue within small communities, as those who sell the quota are often considered to be "betraying the town," given the reduction in baiting, fishing, fish processing, and hence employment that ensues from any such sale. The risk to these small locations, where families or tightly networked groups tend to hold the quota, can and has been devastating. In 2007 the primary quota holder in Flateyri, a small town in the Ísafjarðarbær municipality of the West Fjords, sold his entire holdings at the highest recorded price ever of 4,000 kronur per kilo. Since then, the town has been in a state of terminal decline. The overall trend in Iceland has therefore been for quotas to accumulate in the hands of an ever-decreasing number of large fishing companies whose power to control the industry has been greatly enhanced. In 2010, 73 percent of all quotas were held by fewer than twenty large companies (Íslandsbanki Seafood Team 2010, 14), and it was these companies that tended to rent out a high proportion of their quotas to others, creating social unease and in many cases outright resentment.[11]

The general macro-level effects of this combined ability to sell and collateralize virtual fish were well illustrated in a paper by a prominent fisheries economist written just several months before the crisis. Ragnar Arnason argues that the ability to use virtual fish (my term) to raise financial—or what many would call speculative—capital created up to $5 billion in wealth *"where none existed before"* (Arnason 2008, 37; emphasis added) Moreover, he contends that there is a direct correlation between the creation of this wealth, or *"living capital"* (ibid., 36; emphasis added), as he refers to it, and the growth of the Icelandic economy during the economic boom years.[12] Using the indebtedness of the fishing industry, which doubled from 1997 to 2007, as a metric for how much money flowed from fishing to other industry sectors, his clear inference is that the quota significantly contributed to the takeoff of the economy as a whole. More interestingly, what Arnason's paper hints at, and what I have been pointing toward, is the alternate spatiotemporal scale at which the virtual fish emerges, coming *"alive as capital"* in Iceland in ways that fleshy fish never could.

Emerging from specific scientific practices at a time when a broader neoliberal surge was underway in Iceland, in which leveraging, or the raising of debt capital, was the dominant motif, the virtual fish became enfolded in a broader set of juridical-financial relations in which it became subject to the dominant logics of capital mobility. At the zenith of quota prices in Iceland, the virtual fish could be leveraged at 4,000 kronur per kilo and could, therefore, actualize many multiples of its future self in one transaction. In comparison to fleshy fish, which must be caught through normal fishing practices and therefore incur all of the typical costs of fishing (boat, fuel, labor, etc.), there are no such associated costs with virtual fish. Given their exorbitant market price, the profit to be made from their sale amounted to roughly eighty years' average fishing revenues. My fishing friends always talked about this in terms of taking the profits today of fish that would not hatch until many years hence.

As such, the virtual fish emerges from a future temporal location that has its effects in the present by being actualizable in vast monetary multiplications of itself. Such a temporal form, while blurring causal trajectories, became standard business practice and always sat uncomfortably with my friends who pondered how the benefits and value of future fish could be taken from the seas in the present. It not only violated the basic "catch law" but also "stole" the rights of future generations of fishermen and communities. The virtual fish also emerges at a spatial scale which gives it a unique type of mobility, moving around as it does not in local waters but in a de-territorialized market exchange. The irony of the virtual fish's spatiality (which facilitates an ease of exchange not previously seen) is not lost on locals who become immobilized by its mobility.

POST-CRISIS EFFECTS AND PROPERTY CONCERNS

The response of the fishing industry to the financial crisis was at first somewhat ambivalent, given that the currency's depreciation led not just to an increase in debts but also in a sharp increase in fishing revenues.[13] However, as the extent of the industry's insolvency began to unfold, opinions became less muted. It is estimated that the fishing industry owes somewhere in the region of ISK 465 billion or up to twelve times the industry's annual profits (Íslandsbanki Seafood Team 2010).[14] What Arnason was praising as the natural ability of *"living capital"* to stimulate the economy is now looked upon in many quarters as speculative gambling that has mortgaged the entire industry and future generations of fishermen without any significant improvement in boats, processing facilities, or fishing technology. Despite or maybe because of these issues, fishing, and particularly the conflict over quotas, has once again taken on renewed significance both nationally and in small coastal towns around the country.

The economic crisis that inevitably followed the financial one turned the focus to nonfinancial industries that a small island population can sustain, and fishing was seen as a central component of this plan. The new government set up a parliamentary working committee on fisheries consisting of twenty members from political parties, industry groups, and academia. The commission was tasked with nothing less than "defining the main conflicting areas within the fisheries and to come up with sustainable solutions that would win the broadest support of the nation."[15] The dealings of the commission crystallized around two pertinent issues. First, a debate ensued as to whether the first article of the fisheries law, which designates fish as the common property of the nation, should be enshrined in the constitution as a way of unambiguously clarifying its property status. Second, and more contentious, was the proposal to revoke the quota, a move that would allow currently excluded fisherman to regain access to the sea.[16] Although many groups have given voice to this suggestion in the past, it was the post-crisis reconfiguration of fishing that created an environment, or a "generative moment," as Bruce Kapferer (2005) puts it, in which the tensions around fish began to fully play out, and it was a series of antecedent legislative measures on the status of fishing rights as property around which such tensions coalesced.

The typical anthropological understanding of property ranges from a relationship between persons and things, a person-to-person relationship mediated through things, or a relationship between persons in relation to a thing. Of course these definitions all raise the question, what is a person, thing, or even, for that matter, a relation? I would like to temporarily park these more vexing issues and focus right now on how legal and economic concepts are based on a similar type of understanding. The standard legal register of property is one of rights; rather than property being an actual thing, it is seen as a relationship that a person has toward a thing, wherein a critical mass of rights—or a bundle of rights—accrues to someone in relation to it. So if a person can possess, enjoy, and change a thing, then they have certain types of rights over it to the exclusion of others.

Property is also said to enjoy certain characteristics, so, for example, the more secure, exclusive, permanent, and transferable one's rights are, the more perfect the property right is said to be. This bundle-of-rights approach is common in fisheries management, where the tendency has been toward ever-increasing propertization, mainly as a response to Garrett Hardin's "tragedy of the commons" scenario (Feeny et al. 1990).[17] The 1991 Fisheries Management

Act in Iceland—amended and updated in 2006—classifies the fish stock within Iceland's 200-mile exclusion zone as being the common property of the nation. While allocating harvesting rights to quota holders,[18] it clearly states that these rights do not constitute permanent property rights (see Ministry of Fisheries and Agriculture 2006). So, somewhat paradoxically, the ITQ system allows individuals to buy, sell, and rent these rights even though they are not classified as individual property.

Additional legislative measures have been passed that further this property-based conundrum. In 1997 the government passed a collateral law whose first line states that quotas, as the common property of the nation, cannot be used as collateral to raise capital. However, the very next sentence of the article provides a mechanism to do just that. It stipulates that if a quota holder has mortgaged a property that has use rights attached to it, then the holder is prohibited from separating these rights from the property without recorded approval from the mortgage giver.[19] So, in effect, although you cannot technically mortgage the quota, the quota becomes an irremovable part of the mortgage.[20] In addition, the courts have ruled on two other issues that also have a bearing: in 1993 they ruled that the profits from the sale of quotas are subject to taxation, and later in the same decade they allowed a woman to successfully lay claim to quotas as part of a divorce settlement (Eythórsson 2000, 17). So, in practice, harvesting rights can be bought, sold, rented, leveraged, taxed, and inherited; in effect expressing all the characteristics of individual property to a strong degree while legislatively remaining common property.

My fishermen friends in the West Fjords constantly puzzled over this question of fish being both the common property of the nation, which they talked about in terms of fleshy fish swimming in the seas that any Icelander has the right to fish, and individual property, which they saw as being the provenance of only a select few who had saleable and mortgageable rights over fish. The common rationale for the conflicting, almost paradoxical status of the simultaneous existence of two mutually exclusive property forms tended to remain political. Fishermen saw contradictory legislative measures to be the result of interest-based affiliations and ethically suspect, albeit savvy, political maneuverings among closely interlocked networks of political parties, bankers, and fisheries lobbying groups.

However, these fishermen regularly expressed their bewilderment at how fish, which were as of yet unhatched, could make claims on the world in the present. "How can one make so much money from something that does not yet exist? If you go out and fish real fish in the sea, you cannot get a fraction of the same value that you can from selling quota." Yet they acknowledged that despite the sheer incomprehensibility of this setup, it was still possible to gain the benefits of fish in the present that would not exist for eighty years in the future.

Although the enormous quantity of present money raised from future entities was a real issue for people in the West Fjords, it was not only this temporal dislocation that created consternation among my friends. It was also the virtual fish's spatial scale and its ability to "move away" through de-territorialized exchanges, or those no longer reliant upon geography, that aggrieved them. While fleshy fish still remained "out there in the sea," the mobility of the virtual fish has left coastal communities abandoned in its wake. The small town of Flateyri is a good case in point. When the virtual fish was sold away in 2007, not only did the local processing plant collapse, but almost all of the town's ancillary industries suffered as a result. The fall in employment and the ensuing collapse of the property market left people with no jobs and no obvious way to relocate. They became "stuck," as they put it. In early 2009 a group of locals got together and bought the processing factory without quotas, but this operation went bankrupt in April 2011. It wasn't sustainable to rent quotas from the market and sell them to foreign customers.

Although the spatiotemporal scale of the virtual fish is unlike that of the ordinary fleshy fish, both types have a unique "mode of existence" (Latour 2011). In an interesting take on the philosopher Etienne Souriau, Bruno Latour argues that entities, from microbes to horses, can undergo transformations and alterations through certain practices and as such can enter into new pathways in which they circulate along different "chains of experience" (Latour 2008, 90). For Latour, enquiries into modes of being are ultimately enquiries into different ways of altering, suggesting that each mode contains a specific ontological pattern. Similarly, the virtual fish emerged at its own spatiotemporal scale. The entity was altered, and ultimately transformed, leaving the seas and becoming enfolded into new chains of legal and financial experience via particular scale-switching practices—from index to stock to biomass to virtual.

Fish, rather than being a singular phenomenon, can in fact be multiple, existing in different modes and circulating along different chains of experience. As such the coexistence of two "versions" (Mol 1999) of fish, each with its own spatiotemporal scale, creates certain tensions that have played themselves out both in the everyday considerations of fishermen and, strikingly, in a legal property-based idiom. Karen Sykes argued in a recent Manchester debate that "culture is a creative process by which members of a society inventively answer ontological questions"(Carrithers et al. 2010, 169). Using as an example the *malanggan*, a carved sculpture from the New Ireland province of Papua New Guinea, she suggests that the act of carving answers the ontological question "What is a life?" I am suggesting, therefore, that the reconfigured post-crisis setting in Iceland was one in which people's *concerns* with fish were realigned and more fundamental questions were raised. It is in this regard that we can consider the legislative amendments around the quota as a creative cultural response to the ontological question "What is a fish?"

If this is the case, then the simultaneous existence of alternate property forms (common and individual), while appearing mutually exclusive, could be seen as a response to the multiplicity of fish. Rather than contradictions leading to mixtures or multiplicities, as standard dialectical approaches would have it, it is in fact the multiplicity of the world that enables paradoxes to proliferate and be sustained (Webmoor and Witmore 2008, 60). The puzzling paradox that straddles several pieces of fisheries legislation, in which fish are de facto individual property while remaining de jure common property (Pálsson 1996), is not therefore a formal contradiction attributed to sleight-of-hand political maneuverings or unethical lawmakers but rather is more productively construed as an ontological tension that enables the seeming contradiction to be reformulated. Rather than the irreconcilability of the existence of simultaneous property forms, it is the multiplicity of fish that holds the contradiction in a type of unresolved tension or dissonance. The existence of fish as simultaneously virtual and fleshy allows people to conceive of them as either common or individual property. Thus their status as property is indeterminate.

CONCLUSION

In recent times many countries have found themselves entangled within the logics of the new "financial economy," the complexities and consequences of which are still being felt around the globe. While Iceland only recently subscribed to such processes and practices, it embraced these logics with a speed and fervor that indebted and unsettled the entire population in equal measure.

Virtual fish were transformed into being through various scientific scale-switching practices and entered into the lives of ordinary Icelanders through various legal and financial practices and relations. The collective concerns of the scientific, financial, and legal communities, or what Latour calls "communities of affirmation" (cited in Bell 2012, 114), throughout the 1990s and 2000s enabled the virtual fish to sustain their mode of existence, which while not actual was nonetheless real. As Alfred North Whitehead succinctly puts it, "through the relations or concerns between the emergent entity and its environment, the entity achieves its decisive moment of absolute self-attainment and stands out for itself alone" (Whitehead 1933, 177).

The Icelandic financial crisis, while having many alternate trajectories and consequences, opened up a generative moment in which a fundamental onto-logical question was posed about fish. The creative cultural response to such musings was framed in a legal idiom in which the multiplicity of fish was brought to the foreground and as such allowed for an alternate reading of the property paradox at the heart of fisheries legislation. Instead of the simultane-ous existence of two mutually exclusive property forms (common and indi-vidual) being the result of political machinations, I have argued that it is the multiplicity of fish that allows the paradox to continue in abeyance.

There is no doubt that Iceland has been going through a process of refor-mulating its own collective self-identity in the wake of its rapid engagement with transnational capitalism, and as such the concerns of the country have been altering. The pre-crisis discourse in which the media "forged ideologi-cal links with Iceland's first settlers and their presumed independence spirit" (Loftsdóttir 2010, 11) constantly referred to the prowess and risk-seeking men-tality of the *útrásarvíkingur* (Business Vikings). The post-crisis sentiment has opened up a space of national reflection in which the characteristics of the financial economy are now being thoroughly reevaluated. It is in this context that the virtual fish and its simultaneous individual property form has become a mode of existence that may be difficult to sustain in the future.[21]

Thanks go to the group of anthropologists at the Waterworlds project in Copenhagen, Denmark, for providing essential feedback on an earlier draft. In particular, I thank Kirsten Hastrup for encouraging me to write the paper and Frida Hastrup for her generous and close reading of the second draft. Finally, I thank Brit Ross Winthereik for a valuable and constructive discussion of the text's key ideas.

NOTES

1. Despite the fact that there is still a lot of dispute as to the quantity of fish in Icelandic waters, there is almost no dispute that coastal waters could support a healthy local fishing industry and, by extension, maintain a solid municipal infrastructure.

2. Zizek explains his ideas in the filmed lecture *Slavoj Zizek: The Reality of the Vir-tual* (Olive Films, 2004). For part 1 of the documentary, see http://www.youtube.com /watch?v=KdpudWL5i68.

3. Pálsson and Helgason (1998) utilize "virtualism" in similar terms in relation to Icelandic fish stocks, as do Minnegal and Dwyer (2011) in their discussion of fishing in

Australia, but again my difficulty lies in the conflation of "virtual" with "abstract," set in contradistinction to the real.

4. In the annual assessment of codfish stocks, the MRI used two independent data sets: an analysis of actual landing statistics and a set of fish samples taken from an annual trawl survey. This latter measure was introduced in 1985 as a response to the perceived lack of reliability of the landing statistics as a stand-alone technique. Every March five trawlers are used to trawl 600 stations located around Iceland. The same stations are used every year in order to provide for sampling consistency and were chosen partly by the MRI and partly by an original group of trawler captains based on their knowledge of good fishing spots. The boats trawl for an hour at each station, and the ensuing catch is analyzed by onboard MRI scientists.

5. Generating a yearly fish index is an important component in assessing the overall fish stock levels. Such data are necessary to create a historical correlation coefficient between population size and index, which can then be applied to the current year's survey index to arrive at an estimate of the stock in the sea.

6. Genetic methods include assessing protein variation, chromosomes, mitochondrial DNA, and nuclear DNA.

7. The quota system has expanded to include many fish species and is not just limited to cod.

8. Over the coming pages I will use the terms collateral, mortgage, and leverage relatively interchangeably.

9. By local waters I mean the distance that small-scale fishing boats travel on an average daily trip (anywhere up to twelve miles from shore). In order to be eligible to go to sea, a seaman must have a captain's license and a seaworthy boat and must maintain different sets of economic and social relationships necessary for baiting, processing, and selling capacities.

10. LÍU is one of the central players and lobbyists in the fishing industry. There is also a small boat owners association, Landssamband smábátaeigenda, which lobbies on behalf of small boats under 15 tons.

11. Several authors (Eythorsson, Pálsson, Helgason) have commented on a range of narratives that have developed in response to such renting, in particular noting the development of a feudal fishing system consisting of "lords of the sea" who reap the benefits of using the quota as a purely financial tool and "tenants" who have to "fish for others" at reduced incomes.

12. Arnason does acknowledge that there were other contributing factors, such as the growth of the aluminum industry.

13. Although accurate figures are unavailable given the confidential nature of the transactions, a significant percentage of the money raised by the mortgaging of quotas is believed to have been secured via non-Icelandic banks, denominated in foreign cur-

rency. The devaluation of the krona, therefore, led to a sharp increase in the indebtedness of many fishing companies. At the same time, however, fish prices (mostly traded in sterling, euros, and dollars) delivered higher krona revenues.

14. The report was prepared by a division of Íslandsbanki (formerly Glitnir). While I do not doubt the integrity of the numbers presented in the report, there are some issues regarding the selectivity of the data. Many commentators put the debt figure at up to ISK 1 trillion.

15. This is a quote from a conversation with a parliamentary committee member. The final report was delivered in September 2010 (Sjávarútvegs- og landbúnaðarráðuneytið 2010).

16. My fieldwork entailed attendance at several meetings where the possible consequences of a quota repeal were debated. As is almost always the case at such meetings, positions were strained and tensions ran high. As quota was being treated "as if" it were individual property, any attempt to reappropriate it was considered by many legal experts to be in violation of the primary property clause within the constitution, and as such any breach would necessitate redress by compensation. There were of course many counter opinions. For an excellent summary of the human rights and equality implications, see Einarsson 2011.

17. Hardin (1968) suggested that all resources held in common, such as oceans, rivers, air, and parklands, are subject to ever-continuing degradation due to people's proclivity to take any extra profit available from such resources, but their unwillingness to bear more than a fraction of the cost. In essence, freedom in the commons would "bring ruin to all." Private property rights are seen as the antidote to such a scenario, whereby resources become more economically efficient the greater the degree of property rights attached to them.

18. The original allocation was made to boat owners—itself a contentious issue—in 1984 based on the average of their previous three years of fishing experience. In addition, the term "harvesting rights" is interchangeable with "fishing rights."

19. See http://www.althingi.is/lagas/nuna/1997075.html, paragraph 3, article 3.

20. In practice this means that a quota holder can borrow money from a bank equivalent to the value of the boat plus the market value of the quota, using only the boat as collateral. However, the quota holder is not allowed to sell the quota without the prior approval of the bank, hence locking the quota to the boat without technically using it as collateral.

21. Leaving Iceland in late 2010, I had the distinct impression that the days of the virtual fish were numbered. However, following the media reports on the turbulent passage of the new fisheries law, which was being pushed through Parliament at the time of finalizing this chapter, it could well be that my response was slightly optimistic.

11

*The Resilience of
Rural Iceland*

*Margaret Willson is an anthropologist at the University
of Washington, Seattle, and Birna Gunnlaugsdóttir is a
teacher of continuing education in Iceland. In this chapter
they describe the awakening of a small fishing community
after the crash, after it believes it has escaped the worst.
The authors argue that the notion of small-town resilience,
without larger government support, conflicts with the basic
tenets of capitalism.*

● ● ● ● ● ● ● ● ● ● ● ● ● ● ● ● ● ● ●

A persistent question of the last several decades has
revolved around why regions or communities economically or systemically "succeed" or "fail" (Hassink
2010). Concepts of sustainability, with an emphasis on
future generations, became a popular means of grap-
pling with this question in the 1990s. These concepts
were superseded in the early 2000s with the conceptual
framework of resilience. A resilient system is defined as
one that can continue to function when faced with the
pressures of outside change (Hassink 2010, 46). Rooted
in engineering and taken up by ecology and the social
sciences (including psychology, economics, and, more
recently, geography), resilience has been used particularly in relation to a community's or region's vulnerability or stability when confronted with outside influences
such as environmental or economic crisis (Adger 2000;
Pike, Dawley, and Tomaney 2010; Raco and Street 2012,
2).

Proponents of the concept of resilience have generally presented it as apolitical or neutral, a useful

DOI: 10.5876/9781607323358.c011

way to explain why some regions are able to adapt, reinvent themselves, or adjust when confronted with outside disturbances, while others are not. A small group of critics, however, have noted that focusing on resiliency places the onus of success on the region in question (Hudson 2010, Raco and Street 2012), allowing neoliberal policy makers to use the concept to bolster their arguments supporting policies of "self-help" and "competitive fitness" (Martin 2012, 2). Previous studies on resilience have also tended to focus on urban environments, thereby neglecting the diversity of place and relational power structures (Pike, Dawley, and Tomaney 2010).

In this chapter we join these critics and, using a detailed ethnographic examination of the West Iceland rural community of Grundarfjörður, build upon the queries of Pike and colleagues (2010) regarding larger political and power dynamics that may affect community sustainability in times of uncertainty and crisis. This is where the global stretches its fingers to encircle the most intimate and human, where permutations of power and policies collide in a personal and even individual form.

THE URBAN AND THE RURAL

Much of the international attention Iceland received following its economic crash tended to conflate Iceland with its capital, Reykjavík, and assumed that because the country's population of 322,000 is comparatively small and ethnically homogeneous, it is culturally homogeneous as well: ". . . a country so tiny and homogeneous that everyone in it knows pretty much everyone else. . . . Really, it's less a nation than one big extended family" (Lewis 2011, cited in Cartier 2011, 170). Much of the mainstream literature by Icelandic writers, most of whom lived in Reykjavík, reinforced this impression, so that everything regarding the crash, including the bankers' actions, houses lost, wealth made, and protests, all seemingly occurred in Reykjavík. This dominant voice defined the country's experience related to the crash as an urban one.

For centuries, the majority of Iceland's population, with the exception of merchants and large landowners, lived in poverty (Magnússon 2010). After World War II, the division between the urban and rural populations increased as more Icelanders flocked to the capital city. At the beginning of the twentieth century, 88.1 percent of Icelanders lived in the rural countryside. By the end of the century, 70 percent lived in the urban center, 9.3 percent lived in the countryside, and about 20 percent lived in small coastal communities (Hafstein 2000; Skaptadóttir 2000). This demographic shift turned Iceland's rural communities into a minority population geographically isolated from the urban seat of power and with less access to government policy and politics.

THE PRE-CRASH DECADE: OPPORTUNITIES
FOR MOBILITY AND DEBT

The kind of debt many Icelanders incurred before the crash is specific to the Icelandic context. Because of previous high inflation, Icelandic banking systems, unlike those of many other industrialized countries, offered "inflation-indexed loans." These loans imposed a second fee that was subject to rises with inflation on top of the interest rate of the regular loan. This second fee means that a nominal amount of debt can continue to rise even though the borrower continues to make regular payments. To avoid paying the second fee, many Icelanders invested in foreign-currency-indexed loans. Although speculating on the foreign currency market is potentially risky, investors were encouraged to do so by the banks and a strong Icelandic currency.

For pre-crash Grundarfjörður, this kind of debt and the need for fish quotas went hand in hand. In 1991 changes in government fisheries policy cut the total allowable yearly catch size (TAC). This law was especially hard on small-scale quota holders. In order to maintain a constant level of catch-share, boat owners had to buy increasing amounts of quota (see Pálsson and Helgason 1996). To buy this additional quota, small-scale operators took out loans. In the early 2000s the price of quota increased dramatically, while at the same time, because of the high international value of the krona, the export price of Icelandic-caught fish was low. By 2006, the cost of quotas was higher than the value of the fish yield. On August 1, 2007, the government cut the TAC by one-third (Karlsdóttir 2008, 112). Icelandic banks made it easy for quota holders and farmers to borrow huge amounts of capital, most of which had little hope of ever being repaid.

At this point, the four or five comparatively small local quota holders who owned the major local fisheries companies in Grundarfjörður made different choices (larger outside firms own two additional companies in the town). Those who had been buying small amounts of quota gradually over the years stopped purchasing quota because their businesses were becoming too small to be viable. Others bought more quota while incurring increasing debt. One local quota-holding family, which had been given a ISK 100 million bank loan, was literally unable to buy quota because the price had risen by the time they could put in a bid. Despite the bank offering them another 100 million, they decided to sell their quota and leave fishing.

So in 2007, the fisheries in Grundarfjörður, which employed about 300 people—or about a third of the total local population—were struggling because
of high debt, shifting regulations, and a system that put local companies in
direct competition with the largest consolidated companies that controlled
the bulk of the market share and government influence. Therefore, many in
Grundarfjörður feel that 2007, not 2008, was the year of their rural crisis.

During this time banks were also soliciting local farmers in the area, who
were struggling to survive under the new regulations, policies, and economics (Bændasamtök Íslands 2010). In the early 2000s, banks encouraged these
struggling local farmers to take out increasingly larger loans. "[At the time],"
said one local farmer, ". . . we trusted the banks."

For example, in 2006 a bank encouraged one local farmer to take out a loan
to build a larger cowshed, which he did not do. Then in 2007 a farm machinery
company (of which the Icelandic bank Glitnir had recently acquired a major
share) invited him and other farmers go on a trip to Europe to attend a big
farm machinery exhibition. The farmers were pleased that the company was
giving them personal service and attention. A representative from Glitnir, one
of the three banks to collapse and be nationalized after the crash, accompanied the farmers on the trip and encouraged them to take out foreign currency–indexed loans. The banker said that he himself was paying on loans
for everything and that this was "normal." Just months before the crash, a
representative of this company again approached one of the farmers, calling
him frequently with increasingly large enticements to take out loans for large
machinery. The repeated solicitation by large banks began to send a message to
the local residents that taking out large loans was normal and desirable.

In the early 2000s Grundarfjörður, along with adjoining municipalities, invested in a local upper-secondary school (for students ages 16–20).
For small rural towns, having an upper-secondary school close to home is
advantageous for the community because it limits the outmigration of young
people. When rural communities don't have access to these schools, students
often leave the area to continue their studies in Reykjavík or other distant
locations, thereby draining the local population of young people (Bjarnason
and Thorlindsson 2006). The school project and two large housing projects
financed by nonlocal investment firms was a sign to local residents that the
building trade was doing well in their town. Local restaurants benefitted
from workers who came in for lunch. "They would line up just as [the stu-
dents] do in the school lunch line, waiting for their meal," said one restaurant owner. The two local banks employed four or five people each and were
also doing well. Tourism was not a major industry of the town, and a couple

who had bought the local hotel in 1998 sold it to a local fisherman who used money from selling his fishing quota. In April 2004 unemployment in Grundarfjörður stood at seven people, rising slightly to eight in April 2007 (Vinnumálastofnun 2012).

Increasingly through the late 1990s and early 2000s, Icelandic residents of Grundarfjörður, like those in other coastal communities (Karlsdóttir 2009; Skaptadóttir 2007), found new economic opportunities beyond fishing (mostly done by men) and minimum-wage fish factory work (mostly done by women). At the local fish factories, again following a national pattern of economic migration (Skaptadóttir and Wojtyńska 2008b), foreign migrant labor filled the resulting labor shortage, and by 2007, according to local fish factory owners, about 60 percent of the fish factory workers in Grundarfjörður were foreign, most of them Polish. Local residents began to look beyond Grundarfjörður for their business and social life, driving the two hours to Reykjavík in one evening for shopping and a movie. Young people no longer considered the fisheries prime career options. Many, once they finished school, moved to Reykjavík in search of new opportunities.

Residents began to think of themselves as participating in the bustling big-city life. Some, like their city counterparts, began taking overseas trips. They also began to demand that their village offer them the same benefits that the city did. The local bookstore owner said there was a strong sense of urgency during these years, that if one of his customers wanted something, he or she wanted it *now*! So he often ordered single items to be delivered the next day from Reykjavík. He felt pressured to provide this kind of service if he was going to be able to satisfy, and keep, his local customers.

The infrastructure of a rural community is central to its ability to survive, and over the previous several decades, while the state government improved access to the town through roads and bridges, the Grundarfjörður town council paved local roads, built a swimming pool (1976) and gymnasium (1980), fenced areas of town to keep out sheep, planted trees as windbreaks, established a small kindergarten, installed drainage pipelines, and established regular garbage pickup (Njálsdóttir 2012, 51). Improvements decreased in subsequent decades but picked up again in the early 2000s. In 2001 the town built a library; in 2004, in cooperation with three adjacent municipalities, the upper-secondary school was completed; and then beginning in 2006 residents approved more construction. As one town official noted: "Everyone was optimistic. In 2006 the kindergarten was renovated and for the primary school we bought the land it is on from the government. . . . It was a good price. It was good; it all had to be done. We fixed up the harbor, a million here or there."

Bank loans from Reykjavík seemed almost limitless and were easy to obtain. In 2006 townspeople began planning a large sports center, spending a few million kronur on the planning alone, and began talking about holding a large track and field competition. The Grundarfjörður town council paid for nearly all of the projects with foreign currency–indexed loans.

In pre-crash Grundarfjörður, the fisheries, the main source of community stability, were struggling to balance quota and debt. Construction workers had jobs while local businesspeople struggled to provide services on par with the urban center. Greater opportunities seemed possible to residents as they turned increasingly outward. But the new access to capital, for quota holders, individuals, and town council members alike, was rooted not in growing local wealth but in unstable loans that the banks made easily accessible and described as the way things were done. This pre-crash rural experience, distinct from that of urban Reykjavík, was reflected throughout Iceland:

> The brave new financial world was almost entirely centered on Reykjavík
> and neighboring areas. The role of the fisheries communities, previously the
> backbone of production for commodity exports, declined when considered
> in relation to the national economy as a whole. . . . The perceived glamour of
> wheeling and dealing sidelined the rural resource-based occupations even fur-
> ther. Existing regional inequalities were thus greatly amplified in the neoliberal
> regime. (Benediktsson and Karlsdóttir 2011, 231)

A NATIONAL CRISIS ON A RURAL LOCAL LEVEL

For residents of Grundarfjörður, the immediate reaction to and effects of the crash varied. Many immediately noticed the difference between Reykjavík and their community:

> I was in California when our prime minister said, "God bless Iceland!"
> [announcing the crash]. I was just in the process of trying to use my credit card
> and had this sudden feeling that the machine would reject it. I could almost feel
> the shock of Reykjavík across the world, but then when I arrived in our small
> village of Grundarfjörður, it seemed that nothing had changed.

Local non-fisheries-related businesses were hit immediately and hard by the crash. The few bankers in the small Grundarfjörður branches had no idea the crash was coming:

> I was on vacation abroad when it happened. I learned about Landsbanki that
> day after it closed, October 4. . . . I don't quite remember my first thoughts, I

was too much in shock. I just remember I thought, Will I have a job? Will my bank stay open? . . . Very soon after the crash, they were closing the small offices. You didn't know who was going to be fired and who wasn't. . . . People were angry . . . I think the blame was less on people in the smaller communities, [but] . . . at the first, right after the crash, most of us [at the bank] took our work home and didn't get much sleep.

Building construction stopped almost immediately. Local unemployment instantly doubled to sixteen people; in the West Iceland region the percentages went from 0.5 percent unemployment for men and 1.5 percent for women in 2007 to 5.2 percent for men and 5.1 percent for women in 2009 (Directorate of Labour 2012), numbers that were still less dire than the 8.8 percent and even 12.8 percent unemployment in the Reykjavík area (Benediktsson and Karlsdóttir 2011). The restaurant owner said she had fifty people a day for lunch before the crash, then ". . . in one day lots of people, the next day, nothing. No one came. It was that quick." The bookstore owner stated: "The companies had to go on the same, but the people just waited to see what was happening before they bought anything. It was also difficult . . . because we couldn't get things from overseas for a time."

Because the value of the Icelandic currency almost immediately halved, everyone who held a foreign-currency-indexed loan saw it double. While in Reykjavík large numbers of people were unable to pay their house loans, in Grundarfjörður a combination of lower house values and bank policies that made 100 percent loans on rural houses harder to get meant that only a couple of people lost their homes. Farmers who had taken on big debt lost their farms to the banks and began working the land as tenants. The large foreign-currency-indexed loans the town council had so blithely taken out were now massive.

The one business that immediately benefitted from the crash was the fisheries, since the drop in the krona meant that exported fish prices now suddenly doubled. But so did the debts for those who had recently bought quota or invested in new ships. While in Reykjavík large numbers of migrant workers lost their jobs (Skaptadóttir, this volume), migrant workers in Grundarfjörður were still employed, but the international value of their wages halved. These workers said that Icelanders quickly became more reserved and that they felt immigrants were being blamed for the crash. A short time after the crash, a website called "Fucking Poles" appeared. Although relieved to see a general outcry in reaction to the website, Polish migrants said that they felt increasingly isolated and, being from a country with a history of sometimes brutal repression, were concerned about their position and even safety in Iceland.

Economically speaking, the rural residents of Grundarfjörður never benefitted from much of the money that urban people were making before the crash, so they didn't feel the loss as keenly. As one resident stated, "We never really had a boom so the crash didn't affect us so much." The residents of Grundarfjörður considered the sudden high debt a major setback, but viewed in the context of a history of poverty, struggle, and survival, they were confident the crisis would not seriously threaten their community stability. It certainly wasn't as bad as losing their area-based quota, a situation that had destroyed the economies of many other rural communities over the past twenty years (Einarsson 2011; Pálsson and Helgason 1996). They also saw the crash as a wake-up call. The attraction of money and city life had lured them away from the good life they had in their town. They suddenly realized once again that they were a community whose members relied upon each other and were united. Even the town council found sympathetic ears when it revealed the large collective debt. Still infused with the optimism of the past few years, the community felt, after a short period of fear and instability, that ultimately the crash was not about them but something they would watch unfold in Reykjavík.

FOUR YEARS LATER: INCREASED VULNERABILITY AND ERODING RESILIENCE

Grundarfjörður in 2013 still has the six fisheries companies it had before the crash, but some ownership has changed. One family ran into post-crash debt and sold to a non-local company in 2011; this company is still located in Grundarfjörður, although staff has changed. Another company that had invested heavily in stocks before the crash now saw its future as unclear. A third small company, which hired three to five people before the crash, now employs only one. One small family company, which sold its quota in 2006, has recently been able to buy some of it back and is now also running a small factory that processes lumpfish roe. The owners of the larger family companies, which hire about ninety people each, see their position as tenuous, mostly because of government regulations and taxes they believe favor the huge fisheries companies, banks, and the Reykjavík-led federal government.

In 2012, according to the local harbormaster, the herring catch from the waters of Grundarfjörður brought in a total of more than ISK 25.5 billion. Such healthy herring stocks have previously made rural communities rich, but current post-crash regulations, taxes, and a quota system that allows non-local boats open access to the fish (during the season, the bay was carpeted with non-local boats) now means that little of this fish revenue stays in Grundarfjörður. In a trend that began for Grundarfjörður in the early 2000s, the boats now unload elsewhere or process their fish onboard, taking the attendant dock and transport jobs away to mostly Reykjavík-based fish auction houses to which the fishing vessels are legally required to sell their fresh fish. Governmental and environmental influences, including the quota system, restrict the time allowed for fishing to short scattered periods, resulting in an overabundance of available stock, followed by periods of no fish stock. This in itself creates price fluctuations when everyone tries to sell their fish on a glutted market. To avoid this situation, quota holders often hold their fish, distributing it over a longer period as needed.

In 2012, due to the economic crisis in Europe, the price and demand for imported Icelandic fish began to fall. The local Grundarfjörður quota holders, however, were less alarmed by what they saw as "normal" price fluctuations than by a new post-crash government regulation that no longer allows them to "hold" stock. All small quota holders must sell at the same time. The result, according to these quota holders, is uncontrolled and even steeper price fluctuations. In addition, government-imposed currency regulations continue to favor the banks and the largest fish companies by giving them preferred exchange rates when transferring foreign currency back to Iceland after fish export sales in Europe. All these influences ensure that most of the highly profitable fish catch revenue goes directly to the largest fish companies and to Reykjavík instead of staying in the rural countryside where it was generated.

In 2012, because some of the foreign-currency-indexed loans were declared illegal, the Grundarfjörður town council received some repayment on its loan debt, a payment repeated in 2013. Their uncertainty reflects a general lack of transparency regarding a host of banking and legal policies, including which bank debts are being forgiven and which ones are not. Despite regular payments and a 13 percent rise in the municipality's income (mostly from fisheries), Grundarfjörður in 2012 owed 250 percent of its income to loan debt. In 2012, instead of restructuring these loans (which earn huge profits for Icelandic banks), the government passed new regulations on municipalities, requiring them to reduce their overall debt to 150 percent of local income over the next ten years.

Municipalities in Iceland are also not allowed by law to declare bankruptcy. The council is evaluating its options: raising local taxes further will make the area less attractive for new residents or businesses. It has cut road maintenance, but cutting services further will, in the words of the state auditor who came to advise them, make the town "uncompetitive."

Unemployment in Grundarfjörður has grown worse over the past few years, rising to twenty-six people in 2010 and twenty-one in 2011, mostly men from the building trade. The two large housing projects remain uninhabited despite a local housing shortage. Deckhand jobs pay well right now and are prized, making it hard for young inexperienced people to get jobs unless they are related to the skipper. One of the two banks closed in 2012. The post office has been incorporated into part of the grocery store and is open only four hours a day. Unable to find work, a few families have moved, some to Norway, as it offered them better opportunities than Reykjavík. The state government has proposed reducing health care services to the town. In part because of the cycle of age, but also because so many young people left in the years around the crash, the number of elementary school children has almost halved. Upper-secondary schools have seen cuts in their budgets, especially since October 2008. If the upper-secondary school in Grundarfjörður fails to increase its student numbers, the school will likely be merged with larger regional schools an hour or more away. The town's population has fallen from 952 in 2000 to 903 in 2012. The townspeople are very aware that if this trend continues, their town will no longer be viable.

Despite restrictions, fishing still brings income to the town, and unlike Reykjavík, nearly all the local migrant fish factory workers are still employed. As one Polish fish factory worker who has worked in the area since before the crash said, "It is not a tragedy [for us]. We are still here." And, in the words of another longtime local Polish factory worker, "Poles are everywhere around the planet. People in Poland have always emigrated. . . . We have had several wars, and we know this is not the fault of the people but of governments and those in power. So we have thick skins for this kind of shit."

Tourism has also increased. The fishing family that bought the hotel in 2006 has seen its profits double every year since 2008. They bought one whale-watching boat and then a second one in 2013. The local youth hostel caters to an increasing number of people, as does a new guesthouse, which opened in 2010. Cruise ships stop at the harbor, paying fees that go directly into the council's coffers. The restaurant is expanding its services, offering sports telecasts and catering to seamen who want burgers and a beer. "Sometimes they call me from sea to ask if I'm open," said the proprietor. "I don't care if I'm in bed when they call. By the time they reach shore, I'm open." The restaurant also supplies lunches to the upper-secondary school and tries to appeal to the tourists.

After a severe post-crash drop, the bookshop stabilized except for a decrease in all-important school supplies. But buying habits have changed, and customers are no longer in a hurry to receive ordered items. Because of increased transportation costs, the bookshop owner now bundles requests before he orders and often drives to Reykjavík himself to buy goods wholesale. Sales of Icelandic wool are booming. Since 2008 the local grocery store has been doing better, selling food and souvenirs, and with increased cooperation from local fishing vessels, the store now sells food and supplies to fishing boats.

According to the local police and upper-secondary students, violence, robbery, alcohol use, and drug abuse have actually decreased in the last few years. There are strong indications that an increasing number of young people, particularly women who had moved to Reykjavík and had children, are finding it too hard to live there and are moving back. Although the number of elementary school children is still low, the number of kindergarteners is rising. In 2012 fourteen children were born in Grundarfjörður.

Grundarfjörður residents, newly galvanized and politicized, are eager to sustain their community. They blame the post-crash, Reykjavík-based government, replete with corrupt banking and Quota King favoritism, for using their local resource-based wealth to prop up "an otherwise ailing economy" (Benediktsson and Karlsdóttir 2011).

RESILIENCE, POLITICS, AND POWER

In discussions of economic crises, such as the 2008 Icelandic crash, the blame is often placed on a number of rogue individuals. Seldom is a financial crisis "conceptualized as a structural feature of capitalism or a consequence of neo-liberal programs of reform" (Raco and Street 2012). Likewise, while residents of the Reykjavík region made a sharp distinction between themselves and the bankers who perpetrated the crash, residents of Grundarfjörður conflate "Reykjavík" as a single systemic force that continues to favor itself and the bankers who feed it.

Grundarfjörður residents' disconnection from the crash as it was experienced in Reykjavík relates also to a feeling that their very existence as an embodiment of rural Iceland, including its fisheries and agricultural products, is undervalued. The inequality of population, representation, power, and the ability to determine resource distribution disenfranchises them from the concerns of an urban-directed nation. It is this attitude, they say, that fosters the consolidation and quota policies that undermine their local economy and resilience.

Hudson (2010, 12) recognized that a central weakness of the conceptualization of regional resilience in times of crisis is its lack of "recognition and treatment of power." Minsky (2008) also made the point that it is erroneous to consider booms and busts as outside forces when they are intrinsic to the capitalist system. The ability of a region or community to be resilient is either bolstered or undermined through government planning policies and spending priorities. As long as the larger system remains unchanged, regional resilience planning and policy is not viable. Ultimately it is national policy that controls a subregion's ability to adapt in the face of change (see Pike, Dawley, and Tomaney 2010). Under neoliberal forms of governance, areas deemed most "efficient" are supported and favored as a means of making the national economy more resilient. As a result, peripheral areas become less significant (Raco and Street 2012, 4). In this way, Reykjavík's road to recovery is coming at the expense of community stability.

Within this relationship, local residents are expected to "adapt," with adaptation being defined as "the capacity of actors in the system to influence resilience" (Hudson 2010, 12). Residents of Grundarfjörður are trying to compete in the global market by investing in their fisheries, tourism, innovative education, and strong community cohesion. Before the crash, increased mobility over several decades combined with the pre-crash national excitement about abundance encouraged many residents to look beyond their own community for well-being. When the crash hit, they reassessed this relationship and now look to the local community for their well-being. But their lack of autonomy in determining their economic future has made this adjustment difficult. They are being expected to be resilient and adaptive without representation or power.

Aside from the potential loss of their quota, Grundarfjörður residents see the loss of fundamental state-funded social services as their greatest postcrash threat. Several local residents remarked that since nearly all decision-making power emanates from Reykjavík, when Parliament makes cuts, "It is easier to cut what is farther away," and "If you are going to think about votes, the countryside is not efficient." Icelandic national policy makers are indeed questioning the need for small communities because, under neoliberalism, they are deemed inefficient. Grundarfjörður residents see such weakening of federal structural support as placing money before the interests of society, a continuation of the same thinking that brought about the crash.

Grundarfjörður residents say this is nothing new. They saw little of the pre-crash prosperity enjoyed by the city, while post-crash Reykjavík-directed government cuts and regulations, fisheries policy, and bank decisions jeopardize their community survival. Grundarfjörður is now competing with the Reykjavík region for services and investment, and as a minority, it will lose. As one local resident, who had also lived for a few years in Reykjavík, said,

In the metropolitan areas, people are concerned about their own welfare, their individual survival. In the countryside, people are concerned about the larger environment, about the survival of the entire community. This is because the people's individual survival in the countryside depends upon their community's survival, and in the countryside, unlike the city, this is always in danger. People in Reykjavík may have felt worried right after the crash that Iceland's survival was in danger, but that passed. As much as everyone there is angry about the bankers, they don't now fear for the survival of their entire community.

Hudson (2010, 16) advocates "more place-based, localized, and regional ways of living" to increase resilience. But expectations of recovery of small communities come directly in conflict with the success of a capitalist economy, which routinely creates "vulnerability and crisis in regional economics precisely because processes of combined and uneven development lie at the heart of capitalist social relations" (ibid., 11). If rural communities are to have any chance at becoming resilient, the government must lead the way. Only the government can give local regions the power of self-determination and self-dependence.

We would like to thank the many people of Grundarfjörður and the surrounding areas who contributed to this article, particularly the Fjölbrautaskóli Snæfellinga (upper-secondary school) who treated us with great generosity, and local librarian Sunna Njálsdóttir for her considerable assistance. Margaret Willson would further like to thank the participants and organizers of the "Icelandic Meltdown" workshop, who inspired this research, and Ágústa Flosadóttir for her hospitality. Numerous people offered much-appreciated comments on earlier drafts, making this a much better chapter. Responsibility for the contents of this article is, of course, solely our own.

12

When Fishing Rights Go
Up against Human Rights

Anthropologist Níels Einarsson is the director of the Stefansson Arctic Institute in Akureyri, Iceland. Here he discusses the implications of Iceland choosing not to reform its fisheries management even in light of a 2007 United Nations Human Rights Committee decision that the system violates basic human rights. He warns policy makers that turning local fishing rights into a transferable financial commodity could cause potentially irreversible damage to the people and communities of Iceland and other countries where the "Icelandic model" is expected to be applied.

· · · · · · · · · · · · · · · · · · · ·

Fishing has been the mainstay of the Icelandic economy since the early twentieth century and continues to provide almost half of the country's export value in terms of products. Two-thirds of Icelandic fish products are sold within the European Union (EU) (see Bjarnason 2010, 203). After the short-lived financial boom and collapse in the 2000s, fishing regained its role as Iceland's main economic activity, together with industrial aluminum smelters and tourism. The Icelandic economy is fundamentally different from that of its neighbors in Western Europe and the EU, of which Iceland is not a member but has rights and responsibilities under the European Economic Area (EEA). In Iceland fishing contributes about 6 percent of GDP (down from 10 to 12 percent in the last decade), compared with an average of only 0.25 percent in the EU. Iceland ranks among the leading

DOI: 10.5876/9781607323358.c012

fishing nations of the world with an annual total catch of over a million tons (ibid., 203–4).

Iceland is often held up as an example of best practices in international fisheries management. This "poster child" reputation is less than convincing to many Icelanders, however: in a recent opinion poll, the overwhelming majority of respondents agreed that the current system of fisheries management should be fundamentally changed and property rights in fish stocks recaptured and reallocated. In the poll, taken in September 2010, 71 percent gave their support or strong support to such a transformation; an increase of 10 percent from February 2009.[1]

Before Iceland's version of fisheries management is held up to the world as a universally ideal model, as proponents of Individual Transferable Quotas (ITQs) advocate (see Auth 2012; Eyþórsson 1997; Pálsson and Helgason 1995; Pálsson and Helgason 1996; Árnason 2008; Hannesson 2004), anthropologists and other social scientists who have studied private property rights used in Icelandic fisheries governance have some serious questions that should be addressed. Foremost is how the present system squares with human rights and social equity.

HUMAN RIGHTS

In 2003 two Icelandic fishermen brought a case against their government to the United Nations Human Rights Committee (HRC), arguing that the ITQ system used for managing Iceland's fisheries was unfair, unconstitutional, and illegal. Until then, Iceland had consistently placed at the very top of the United Nations Human Development Index, so the accusation at the international court was a national embarrassment. In 2007 the HRC issued its decision supporting the fishermen's charges, adding more fuel to the fire in an already inflamed social debate about the legitimacy of ITQs.

The conflict began in September 2001 when the fishing vessel *Sveinn Sveinsson* from the coastal village of Patreksfjörður in the West Fjords sailed several times to fishing grounds to catch fish. What made these trips unusual was that the boat's owner and crew were publicly defying laws laid down by the Icelandic Fisheries Management Act (FMA) of 1990, which firmly established the ITQ system. The fishermen had notified the authorities of their intentions in advance, planning their outings as a protest against the FMA. They claimed the act was illegitimate and unethical, and they believed it was undermining not only their own livelihoods but also the economic and social viability of fishing communities around Iceland.

The inherent inequity of ITQs and the privatization of the commons in Icelandic fishing communities has been well documented by anthropologists and other social scientists. In the 1990s anthropologists Gisli Palsson, Agnar Helgason, and Einar Eyþórsson reported on how the unfettered transferability and commodification of fishing rights was affecting fishing communities and how catch quotas accumulated quickly into the hands of a few large companies. The consequences for small fishing communities were severe (see Eyþórsson 1997; Pálsson and Helgason 1995; Pálsson and Helgason 1996; Auth 2012.)

In 1995 twelve of the fifteen villages that lost more than 60 percent of their quotas had a population of less than 1,000. Iceland's West Fjords were hit particularly hard: by 1995, four villages had lost 70 percent of the quotas they had had in 1984 (Eyþórsson 1997, 117). When coastal communities dependent on these resources lose their quotas, it translates into insecurity, unemployment, depopulation, outmigration of young people, valueless homes, and social alienation (Skaptadóttir 2000). In these communities fish stocks have from the time of settlement been open and common property. Now they face a social reality of fenced and enclosed commons regardless of the conditions of the fishing grounds and abundance of fish close to home, and irrespective of local needs and aspirations. (For a history of access rights and Icelandic fisheries see Þór 2002, 37.)

The Icelandic Fisheries Agency filed suit against the two protesting fishermen. In August 2002 the two men pled guilty but claimed the laws were unconstitutional. They were found guilty by the West Fjords District Court, which based its decision on the precedent of the April 6, 2000, Supreme Court decision in the so-called *Vatneyri* case. The two men were sentenced to pay a fine of one million kronur each, or be imprisoned for three months, and pay the costs of the trial. In their subsequent appeal, the Supreme Court upheld the decision of the district court.

However, the two fishermen pursued their legal battle and took their predicament to the HRC, claiming to be victims of a violation of article 26 of the International Covenant on Civil and Political Rights (United Nations Human Rights Committee 2007).

They were acting on the culturally and historically ingrained assumption among many Icelanders that the fisheries cannot belong to any one person. They are a commonly held resource equally accessible to all Icelanders. Therefore, the men argued, their protest was ethically justifiable. (For an ethnography of the moral discourse on privatization and property rights in Icelandic fishing see Óðinsson 1997.)

Although the Fisheries Management Act of 1990 has been amended several times since it was first adopted, it still starts with a stipulation stressing that the fish stocks in Icelandic waters are the common property of all Icelanders and not the private property of any group of people. It states:

> The commercial fish stocks in Icelandic waters are the common property [*sameign*] of the Icelandic nation. The goal of this Act is to support their conservation and efficient use and thereby secure employment and settlement in the country. The allocation of fishing licenses according to this Act shall not give rise to property rights or irrevocable control of individuals over fishing licenses.[2]

Despite this preamble, most of the FMA describes the administration and allocation of common property resources within an ideology of transferable private property rights, or ITQs. The FMA defines which stocks it covers, delimitation of the jurisdiction, and how annual total allowable catch (TAC) is determined for each so-called fishing or quota year, which starts annually on September 1. Harvest rights or individual catch quotas within the TAC are calculated on the basis of this total amount, and each vessel receives its share on this basis. Change in annual TAC means a change in the quota share. Originally quotas were allotted without a fee, so in fact they were given to those firms engaged in fishing in 1983, based on the fishing record of 1981 to 1983. In the literature of fisheries governance this method is sometimes referred to as "grandfathering of catch rights." Article 4 of the FMA stipulates that no one is allowed to undertake commercial fishing without a fishing license. Penalties for violating the act include fines and imprisonment of up to six years.

In their appeal, the fishermen argued that according to law, Icelandic fish stocks were defined as common property. However, they were in fact treated as private property and given free every year to a select group; thus, in reality, they were donated to a privileged few. Other fishermen were forced to lease or buy quotas from this group. The income from the sale and lease of fishing rights benefited the sellers directly and not the nation as a whole. This ability to buy and sell fishing rights, plus the fact that quotas can be used as collateral, inherited by spouses and offspring, and are subject to property tax shows that they are treated as de facto private property.

Bringing cases to the HRC is a slow and stately business, but six years after the two fishermen went fishing without stipulated appropriation of fishing rights, the committee concluded that the Icelandic state had indeed violated the rights of the two men and that they were victims of discrimination in violation of article 26 of the covenant (see United Nations Human Rights Committee 2007, 13, clause 10.2). The decision rested on the fact that the two fishermen were obliged by the FMA to buy fishing rights from other citizens to gain access to resources that were declared by law to be the common property of the Icelandic nation.

Furthermore, the committee pointed out that the FMA differentiated between those fishers who were fishing at the time of the initial allotment in early 1980s and those who started fishing later. Those who enjoyed the initial allocation are able to use, sell, and lease their catch shares, whereas those who took up fishing later had to buy or rent from the former (ibid., clause 10.3). The committee acknowledged that the protection of fish stocks is a legitimate, reasonable, and objective goal. But it also pointed out that the quota system had been introduced as a temporary measure, that in fact its provisional character was a key precondition for adoption by the Icelandic Parliament, which was initially reluctant to allow ITQs in 1983 (Helgason 1995). The committee stated that the nature of the quota system changed with the FMA:

> ... [it] became not only permanent with the adoption of the Act but transformed original rights to use and exploit a public property into individual property. Allocated quotas no longer used by their original holders can be sold and leased at market prices instead of reverting to the State for allocation to new quota holders in accordance with fair and equitable criteria. . . . in the particular circumstances of the present case, the property entitlement privilege accorded permanently to the original quota owners, to the detriment of the authors, is not based on reasonable grounds. (United Nations Human Rights Committee 2007, 13–14, clause 10.4)

The committee cited the International Covenant of Civil and Political Rights in stating that that Iceland must not only compensate the two fishermen but also revise the Icelandic fisheries management system in accordance with human rights. The committee made a point of reminding Iceland that it is party to the Optional Protocol of the covenant, which means that Iceland recognizes the HRC as competent to determine human rights violations and has undertaken the obligation to guarantee its citizens rights under the covenant. Needless to say, the HRC's ruling has put a dent in Iceland's image of itself as a civil society accustomed to enjoying a top spot on the United Nations Human Development Index.

COLLATERALIZED FUTURES

The ITQ fisheries management system not only has led to international allegations of human rights abuses but also is directly linked to the country's economic boom and subsequent bust. Before the ITQ system was introduced by law in 1983, and also before the 1997 act that allowed fishing rights to be used as collateral (albeit supposedly connected to the physical properties of boats), the only value fishing firms had was in their fishing vessels, gear, and facilities on land. After 1997 companies and individuals with fishing licenses were allowed to use them as monetary collateral, or "paper fish," creating a heretofore nonexistent source of financial capital. With the ability to use fishing rights as collateral, the value of firms multiplied, and the price of stocks and markets in the 1990s and 2000s skyrocketed. Icelandic banks also greatly benefited, because they now had enough assets and equity to draw the attention of foreign investors.

Outside of the fisheries industry, Iceland had few other assets that could be manipulated into capital assets of collateral equity. The danger facing financial institutions using fishing rights as mortgages had, however, been known for some time. In a newsletter dated as early as 2000, the Central Bank of Iceland warned against using the volatile collateral of quotas, because the market price of fishing rights was deemed to be overly inflated (Seðlabanki Íslands 2000, 22–23).

Nevertheless, before the collapse of 2008, Icelandic banks, largely owned and operated by the newly rich "Quota Kings," were eager to buy fishing firms and their quotas from small-scale operators who had gradually joined the ITQ system. The banks also fueled quota transactions by offering, sometimes insistently, what looked like lucrative loans in foreign currency for investments in catch quotas. The impact of this policy was to raise the prices of quotas and their collateral equity, thereby inflating the banks' balance sheets with "paper fish" assets.

Risk-taking in the Icelandic banking system increased even further with the privatization of the two state-owned banks in 2003. These banks were handed over to political allies of the ruling parties, as described by Már Wolfgang Mixa in this volume. Within a few years, the system had escalated into an all-out reckless international market raid, leading to a rise in assets from 100 percent of the GDP in 2000 to over 900 percent in mid-2008 (Gylfason et al. 2009, 149).

In 2000, when the Central Bank warned that the price of quotas was unsustainably high, the price of so-called "cod equivalents" was just over ISK 800 per kilo. By 2008, just before the collapse, the price had risen to a flabbergasting ISK 4,400 per kilo, far more than any existing fishing operator or new entrant could hope to see as a reasonable investment in catch rights or a viable business. In 2007 and 2008 the total value of quotas in the Icelandic fisheries reached what one economist calls the "ridiculous" level of approximately ISK 2,000 billion, or fifty times the annual profit of the fishing industry (Steinsson 2010, 7). This inflation reflected the willingness of the banks as institutions of financial capitalism to offer loans based on quota acquisitions in the industry rather than on the real productive value of the fishing rights. By the time of the economic meltdown, when the money dried up, the price of permanent quotas had dropped to half of their previous value (ibid., 3). In the spring of 2012, the market value of one kilo of permanent catch rights in cod equivalent was around ISK 2,000. However, the price lacks transparency and seems to be kept afloat by a tacit agreement between banks and fishing firms.

HUMAN RIGHTS AND MARINE POLICY

One crucial outcome of quotas as mortgage collateral is that banks and quota holders have vested interests in keeping the inflated value up and working against any attempt by authorities—as the HRC ruling called for—to recapture and reallocate the quotas, which in practice are now private property. Any such change could immediately affect the status of quotas as collateral and lead to a drastic collapse in the value of financial assets in quotas. This is explained in a report by the so-called Resource Committee (Auðlindanefnd), which, in 2000, was asked to review the impact of capturing resource rent from Icelandic natural resources, including fish stocks. It concluded that recapturing quotas at as little as 5 percent per annum would lead to a 42 percent decrease in the overall capital value of fish firms and cause much "unrest" among financial institutions (Auðlindanefnd 2000, 35–36).

In this context it does not come as a surprise that Icelandic banks take an avid interest in the current fisheries policy and campaign against any changes. Many of the assets of the new, refinanced banks in post-meltdown Iceland are also tied to quota collaterals. Icelandic banks were active in advising the so-called Reconciliation Committee (Sáttanefnd), appointed by the post-crash government to discuss reformation of Icelandic fisheries governance. This committee commissioned several assessments of the economic impact of recall and redistribution of the fishing rights. One of the reports, echoing the 2000 report mentioned above and the concerns of the fishing industry, concluded that with 5 percent recall per annum, the value of quotas and thereby collateral equity would immediately decrease by 57 percent. A 10 percent recapture would lead to a 75 percent fall (see Gunnlaugsson et al. 2010, 32–33). These numbers are hard to believe, since the forecast applies to post-crash conditions when quotas have already lost half of their value, though it may well indicate that quota prices are still too high. But this does support the Central Bank's reasoning in its 2000 warnings on the financial dangers of inflated quota prices and the risky nature of quotas as collateral.

In the end of 2008 the fishing industry owed the banks ISK 560 billion, and since the industry was in dire straits, the banks needed to secure the loans for themselves and their foreign lenders. Fishing industry profits in 2008 were ISK 33 billion, and by 2009 it they had increased to ISK 45 billion (Hagstofa Íslands 2010, 12). These enormous loans also had to be kept intact, as the income the banks receive annually from the fishing firms in the form of interest and other payments are vital for the banks' stability. There seems to be a real fear of another financial collapse in the banks and, by default, among political decision makers who have been given the task of resurrecting the nation's economy. The International Monetary Fund, which Iceland called on for help during the crisis, required the rebuilding and strengthening of the financial system as a key component of its adjustment program (International Monetary Fund 2011). Ultimately, the majority of the Reconciliation Committee rejected any radical change in quota rights involving recapture and equitable reallocation of privatized common property that would have been in accordance with the demands of the HRC. The banks and quota holders could trust in the relative status quo.

In March 2012 and again in the spring of 2013 the Left-Green/Social Democrat government put forth bills, which were not approved by the Icelandic Parliament, that essentially would have prolonged neoliberal governance of the Icelandic fisheries by recalling in name all the quotas, but at the same time and in one fell swoop reallocating for the next decades some 93 percent of the TAC to present quota recipients, who now generally refer to themselves as quota "owners." The new allocations were to be tied to twenty-year contracts, which could be renewed for another twenty years. But, importantly, fishing rights were to continue to serve as financial products and collateral, a key element for the financial system, including the international hedge funds that own some of the banks, as well as debt-ridden fishing companies. However, the holders of resource-use contracts in fisheries were to sign a declaration in conjunction with the allotment of the (new) rights, stating that the fish stocks are indeed the property of the Icelandic nation. To many, this recognition of the national property quality of fish may seem peculiar, since it is already stated in the current FMA. However, the clause in the law declaring the fish stocks to be in national ownership was, according to the new but failed bills, semantically strengthened by the word *ævarandi*, which means "forever."

The new bills were harshly criticized by politicians and lobby groups representing the majority of the fishing industry as well as those who point out that the new law made no fundamental change and that the government was backing down from its election promises of a complete revision of the governance regime. Emotions ran high. The issue was of such gravity that the president said he would call for a national referendum if the bill became law.

CONCLUSIONS

The privatization of common-property resources in Iceland and the giving away of what was never a *res nullius* runs counter to the basic principles and preconditions of human development as defined in the 1990 Human Development Report (HDR), i.e., as "A process of enlarging people's choices" (United Nations Development Programme [UNDP] 1990, 12). For this to happen, people must be free to make choices and have the opportunity to realize them. The concept has evolved as the world has changed, with increased attention to sustainable human development and equity factors, but the fundamental principle of making people the center of development remains (ibid.). Given the human ecology of Icelandic fishing communities with their reliance on few employment options apart from fishing, the impact of ITQs is a matter of grave concern. They not only decrease the social and economic flexibility of fishing communities but limit personal and cultural self-realization as well. But the quota system impoverishes all Icelanders by depriving them of equal access to the nation's most important resource.

The system introduced in Iceland to manage human environmental relations in the fisheries was part and parcel of reductionist economic tools and policies guided by market fundamentalism, lack of foresight, and perhaps even lack of interest in the well-being and viability of the societies so deeply affected by policy and politics beyond their control. Some economists quite honestly admit that privatization of the commons inevitably causes smaller communities to lose out. They have even questioned whether fisheries-dependent communities are actually part of the fishing industry proper. They see the exclusion of these communities as not just logical but also justifiable, rational, and necessary (Hannesson 2004).

Human development relies on human rights and access to limited resources. The closing of commons, such as fish stocks or water, and the giving away or selling of the commons to a small group of privileged few may be not only unethical but also highly detrimental to the ability of those excluded to determine their own fate, nurture their cultural integrity, and indeed interact with

nature in the pursuit of appropriating resources for livelihood and the fulfill-
ment of their needs. In the ecological context of Arctic regions, access to local
resources is a key to human welfare.

The reprimand from the HRC should be a wake-up call to Icelandic officials that fundamental change in the system needs to occur if they do not
want to see the country placed on par with Myanmar or Zimbabwe when it
comes to human rights. The views of the HRC should be a warning to other
countries that are considering introducing the "Icelandic model" to their fishing economies.

Heeding the views of the HRC and setting a course for future action could
make a real difference in the development of Iceland. Following the committee's recommendations would be a meaningful pragmatic political act in what
appears to be an irreversible process that has transformed public resources into
private assets, wealth, and power. But in the realpolitik of post-crisis Icelandic
society, marked by the dominant realities and logic of fishing rights as financial
products, the message seems to have been lost. It remains to be seen whether
Icelandic society has the political and moral capacity to change its economic
course and privilege once again human rights over fishing rights.[3]

NOTES

1. The findings of the opinion poll, conducted by Market and Media Research,
are available from http://www.mmr.is/frettir/birtar-nieurstoeeur/157-stueningur-eykst
-vie-afturkoellun-fiskveieiheimilda.

2. Author's translation. For the Icelandic legal text, see "Lög um stjórn fiskveiða,"
no. 116, August 10. http://www.althingi.is/lagas/138a/2006116.html.

3. For an earlier version of this chapter, see Einarsson 2012.

*The Crash and
Communities*

13

Schools in Two
Communities Weather
the Crash

Guðný S. Guðbjörnsdóttir and Sigurlína Davíðsdóttir are
both professors of education at the University of Iceland. In
this chapter they analyze the effects of the crash on schooling
in two different Icelandic communities and how sometimes
crisis doesn't have to end in disaster.

·····················

In this chapter we investigate how the Icelandic economic meltdown impacted schools in two different
communities. To what extent has the economic meltdown in 2008 disrupted education in schools in these
two locales? Is the situation different in preschools,
primary schools, and upper-secondary schools? How
different is the situation in the two different communities? Have school leaders dealt professionally with
the situation? Has the economic crisis resulted in a
school or educational crisis or have efforts to protect
the schools been successful in these two locales?

The Center for Public Education (2010) recom-
mends focusing first on measures not considered to
have a direct effect on student outcome, such as reducing central office staff, eliminating nonessential travel,
deferring maintenance, reducing supplies, and saving
on heating and cooling costs, and trying to avoid more
severe measures, such as increasing class size and cutting extracurricular activities, necessary transportation,
and, possibly, school hours or days. Typically, a recession's greatest impact on community budgets comes
one or two years after the recession ends.

DOI: 10.5876/9781607323358.c013

According to the literature on leadership during crisis, all the signs of crisis were present in Iceland in 2008 (Flannery 2010; Gísladóttir 2010). Political leaders and financial leaders both showed signs of pre- and post-crisis leadership, as described by Hackman and Johnson (2009). Some leaders were more alert to the warning signs than others; some had a crisis management plan; and some showed signs of overconfidence. Other signs of crisis included the punishment of whistle-blowers and an emphasis on creating trust. After a crisis, the reconnection with visions and values is important, then comes the denial and evading of responsibility, reduction of offensiveness, emphasis on corrective action and learning from experience, and finally the promotion of healing (ibid.).

Right after the collapse of the Icelandic banking system, the country showed characteristic signs of post-crisis leadership; specifically, there was a general emphasis on reconnecting better with national visions and values. A national assembly of 1,500 randomly selected people discussed the most important values of Icelanders on January 20, 2009. The four values favored most by the assembly were integrity, equal rights, respect, and justice (National Assembly Iceland, 2009).

There is not much literature available on symptoms or definitions of crises in schools or on how to lead schools during a crisis. In a recent attempt to conceptualize a theory of crisis within education, Pepper et al. (2010, 6–7) proposed a three-part unified theory. First, a school crisis is "an event or a series of events that threaten a school's core values or foundational practices." These include underlying assumptions, school culture, and professional practice of teachers, replicated by parents and students. Second, a school crisis is "obvious in its manifestation but born from complex and often unclear or uncontainable circumstances." The circumstances may include politics and diverse community needs and demands. In addition the schools must meet local and state demands while at the same time they are constrained by varying needs of different individuals, staff, and students. Third, a school crisis demands urgent decision making. There are many types of crises: economic, informational, physical, human resources, reputational, psychopathic acts, or natural disasters (Hackman and Johnson 2009). School crises have been classified on the basis of their origin, internal or external, and if they were predictable or nonpredictable (Pepper et al. 2010). The situation in Iceland suggests a predictable, external, economic crisis. These authors recommend that immediately following such a crisis event, the leaders should use prevention strategies to strengthen the school's resilience and prevent a real crisis from developing.

After analyzing different cases of crisis situations in twelve different schools, Pepper and colleagues (ibid.) concluded that school leaders should follow six principles: respond to the situation before it becomes a real crisis; identify truly immediate priorities; let time, efforts, and resources flow in proportion to prioritization; communicate constantly; be flexible; and do not personally give in or surrender to the crisis. Smith and Riley (2012) proposed similar guidelines for school administrators in times of crisis. These principles will be used here as guidelines for appropriate leadership behavior in schools.

Shafiq (2010) has provided a conceptual framework for understanding how crisis conditions affect children's educational outcomes, suggesting both negative and positive effects. Available studies suggest that primary education is not hit as hard as secondary education, partly because enrollment decreases more in secondary schools. That can be related to socioeconomic status, parental employment, and the possibility of student employment. Shafiq also mentions evidence from the United States during the Great Depression, the Mexico crisis in the 1990s, and the Peruvian crisis in 1987–1991 indicating that educational outcomes can improve during a crisis, in the sense that more secondary school students remain in school because of few opportunities to work.

One comparable Icelandic study suggests a very minor effect of the Icelandic meltdown on schools in the fishing community Hornafjörður (Illugadóttir 2011). This community did not experience the same degree of hype conditions as the capital area did before 2008, and after the meltdown the net income of this town did not diminish since fishing exports are paid for in foreign currency, which made a big difference due to the devaluation of the Icelandic currency, as we discuss below.

In 2007 and 2008 Iceland spent more on education than any other OECD country (OECD 2010; 2011a). This is partly explained by the country's age distribution, since expenditure is usually higher in countries with a young population and where students are a large proportion of the population. Iceland's expenditure on educational institutions amounted to 7.8 percent of GDP in 2007, ranking Iceland first among OECD countries. Local authorities run preschools and primary schools in Iceland, so their policy is important. After the meltdown, the Icelandic Association of Local Authorities (2008) agreed on the priorities that schools should have during the recession. It recommended that basic services of the primary school and, to a certain extent, the preschool should be protected as much as possible. In January 2009 the new coalition government of two left parties, formed after a general election, issued a policy statement that stressed the importance of free basic education as the key to social equality and the prosperity of the nation (Government Offices of Iceland 2009).

THE STUDY

The study described in this chapter was conducted from 2010 to 2012 in two communities that were known to be hit hard by the crisis but that are economically dissimilar. The purpose of the study was to ascertain what difference, if any, the crisis had on each. One is in the middle of a farming community and the other bases its income on services, fishing, and transport. The researchers went into the communities and collected data and conducted interviews and focus groups with administrators of preschools and primary and secondary schools, teachers, parents, and pupils and gained access to school expenses from the local authorities. The research group included seven academics from the School of Education, University of Iceland, including the authors.

The number of pupils in both communities dropped by 12–13 percent from 2007 to 2010 (Table 13.1). In the farming community both the number of administrators and teachers went down. In the service community the pattern is different: the number of administrators went up from three in 2007 to four in 2010–2011, while the number of teaching posts remained the same, at thirty-eight, in 2007 and 2010, despite fewer pupils.

The pupil-to-staff ratio in the rural school went from 1:7.8 in 2005 to 1:5.9 in 2007 and 1:6 in 2010. In the service school the pupil-to-staff ratio was 1:7.4 in 2005, 1:7.3 in 2008, and 1:6.5 in 2010, suggesting an earlier change in the farming community.

The cost of running the schools is presented here in Icelandic kronur (ISK), which saw a devaluation of 83 percent from October 2007 to October 2010, and over 100 percent from 2007 to 2012 (Central Bank of Iceland 2012). This devaluation affects both the cost of the schools and the cost of living for teachers and others in the country.

Our interviews and focus groups yielded the following information on how the economic crisis affected the two target communities: we learned what the antecedents were in each community; what was cut from the schools and how; the effects of the cuts on schooling; and new opportunities created by the crisis.

ANTECEDENTS TO THE MELTDOWN

Prior to 2005, the farming community consisted of a number of smaller communities. Due to economic difficulties in 2006, the communities were merged that year. Throughout the process, residents discussed what to do with the educational system, including merging the schools. Although the communities did not physically merge the schools at the time, some of the rural

	Farming Community			Service Community		
	2007	2008	2010	2007	2008	2010
Number of pupils	320	301	279	467	465	412
Administrators	5.5	5.1	2.8	3.0	3.0	4.0
Teachers	33.4	34.3	28.3	38.0	40.3	38.0
Support staff	6.2	7.8	3.2	9.7	12.0	13.5
School helpers	3.8	5.2	6.2	4.75	3.5	3.25
Other staff	5.6	5.5	5.6	5.8	4.5	5.0
Number of staff	54.5	58.0	46.2	62.25	63.3	63.75
Pupil/staff ratio	1:5.9	1:5.2	1:6.0	1:7.5	1:7.3	1:6.5
Total cost of the schools (million ISK)	289	298	326	356	429	438

schools did merge their administration. Educators found this process challenging, more value-laden and difficult to negotiate than the meltdown itself. One of the respondents stated: "They began immediately calculating what could be cut; the atmosphere in the community became quite stressed. One of the school sites was supposed to shut down; nobody knew what would happen. Many meetings were held; people were very upset here." The economy of this community had been sliding for some years before the meltdown, resulting in a lower number of students because lack of job opportunities had caused families to move away. In 2007 an upper-secondary school established itself in the community as an independent association, but when its savings bank crashed relatively early in 2008, that school became a burden for the community.

For the service community, the crash seemed to come as a complete surprise, at least to the parents. One of them said simply: "No, there was no preparation or any antecedents. All of a sudden, the economy here had crashed completely." Teachers and administrators were not of the same opinion as the parents; they thought the recession in the community started before 2008. So it seems the farming community had inadvertently prepared for cuts in the school system and had even completed many of the necessary cuts before the meltdown happened, where few actions were taken in the service community, leaving it less prepared for the shock. The latter community had already suffered a severe drop in employment in 2006 due to a major employer moving out of the area, making it more susceptible to the lure of the economic boom. The local savings bank made loans that allowed the unemployed to find jobs building new houses and factories, and those newly employed workers took out loans themselves that later they were unable to repay in a story that played itself out across Iceland.

WHAT WAS CUT AND HOW?

In the farming community, there were discussions between the local authorities and the schools about what should be cut and how, but no school was ready to commit to cutting its own funding. In the end, community leaders decided what should be cut. Mostly, these cuts could include what was not decided beforehand or protected by law, as much of schoolwork is. Choices included providing less expensive food, less specialized assistance such as psychologists and speech therapists, less continuing education of staff, and less extra help for students as well as reducing administrative costs, all of which translated into administrators taking on more work with less pay, including substitute teaching. Support staff was hired on a part-time basis and extracurricular activities and after-school services were cut, as well as equipment and building maintenance. Monitoring of school financing also became much stricter than before, with no tolerance for slack.

The meltdown hit the service community harder than the rural community. The service community thrived during the economic hype around 2007, but after the meltdown it had trouble paying off loans. However, in spite of the grave situation it found itself in, the general consensus was that the schools should be protected. Their funding was cut, but less than expected, given the severity of the situation. "The first and greatest cut was in 2009, and the last three years we are getting less and less money to run the school," said the headmaster of the grade school. The schools adopted measures that would affect the students the least and asked parents to participate more than before in bearing the costs of activities such as crafting, student trips, and monitoring during breaks. One of the parent committees negotiated with the oldest grade school students to help pay some of the cost of their yearly graduation trip if they would help with break monitoring. Parents understood that costs had to be cut, and they seemed to feel that the schools were doing what they could to prevent negative consequences for the children.

There is much more joblessness in this community than before, so the parent committee is reaching out to those parents who need help. However, they feel that the situation has changed. One parent said, "This is the first Christmas when we are asked to have the students bring materials from home to use for

Christmas crafting and decorations." In the upper-secondary school, class size increased when the school participated in a governmental plan to provide schooling for the unemployed. Students in the lower grades did not notice many changes, except for less specialized help. They are still able to come up with money to have expensive dances and trips, but they need to work harder to finance them than before, they said.

Both communities have had to cut costly extras from the schools. In the farming community, there was a popular center attached to the school with lots of recreational opportunities for the students. This had to be changed to more of a child-care facility, with fewer recreational options. Both communities cut down on trips. In the farming community, the students told us they understood this decision and agreed with it. "What we were doing before was simply much too expensive. We can still have fun if we take our graduation trips inland rather than going abroad," they said. In both communities the preschool teachers had fewer possibilities for meetings, cooperating and offering specialized help, and in both communities the parents rose to the occasion.

In general, it seems that both of the communities went the extra mile to protect their schools, even if they had to cut costs. This was especially noteworthy in the harder-hit service community. The schools there seemed to be thriving, optimistic, and productive, in spite of the economic situation.

EFFECTS OF THE MELTDOWN ON SCHOOLING

In the farming community the number of administrative posts decreased both in the grade school and in the preschools. The service community saw an increase in grade school administration from three to four in 2010, at the time of the most serious cuts. There was an increase in the number of children with special needs, so one administrator was dedicated to that area. The school administrators refused to take a 10 percent salary cut but agreed to give up their transportation expense benefit. The preschool administrators, however, took a 10 percent salary cut, as did most administrators in the community. Generally, administrative cuts are seen as the first place to tighten the budget, even if the need for administration does not diminish during these times.

In both communities, the pupil-to-staff ratio has risen slightly. Administrators take on more work than before without getting raises. The preschool teachers are fewer and complain about doing less professional work, particularly in the afternoon when just the basic needs of the children are attended to. The special education services have been cut in all the schools in both communities. In the service community, class sizes are larger in the upper-secondary school because of more students. Children in the upper grades are sent home if their teacher gets sick, but the lower grades have substitute teachers. Parents participate as best they can. Thus it seems there is a concerted effort to prevent negative cost-cutting effects on teaching or learning.

The grade school in the harder-hit service community had been ambitious in increasing reading and math proficiency for the last five years and have kept the full-time special teaching director for that. The school's ranking on a national test for grade 4 has improved considerably in reading and even more in mathematics. The teachers are now happier about their secure jobs and salary than before, and now all the teachers have full teaching qualifications, compared with only 48 percent in 2006.

With fewer teachers, each teacher does more work and has fewer hours for collaboration than before, particularly in the preschools in both communities. There are also fewer possibilities for continuing education. In the harder-hit service community, cooperation between teachers and with parents has, however, become more school-oriented and improved, according to the principal. "We see ourselves as a community, the school and the parents." Educational evaluation was thriving in at least some of the schools, and now evaluations are minimal, only enough to satisfy the letter of the law. It is clear that in order for cooperation and collaboration to take place, there must be time for meetings. This has become more difficult.

OPPORTUNITIES IN THE WAKE OF THE MELTDOWN

In both communities parents seem to have more time to spend with their families. When it is because of joblessness, it may have some negative as well as positive consequences, but, in general, people seem to see increased family time as a positive development. The school and the welfare services cooperate in the harder-hit service community to make sure all children have proper clothes and school equipment and are able to buy school lunch. Parents are more cooperative with the schools than before, spending more time and effort. They also help with entertaining their children during festivals rather than hiring entertainers for that. They go on field trips instead of paying teachers for those trips. The schools do not print more than absolutely necessary and monitor their spending diligently. The children seem to be just as happy now as before, even happier with more time and attention from their parents. Some of the respondents in this study saw these developments as opportunities to reevaluate the setup of our communities, with values other than grasping for material goods.

The future looked different in the two communities. In the farming community people believed that they had already cut as much as they needed for seven years and the only way now was up. The harder-hit service community had only been cutting for three years when the interviews took place, and the respondents were not as optimistic, particularly for the community as a whole. Some were of the opinion that the cuts were there to stay, at least for some years, but others thought they had already hit bottom in terms of cuts. The parents worried mostly that teachers they appreciated might tire of the situation and morale might deteriorate.

Another opportunity created by the meltdown was reorganization of specialist teaching in the grade school, which now focuses on small groups more than individuals. In the farming community's upper-secondary schools, an interest in cooperating with neighborhood schools has increased. In the service community, new curriculum tracks and courses were created in cooperation with the unemployment services. In both communities, parent committees were ready to chip in with smaller issues, but people were worried about the bigger picture, especially in the harder-hit community.

CONCLUSIONS

As expected, there have been cuts in the Icelandic school system, and the devaluation of the Icelandic currency without comparable salary increases has been dramatic (Central Bank of Iceland 2012). This agrees with findings such as those from Education International (2010). Both the Icelandic government and local governing bodies have, however, prioritized to protect the preschools and primary schools as much as possible. So far, teachers have not been laid off in the communities discussed here. So far, extra costs have been "cut to the bone," as some participants phrased it, but the basic functions of the schools have been protected as much as possible. This was possible because, before the crisis, Iceland was spending so much on preschool and primary education and ranked very high among the OECD countries in 2007 (OECD 2010) and in 2008 as well (OECD 2011a).

DIFFERENT SCHOOL LEVELS

Disruptions to the general running and basic values of the schools have been minor. The grade school investigated in the service community had already taken on an extra goal to increase achievement in reading, math, and student health. This has continued after the crash and probably counteracted the adverse effects of the crash. Morale in the school community is high, with more parental participation than before. They have managed to create a community of practice with the parents.

In the preschools there is more disruption of the daily work, more so in the farming community. The fees have gone up, and the length of the school day has been shortened. Meetings and preparation time of teachers are difficult during normal working hours. Parents complain about shorter hours and lower-quality food for the children, but nevertheless they cooperate well with the preschools.

The upper-secondary schools are run by the state, and in these two communities the situation is very different. In the farming community a new school was founded and built during the economic boom in 2007. It was backed by private investors and the local service bank, which ran into difficulties and collapsed early in 2008. At the same time, the area is losing pupils as unemployment sets in, so running the school is difficult with fewer students. In the service community, there was an established upper-secondary school before the hype and the crash. After the meltdown this school cooperated with the government and the Directorate of Labor on the education of unemployed young people in an attempt to reduce unemployment. This has put the school in demand and made it more economically efficient, but at the same time there is more demand for counseling services, and new short tracks have been created. In this sense, the situation is similar to the findings of Shafiq (2010), where more secondary school students remain in school because of fewer work opportunities.

PROFESSIONAL WORK

In both communities the grade school leaders showed active leadership skills and are considered by their teachers to be fair. The headmaster of the rural grade school was seen as good at negotiating with the local authorities and in charge of choosing where to cut costs. In the service community the principal saw the amount of money the school got each year from the town as fixed, and his role was to communicate well with the teachers about how to make the most of that money and create a learning community that included the parents. He was seen as a fair and trustworthy leader. The leaders of the upper-secondary school in the service community were active in participating with the government unemployment office. Their program admitted more pupils and thereby strengthened the school, benefited unemployed individuals, and reduced national unemployment. This cooperation is a win-win situation and a sign of good leadership. The rural upper-secondary school was waiting for a new leadership team.

The political leadership in the farming community was more alert to the early warning signs of the crisis and started to cut the cost of education well before the meltdown. In the service community there were signs of overconfidence in the economic boom, and cuts were directed to other areas, such as administration. Their aim has been to protect the schools as much as possible. This meant that cuts in the schools came late in view of the grave financial situation. It is still not clear if they have reached the bottom yet.

A SCHOOL CRISIS?

A school crisis has been defined as an event that threatens the basic or core values of the school and its administration and foundational practices (Pepper et al. 2010). In both communities the professional practice of preschool teachers was disrupted, but the professional learning community in the grade schools was not seriously disrupted. Both in preschools and primary schools the teacher-parent relationship improved, and in the upper-secondary school the cooperation with the welfare and unemployment authorities strengthened the school in the service community and made the teachers more committed to their work than before. This is in agreement with ideas of Ranson (2008) on changing governance in education, where collaboration in creating a community of practice with families is prioritized over focusing on comparison and competition between schools.

Second, a school crisis is often born from uncontainable consequences, which is clear in this case. The political situation is different in the two communities, and the aims of the national government and the unemployment services helped to prevent problems from getting bigger. Third, a crisis demands urgent decision making, which was clearly met in the farming community and probably in the service community as well. In the latter community, the community leadership has focused its savings first on other areas in order to protect its schools, and the school leadership has coped well with unavoidable cuts. The financial meltdown in Iceland was an external consequence to the school. The problems of these communities and the economic boom conditions in Iceland as a whole helped to trigger the meltdown, which seemed to be foreseen better in the farming community than the service one.

Did the community and school leadership respond appropriately to the situation in view of the principles recommended by Pepper et al. (2010)? The farming community clearly saw early signs of a crisis and responded; both communities as well as the association of local authorities and the Icelandic government (Icelandic Association of Local Authorities 2008; Government Offices of Iceland 2009) all agreed to prioritize preschools and grade schools, and have protected those as much as possible. The emphasis on cooperation and communication was clear in both communities, though it could have been better in the rural community. In the service community communication and cooperation between teachers and among teachers, parents, and the community is highly prioritized. Flexibility and resilience are emphasized, particularly in the service community. There are probably more signs of a crisis in the schools of the farming community at the present time, but they started cutting earlier. It remains to be seen if the service community will manage to avoid a real crisis in the years to come, but the financial situation of that community is rather bleak.

This study was conducted on behalf of the Center for Research on School Administration, Innovation, and Evaluation at the School of Education, University of Iceland. Other members of the research team were Anna Kristín Sigurðardóttir, Arna H. Jónsdóttir, Börkur Hansen, Ólafur H. Jóhannsson, and Steinunn Helga Lárusdóttir.

14

What Happened to the
Migrant Workers?

*Unnur Dís Skaptadóttir earned her anthropology degree
from the City University of New York studying women in
Icelandic fishing communities. Here she documents how the
boom's jobs with good wages drew immigrants, particularly
men in construction, and how the crash, and Icelanders'
response to it, hit them disproportionately harder.*

••••••••••••••••••••

In this chapter I examine the effects of the 2008 economic crisis on immigrants, especially those facing the
challenges of unemployment. From the 1990s until
the end of the economic boom, Iceland had a growing
immigrant population. This trend mirrored international work-related migration, an important aspect of
global capitalism at the beginning of the twenty-first
century.

During this period men migrated to countries experiencing an economic upswing, such as Ireland, Spain,
and Greece, predominantly to work in construction
(Martin 2009; Wilson 2009). Women also migrated
in greater numbers to engage in industrial production,
service, and care work (Koser 2007; Mahler and Pessar
2006; Skaptadóttir and Wojtyńska 2008a). The majority of jobs in Iceland were low-paying for Icelanders,
but higher-income for the immigrants who took them
due to the favorable exchange rate.

The economic crash hit recent migrants hard, resulting in unemployment (Skaptadóttir 2010a). An important goal for many migrants moving to high-wage
countries is to provide for family members back home

DOI: 10.5876/9781607323358.c014

(Brettell 2007; Guarnizo 2003; Olwig and Sørensen 2002; Vertovec 2004). Martin (2009) has pointed out the significant increase worldwide in remittance flows in the years preceding the economic crisis in 2008. Given the gravity of the economic crisis, many feared that migrant remittances would severely decrease following the meltdown. However, the decrease was less than had been expected (Tilly 2011). This corroborates the findings of Fix and colleagues (2009) that conclude that while remittances have diminished on a global basis, they remain a significant source of income for the countries receiving them.

There is no doubt, however, that the current recession has had a negative effect on the financial status of immigrants and their families. Data on poverty from the period leading up to the economic crisis show that immigrants are more likely to fall into the low-income bracket than native inhabitants. In Iceland unemployment hit the construction industry and those dependent on foreign laborers harder than other labor sectors. It can be assumed that poverty among labor migrants has grown as a consequence of the meltdown (ibid.). A large number of migrant laborers lost their jobs, reducing remittance flows considerably.

The discussion in this chapter is based on a number of research projects that I have conducted since 2003.[1] All the projects have been conducted in Reykjavík, the surrounding municipalities, and in three towns in Iceland with a relatively high percentage of migrants. The majority of research participants were Poles, who are the largest immigrant group overall, and Filipinos, who form the largest Asian group in Iceland. I included representatives from organizations, state and municipal institutions handling immigrant issues, as well as language teachers and representatives from trade unions and charities. The findings from the different studies span a decade, thus providing important insights into developments before and after the meltdown.

RISING INTERNATIONAL MIGRATION
WITHIN A BOOMING ECONOMY

The growth in migration had already begun in the late 1990s with Iceland's 1994 decision to participate in the European Economic Area (EEA) with its agreements regarding a single labor market. But it accelerated in 2006 when the window given to new EU members limiting access to Iceland's labor markets expired (Dustmann, Frattini and Halls 2009; Sigurðsson and Arnarson 2011). This coincided with a great need for workers in mega projects in Iceland and the booming construction industry. In 1996 the number of immigrants (defined as people born abroad with parents born abroad) accounted for approximately 2 percent of Iceland's population, with 30 percent coming from other Nordic countries. Immigrants from Asia accounted for only 15 percent. In 2008, just over a decade later, the number of immigrants had skyrocketed, representing 8.1 percent of Iceland's population. The majority, 68 percent, came from Europe, while the number of Nordic immigrants had decreased to 7 percent. Although the number of Asian immigrants had grown, they continued to account for only about 15 percent of all immigrants (Garðarsdóttir, Hauksson, and Tryggvadóttir 2009). People from outside of the EEA coming to work in Iceland require a work permit prior to entering the country. Thus, those coming from outside Europe arrive increasingly to reunite with their families.

As discussed by Fix and colleagues (2009), immigrants are vulnerable for many reasons. They may have little education and poor host-country language skills. The practice of hiring immigrants in large groups on provisional contracts in sectors often referred to as boom-bust industries, such as construction, can weaken their position further. In the 1990s a large number of people arrived in Iceland to work in the fisheries. Most of them were women taking jobs previously held by Icelandic women. By 1996, 70 percent of all work permits were granted to fish processing plants, the majority for women from Poland. High unemployment among women in Poland at the time, the transformation to a market economy, and the opening of borders of Western Europe following EU membership in 2004 were all factors that stimulated migration from Poland to countries within the EEA, including Iceland (Skaptadóttir and Wojtyńska 2008a).

People from the Philippines were also migrating to Iceland to work in the fisheries, since most of the jobs vacated by Icelandic women were originally filled by women from these countries who had immigrated because of marriage. Subsequently, they would find employment for friends and family members who wished to join them. These women thus became central agents in the chain migration that took place during the economic boom. Johanna G. Bissat (2013) found that Thai women had the same role in the migration of people from Thailand to Iceland.

Women migrants were no longer the majority once migration increased significantly after May 2006, when people from the new member states of the EU no longer needed to secure work permits to come to Iceland. The majority of migrants arriving after the simultaneous EU accession of former Eastern Bloc countries in 2004 came from Poland. Immigrants from countries such as Portugal and Lithuania arrived in increasing numbers as well. In 2007 alone, the number of Polish immigrants in Iceland rose from 3,629 to 5,627, of which 73 percent were men. Several massive construction projects, including a large power plant and an aluminum smelter, explain the prolific increase of male immigrants in 2006, 2007, and 2008 (Skaptadóttir 2011). In 2007, at the height of the Icelandic economic expansion, the Directorate of Labor reported that 9 percent of the Icelandic work force was composed of foreign citizens. In 2007 and 2008, 36 percent of all foreign workers were employed in the construction industry (Sigurðsson and Arnarson 2011). Most people who moved to Iceland at this time were twenty-five to thirty years old. That meant that, in 2010, 15 percent of the Icelandic population in this age range was foreign-born. The escalating economy also created jobs in services, and thus many of the immigrant women became visible in service jobs (Skaptadóttir 2011).

During this period unemployment was almost nonexistent among immigrants who came to Iceland for work (Skaptadóttir 2010b; Wojtyńska 2011). However, migration was not driven solely by unemployment in the country of origin; a survey from 2009 shows that the majority of immigrants were employed in their country before moving to Iceland (Jónsdóttir, Harðardóttir, and Garðarsdóttir 2009). My interviews with immigrants in recent years show that the higher wages, due to the very high value of the Icelandic currency at the time, was an important factor in the decision to migrate. For example, Poles could multiply their salaries by working temporarily in Iceland. Many of them were sending money to their parents or children, and some were saving for a house back home. The difference is even higher for Filipinos, who in some cases could multiply their salaries by taking on even low-wage employment in Iceland. Unlike the Poles, people from the Philippines are more likely to define their stay as long-term and plan accordingly but continue to place great emphasis on sending remittances to relatives, such as elderly parents, children, siblings, and in some cases nephews and nieces (Skaptadóttir 2010b). As citizens of the new EU member states have received higher priority in the labor market in recent years, people from the Philippines increasingly indicate uniting with family as a reason for migrating to Iceland.

Many of those who first arrived in Iceland and started working in fisheries and later in the service, caregiving, and construction sectors saw their stay as temporary. Since there was a demand for labor and it was relatively easy to get work for relatives and friends, many of them extended their stay (Skaptadóttir and Wojtyńska 2008b).

FOREIGN WORKERS FEEL THE CRASH

The economic collapse in Iceland affected immigrants adversely in many ways. Unemployment in the Icelandic construction sector rose dramatically, causing unprecedented unemployment among male immigrants and making them the majority in the aftermath of the collapse. Immigrants, primarily women, working in service-sector jobs suffered the least, but they nevertheless faced reorganization and the threat of layoffs. In 2010 the immigrant unemployment rate was 14.5 percent, twice as high as that of Icelandic citizens (Sigurðsson and Arnarson 2011). Approximately 90 percent of unemployed immigrants came from Europe, with 60 percent of those from Poland (Sigurgeirsdóttir 2011; Skaptadóttir 2010a).

While unemployment among Icelanders decreased in 2009–2010, unemployment among foreign residents increased. There is no single explanation for the continuing higher rate of unemployment among immigrants. However, there are a number of factors that normally influence a person's chances of getting a job, such as nationality, interpersonal skills, and length of time in the country (Wojtyńska 2011, 47–48; Tilly 2011, 685). Immigrants' chances of getting a job in Iceland were already limited since their work experience was generally not recognized in Icelandic society. Immigrants also tend to receive inadequate information about available jobs and employers' requirements for jobs. Before the crisis, not knowing Icelandic did not keep immigrants from securing at least low-wage jobs. However, that lack of knowledge is also the main obstacle in acquiring a job at a time of high unemployment; thus recent immigrants are the first to lose their jobs during a recession.

Although migration is a fairly new experience for Iceland, immigrants have commonly been discussed in terms of "foreign labor power" (*vinnuafl*) that is expected to leave in times of employment shortages. The media headlines immediately following the bank crash in 2008 depicted a mass exodus of both foreigners and Icelanders without work (Garðarsdóttir and Bjarnason 2010). Emigration from Iceland has in fact increased since the crisis, although not as much as expected. After the collapse some immigrants chose to return home, and the ratio of immigrants in Iceland declined. At its height in 2009 at 7.6 percent, the foreign population dropped to 6.6 percent in 2012 (Statistics Iceland 2012).

These figures indicate that despite the escalation in the unemployment rate among foreign residents, there has not been a significant decline in the immigrant population. More foreign men (mostly European) than women have left, which may be explained by the fact that they arrived more recently, just before the economic meltdown, so were less settled than the women. Given the global nature of the current economic crisis, many foreigners may remain in Iceland because they do not have a job back home. Unemployment is on the rise in eastern Europe and in the Baltic countries, which have been experiencing severe a economic crisis since 2008 (Masso and Krillo 2011). The global socioeconomic situation is likely to be relevant since the positive net migration among women to Iceland in 2010 was mainly from the Baltic countries.

Despite persistent unemployment in Iceland, there are certain jobs that Icelandic women and men are shunning, and openings in fish processing and caregiving work still remain. Hence, foreigners have continued to move to Iceland after the economic crisis, albeit in much lower numbers (Garðarsdóttir and Bjarnason 2010; Júlíusdóttir, Skaptadóttir, and Karlsdóttir 2013).

NEW OBSTACLES TO EMPLOYMENT

Immigrants mostly came to work in formal employment; therefore they have been members of unions since they began working in Iceland. The employers, based on an agreement with the labor unions, pay a certain percentage to the unemployment fund on behalf of each unionized worker. Like their Icelandic counterparts, these workers are entitled to unemployment benefits. In most cases, these benefits pay more than many of the recent migrants would receive for employment in their countries. Poles and other Europeans can take their unemployment with them back to their country of origin but will then receive the given unemployment benefit in that country, which is much lower than in Iceland. The payment of unemployment benefits is in the hands of the Directorate of Labour.

Those who are not unionized and who are seeking work need to apply to the municipality where they live for assistance. Although job seekers are offered various free courses to aid in finding work, the courses are in Icelandic and are therefore inaccessible to many foreigners. Prior to the financial crisis, foreign workers were usually not required to have any knowledge of Icelandic; newspaper advertisements for available jobs could often be found in Polish. The construction industry often hired large groups of workers who spoke neither Icelandic nor English and provided them with a translator. Since the crash, this trend has shifted and employers now often expect immigrants to master Icelandic if they are to employ them (Wojtyńska 2011).

A recent study among unemployed immigrants (Wojtyńska, Skaptadóttir, and Ólafs 2011) shows that only 14 percent of respondents considered themselves fluent in Icelandic. Hence, the unemployed are directed to Icelandic language courses by the Directorate of Labour with the goal of making them more employable. People can take other courses, but over 90 percent of participants in the aforementioned study had enrolled only in courses suggested to them by the Directorate of Labour. In open answers in the survey, many participants said they would like to take courses in driving special vehicles or in operating machines, computer design or programming, and in languages other than Icelandic. The same study showed that 63 percent of the unemployed want to stay in Iceland and 87 percent were actively searching for work, primarily in Iceland. However, the survey also showed that three-quarters thought it would be very difficult or rather difficult to get a job in Iceland, and 71 percent named lack of fluency in Icelandic as a reason. Furthermore, 62 percent answered that employers were not eager to hire foreigners. The great majority, or 72 percent, agreed with the statement "Since the onset of the financial crisis, Icelandic employers prefer to hire Icelanders rather than foreigners" (ibid.).

It is evident from interviews with immigrants, language teachers, and various service providers that since the crisis there has been an increased emphasis on knowledge of Icelandic as a job requirement. Some immigrants complained in the interviews that they could no longer get the kind of job they had when they first came to Iceland, such as in cleaning or food production, because they do not speak the language well enough. Almost all advertisements for jobs are in Icelandic, and many specify Icelandic as a requirement, although there are a few recent exceptions where advertisements have been in Polish. Representatives from trade unions and state and municipality offices further indicated that immigrants commonly sought assistance because they were unable to understand the information sent to them, which was usually in Icelandic.

OBLIGATIONS

Immigrants have been affected not only by unemployment. Like Icelanders, many of them had taken out loans for cars and housing, and their ability to pay was damaged by higher interest rates, inflation, and depreciation of the Icelandic currency, which led to a devaluation of their salary in terms of remittances. The majority of Poles are supporting their partners, elderly parents, and children in Poland. Filipinos have hospital bills, expensive medication, and college education to pay for their children or younger siblings. In many cases, immigrants from both Poland and the Philippines have invested in housing at home. Thus, it was difficult for them to cut their remittances, since the people depending on them tended to be ones with whom they had emotional ties. In some cases, as with the Filipinos, the roles had been reversed. Parents, uncles, or aunts now receiving the remittances had previously supported those now bearing the responsibility of remittance flows. Hence, people felt obliged to continue to send money despite decreasing wages or unemployment benefits.

It was inevitable that they would have a hard time making ends meet given the rising living costs in Iceland.

This may be one factor that explains why unemployed immigrants seek aid from charities that distribute food and cheap clothing. Representatives from the two main charity organizations expressed their concern during interviews about the growing number of foreigners seeking assistance after the crisis. A 2010 study showed that one-third of those seeking help from charities had foreign citizenship, the majority of them unemployed Poles (Dofradóttir and Jónsdóttir 2010). Most of the Poles participating in this study had lower incomes but more education than the Icelanders and other foreigners receiving aid. Unlike the Icelandic participants, they lived in rented housing, which was not subsidized. In the same study, some Icelanders expressed concern that they were receiving less food because foreigners were getting assistance. Poles felt that they were subjected to prejudice and suspected that Icelanders had access to better food bags. Charity representatives told us in a 2011 interview that in response to the growing demand, they had decided that foreign men would be entitled to monthly food rations only, whereas others could receive it weekly. Their argument was that single men, who might be sharing a house, could survive on unemployment benefits and could get warm meals elsewhere. The women we interviewed showed more concern for helping women than men, even though they were aware of higher unemployment among men (Wojtyńska, Skaptadóttir, and Ólafs 2011).

CHANGING VIEWS TOWARD IMMIGRANT ISSUES

Tilly (2011) points out that public opinion in Western Europe seems to have turned against immigrants during the financial crisis. It is difficult to ascertain whether this is the case in Iceland because of a lack of pre- and post-crisis studies of the general view of immigrants in Iceland. However, the survey I conducted during the summer of 2012 on the views toward immigrants showed that the majority of respondents were positive toward immigrants coming to work in Iceland. But those making the lowest wages were most likely to agree with the following statement: "Icelanders should have more right to work than immigrants when there are few jobs available." The same survey showed a difference in views based on education, with 39 percent of people who had finished compulsory education agreeing that it was very good or rather good for the Icelandic economy to have immigrants move to Iceland. However, 83 percent of those with a postgraduate degree agreed. People in urban areas are also more positive than those in rural areas.

There is evidence that interest in immigrant issues has diminished and that the state has been unable to adequately fund agencies and organizations that work directly with immigrants to address their specific circumstances. Immigrants, like other groups, have had to bear the consequences of the pervasive cuts to public institutions. Yet some budget reductions hit immigrants disproportionately, such as funding for Icelandic courses and savings on translation and interpretation for immigrants. Many schools have also reduced their services for immigrant children.

The decreasing interest in immigrant issues is clear in the media. There has been a general reduction of local newspapers in Iceland, and immigrant issues are generally covered less. At the same time, similar to many European countries, immigrant issues are increasingly being depicted in relation to crime (Wojtyńska, Skaptadóttir, and Ólafs 2011), thus reinforcing the stereotypes of immigrants as threatening and Eastern European men as connected to organized crime, rape, and violence. The only newspaper covering news in Polish has since ended this service, thus diminishing the possibility for those not fluent in Icelandic to follow political, social, or cultural events in Iceland (Wojtyńska and Zielińska 2010).

A changing nationalist discourse may also affect immigrants and their inclusion in society. During the economic boom, the nationalist discourse of Icelanders as "the best in the world" was outward-looking (Loftsdóttir 2009). However, since the meltdown, the nationalism has become more inward-looking, with a focus on the common history of Icelanders. This affects the way native Icelanders view foreign workers, who cannot easily claim to be a part of the old traditions, such as knitting Icelandic designs and cooking traditional "national" food, practices that have become more important during the crisis. Thus, the current nationalist discourse is more exclusive.

Immigrants talk to me about experiencing more negative attitudes after the recession set in. However, prejudice toward foreigners did not begin with the crisis. In 2006, when immigrants were becoming more visible, moving from closed-off factories into services, working in shops or restaurants, or driving buses, the media were already publishing negative perspectives. Yet when asked about the effects of the crisis, some immigrants say they have experienced a change of attitude toward them. Many, including those who are settled with families, said they had been asked after the crisis when they would be leaving. Wojtyńska and Zielińska (2010) explain how the majority of Poles they interviewed said they had a positive experience of Icelanders, but recently some had noticed a shift toward a more unwelcoming attitude and claimed that Icelandic employers preferred native workers.

Similar concerns came up in my interviews with people from the Philippines. One man, for example, said, "They blame us for the crisis. They do not understand that we have contributed to the economic well-being of this country and that we have been paying our taxes, and they do not understand that we have to send money to our families. It is very difficult to turn back and no longer be able to help our families who depend on us." A woman from the Philippines, who had been working for five years in caregiving work, claimed that, after losing her job in 2009, she is unable to find work again only because she is Asian.

CONCLUSION

A great number of people moved to Iceland during the economic boom to work in low-income jobs that Icelanders no longer wanted. Salaries were low, but with overtime and the increasing value of the Icelandic krona, they could earn much higher wages than in their country of origin. Many also came to be with relatives in Iceland.

The working conditions of foreigners have worsened since the crisis. There is higher unemployment, reduced working hours, and lower salaries. Knowing Icelandic is increasingly a precondition for getting a job. So although unemployment is dropping, it remains high for immigrants. The government's main method to address unemployment among immigrants is to offer courses in Icelandic. Many Poles feel disillusioned and cheated by the banks, politicians, and the media after the crisis (Wojtyńska and Zielińska 2010). Thus, in many ways, the experiences of immigrants are similar to those of Icelanders, but their weak position in the labor market makes their situation much worse. Although unemployment benefits are better in Iceland and their situation in many cases is better than at home, many experience discrimination and exclusion from the labor market.

NOTE

1. My discussion is primarily based on the following studies: "The Construction of Diversity in a Global Context. Immigrants in Iceland: Opportunities and Obstacles" (2002–2006), funded by the Research Fund of the University of Iceland and RANNIS, the Icelandic Center for Research; "Transnational Ties and Participation in Icelandic Society. Women and Men from the Philippines in Iceland" (2008–2012), funded by the Icelandic Center for Research, the University of Iceland Research Fund, and Þróunarsjóður innflytjendamála; and "The Participation of Immigrants in

Civil Society and Labour Market in the Economic Recession" (see Wojtyńska, Skaptadóttir, and Ólafs 2011), which is part of a larger project, "The Path to Equality: Promoting Diversity and Breaking Down Stereotypes in Iceland," financed by the European Commission's PROGRESS program "For Diversity / Against Discrimination."

15

Icelandic Language
Schools after the Crash

Pamela Joan Innes is a linguistic anthropologist and author of Beginning Creek: A Basic Introduction to the Language and Culture of the Muskogee (Creek) and Seminole Indians. *Here she describes the struggles of Icelandic language schools after the crash and their efforts to live up to the general public's and Parliament's expectations while juggling legislative mandate, tight budgets, and limited class time.*

• • • • • • • • • • • • • • • • • • • •

As several of the other chapters in this volume demonstrate, the crash of 2008 affected many areas of Icelandic life outside of the economic sector. Cutting financial support for programs and institutions working with immigrants was one realm where the government could institute change immediately with little worry of public outcry, partly because people had voiced concerns since the mid-1990s about rising immigrant population numbers and their effect on Icelandic society. Schools teaching Icelandic to foreigners were among the programs facing cutbacks and limitations.

One of the desired outcomes of language schools is helping foreign workers to develop sufficient fluency in Icelandic to find gainful employment. They are also, for some students, a means of satisfying requirements necessary to receive unemployment benefits from the state. They appear to some in the Icelandic public to be akin to the charitable organization described by Rice (this volume) because they can be considered as

DOI: 10.5876/9781607323358.c015

providing services to individuals who should be actively seeking work, not taking courses.

The schools also are a locus for discussions about Iceland's position vis-à-vis the European Union and the United States, particularly concerning Iceland's ability to support an immigrant population and whether the nation has an obligation to recognize and integrate this group (see also Loftsdóttir's and Skaptadóttir's chapters, this volume). And exploring how Icelandic language schools have weathered the storm provides a comparison with the study by Guðbjörnsdóttir and Davíðsdóttir (this volume).

Classes teaching Icelandic to foreigners also raise issues that have long been topics of public discourse, including language purity, control and evaluation, and the position of Icelandic language as a marker of Icelandic identity (Corgan 2004; Hálfdanarson 2003; Skaptadóttir 2008). People frequently raised these issues in interviews and conversations. As a nexus point where immigration, integrative services, and identity-changing practices come together, discussants found it natural to speak about these issues while talking about the schools. Interview and conversational data focusing on language schools thus provide other pathways through which we may gauge the influence of the economic crash on Icelanders' perspectives on a range of social, cultural, and linguistic topics.

A BRIEF HISTORY OF ICELANDIC LANGUAGE TEACHING

The Icelandic language has long been an area of interest for linguists concerned with the evolution of the Scandinavian languages. An extensive collection of early manuscripts written in Icelandic makes knowledge of early Icelandic a useful skill for those interested in medieval studies. Universities within and outside of Iceland have offered courses in early Icelandic for many years, and a range of textbooks has been developed since the early twentieth century. However, there had not been a great call for schools presenting colloquial Icelandic to learners outside of academia until the mid-1980s. At that time, the numbers of foreigners in Iceland had increased enough that individuals began to offer informal conversational courses in their homes (interview with Ingibjörg Hafstað, January 18, 2012). These classes varied in content and length, and the courses were not assessed.

In the mid- to late 1990s, as the numbers of immigrant workers rose, employers began to offer language classes. According to two instructors, these classes most often focused on work-related vocabulary and making communication between managers and line workers easier. The instructors noted that the teachers were not always required to have received language instruction training and that the quality of instruction was variable. Again, instruction assessment mechanisms were not in place.

By the early 2000s, the number of foreign workers in Iceland had reached a level where a need for organized, stable language-teaching institutions was evident. Schools devoted to teaching colloquial Icelandic were established. There was no governmental oversight yet, but its attention began to turn to the language skills of immigrants, particularly those seeking permanent residence and citizenship. Icelandic immigration policy began to push foreigners to language schools with a new requirement of 150 hours of language courses to receive a permanent residence visa. This requirement came into play at about the same time as the citizenship law was changed to institute a language test.

The Icelandic Parliament (Alþingi) passed Law 81 in 2007, amending an earlier version of the citizenship act dating from 1952. In these amendments, the Alþingi determined that "What matters most, and what is going to change in practice, is the requirement that applicants should in the main have shown some skill in Icelandic" (Alþingi 2007, 5, paragraph 1). The existing facilities were not adequate to allow foreign applicants for citizenship to reach this goal, so the Alþingi allowed two years, which spanned the economic crash, during which schools were to be well funded, curricular standards developed, and the language test for citizenship created. While funding for schools decreased after the crash, the other two portions of the plan were achieved. But the meltdown affected the ways in which schools responded to the curricular norms and the language test.

GOVERNMENT ACTION

Language had never before been part of the evaluation process for citizenship. With rising numbers of foreign nationals applying for citizenship, from 288 in 1996 to 774 as of October 23, 2006 (Alþingi 2007, 13), the Alþingi increased the requirements with a language test. Instituting this test required the development of a new testing instrument as well as guidelines for language classes. Those taking the language test are not required to take any courses, but they are strongly encouraged to do so. The Alþingi laid the responsibility for overseeing the testing and creating a comprehensive language curriculum on the shoulders of the Ministry of the Interior.

The Ministry of the Interior accomplished both of its responsibilities before the crash occurred. A testing center developed and administered the language test. Although the statisticians and psychometricians at the testing center consulted with language teachers and specialists and were aware of the work being done by the Ministry of Education, Science, and Culture (MESC) to formulate the school curriculum, they ultimately developed a test structure that does not satisfy many specialists.

By 2008 testing was underway. From the outset, applicants were required to pay a fee, which an employee at the testing center said covered the costs for the center. However, the test is administered only when enough employees from the center can monitor the test session, a restriction that may cause a slight decrease in test offerings if overtime pay and staff shortages restrict employee availability for weekend tests. No employee shortages were reported to have occurred after the crash, but the person with whom I spoke hinted that limits on overtime were becoming a problem.

The numbers and curricular strength of language classes targeting foreign learners was a prime area of concern for the Alþingi as Act 81 of 2007 was debated. During the debate, it became clear that the number of credible schools teaching foreigners was too low. Along with increasing support for such schools, the Alþingi determined that there was a need to establish course content standards. The Ministry of the Interior called upon the MESC to develop a curriculum to which all institutions advertising language classes would be held.

A committee created the curriculum, published by the MESC in 2008. The document presents content areas and assessment points for four levels of Icelandic language courses. Students completing the course outlined in the document earn 240 hours of credit and should be able to demonstrate ability in Icelandic equivalent to the lowest levels (A1 to A2) of the Common European Framework for the Reference of Languages, a framework developed to standardize language assessment among the forty-seven member countries of the Council of Europe (Menntamálaráðuneyti 2008, 4; Council of Europe 2001, 1–4). Classes must cover items such as health and illness, job and school activities, clothing, food, and other common household terms and the activities within these domains. The curriculum is intended to give all students a grounding in commonly used vocabulary, phrases, and interactive routines, providing them with both grammatical competence (Chomsky 1969, 4) and communicative competence (Hymes 1971) so as to prepare them to use and comprehend Icelandic in a wide range of situations.

The curriculum has guided the content and organization of several language textbooks, with all following the order of topics and grammatical forms presented in the curriculum (e.g., Arnbjörnsdóttir et al. 2003; Jónsdóttir and

Halldórsdóttir 2011; Einarsdóttir et al. 2009). In schools students are placed into language courses based on their existing level of knowledge assessed against the four language skill levels presented in the curricular document. The content covered in classes is identical to that specified in the curriculum. Schools and textbook writers attend to the requirements imposed by the MESC document.

IN THE CLASSROOM

It is within the schools themselves that one finds the greatest evidence that the economic crash has affected the way Icelandic is taught. Schools are dependent, in part, on government support since student fees do not cover all costs. Also, given that language schools are places of contact for students and teachers from very different backgrounds, schools can become sites of friction, contestation, agreement, and empowerment, as Freire (1993) and hooks (1994) argue is true for public schools where minority students are subject to a system created and governed by the majority. Teachers and school administrators have had to react to the stresses on students and colleagues over the course of the economic meltdown in ways that have influenced what is covered in classes and how.

Conversations with those who work at language schools make evident the powerful effects of the economic crisis, often in very personal ways. One thing these conversations revealed, but which will not be discussed in great detail here, is that school employees are concerned about their job security. When discussing their use of alternative pedagogical methods, seven of the nine teachers interviewed said that they were anxious that releasing this information could jeopardize their employment. Three of the five school administrators interviewed also expressed concern about continuing support from the government to keep their school open and wanted assurance that their opinions would not be traceable to their school. They explained that their school budgets are so reliant on government funding that any decrease affects some aspect of the operation, even causing layoffs. Therefore, all school employees' identities are anonymous.

When students enter the language schools, the first requirement is to place them into the appropriate course level. This is achieved primarily through conversation with the student, during which a staff member determines the student's command of grammar and lexical forms. Placement is an inexact science, though this is not often a problem since students are allowed to move either up or down in level during the first week or two of classes. However, it does appear that there are times when staff place students in particular classes to keep one teacher's load fairly equivalent to the others'.

Three teachers in one language school and one from another school spoke to the issue of student placement. One suggested that students are placed not according to their skill level but according to what administrators think will make a student happiest and most comfortable. The teacher said that she had students in a second-level course who did not know the skills and vocabulary from the first level. She felt compelled to do extra work to bring these students up to where they could participate, rather than asking that they be moved. The primary reason, she said, was to encourage those receiving unemployment benefits to keep attending. She was concerned that these students, who were doing what the system required, would get discouraged and then assume the negative characteristics she feels most Icelanders assign to immigrants, especially those from Eastern European countries (a view supported in Robert [2008] and Ólafs and Zielińska [2010]).

This teacher, and the three others who experienced ill-prepared students, said the second important reason was to maintain student numbers. One foresaw that if student numbers decreased at the schools for any reason, including discontent at being held back, government support and tuition would decrease enough to cause layoffs. School administrators provide enrollment figures as part of their requests for government support, and one administrator agreed with the teachers' belief.

The placement procedures in all three of the largest language schools have been directly affected by the economic crash. The crash and resulting fiscal conservation have kept the schools from developing and implementing more robust placement mechanisms. One administrator admitted that she had weighed the costs of creating and instituting a regularized placement test but could not justify the expense in the current economic environment. She thought that better placement of students would increase the morale of her teaching staff and would lead to greater satisfaction among students, but there simply was not enough money in her budget for such a project. She also thought that students would walk away if they believed the placement test results placed them in low-level classes. She acknowledged that student enrollment numbers are so critical that instituting a stricter placement policy would not be in the school's best interest if it led to a decrease in the student population. Economic considerations thus work directly against the adoption of mechanisms to put students in the classes for which they are best prepared and are affecting the overall teaching effectiveness in the schools.

Class content and topic coverage in each class is also affected by the economy. The curriculum developed by the MESC presents a range of pedagogic topics and discursive forms that students must master. Commonly used textbooks follow these guidelines, though each takes a slightly different approach. Individual teachers are aware of the topics they are to cover, but all mentioned that they paid particular attention to those they believed would help their students the most in their work and home life. The topics chosen by the teachers did not always correspond to those identified by the curriculum committee.

For instance, the second-level textbooks include sections about calling in sick to work and asking coworkers to take one's shift because of illness or previous commitments. One teacher was observed covering both topics, but very quickly. She mentioned to her students that she thought very few of them would ever feel so secure in their job that they would hazard using these phrases. She added that knowledge of these phrases would help them respond appropriately when a coworker asked them to cover a shift, as if the students would ever be only receivers of the requests. Students agreed with their teacher that they would not make the requests of others. One of the students mentioned that his friend lost his job because he had asked for time off because of illness. This student vowed he would never give his employer the same reason for firing him.

In the same class, the teacher told students where car-related vocabulary and phrases were located in the textbook and asked whether any students required such information. The students almost unanimously replied in the negative, with two women saying that they were in no position to afford a car. Indeed, as part of an in-class exercise, students were asked to describe how they got to school and other places. All but one student said they took the bus or walked. When the single student mentioned that he drove to school, he felt compelled to add that he needed a car to take his daughter and wife to school and work. Two of his peers nodded and said that having a family made owning a car understandable. The student then responded that his family used the bus system very frequently but that the car was necessary at times. He also mentioned that he often loaned his car to friends and provided a small carpool service for coworkers from his neighborhood. The teacher closed the discussion by pointing out how few of the students needed to know car terminology, merely directing them to the pages where they could find it.

Undoubtedly, the situation is different for those outside of Reykjavík, but students in all classes within the city reported that they relied heavily on public transportation and did not have the resources for a personal vehicle.

Both teachers and students identified the post-crash economic situation as the reason for students' lack of car ownership. Two students who had formerly been employed as auto mechanics blamed the economic crash for the loss of their jobs and their cars. Nearly all of the students in the classes in Reykjavík and the surrounding suburbs agreed with their teachers that most students were not going to use such terminology because they could not afford their own cars.

One last content area directly affected by the economic crash involved review of the daily newspapers. In all but two of the observed second- and third-level classes, teachers incorporated some amount of reading and conversation about the daily Icelandic-language newspapers, including the help wanted advertisements. The variation in the advertisements concerning the applicant's training or certification, Icelandic language skills, and willingness to work a variety of shifts allowed teachers to address a number of grammatical and lexical issues. Each teacher asked students whether they considered themselves appropriate applicants and talked with students about skill development and ways to phrase application letters to present their qualifications for positions. None of the teachers said they had used this exercise before the crash but incorporated it to help their students with job-seeking skills after learning that most of them were under- or unemployed. Teachers noted that these exercises increased students' reading abilities and, in two cases, had led students to get jobs. The two teachers whose students got jobs were extremely proud of their role and expressed the wish that it would happen more often.

The lack of in-service or continuing education is another area that teachers believe the economic situation has affected. One administrator corroborated this belief. None of the teachers said that their schools sponsored occasions for teachers to collaborate on teaching methods or deal with concerns in their classrooms. Three of the teachers admitted that they occasionally felt overwhelmed by the demands of their students, particularly those not up to course level, but believed their schools had no resources to promote communication among teachers about such issues. One teacher said she thought schools did not offer in-service days because the government would perceive that the teachers were ill prepared or unqualified. She thought this could lead to decreased funding of her school if government officials began to doubt the efficacy of the school's teaching. She also pointed out that teachers occasionally work for more than one school and may switch from school to school. If administrators at other schools began to doubt the teachers' preparation and skills, individual teachers might lose their jobs or ability to change employers.

The school administrator who spoke about in-service opportunities for teachers said that her school did not have funds available for such activities. Schools would have to pay speakers and moderators honoraria, and teachers would be owed salary for attending such events. The administrator noted that there would probably be requests for multiple presenters on such days and, quite frankly, she did not believe her school's budget would be able to accommodate such an expense. She also thought there was little reason to provide such gatherings because she regarded her teachers as quite gifted and well prepared to teach. Of the three teachers who expressed desire for communal gatherings at which they could discuss methodological issues, two were employed by this administrator.

Comments and observations by teachers and school administrators demonstrate that the economic downturn has had significant effects on morale, decision making, and development. Teachers respond to their students' concerns and desires, all of which are influenced by the state of their finances and employment prospects. Teachers themselves are concerned for the fiscal well-being of their schools and consciously consider their classroom conduct in light of what it means for student retention and their own job security. Administrators are aware of changes that could increase student satisfaction and heighten teacher morale but feel unable to initiate such changes due to tight budgets.

OUTSIDERS' PERSPECTIVES

Finally, one must consider the opinions of members of the general public who have little or nothing to do with the schools. When the author first introduced herself to Icelanders, invariably they would ask questions about what brought her to Iceland and about language schools for foreigners. While I did not record these conversations, I took notes about the opinions I heard and am drawing from that record for this section.

A frequent topic of conversation was whether language schools are necessary and whether they benefit Icelandic society. In all of the notes taken after informal social interactions, a great majority (twenty-seven of thirty-five) contain references to comments that immigrants and long-term foreign visitors should learn Icelandic. These were in line with a policy document published by the Ministry of Social Affairs (2007, 2), which states that "knowledge of the Icelandic language is the key to Icelandic society and can be a deciding factor in the successful integration of immigrants into Icelandic society."

Several members of the Icelandic public said that learning Icelandic was necessary for immigrants to be able to work within society. Comments along this line were often followed by musings about whether the Icelandic state should fund language schools or offer opportunities for education. For most conversationalists, responsibility for language learning fell almost equally on the shoulders of the learners ("They [foreigners] ought to use Icelandic whenever they are in public; they should learn it by speaking with us [Icelanders]") and on the state ("We have to offer school programs for foreigners; the language is too difficult for anyone to learn without a teacher"). The effects of the economic downturn arose when I asked people whether they thought the state was able to provide enough language classes. The majority commented that the financial responsibilities of the state should be directed first to Icelandic citizens and only secondarily to foreigners. The commonly shared perception was that economic resources were too thin to allow Iceland to support enough courses for foreigners who actively sought out language and culture classes and were definitely too thin to support classes for those not seeking them.

There was a shared sentiment that immigrants should know they were expected to contribute to society, not simply to draw benefits from social welfare programs. Interlocutors described schools as places teaching about Icelandic cultural expectations and behaviors. When Icelanders spoke with me about what the schools should present, they frequently mentioned the themes of social cohesion, responsibility and obligations to self and community, endurance, and survival against great odds through personal and communal hard work. The underlying assumption was that foreigners would not share these sensibilities and that the schools were one place where they could learn about such expectations. One speaker noted that immigrants could get the same information from newspapers, the sagas, and interactions with Icelanders, but he thought that language differences made such information unavailable to most. When asked whether translations of the written media presented the Icelandic behavioral ideals, he admitted that they did but said that he was unsure that immigrants from Poland and Southeast Asian countries had access to materials translated into their languages. He was only aware of good translations into English. Therefore, he said, the schools offer the best means of educating foreigners about Icelanders' expectations for behavior and integration.

The schools, then, are to make foreigners realize that they are to contribute to the state by becoming gainfully employed, contributing to local organizations by donating time or money, and seeking to meet their needs without assistance from welfare organizations or the state. In doing this, the schools create people who do not draw from but, instead, contribute to the pool of resources available to Icelanders. Several discussed this in purely economic terms, saying that the schools should change foreigners' habits of draining Iceland's social welfare system. These speakers felt that the social welfare system was first and foremost for Icelandic citizens, especially following the crash. They felt it was inappropriate to help foreigners until the needs of Icelanders had been met.

There was a minority who did not speak in these terms. About one-third of my notes record conversations in which the schools were portrayed as dealing with people behind Icelanders in terms of opportunities and employment. For these speakers, the schools were places of refuge where foreigners could learn how to better fit in and access information about their rights. Several stated that the poor fiscal state of immigrants' native countries drove them to Iceland to seek work, but then they too felt the effects of the financial crash. To these speakers, this left foreigners with few channels offering moral and social support. The language schools, along with charities, emerged as sites that offered assistance to those most often overlooked by state social welfare offices. Those who took this position never considered whether the schools suffered any strain in the midst of providing for the needs of foreigners, so they did not consider how the schools provided such support, who funded it, or whether it was in jeopardy because of the budget crunch. They simply took it for granted that the schools could and should provide support for foreigners.

Members of the Icelandic public spoke about the schools' role in integrating foreigners into Icelandic society, which was always connected to employment. Difficulties in finding a job after the crash were rarely acknowledged. More often foreigners were described as unaware of Icelanders' ideas of appropriate behavior and schools were accorded respect for relaying such information to foreigners. However, some criticized schools for providing unemployed foreigners with a means to continue their unemployment benefits. Some thought that foreigners were excused from looking for work while attending school and drawing benefits, which is not true.

Discussions about language schools caused people to confront their opinions about foreigners and their families, their positions on the role of the state in assisting people through troubled times, and what characteristics distinguish Icelanders from others. Icelandic language schools emerged as places where conflicting ideas and opinions converge, with people's opinions informed by economic considerations colored directly by the crash.

CONCLUSIONS

Dedicated and competent teachers are managing to teach Icelandic to foreigners, despite the downturn. Students continue to enroll, finding the schools useful and productive, whether they do or do not have a job at the time. Government assessments of the schools remain positive, and financial support continues to flow. And the general public appears to think rather highly of the schools' abilities to teach foreigners about Icelandic language and society. Thus, language schools appear to have weathered the economic storm unscathed. A closer inspection tells a different story.

Schools rely on a number of funding sources, including student fees, state monies, and grants. The availability and amount of money from these sources has decreased with the downturn. The uncertainty administrators and teachers feel is reflected in the choices they make about which curricular areas to cover, whether and how teachers are expected to hone their skills, and the ways in which students are assigned to classes. These decisions affect a wide range of constituencies, including the administrators, teachers, and students at the various schools, government officials, and members of the public who reach conclusions about the worth of schools based on interactions they have with students and media reports about immigrant communities. Decisions about what can and should be taught depend upon available resources and teachers' readings of their students' financial state, proving that the economic crash has far-reaching and wide-ranging effects on the schools.

Administrators are extremely cost-conscious and express concern about institutional revenues. Teacher training sessions and school-sponsored instructional seminars are impossible at the present time according to administrators, though they admitted that these would enhance instruction and might raise teacher morale and comfort if discussions among teachers dealt with various ways to ameliorate problems in the classroom. Administrators encourage teachers to discuss such issues among themselves and develop supportive relationships with each other, but no school administrator considered his or her budget large enough to fund a school-wide gathering or in-service day.

These decisions, all influenced by the perceived need to keep expenses low, affect the quality and level of instruction offered in classes. The four-week term structure limits the amount of time spent on any of the topics specified by the MESC curriculum. This causes many teachers to drop or provide only a minimal introduction to certain of the content areas in the textbooks. Teachers make decisions about what to stress and what to minimize based upon their understandings of student need. When students express that their own financial resources are limited, teachers may choose to rush through subjects not relevant to students without means.

Administrators and teachers are aware of how criticism of the schools might cause some government officials and legislators to decrease their funding.

Government officials saw the necessity for well-funded schools before Law 81 of 2007 was passed, well ahead of the economic crash. The structures put in place to direct curriculum were constructed before the economic downturn affected the opportunities available to foreigners to attend schools and students' needs upon completion of the coursework. This is not to fault the curriculum developed by the MESC, but rather to suggest that the curriculum covers too much material for each school term. So teachers are making strategic cuts independently, classroom by classroom, depending on students' needs and time constraints. When Icelanders encounter foreigners with gaps in their linguistic knowledge, criticism is first leveled at the student, then at the schools. There is anxiety among administrators, teachers, and students that such criticism will convince parliamentarians to cut funding for schools.

As recipients of state funding, the fiscal safety of schools was imperiled almost immediately after the crash, though they have continued to receive support. The student community they serve is subject to critical evaluation by Icelanders, and the critical gaze occasionally shifts to the schools as the places most responsible for acculturation. When Icelanders perceive problems with foreigners, schools may be criticized for not doing an adequate job. This perception relates to larger social concerns about financial stability and employment and does not directly reflect schools' success or failure. Schools and teachers continue to offer high-quality language instruction, despite the downturn, and all involved with the schools voiced optimism that conditions will improve and that schools will thrive.

Research for this chapter was supported by a US–Iceland Fulbright Fellowship from January 2011 to August 2012.

16

Charity in Pre- and Post-Crisis Iceland

James Rice is an assistant professor in anthropology as well as disability studies at the University of Iceland. Here he documents the methods and frequency with which Icelandic charities communicate with the public. He concludes that charities, despite their sometimes radical foundations, continue to reinforce the status quo of socioeconomic inequality, even after being rocked by the monumental financial crisis of 2008.

• • • • • • • • • • • • • • • • • • • •

The economic crisis that consumed that Iceland in the early autumn of 2008 coincided with the conclusion of my dissertation research in Reykjavík. I realized that a research project so focused on inequality as mine, on the role of poverty-related material aid charities, demanded that some data collection continue as this crisis unfolded. Here I analyze the practices and the media production of material aid charities in pre- and post-crisis Iceland. I struggled with using the framework of "crisis," however, since the long-standing poverty and marginalization that charities attempt to address existed long before the crisis of 2008 and will most likely persist long after. Marxist-inspired thinkers have long taken exception to the analysis of economic crises as being anything other than utterly predictable given the very nature of capitalist production. Over twenty years ago, Antonio Negri argued that "crisis is both the mode and the specific function of capital's process of production—and it is totally necessary" (Negri 1988, 67). David Harvey similarly argued

DOI: 10.5876/9781607323358.c016

that regularly occurring crises are to be expected in an economic system based upon what he refers to as "accumulation through dispossession," as are the mechanisms employed in response to crisis (Harvey 2005, 162). The events in Iceland in 2008, as seen through the context of material aid charities over the last decade, could be seen as a crisis in terms of being a deviation from the normal and proper order of things. But, following Negri and Harvey, they could also be viewed as evidence of the continuity of the existing socioeconomic order. The work and media relations of material aid charities in Iceland shifted in certain ways in response to the crisis of 2008; yet they also carried on much as they always have. There is no question that "crisis" in the literal sense could be used to describe the series of events that emerged in Iceland in the latter half of 2008.

But in light of the arguments of scholars such as Negri and Harvey, the only unusual aspect of this crisis was the failure on the part of the regulatory mechanisms to contain it from spreading beyond acceptable levels. When considering material aid charities and the daily situations faced by the clients they serve, the analysis of crisis appears to be much less appropriate and perhaps even a little naive. The charity where I conducted my research, Mæðrastyrksnefnd Reykjavíkur (Mothers' Support Committee of Reykjavík), was actually born of a crisis of sorts in 1928. The committee was formed as the focal point for the conjoined efforts of women's organizations in response to the sinking of the trawler *Jón forseti* out of Reykjavík in February of 1928, which claimed fifteen lives. While the accepted narrative that this organization was brought into existence to support the women widowed as the result of this tragedy, the history—told to me by former and current staff members as well from an unpublished history (Gestsson and Hjartarson 2004)—revealed that many members of these women's groups were previously active in lobbying for women's rights, conducting research, and raising awareness about the lack of social supports in Iceland, particularly for widows, children, and elderly people. While a "crisis" may have been the impetus needed to formalize this charity—the accident at sea is often referred to in the hagiography of Mæðrastyrksnefnd—the analysis of crisis or disaster in relation to such charitable efforts is somewhat misleading: the issues these women were dedicated to addressing were persistent, long-standing, and quite predictable given the socioeconomic conditions in Iceland at the time.

Material aid charities are often placed into the framework of "emergency assistance" (Poppendieck 1998), yet the underlying issues of structural poverty that force people to seek such assistance are usually not adequately analyzed as crises or emergencies in the sense of being unexpected or temporary in duration, particularly among marginalized sectors of the population. This understanding is, however, often not reflected in how contemporary charities speak of themselves. In my experience, staff members, volunteers, and donors commonly referred to "helping those in need" in terms of it being the right thing to do, but they rarely made overt references to the structural factors underlying the clients' situations in a coherent or critical manner. Rather, the clients were spoken of as people of certain quasi-demographic categories who were implicitly or explicitly perceived as being expected to be poor—the normative poor—with charity an expected complement to the formal governmental social welfare infrastructure. However, this stands in direct contrast to the early history of this particular organization, which was quite radical for its time. Mæðrastyrksnefnd did indeed accomplish a great deal on behalf of marginalized women and children from the 1920s to the 1940s through lobbying for legal protection and welfare reform, and later with legal counsel to assist their clients (Rice 2007a, 84–88; see also Hákonardóttir 2000). However, without persistent determination, the radical edge of organizations like Mæðrastyrksnefnd can become blunted over time. Without activism to accompany the necessary material assistance—focusing on structural change rather than the congratulatory celebration of donors and volunteerism—charity becomes little more than a regulatory mechanism in the larger framework that works to preserve the status quo.

The rather haphazard response to poverty typical of contemporary material aid charities is particularly apparent in its seasonal orientation. Similar sentiments of "helping those in need" were echoed in the Icelandic media when heightened attention was paid to charities around the holidays of Christmas and Easter. Concerted efforts were made to gather and redistribute resources during these specific times of the year. Inevitably attention waned until the next holiday season. One key effect of the practices and discursive production of material aid charities, I contend, is the way in which public attention is diverted toward activities that soften the immediate edges of material poverty but do little to foment long-term change. Furthermore, when attention is paid during these delimited times of the year, it is the donors who are the primary focus of this attention and much less the clients—even less so the reasons why this assistance is repeatedly sought throughout the year. It took a crisis of a more prominent scale, such as that of 2008, to redefine the work of charities as organizations dedicated to countering the effects of an exploitative and unequal socioeconomic order. However, from the perspective of post-crisis Iceland this redefinition appears to have been short-lived.

THE "GOOD YEARS": CHARITY IN PRE-CRISIS ICELAND

The Iceland that I encountered in my early fieldwork from 2004 to 2006 struck me as one not marked by deep economic divisions. The common narratives relegated poverty (*fátækt*) to a thing of the past or as something found elsewhere. Even discussions of socioeconomic class appeared to be muted, which some scholars have linked to the notions of Nordic sameness or equality (Niemi 1995; Pálsson 1989) and, in the case of Iceland, even the easy availability of credit (Durrenberger 1996). The underlying empirical data, however, did not support the contentions that Iceland lacked economic inequities. Icelandic sociologists have long pointed out the numerous deficiencies of the Icelandic social welfare system compared with those of the other Nordic nations in terms of social welfare spending as a proportion of Iceland's GDP as well as the relatively meager and restrictive disability and seniors' pensions (Njáls 2003; Ólafsson 1993; 1999; 2005; Ólafsson and Sigurðsson 2000; Traustadóttir et al. 2011). While Iceland's social welfare infrastructure is strong in certain respects, in others Iceland fares poor to middling. The OECD's report *Divided We Stand: Why Inequality Keeps Rising* singles out Iceland and a handful of other nations as negative examples of the effects of public transfers in reducing market-income inequality (OECD 2011b, 38). In terms of public social expenditures, Iceland ranks significantly under OECD averages, somewhere between the Russian Federation and Estonia, in contrast to the other Nordic nations, which all rank above the OECD average (ibid., 61).

Very little of this surprised the staff of Mæðrastyrksnefnd. Early in my research the chair of Mæðrastyrksnefnd held up her hand and ticked off on her fingers the key commonalties she found among the clients, naming in particular low education, low income, and little or no property. However, the staff, in communicating with the public, tended to emphasize the demographic categories of their clients (single mothers, disability pensioners, seniors) but left the commonalities among and between these groups unexplored. But these public media accounts differed strikingly from the conversations I was part of during coffee breaks or while we worked. I noticed that some staff struggled with their preexisting beliefs when they conducted their charitable duties. They mentioned stress and sleeplessness as typical when they first began working at Mæðrastyrksnefnd. Some also struggled with their previously held suspicions about those receiving social assistance, particularly disability pensioners and single mothers—the former in terms of the legitimacy of their claims to being disabled and the latter whether or not they lived unofficially with a partner.

While some staff members of Mæðrastyrksnefnd remained firm in their convictions about the scale of clients who took advantage of programs, the views of individuals and the organization as a whole were still open to debate. Even during my fieldwork I was able to discern some shifts in attitudes and policies that influenced how they described their work and clients in the media. By the time my research concluded, the debate over whether Mæðrastyrksnefnd should openly assist single men without children—given this organization's focus on mothers—had more or less concluded and specific food allotments were set aside for them. Single men with children continued to be welcomed, though I learned this practice was not common as recently as the 1990s. It is not accurate to characterize charities as mired in nineteenth-century responses to poverty; they do evolve in response to changes in the larger society. But they also have a strong tendency to preserve the status quo, first in how they insinuate that socioeconomic inequalities are the result of individual moral or behavioral deficits, and, second, in treating as natural the inequalities among specific, delimited groups without reference to common structural factors among them, much less the structural economic and political arrangements that produce inequalities. In this regard such charities are not best interpreted as antipoverty organizations, since the charity discourse generally amounts to calls for more volunteers and donations rather than for change.

When charities in Iceland discussed their work in the media, they spoke of clients mostly as a decontextualized collection of groups of people, what I sarcastically referred to as the holy trinity of "single mothers, disability pensioners, and senior citizens" (*einstæðar mæður, öryrkjar, og eldri borgarar*). Sometimes this included the unemployed and, later, single men. My reference to the "holy trinity" contained a theological connotation that is not accidental. These descriptors (Wagner 2000) of charity clientele serve a dual function, one of which is a discursive tactic in lobbying for support, as charities cannot function without donations and volunteers. This tactic involves referring to categories that are expected to resonate positively with the general public and potential donors. This was truer in Iceland of elderly people than disability pensioners, who remain a somewhat stigmatized group (Traustadóttir et al. 2011). But there is no question that the image of an impoverished senior citizen or a young mother with a child would pull on the heartstrings of donors more than a middle-aged male substance abuser, people with mental health issues, or, to an extent, immigrants. The former prime minister of Iceland, Jóhanna Sigurðardóttir, when in opposition to the sitting government as an MP, was known to invoke such images in her criticism of the government's lack of focus on poverty, as she did in a newspaper editorial from 2002: "The lines at Mæðrastyrksnefnd in reality say everything that needs to be said about poverty in Iceland. For one of the richest nations in the world it is tragic to have to see single mothers with children in their arms waiting in line for food donations" (Sigurðardóttir 2002). The substitution of "single mothers with children on their arms" would simply not work with other demographic categories, something that charities have long known.

The historian Carter Lindberg (1993) notes that in the Judeo-Christian tradition classic categories of the worthy poor, such as widows, orphans, and the sick or lame, were delineated in the Scriptures. The unworthy poor were those who were considered capable of but unwilling to work (Lindberg 1993, 20). Early charity was largely a theological exercise, whereby the poor served as the recipients of alms given by the elites, the giving of which was intended to alleviate the theological dangers associated with the accumulation of wealth. These early charitable practices had nothing to do with altering the socioeconomic order, which was largely perceived to be intended and divinely determined. The historian Robert Jütte (1994) notes that the reasons for the reemerging importance of distinguishing the poor into typologies of degree and causation ranged from the need for labor during periods of depopulation due to famine and disease, to the later need for social order in emerging urban centers and to limit demand on public relief. By the sixteenth century, after a prodigious output of pamphlets, tracts, and decrees dedicated to identifying these subcategories of the poor in an effort to limit begging and demands upon public and charitable relief, "the distinction between the worthy and unworthy poor became a commonplace concept through which contemporaries organized their view of the social order" (Jütte 1994, 12). Iceland did not share this specific historical timeline of mainland European charity, as organized charities of this kind developed in Iceland only in the late nineteenth century. But these categories of the worthy poor appear to have still been a factor in the local politics of charity, welfare, and poverty. My perusal of early newspaper accounts and internal documents from Mæðrastyrksnefnd revealed that prospective aid recipients were often portrayed by their supporters as the unfortunate victims of happenstance, often combined with references to their earlier contributions as "hard workers." These discourses reflected the worthy poor ideology elsewhere and have remained a significant component of charitable discourses through to the present day.

Charity serves to meet a multitude of interests, and therefore it is important to consider broader historical factors as well as issues specific to Iceland, Mæðrastyrksnefnd, and other similar charities in particular. The categorization of the clientele into the typical descriptors of the worthy poor has historical antecedents in terms of theology and disciplinary power as well as strategic importance when soliciting support. The specific emphasis on women is in keeping with Mæðrastyrksnefnd's history. There is also some empirical truth to describing their clients using this set of categories. For example, disability pensioners in the contemporary context made up the bulk of Mæðrastyrksnefnd's clientele, and it would be odd to ignore this factor. But there were also some half-truths and outright distortions contained within charitable public discourses. Senior citizens, for example, figured prominently in the discourse of charities. Yet during my fieldwork senior pensioners never accounted for more than 3 to 4 percent of the overall clientele at Mæðrastyrksnefnd. There were statistically more students and low-income workers who sought assistance from this charity; yet these groups were often downplayed or ignored in media accounts. I interpret the emphasis on seniors, despite their lack of numbers as clients, as linked with the tactics of soliciting for donations. I quickly learned that I could not treat the press releases of charities as scholarly but needed to analyze them as a discourse and focus on their effects rather than be concerned about the truth value of their statements.

My research focused on the firsthand practices of charity as they unfolded around me, both as an observer and direct participant. But for the events during and after the crisis of 2008, I have instead decided to focus more extensively on the discursive production of charity in the media. Charity served as an important focal point through which inequalities and the changing nature of Icelandic society were portrayed, discussed, and interpreted. It is important to consider the impact of this discourse in a historical, cumulative framework rather than as isolated examples of media accounts. Since they began in the late nineteenth century, Mæðrastyrksnefnd and other charities have become part of the normative and somewhat unquestioned urban landscape of Reykjavík—one expects to encounter their work from time to time. When I analyzed six years of reporting on Mæðrastyrksnefnd, I was surprised to see certain patterns emerge and persist; nowhere were these patterns more apparent than the seasonal attention on charity, most notably during the Christmas holiday season.

In the United States the seasonal approach to charity was said to have collapsed in the 1920s as the result of the Great Depression, which required a more "rational" approach to poor support (Waits 1993, 174). It would seem that Iceland is unaware of these developments, as Christmas is, and has always been, the busiest time for charities. One possibility raised in a workshop was that in some countries there is an upsurge in charitable donations at the end of the year as the result of the structure of taxation legislation. However, this would not apply in Iceland. Staff insisted that they do not issue receipts and that tax concessions are not made for charitable donations in Iceland. Further, this heighted attention during the holidays also applies to the kinds of donations made, such as wrapped gifts left in collections at local malls or bags dropped off at Mæðrastyrksnefnd, and are for the most part done anonymously. I also made a specific point of asking the seasonal volunteers—none of whom I saw the rest of the year—and almost all wanted to do something to help those in need during this time of the year.

During the Christmas allocation there were days when we served triple the usual numbers of clients. Spread out over eight days in December of 2004, for example, we assisted 1,155 clients. If one included the members of their immediate families, according to their application forms, this assistance supported 3,233 individuals. This was an enormous logistical undertaking for a group of generally middle-aged and elderly staff members, in addition to one very tired Canadian anthropologist. Other charities do much of the same work at Christmas, so starting from 2005 Mæðrastyrksnefnd joined forces with an organization with links to the national Lutheran Church and the Icelandic Red Cross and have since worked together. Yet from the perspective of charitable discourse production, little else has changed. Beginning in late October to early November in any given recent year, newspaper accounts and advertisements concerning charities begin to appear, alerting those who may need the assistance and to gather support from companies and the public. A large Christmas tree is erected in two area shopping malls to serve as collection points for gifts for needy children. The gifts are then redistributed via local charities like Mæðrastyrksnefnd. In recent years, the wife of Iceland's president has been on hand in a ceremony to light one of these trees. Local artists, musicians, crafts people, and schoolchildren perform activities throughout the city to collect goods and money for charities during this time—all of which abruptly ceases come January. So what effect did the 2008 crisis have on these efforts?

THE CRISIS EMERGES: 2007–2009

The year 2007 began and ended very much like the other years I spent at Mæðrastyrksnefnd. The discursive output included, among other expected components, references to the increasing numbers of clients, usually framed as there being "more need than ever before." I was somewhat skeptical of this, as it had become a common feature of their discourse. However, the basic claim that their client base was growing each year was empirically true. I could discern certain patterns to this. January of 2007 began typically with a few thank-you notes in the newspapers.[1] Afterward there was a quite dramatic and noticeable silence throughout the rest of the year, aside from a few brief mentions about Mæðrastyrksnefnd's operating hours and the occasional piece. Newspaper accounts began to emerge with force once again in November in the lead-up to Christmas. In one such account, on the front page of the widely read national newspaper *Morgunblaðið*, the chair of Mæðrastyrksnefnd articulated her concerns about the increasing numbers of clients and described them as consisting primarily of disability and senior pensioners. The article concludes with a reference to the union of three major charities for the upcoming Christmas allocation. The media accounts over November and December of 2007 focused on announcements about when and where the holiday allocation would be held; Dorrit Moussaieff, wife of Iceland's president, was depicted in two stories lighting the Christmas tree in a local shopping mall. There were also numerous stories about donations of cash or material goods from the business and financial sector, along with the obligatory photo ops of officials shaking hands with charity staff or presenting goods or oversized novelty checks. Included as well were stories about schoolchildren who raised money or goods for charity, artists who donated the proceeds from a concert or exhibition, or homemakers who knit woolen mittens to donate. All of these stories were predictable. There were usually a few deviations from this pattern. The director of the domestic assistance branch of a charity with links to the Lutheran Church could be counted on for her sophisticated insights, and she did not fail in an article where she discussed the psychosocial effects of poverty. But generally 2007 was normal and predictable. I expected that 2008 would repeat the pattern.

January 2008 began typically with the usual assortment of thank-you pieces, including one that was identical to the one from January of 2007.[2] Perhaps the only unusual thing in the early part of 2008 was a number of reports in February that there were actually fewer (8.5 percent decrease) requests for assistance during the 2007 Christmas allocation than in 2006, though the clients were still referred to primarily as disability pensioners and single mothers. But by late summer of 2008 it was clear that things were becoming unsettled. I listened like many others with growing trepidation and shock to Prime Minister Geir Haarde's infamous October 6 speech about the imminent collapse of the financial sector.

From the beginning of October 2008 onward, stories—often in prominent and noticeable places in the newspaper—about the increasing number of people seeking help at charities like Mæðrastyrksnefnd were quite common.

"Families" or "households" became the preferred category of reference rather than pensioners and social assistance recipients, along with a focus on more young people and the recently unemployed as the result of the crisis. One such article reflected on the staff's observation of the increasing presence of newly unemployed white-collar workers now among their clientele, as well as foreign men who had lost work in construction as building projects ground to a halt. More striking was the shift to the interpretation of these donations in light of the crisis, framed in a quasi-nationalistic sense of collectivism. For example, when a manager was asked by a reporter about the donation her company made to Mæðrastyrksnefnd, she commented: "It is in this spirit, as has been recently in Iceland, to stand together and show solidarity." There was also a shift in tone of urgency, as well as an indication that they were dealing with unusual events and not the normative clientele of the past. The typical advertisements used by Mæðrastyrksnefnd in earlier Christmas drives began to appear again in the late autumn of 2008. However, an extra phrase was inserted: "often there was need, but now is necessity" (*oft var þörf en nú er nauðsyn*).

The role of charities in the crisis took on a national scale. Rather than referring to clients as seniors and other pensioners, one newspaper report commented that 2.1 percent of the nation depended upon charitable assistance to survive. Charity was now playing a role that served a nation in crisis rather than just those simply "less fortunate." Local charities in Reykjavík began to take on an international role as well. During the Christmas allocation of 2008 a story ran on the front page of *Morgunblaðið* of a donation to Mæðrastyrksnefnd on behalf of a collection taken up by the Icelandic diaspora in the Canadian town of Gimli, Manitoba, to the sum of Can$15,000. It struck me as sadly ironic to see the descendants of Icelanders who emigrated to Canada to escape poverty in the nineteenth and early twentieth centuries collecting money to help Iceland, when only a few short years ago the so-called *útrásarvíkingar* or "outvasion Vikings" were bragging about their economic conquests abroad.

Despite these noticeable differences in framing, other components of these discursive practices remained stubbornly intact. Aside from the spate of charity-related stories in October 2008 due to the emergence of the crisis, the usual buildup of media reporting increased over November and December and tailed off yet again in January 2009. There were a handful of stories in February but a noticeable silence until the following November. The Christmas season of 2008 saw yet again Iceland's "first lady" lighting the charity Christmas tree in a local shopping mall, and I was able to gather the usual collection of stories and photographs of business leaders and other organizations posing with the staff of Mæðrastyrksnefnd and displaying novelty checks, plaques, or other props to signify their donation.

THE POST-CRISIS CONTEXT: 2010–2012

The media production of charities in 2010 confirmed that the seasonal media coverage of charities in Iceland was more or less untouched by the crisis. There were, however, some important developments. The year 2010 marked a rather dark phase in the politics of charity in Reykjavík. The growing presence of immigrants at Mæðrastyrksnefnd was something that was hotly debated behind the scenes during my fieldwork but rarely went public. Some of the staff, favoring a more material or socio-structural interpretation, recognized the important role that immigrants fulfilled and were aware of the kinds of exploitative, low-paying jobs they occupied. Thus, they saw them as legitimately seeking assistance. Others were more concerned about the potential sociocultural disruption they perceived immigrants posed in a nation not used to high levels of immigration. Opinions were divided, and I felt myself conflicted when I was asked to analyze the number of "foreigners" who sought assistance at Mæðrastyrksnefnd (see Rice 2007a).

Other organizations did not moderate their public discourses or practices as much.[3] In March 2010 there was an increased attention to charity as the result of a number of stories on how one charity—Fjölskylduhjálp Íslands (Iceland's Family Help)—decided to queue its clients based on nationality: Icelanders in one queue and foreigners, mainly unemployed Polish construction workers, in another. In the paper *Fréttablaðið* this news made the front page, alongside a photo of a volcanic eruption. The manager of this charity argued that these foreigners, citing Poles specifically, are often young, healthy men with a different "line culture" in terms of being aggressive and not queuing properly. The manager contrasted these young Poles with older Icelanders who "toiled their whole lives" and with "young mothers with babes in one hand while holding another" leaving in frustration without being assisted. The social welfare services of Reykjavík were furious at this queuing by nationality and many of the general public appeared to be appalled as well, based upon media accounts, blogs, forums, and general discussions.

What struck me about this, and which was ignored in the media outburst, was the age-old reliance upon the traditional categories of the worthy poor— the normative poor—who "rightly" belong as the clients of charity. These Polish migrants, regardless of how they did or did not act in the queues, were nevertheless perceived as the structural victims of the recent economic crisis. I found it staggering that despite the crisis, nothing had really changed. The presence of Poles and other migrants was interpreted through the lens of the labor market and other structural economic factors, yet the plights of native Icelandic seniors, single mothers, and disabled people did not warrant similar analytical treatment.

My analysis of the media accounts in 2011 and 2012 revealed the pattern once again: minor attention during Easter, the rise in charity-related stories in November, a crescendo in attention and activity in December, and silence again in January. Mæðrastyrksnefnd reverted to describing their clients much as they had pre-crisis. One article was entitled, "Large families and disability pensioners seek assistance" (*Stórar fjölskyldur og öryrkjar leita aðstoðar*), noting that there was a noticeable decrease in the number of Poles seeking assistance. Another during the Christmas allocation referred to the clientele as large families, seniors, and "more Icelanders than before." Much the same held for Easter of 2012; charity officials said the bulk of their clientele were families, disability pensioners, and, quite fittingly at Mæðrastyrksnefnd, an increase in the number of young single mothers. From the perspective of 2012, excluding the brief discursive shifts over 2008–2009, it would appear as if nothing of note had happened.

CONCLUSION

The concept of crisis, as well as continuity, in the context of charity needs to be unpacked and analyzed. The notion of crisis as a temporary deviation from the normal order is not a sufficient framework for the analysis of long-term, structural poverty. Such a framework implies that a crisis is only legitimately perceived as such if it impacts those who normally do not require financial or material assistance. I argue at length elsewhere (Rice 2007a; 2007b; 2009) that the material assistance offered by such charities is never sufficient to do more than soften the sharp edges of poverty. The ways charities solicit for donations and explain their work direct the well-intentioned efforts of the public into activities that preserve the status quo. In addition, the accompanying charitable discourse normalizes rather than analyzes the inequalities they purport to address. Such material assistance is necessary given the reality of structural inequality, but it needs to be coupled with an entirely different form of discourse if the reduction of structural inequities is the intended goal. At times I held grave doubts that change was the goal. However, the possibility of a different discourse and a different way of providing charity is not idle fantasy, as the early history of Mæðrastyrksnefnd demonstrated; it is possible as this discourse displays as much capacity for fluidity as it does for rigidity. Whether charities can do so is another matter. The corporations and businesses that are so keen on assisting charities are, in my interpretation, part of the problem of the larger socioeconomic order in which charities and their clientele are embedded. Directly criticizing the financial and business sector, municipalities, and the state, which provide the bulk of the operating funds to charities, is not in the best interest of charities.

While I was disappointed to see the return of the status quo, there still remain glimmers of hope. In the spring of 2012 Mæðrastyrksnefnd promoted a drive to develop an educational fund to assist women. Such an activity recalled for me the early, radical days of Mæðrastyrksnefnd when it actively supported marginalized people with the tools they needed to address the structural socioeconomic barriers they faced, rather than solely doling out food and clothes. This was widely reported on television, radio, all major newspapers, and in various publicly visible drives and events.[4] And best of all, this had nothing to do with Christmas. That year I gladly bought a bouquet for Mother's Day that Mæðrastyrksnefnd sold in a home and garden store, the proceeds of which went directly to this educational fund. I felt relieved that I could support an organization and people that played such a central role in my life in Iceland before, during, and after the crisis without the grave misgivings about charity that I had struggled with for the last decade.

NOTES

1. The following media sources were used in this paragraph: "Mæðrastyrksnefnd Reykjavíkur," *Morgunblaðið*, Jan. 7, 2007, 39; Steinunn Ásmundsdóttir, "Ekki eiga allir fyrir gps-tæki: Þeim fjölgar ört sem leita aðstoðar hjálparsamtaka," *Morgunblaðið*, Nov. 19, 2007, 1; photo of Dorrit Moussaieff and caption, *Fréttablaðið*, Dec. 3, 2007, 1; "Jólapökkum safnað undir jólatré í Kringlunni," *Morgunblaðið*, Dec. 4, 2007, 4; Jóhanna María Vilhelmsdóttir, "Sálrænn þáttur fátæktar," *Morgunblaðið*, Dec. 5, 2007, 9.

2. Media sources for the remainder of this section: "Mæðrastyrksnefnd Reykjavíkur," *Morgunblaðið*, Jan. 2, 2008, 31; "Færri þurftu aðstoð fyrir jólin," *Morgunblaðið*, Feb. 8, 2008, 14; "Færri sóttu um jólaaðstoð," *Fréttablaðið*, Feb. 14, 2008, 13; "Yfir 300 fjölskyldur fá vikulega matargjafir," *24 stundir*, Oct. 2, 2008, 1; "Fleiri leita sér aðstoðar," *Fréttablaðið*, Oct. 18, 2008, 1; Önundur Páll Ragnarsson, "Hátt í þrjú hundruð heimili fá hjálp hjá Mæðrastyrksnefnd," *Morgunblaðið*, Oct. 30, 2008, 2; Bergþóra Njála Guðmundsdóttir, "Það vilja allir hjálpa og gefa," *Morgunblaðið*, Dec. 4, 2008, 26–27; Svanhvít Ljósbjörg, "Nytsamlegar gjafir áberandi," *Morgunblaðið*, Nov. 13, 2008, http://www

.mbl.is/greinasafn/grein/1254733/; "Jólasöfnun" (advertisement), *Morgunblaðið*, Dec. 6, 2008, 14; "Tvö prósent þurftu jólaaðstoð," *Fréttablaðið*, Dec. 24, 2008, 2; "Uppörvandi jólakveðja og góðar gjafir frá Kanada," *Morgunblaðið*, Dec. 15, 2008, 1; "Ljósin á jólatré Kringlunnar tendruð," *Morgunblaðið*, Dec. 1, 2008, 9.

3. Media sources for this section: "Íslendingar í forgang hjá Fjölskylduhjálp," *Fréttablaðið*, Mar. 25, 2010, 1; "Stórar fjölskyldur og öryrkjar leita aðstoðar," *Morgunblaðið*, Apr. 14, 2011, http://www.mbl.is/frettir/innlent/2011/04/14/storar_fjolskyldur_og_oryrkjar_leita_adstodar/; "Þrjú hundruð fjölskyldur leituðu eftir neyðaraðstoð í gær," *Morgunblaðið*, Dec. 29, 2011, 2.

4. *Hádegisfréttir*, radio broadcast, stations 1 and 2, Icelandic Broadcasting Service (RÚV), Mar. 28, 2012; *Kvöldfréttir*, radio broadcast, stations 1 and 1, RÚV, Apr. 19, 2012; *Fréttir*, television broadcast, RÚV, Apr. 19, 2012; "Tekjulágar konur styrktar til náms," *Morgunblaðið*, Apr. 19, 2012; "Stofna Menntunarsjóð fyrir tekjulágar konur," *Vísir*, Apr. 19, 2012, http://www.visir.is/stofna-menntunarsjod-fyrir-tekjulagar-konur/article/2012120418991; "Mæðrablóm til styrktar tekjulágum konum," *DV*, Apr. 19, 2012, https://www.dv.is/frettir/2012/4/19/maedrablom-til-styrktar-tekjulagum-konum/; "Styrkja tekjulágar konur til mennta," *Fréttablaðið*, Apr. 20, 2012, 4.

Summing Up

Dimitra Doukas is an anthropologist and community activist. She is the author of Worked Over: The Corporate Sabotage of an American Community *(2003).*

• • • • • • • • • • • • • • • • • • • •

> In Iceland, a new class came into being,
> that of the super-wealthy who reduced the
> middle class to paupers and made fools of
> the lower class.
>
> Einar Már Guðmundsson,
"The White Book," 14

In this book are the makings of a cautionary tale of the greatest importance to the world, with multiple cautionary tales embedded in it. It is a history of neo-liberal conquest, writ large on a small island nation, compressed into less than thirty years' time (from the founding of the Icelandic Stock Exchange in 1985). People need to know about it.

The participants in the National Science Foundation's "Icelandic Meltdown" conference—Icelanders and internationals—were privileged to gather at the University of Iowa to unravel the threads of the story and begin to reweave them. Most were anthropologists who research the world from distant village peripheries through urban avant-gardes to the distant "pinnacle" of neoliberal power, Wall Street. Add to these an emerging anthropologist / recovering banker with a firsthand story of bubble-building to tell, a sociologist who balanced anthropological impressionism with

DOI: 10.5876/9781607323358.c017

careful quantification, a witty but no-nonsense historian, an honest professor of business, a professor of education and former member of Parliament, a public-spirited philosopher, and a great poet who kept pulling us back from the precipice of academic narcissism.

This epilogue reflects further on the Iceland story as the authors of this volume reveal it, setting their puzzle pieces in an array that shows a pattern of recklessness and bad faith of national elites. To expose that pattern is to be able to raise an alarm when smooth-talking fraudsters, eyeing your commons, your commonwealth, promise you the prosperity of your dreams.

> It is those two political parties, the Independence Party and the Progressive Party, who are most culpable. They laid the foundation for the system of gifting fishing quotas. It is therefore possible to sell fish that has yet to be caught and profit thus from a communal resource of the nation. (Guðmundsson n.d., 15)

The Iceland crash started with a financial bubble. The bubble started with the "virtual fish" of the ITQ system, a so-called market-based solution that was born from the fevered brow of a neoliberal economist in British Columbia. It "solved the problem" there as it did in Iceland, by financializing the public right to fish and turning it into private tradable shares that would inevitably gather in the hands of the wealthiest participants in this new market (Pinkerton, Maguire, this volume).

It was virtual fish in Iceland, but it might have been virtual mortgages, like the bubble that neoliberals blew up in the United States. It might have been virtual tulips (Goldgar 2007). Virtual carbon credits might be next. The important point, if you want to blow up a financial bubble, is to create a large new fund of fictitious capital or virtual value that is credible enough to borrow on, that is, to collateralize new loans.

"Market-based solutions" will be the "solutions" of a neoliberal con game that will end with the marks or suckers, the targets of the con, losing their resources, public and private. So-called market-based solutions are actually faith-based. The self-correcting, equilibrium-finding, know-all, be-all Market is the cornerstone of the neoliberal faith, the conceptual framework of the neoliberal con game.

> When neo-liberals speak of the market, they resort to religious terms. They say: "This is up to the market." Or: "We'll let the market decide that." One only needs to replace the word "market" with "God" and the religious content of neo-liberalism manifests itself. . . . But Mammon is shrewd and assumes many forms. (Guðmundsson n.d., 14)

There is bitterness about it now, but many Icelanders lived well under neoliberal rule. They felt they worked hard. They felt they deserved to live well. They felt they had thrown off the historical curse of poverty. If they were bold enough, some said, they could throw off of the yoke of peripheral status and become an important player on the international stage.

The financial bubble, like any con game, depends on credulity, the force of wanting to believe. Successful fraudsters tap into our dreams. Who could resist living better and more securely, being able to give more to their children, and being more important? If a few people of questionable character are getting insanely rich—well then, maybe it's like those financial geniuses say: the risky deals and spectacular profits tend to benefit the society as a whole (Ho 2009).

That's what seemed to have been happening in Iceland. Pension funds grew. Property values soared. A construction boom pulled workers from Europe and Asia (Skaptadóttir, this volume). Icelanders spent more per child on education than any other country in the European Union (Guðbjörnsdóttir and Davíðsdóttir, this volume). Iceland was a success!

Wasn't it? Of course it was! Even a small country can do it! Everybody wanted to believe in the financial miracle. Because they wanted to believe, they did not ask the hard questions. They were not put off by the improbability of Iceland's financial resources growing to six, seven, eight times their pre-bubble values, and so were not inclined to question the miracle's foundations in reality. The con played out by diverting public attention to a different question: "*Why us?* Why are we Icelanders so favored by fortune?"

The neoliberal public relations shops were ready with an answer. Icelanders were special! They were Nordic. They were bold and daring. They had a special relation with nature. They were smarter than other kinds of people (Loftsdóttir; Jónsson and Sæmundsson; Mixa; Grétarsdóttir, Ásmundsson, and Lárusson; this volume). Across the media, a new entrepreneurial Viking (a being of evolutionary superiority) was urged out of the collective unconscious.

This must be in the neoliberal playbook, this flattering of the marks to circumvent their common sense and soften their resistance. Imagine what the delegation from Goldman Sachs told the Greeks about their national genius. Or the Spanish: not since 1492 have you had a chance for such glory!

Remember, World: you will be tempted with all sorts of improvements to your status and standard of living and a better life for your children—or *whatever* you dream of—if you just sign here on the bottom line. You will be flattered, individually and collectively. All of your people's traditions will be brought to bear on the task of flattering you, until you are swollen and swaggering and ready to believe the improbable.

"The last bank that couldn't lend me any money bankrupted me!"
(Guðmundsson n.d., 25)

When the bubble burst and the banks came crashing down, what you heard in the streets was "*Helvítis fokking fokk!*" Icelandic *Helvítis* is "devil" in English. I'll leave the rest to (English-speaking) imagination. A polite translation, Icelanders winked, is "What a shame!" But people were shocked. They couldn't believe it at first, so well had the con been constructed.

When they found out, they felt violated, and the feeling only got stronger as more information came out. Iceland is a small country, a highly literate one, and a highly computer-literate one. Information spreads quickly—the cheating, the corruption, the cronies, the names and dates.

The miracle, the new Vikings, the new affluence, the evolutionary superiority—the whole thing was delusional. Icelanders were up to their eyeballs in debt. The emperor was naked. Those six-, seven-digit figures on your account statements? Computer-generated fantasy.

The shimmering veil of wanting-to-believe was pulled away abruptly and cruelly to reveal deceit, inequity, desperate acts of treachery, and the elegantly clothed backs of run-away billionaires. *Helvítis fokking fokk!*

Some quarter of Icelanders was mad enough to get out into the streets in protest, and at least that many more supported the protesters (Bernburg, this volume). Calling on a symbolic vocabulary older than history, they came out of their houses banging the pots and pans of household economies that were stressed or shattered by the crisis. The protesters banged their pots and pans until the government resigned.

With both parties implicated in the corruption, who would form a government? Who could be trusted? When a slate of public personalities, led by a beloved comedian, offered themselves as a radical alternative, the scramble to their side in the Rekjavík municipal elections was so clamorous that it looked at first like their party, the Best Party, would take a clear majority (Proppé, this volume).

Members of the Best Party wouldn't do politics-as-usual, wouldn't be categorized, wouldn't play the blame-game with their opponents. They saw a new way. Best Party delegates disarmed their opponents before meetings with kisses and hugs! The Best Party organizers didn't just talk about change, they *were* change.

But in the end even the Best Party had to toe the punishing line of austerity, cutting public services at a time when people were already struggling. How disappointing that must have been, like watching the newly elected Barack Obama pick his cabinet in 2008.

Wrenching self-criticism surfaces. The Vikings? They were murderous bar-barians—the "terrorists of their day!" (Jóhannesson, this volume).

But Icelanders shouldn't take it so personally. This is how the neoliberals operate. Ask the Greeks. Ask the Irish. You've been conned, but you've been conned by the best con artists in the modern world.

BLOWING BUBBLES

Financial bubble-blowing of course long predates neoliberalism. The out-lines are always the same. It begins when a crew of financial elites seeks to generate a swirling speculative market around a credible virtual commodity—fishing quota, tulips, carbon credits, whatever. Bankers, wanting in on the action, play a crucial part. Banks allocate credit. To encourage the emerging market, they open the spigot, making credit cheap and easy.

You too can get in on the windfall, the bubble-blowers say, and make your dreams come true! Borrow, sign here! It's easy!

If the bubble takes off, masses of people borrow to speculate on the virtual good. As long as the bubble is expanding, the speculative bets seem to be pay-ing off—the public mood reaches euphoria (Galbraith 1994).

Then something happens. Could be a scandal. Could be a "leak." Could have been the plan all along. Behind the scenes, the big players move to cash out and stick the multitudes with bad news. At some point, bankers close the spigot and "tighten" credit. Gamblers whose pockets are not deep enough, whose assets do not cover their debts, will not be able to hold on to what they have gained, which "flows upward" to the large creditors who put the bubble in motion and kept it going.

The great multitude of investors should not be playing in such gambling games at all because they cannot afford to lose. They are "suckers"—sucked into a con. Suckers always lose, and may lose everything. Winners, on the other hand, walk away with many times their original investment (Jónsson and Sæmundsson, this volume).

Bubble-blowing is an old game. The amazing twist of the neoliberal con has been to turn nation-states into gamblers on speculative markets and make whole peoples responsible for the debts of elite gamblers.

Among the multiple ironies, the neoliberal con wants to bring states to the rigged tables of casino capitalism because states have, or had, solvent financial commons, public investment funds that neoliberals lusted to "privatize." They sucked states into the game through the very social insurance programs that, as politicians, neoliberals always resist and try to dismantle. Don't they?

THE NEOLIBERAL BACKSTORY

How far back does the neoliberal story go? It must go back to a liberalism that some wanted to modernize, hence the *neo*. The term "neoliberalism" was coined by German economist Alexander Rüstow in the anti-capitalist 1930s, not as a call for privatization but as an improvement on the laissez-faire liberalism that so grandly failed in the 1930s. Don't turn to socialism, Rüstow argued, but upgrade liberalism with stronger state-imposed rules over economic activity. Rüstow believed in "freedom" and the "laws of the market" but believed that those were not enough—a "market police" would be required to enforce good behavior. His books and articles had strong appeal for anti-socialist intellectuals like Ludwig von Mises and Friedrich Hayek in Austria and Walter Lippmann in the United States (Hartwich 2009; Foucault 2010; Harvey 2005; George 1999). After World War II the neoliberal movement was joined by Milton Friedman from the United States and Ludwig Erhard, the West German finance minister and chancellor who popularized neoliberalism under the header of the "social market economy" (Henderson 2008).

It was, after all, the "Iron Chancellor," Count Otto von Bismarck, whose government gave the world its first social welfare state in the 1880s. The original neoliberals had no objection to social programs of this kind. Their political enemies were the same as Bismarck's—the socialists.

And this is the point. Neoliberalism is an ideological con as well. It is the ideology of money. It is whatever it has to be in any given political situation. The term lives on today, repurposed as a pejorative by Latin American intellectuals who saw their democratically chosen mixed economies overturned by military coups (Klein 2007; Guðmundsson, this volume). Meanwhile, the neoliberal movement let its old label drop down the memory hole.

What's at stake for neoliberals today is the same thing that was at stake for their predecessors and allies. The question is not social programs, or no social programs, but how government can be used for what's really important: maintaining the flow of wealth to the "right" people.

You can't spot neoliberals by party names or promises. Both parties in Iceland, as in the United States, came to serve high finance, helping to blow up bubbles and protect the big speculators. Promoters of social programs may not be, as they often represent themselves to the public, the loving, caring alternative to the party of the cruel rich.

It is too easy to say that neoliberalism is just a pack of lies. Even if that's true, it is more than that. People want very much to believe that their wealth is part of a fair system, that there's enough for everybody (unless they are "lazy"). Neoliberalism gives them what they want, a belief system in which a vastly unequal distribution of wealth, like we see around us in the early twenty-first century, is good for society.

From boom to bust, neoliberal economic strategies take from the vulnerable and give to the powerful. They aggravate inequality. The very Icelanders who never benefited from the boom—fishing villages, "guest" workers, the structural urban poor—are the hardest hit by austerity measures (Maguire; Rice; Willson and Gunnlaugsdóttir, this volume).

The myth of industrialization, the machine age, the original "liberalism," still held out the ideal of prosperity for all—mechanical production would bring abundance and liberate humanity from toil. Bodies politic were asked to imagine trainloads of desirable manufactured goods pouring out of the factories and into their homes. There was gritty work involved, as people knew (labor unions made sure they knew), but even factory labor could be made humane when a whole nation lived in abundance.

The neoliberal ideal, by comparison, is a cargo cult capitalism. It is the ideal of high finance, uninterested in the mess and risk of actual production. Just invest, we are asked to believe, and your money will miraculously "grow." How cool is that!

We want to believe in financial miracles because most of us can't quite go as far as Carnegie and his Wall Street successors. We are ripe for the neoliberal con precisely because we can't quite abandon some shadowy ideal of equality. We just couldn't enjoy what we have if we thought that it wasn't fair for us to have so much.

IT *WAS* A CONSPIRACY

Banker-turned-anthropologist Mixa (this volume), working a couple of echelons down from the really big bankers, was aware of extreme imbalance in the system two years before the crash. He dutifully tried to point out the problem to those in authority, but they just looked at him, he said, like he was crazy. Everybody wanted to believe in the financial miracle, even bankers—maybe especially bankers.

But, as Mixa reports, the "highest" in-crowd knew the ugly truth, knew who really owned what, knew that the apparent prosperity was just a pyramid of debt piled on debt that would have to collapse eventually—the art of the bubble is in guessing just when the price of your holdings is as high as it will go. The in-crowd created the bubble for the usual reasons, to reel in suckers and extract their wealth. They faked exponential "growth" by lending to paper holding companies that were owned by their own family members and cronies! They committed fraud.

Identifying the conspiratorial element does not blunt the force of Árnason's "friendly power" (this volume), the tacit agreements that normalized wild and risky behavior. So "horizontal power" was internalized and came to comprise the environment that the "Vikings" needed in order to work their miraculous schemes, and work them in the confidence of secrecy.

We can't reject an explanation on the grounds that it is a "conspiracy theory." Things happen in human social life because of social agents. We can fairly call it a conspiracy when those agents work in secret to cheat others.

> Many of the filthy-rich have fled the country and are nowhere to be seen or surround themselves with bodyguards. They do not comment on the situation but try to wait it out in silence, many of them prepared to return home and give a repeat performance in the spirit of capitalist shock treatment which now seems to be wreaking havoc in many corners of the world. (Guðmundsson n.d., 20)

This is a dangerous situation. The bankers and their cronies *will* be back, unless we refuse to let them in. They are not done with you, Icelanders, not with you or any of us, not while there is a breath of air that remains unfinancialized. There's nothing like the aftermath of collective crisis for "disaster capitalism," poised to scoop up the wealth of the disoriented and vulnerable multitudes (Klein 2007).

> The ones who gambled with the [fishing] quota were playing with something of real value not just fictive capital like the financial companies. As a result we are left with a fishing industry on the verge of bankruptcy—and the billions have disappeared. (Guðmundsson n.d., 54)

Keystrokes and electronic numbers are not real wealth. The perpetrators of the bubble floated fictitious capital on the water as *bait* in order to attract the big fish of the real economy. The winners filled their hulls in the messy post-bubble moment, when the suckers had to dump real wealth for a fraction of its value in order to pay off their gambling debts.

> There is a great awakening taking place and many things point to that it will take place all over the world. It isn't just the wheels of industry that need to turn. The wheels of history also turn, even if the tires are damaged and the spokes broken. (Guðmundsson n.d., 99)

Obsession with growth was the problem, Maguire (this volume) observes—now it's being touted as part of the solution, so nothing's changed. It does appear as though nothing has changed in the halls of power. What *could* change, though, is the credulity of the public, and social researchers are uniquely positioned to move that process along. Isn't it the basic job of the social sciences—why our societies support us—to gather together the necessary information and ponder it in order to solve social problems?

One place to start is by seeing the invisible. It comes up in almost every chapter—Skaptadóttir's invisible immigrants, Willson and Gunnlaugsdóttir's invisible factory workers, Rice's invisible poor Icelanders, Maguire's and Pinkerton's invisible fish. What makes them invisible? Invisibility is a property of something we *don't* want to believe.

Don't shoot the messenger. The social researchers who reveal the culturally "invisible" are showing us where our model of social life does not correspond with social reality. They are our friends.

The bubble cycle is utterly predictable. It has nothing to do with economic theory, really, or the neoliberal faith. It has to do with elite competition. It is a form of organized crime. It is a power grab. Today it dresses in the neoliberalism of privatization. Yesterday it dressed in the liberalism of the industrial revolution. It will dress in whatever we are willing to believe.

It's our choice not to believe. Let the Iceland story stand as a caution to all of us. Neoliberals do not deliver on their promise, the prosperity of our dreams. They will *seem to*, for a while, long enough for enough of us to believe in financial miracles that the bubble can fatten on our credulity. If we don't believe, they cannot run the con.

James G. Carrier is an honorary research associate at Oxford Brookes University, associate at the Max Planck Institute for Social Anthropology, and adjunct professor of anthropology at the University of Indiana. He is the editor of Meanings of the Market: The Free Market in Western Culture *(1997), co-editor with Daniel Miller of* Virtualism: A New Political Economy *(1998), and co-editor with Deborah B. Gewertz of* The Handbook of Sociocultural Anthropology *(2013).*

· · · · · · · · · · · · · · · · · · · ·

The quality and breadth of contributions to this volume speak for themselves. Here I want to consider their context, the nature of the project that E. Paul Durrenberger and Gisli Palsson put together that led to those contributions. When seen from the perspective of the more visible currents of anthropological thought over the past few decades, this project exemplifies what the discipline might become.

I will start that consideration by pointing to Thomas Hylland Eriksen's well-known introduction to anthropology and the argument contained in its title: *Small Places, Large Issues* (Eriksen [1995] 2010). For a long time, anthropologists did research in small places: Malinowski (1922) on an island in the Trobriands, Evans-Pritchard (1940) in a small village on the upper Nile, and Mead (1930) on a small island in the Admiralties. For a long time, anthropology has been associated in the public mind with the study of such places. When those small places were considered primitive, the discipline

DOI: 10.5876/9781607323358.c018

could justify itself by, and be justified by, the study of human life free of the distortions that come with the rise of civilization of whatever sort. Those in the countries that produced anthropologists could use what, for instance, Malinowski said of Kiriwina to reflect upon themselves, whether to laud their own achievements or to bemoan their own inadequacies. As well, of course, the anthropologists in those countries could use that knowledge to reflect upon the nature of human existence in general (e.g., Mauss [1925] 1990) and of society in particular (Durkheim [1893] 1984).

Anthropologists have long worried about the disappearance of the relatively untouched societies in those small places that were their conventional topic of research (Münzel 2011). That worry became more insistent, and more justified, after World War II. With the fall of colonial empires, improvement in transportation and communication, and expansion of trade, the gradual disappearance of those societies turned into something like a rout. Members of the discipline knew that they were increasingly living in a "runaway world" (Leach 1967), and many lamented that their field sites were part of a "world on the wane" (Lévi-Strauss 1961). At the same time, anthropologists and many other people were decreasingly happy with the sort of grand evolutionary approaches that sought, in an island in the Pacific or a village in Africa, information about an earlier stage of Western society. Evolutionary thinking may never have been universal in anthropology, but its lingering influence was dying out, both within the discipline and in the public mind. The Primitive or the Simple, that is, turned into the Exotic or Alien, which turned into the Different or Diverse.

This change left the discipline in a difficult position. Many anthropologists may have been happy to do conventional, village-based field research, even though more and more of their colleagues were shifting their focus from villages to plantations, squatter settlements, ghettos, and immigrant enclaves. But however happy they may have been, some of them, like a growing number of their public, wondered what difference their research and writing made, why it was worth pursuing, and, crucially, whether it was worth paying for. The answer to their questions lay in the argument in Eriksen's title. The places may be small, the field research may be restricted to a particular locality, but in those small places anthropologists could address general questions that were of interest to those concerned with social life in other places, whether small or large.

I do not mean that anthropologists of the older generations had not sought to do this, for clearly they had. Malinowski (1921) used his work on the Trobriands to reflect on common themes in Western economic thought;

Margaret Mead (1949) waded into the debate about nature and culture in a work with a subtitle that clearly indicates those she sought to address: *a psychological study of primitive youth for Western civilization*; Lévi-Strauss (e.g., 1966) was interested in the fundamental nature of human thought. While these older anthropologists did use small places to address large issues, the discipline was able to survive perfectly well without them. When they wrote, the need to justify the discipline, either to itself or to its public, had not yet become as pressing as it would become.

Unfortunately, however, after it did become more pressing, anthropology came very close to ruling out the use of research in small places to address those large issues. That began to happen in the middle of the 1980s, with the emergence of postmodernism, associated especially with *Writing Culture* (Clifford and Marcus 1986) and heavily influenced by the cultural turn. Postmodernism flourished at least until the end of the century, and its effects on the discipline remain strong. While the early postmodernist concern with the production of text has weakened, its challenge to the idea of anthropology as a sustained effort to learn about society and culture is still potent. One basis of that challenge emerged from the cultural turn, expressed in the work of Clifford Geertz, especially his book *The Interpretation of Cultures*. Geertz argued that the anthropological task was one of appreciation of people's activities as expressions of their culture, rather than one of explanation. He rejected the more purely sociological ("functionalism") and psychological ("psychologism") approaches, which, he said rather dismissively, only offer "reductive formulas professing to account for" what people do (Geertz 1973, 453).

As shaped by Geertz's arguments, the postmodernist challenge had two main elements. One was a rejection of the idea that there are such things as societies or cultures; the other was the rejection of the idea that we are equipped with the tools that would allow us to try to make sense of these things. The consequence was that many anthropologists retreated. Some retreated into a celebration of Otherness, together with a rejection of the idea that we should try to understand it. Or, as Patricia Spyer (2011, 62) put it, in terms about as dismissive as Geertz's, "any attempt to domesticate such otherness by either explaining it away or reducing it to something already known and commonsensical is eschewed." Other anthropologists retreated into a concern with detail, denying the reality of the forest while seeking to describe minutely the individual trees—such as "What it means to be a woman in all its complexity" (Brownell and Besnier 2013, 240).

A commentator has observed that "anthropologists have perhaps been exceptionally prone to feel that their enterprise has developed in relative isolation from the general intellectual culture around it" (Collini 1999, 280; quoted in Mills 2013, 580). However, it is important to recognize that this sense of intellectual isolation is more fancy than fact. Anthropology's post-modernist wave demonstrates this, for it resembled what happened elsewhere in the social sciences. More intriguingly, it also reflects the emergence of a more general intellectual movement that many anthropologists saw as anathema. That movement was neoliberalism, and especially the neoclassical economics that was its intellectual core.

Neoliberalism rose to prominence around 1980 because the older reigning political-economic orientation was seen to have failed. That older orientation was Keynesianism, a variety of macroeconomics that sought to generate summary understandings of a nation's economy and guide government policy accordingly. The failure was the Keynesian inability to predict or control stagflation, the combination of economic inflation and stagnation that appeared in many Western countries around the middle of the 1970s. The neoclassical economics that rose to replace it did not seek either to improve Keynesianism or to lay out a better macroeconomic model. Instead, it rejected macroeconomics itself, echoing von Hayek's (1944, 204) assertion that governments and people should resist "the craving for intelligibility" about how the economy operates and why.

Like economics, anthropology was having a troublesome 1970s and a portentous 1980s (some of the trouble is described in Carrier 2013, 3–12). Many in the discipline heeded the argument, made most cogently by Talal Asad (1973), that anthropology was a creature of colonialism. They applied to themselves the argument made by Edward Said (1978) and those in the subaltern studies school (e.g., Guha 1982) about the dangers of those in the center of power producing essentialist, timeless renderings of alien and subordinate Others (e.g., Fabian 1983). These arguments were made against the background of the social ferment that existed in many Western countries: civil rights, women's rights, protests against the Vietnam War. Together, they led many in the discipline to conclude that the predominant approaches in anthropology needed to change. One of the more influential critics of these approaches was Sherry Ortner, who saw them as being concerned with the properties of systems, whether cast in terms of structural functionalism, Marxism, Lévi-Straussian structuralism, or a Boasian cultural order. She said that this left people out, or at least people who could think and act. As she put it, the important question is "the relationship(s) that obtain between human action, on the one hand, and some global entity which we may call 'the system,' on the other" (Ortner 1984, 148).

The discipline's response was a flurry of work that attempted to link the system and people's ordinary lives, but by the end of the 1980s many in anthropology had abandoned the attempt, and the postmodernist view came to predominate. That view looked a lot like the view of neoclassical economics. We should not seek to improve our stock of macroscopic models; we should resist the craving for intelligibility. Instead, we should recognize the primacy of people over systems, of lived experience over social or cultural order, and consequently should foreswear the search for cause and effect (see Carrier 2012). For neoclassical economists, this stance took the form of a model that accounted for people's market transactions as the consequence of their individual preferences or utility functions, which were not to be explained but taken as given. For many anthropologists, it took the form of a view that people's actions were expressions of their personal orientation, which also was not to be explained but taken as given. One common result, as I have indicated, amounted to a fixation on the trees rather than the forest, with a principled refusal to explain how those trees came to be as they are, in other than simple narrative terms.

Both the postmodernists and the neoliberals seemed vindicated by the fall of the Berlin Wall in 1989. The macroscopic orientation, the concern with system, that the Soviet Union was said to exemplify was shown to be fatally flawed. Instead, postmodernists and neoliberals celebrated the fragmentation that allowed individual freedom, whether in the form of market choice, cultural diversity, or the liberating disjunctions that came with emerging global flows. In such a climate, Eriksen's small places may have been useful for providing yet another example of human diversity, but appeared to lead to no large issues.

Neoliberalism became less secure by the turn of the century. The Washington Consensus was looking distinctly tattered, the promised freedom and prosperity in the former Soviet Bloc looked increasingly delayed. Even the claim that reducing state power in favor of the market would increase personal freedom looked suspect in the face of high and rising rates of imprisonment in neoliberalism's home country, the United States (see Wacquant 2010), while England and Wales, a bastion of neoliberalism under Thatcher, had higher rates than almost all of Western Europe (Walmsley 2011).

On the other side of the disciplinary divide, anthropologists appear to have been having doubts about their own variant of neoliberalism, postmodernism. The 2009 meeting of the largest body of anthropologists, the American Anthropological Association, had as its title "The End/s of Anthropology." That may have marked concern about the future of the discipline or uncertainty about that old question of what it is for; both concerns speak of a discipline that sees itself as being in trouble. That same view was expressed in an interview with one of the more influential advocates of postmodernism, George Marcus. He said that the discipline is "in suspension," with "no new ideas and none on the horizon" and with "no indication that its traditional stock of knowledge shows any signs of revitalization" (Marcus 2008, 2). And just as anthropology is not an intellectual island, such a view was not restricted to it. For instance, in a recent evaluation of his own field, criminology, Steve Hall (2012, 1) said that "the restrictive intellectual current that has been dominant since the 1980s is running out of momentum." In a review article that appeared near the end of the century, a pair of sociologists put it more starkly, suggesting that postmodernism in their discipline seems to be leading to the "dissolution of sociological theory" (Camic and Gross 1998, 466).

This loss of momentum, this sense of being in suspension, appears to mark a weakening of the hold that postmodernism has had on the discipline. That hold, however, has never been total, and some of the more visible alternative bodies of anthropological work over the past couple of decades are revealing. I said that the Washington Consensus was looking tattered by the close of the twentieth century. That was not brought about by quiet processes but by substantial shocks in the world, most notably the East Asian economic crisis that began in 1997. Those shocks, and the associated unraveling of the Consensus, led to a minor boom in economic anthropology. While some of that boom concerned itself with small places (e.g., Zaloom 2006), a significant portion of it looked at large issues (e.g., Gudeman 2009; Hann and Hart 2009). Similarly, the failure of the promised freedom and prosperity to appear in the former Soviet Bloc led to a minor boom in work on Eastern Europe, and again much of it looked at large issues (see Hann 2005; Rogers and Verdery 2013). These large shocks seem to have jarred at least some anthropologists out of their concern with small places and their rejection of large issues. They seem to have led at least some anthropologists to recognize that even if the relationship between Ortner's system and human action may be difficult to describe, there is no warrant for ignoring that system.

The economic crisis that began in 2008 is another large shock, the biggest that most people in most Western countries have ever experienced. It, too, has led anthropologists to consider those large issues (e.g., Ho 2009; Ouroussoff 2010). That crisis affected different places in different ways, but one of the most profound shocks occurred in Iceland. That place is large compared with many of the places anthropologists have studied, but it is small compared with many of the places currently in the news because of their economic troubles. In being small in that way, scholars can reasonably hope to grasp the predominant features of its history, the way those features shape the present, how that present has been affected by the global economic crisis, and how those in that small place have responded. The results of that effort are the contributions to this volume.

I said at the outset that this project is important as an example of what anthropology might become. I do not mean by this that it should become a discipline that studies people in Western societies, for it has been doing that for some time. Rather, I mean that it should become what it set out to be, but foreswore with the ascendance of postmodernism and neoliberalism. That is, a discipline that addresses large issues, whether they loom large in the world or in the discipline. *Gambling Debt* is an example of that becoming.

In the reference entries below, Icelandic patronymic names are treated as surnames. Icelandic characters are used if they appeared in the original publication. Characters that do not occur in English are alphabetized as follows: *ð* as *d*, *Þ/þ* as *Th/th*, *Æ/æ* as *Ae/ae*, and *Ö/ö* as *O/o*; accented vowels are disregarded for alphabetization purposes.

Acheson, James. 2006. "Institutional Failure in Resource Management." *Annual Review of Anthropology* 35 (1): 117–34. http://dx.doi.org/10.1146/annurev.anthro.35 .081705.123238.

Adger, W. N. 2000. "Social and Ecological Resilience: Are They Related?" *Progress in Human Geography* 24 (3): 347–64. http://dx.doi.org/10.1191/030913200701540465.

Agrawal, A. 2002. "Common Resources and Institutional Stability." In *The Drama of the Commons*, edited by E. Ostrom, T. Dietz, N. Dolsak, P. C. Stern, S. Stonich, and E. U. Weber, 41–85. Washington, DC: National Academy Press.

Ágústsson, Karl. 2010. "Sögukennsla og söguviðhorf: Um þjóðernisleg viðhorf og fræðilegan samanburð í sögukennslu í framhaldsskólum, almennum viðhorfum og opinberri orðræðu." M.Ed. thesis, University of Akureyri.

Albro, Robert. 2005. "The Water Is Ours, Carajo! Deep Citizenship in Bolivia's Water War." In *Social Movements: An Anthropological Reader*, edited by June Nash, 249–71. Malden, MA: Blackwell Publishing.

DOI: 10.5876/9781607323358.c019

Alþingi. 2007. *Frumvarp til laga um breytingu á lögum um íslenskan ríkisborgararétt, nr. 100 23. desember 1952, með síðari breytingum* [Parliamentary bill to make changes to the law concerning Icelandic citizenship, no. 100, December 23, 1952, with later changes]. Reykjavík: Alþingi.

Anderson, Benedict. 1983. *Imagined Communities: Reflections on the Origin and Spread of Nationalism.* London: Verso.

Andresen, Jesper, and Thomas Hojrup. 2008. "The Tragedy of Enclosure: The Battle for Maritime Resources and Life-Modes in Europe." *Ethnologia Europaea* 38 (1): 29–41.

Andrews, Kenneth T., and Michael Biggs. 2006. "The Dynamics of Protest Diffusion: Movement Organizations, Social Networks, and News Media in the 1960 Sit-ins." *American Sociological Review* 71 (5): 752–77. http://dx.doi.org/10.1177/000312240607 100503.

Appadurai, Arjun. 1996. *Modernity at Large: Cultural Dimensions of Globalization.* Minneapolis: University of Minnesota Press.

Arendt, Hannah. 1963. *Eichmann in Jerusalem: A Report on the Banality of Evil.* New York: Viking.

Aretxaga, Begoña. 2005. *States of Terror: Begoña Aretxaga's Essays.* Reno: Center for Basque Studies, University of Nevada.

Aretxaga, Begoña. 1997. *Shattering Silence: Women, Nationalism, and Political Subjectivity in Northern Ireland.* Princeton, NJ: Princeton University Press.

Armitage, D., F. Berkes, and N. Doubleday, eds. 2007. *Adaptive Co-management: Collaboration, Learning, and Multi-Level Governance.* Vancouver: University of British Columbia Press.

Armstrong, C. W., and U. R. Sumaila. 2001. "Optimal Allocation of TAC and the Implications of Implementing an ITQ Management System for the North-East Arctic Cod." *Land Economics* 77 (3): 350–9. http://dx.doi.org/10.2307/3147129.

Árnason, Ragnar. 2008. "Iceland's ITQ System Creates New Wealth." *Electronic Journal of Sustainable Development* 1 (2): n.p. http://www.ejsd.org/public/journal _article/9.

Árnason, Vilhjálmur. 2010. "Moral Analysis of an Economic Collapse—An Exercise in Practical Ethics." *Etikk i Praksis. Nordic Journal of Applied Ethics* 4 (1): 101–23.

Árnason, Vilhjálmur, Salvör Nordal, and Kristín Ástgeirsdóttir. 2010. "Siðferði og starfshættir í tengslum við fall íslensku bankanna 2008" [Morality and working practices in relation to the collapse of the Icelandic banks 2008]." In *Rannsóknarnefnd Alþingis 2010*, vol. 8, annex 1.

Arnbjörnsdóttir, Birna, Ingibjörg Hafstað, and Helga Guðrún Loftsdóttir. 2003. *Af Stað: Kennslubók í íslensku fyrir byrjendur.* Reykjavík: Fjölmenning.

Asad, Talal, ed. 1973. *Anthropology and the Colonial Encounter*. London: Ithaca Press.

Áskelsdóttir, Alda G. 2010. "Áhrif eigenda á íslenska fjölmiðla." MA thesis, University of Iceland. http://skemman.is/handle/1946/6145.

Ásmundsson, Ásmundur. 2008. "LÍ-ALCOA-SÞ." *Viðskiptablaðið* 16 (May): 20.

Ásmundsson, Ásmundur, Hannes Lárusson, and Tinna Grétarsdóttir. 2011a. *Koddu* (catalogue). Reykjavík: Living Art Museum.

Ásmundsson, Ásmundur, Hannes Lárusson, and Tinna Grétarsdóttir. 2011b. "The Cultural Worker." In *Þjóðarspegillinn, Rannsóknir í Félagsvísindum XII: Félags- og mannvísindadeild*, edited by Ása. G. Ásgeirsdóttir, Helga Björnsdóttir, and Helga Ólafs, 606–15. Reykjavík: Félagsvísindastofnun.

Auth, Katie. 2012. "Fishing for Common Ground: Broadening the Definition of 'Rights-Based' Management in Icelands's Westfjords." Master's thesis, Faculty of Business and Science, University of Akureyri, University Centre of the Westfjord's Coastal and Marine Management Programme, Ísafjörður.

Auðlindanefnd. 2000. "Auðlindaskýrsla 2000: Álitsgerð auðlindanefndar um stjórn auðlinda Íslands" [The Icelandic Natural Resources Committee report]." http://www.forsaetisraduneyti.is/media/Skyrslur/Skyrsla_Audlindanefndar_final.pdf.

Bændasamtök Íslands. 2010. *Hagtölur landbúnaðarins*. Reykjavík: Bændasamtök Íslands. *http://bondi.is/lisalib/getfile.aspx?itemid=2824*

Ban, Natalie, Louise K. Blight, Sarah J. Foster, Siân K. Morgan, and Kerrie O'Donnell. 2008. "Pragmatism before Prescription for Managing Global Fisheries." *Frontiers in Ecology and the Environment* 6 (10): 521. http://dx.doi.org/10.1890/1540-9295-6.10.521.a.

Barad, K. 2007. *Meeting the Universe Halfway: Quantum Physics and the Entanglement of Matter and Meaning*. Durham, NC: Duke University Press Books. http://dx.doi.org/10.1215/9780822388128.

Bauman, Richard. 1986. *Story, Performance and Event: Contextual Studies of Oral Narrative*. Cambridge: Cambridge University Press. http://dx.doi.org/10.1017/CBO9780511620935.

Bauman, Richard. 1975. "Verbal Art as Performance." *American Anthropologist* 77 (2): 290–311. http://dx.doi.org/10.1525/aa.1975.77.2.02a00030.

Baumol, W. J. 1990. "Entrepreneurship: Productive, Unproductive, and Destructive." *Journal of Political Economy* 98 (5): 893–921. http://dx.doi.org/10.1086/261712.

Baumol, William, Litan E. Robert, and C. J. Schramm. 2007. *Good Capitalism, Bad Capitalism, and the Economics of Growth and Prosperity*. New Haven, CT: Yale University Press.

Bavington, Dean. 2010. *Managed Annihilation: An Unnatural History of the Newfoundland Cod Collapse*. Vancouver: University of British Columbia Press.

Bell, V. 2012. "Declining Performativity Butler, Whitehead and Ecologies of Concern." *Theory, Culture & Society* 29 (2): 107–23. http://dx.doi.org/10.1177/02632 76412438413.

Benediktsdóttir, Sigríður, Jón Daníelsson, and Gylfi Zoega. 2011. "Lessons from a Collapse of a Financial System." *Economic Policy* 26 (66): 183–235. http://dx.doi.org /10.1111/j.1468-0327.2011.00260.x.

Benediktsson, Jakob. 1971. "Formáli." In *Íslandslýsing: Qualiscunque descriptio Islandiae*, 1–17. Reykjavík: Bókaútgáfa Menningarsjóðs.

Benediktsson, Karl, and Anna Karlsdóttir. 2011. "Iceland: Crisis and Regional Development—Thanks for All the Fish?" *European Urban and Regional Studies* 18 (2): 228–35. http://dx.doi.org/10.1177/0969776411402282.

Bergmann, Eiríkur. 2014. *Iceland and the International Financial Crisis: Boom, Bust and Recovery*. Basingstoke, UK: Palgrave Macmillan.

Berlin, Isaiah. 1969. "Two Concepts of Liberty." In *Four Essays on Liberty*, 118–72. New York: Oxford University Press.

Bernburg, Jón Gunnar, Thorolfur Thorlindsson, and Inga Dóra Sigfusdottir. 2009. "Relative Deprivation and Adolescent Outcomes in Iceland: A Multilevel Test." *Social Forces* 87 (3): 1223–50. http://dx.doi.org/10.1353/sof.0.0177.

Besti Flokkurinn. 2010. "Stefnumál." http://bestiflokkurinn.is/um-flokkinn/stefnumal.

Bissat, Johanna G. 2013. "Effects of Policy Changes on Thai Migration to Iceland." *International Migration* (Geneva) 51 (2): 46–59. http://dx.doi.org/10.1111/imig.12017.

Bjarnason, Magnús. 2010. *The Political Economy of Joining the European Union: Iceland's Position at the Beginning of the 21st Century*. Amsterdam: University of Amsterdam Press.

Bjarnason, T., and T. Thorlindsson. 2006. "Should I Stay or Should I Go? Migration Expectations among Youth in Icelandic Fishing and Farming Communities." *Journal of Rural Studies* 22 (3): 290–300. http://dx.doi.org/10.1016/j.jrurstud.2005.09 .004.

Björnsdóttir, Inga Dóra. 2001. "Leifur Eiríksson versus Christopher Columbus: The Use of Leifur Eiríksson in American Political and Cultural Discourse." In *Approaches to Vínland: A Conference on the Written and Archaeological Sources for the Norse Settlements in the North-Atlantic Region and Exploration of America*, edited by Andrew Wawn and Þórunn Sigurðardóttir, 220–30. Reykjavík: Sigurður Nordal Institute.

Bogason, Arthur. 2007. "The Quota Conundrum." *Samudra Report* 47:22–27.

Bond, George D. 2005. "The Sarvodaya Movement's Vision of Peace and a Dharmic Civil Society." In *Social Movements: An Anthropological Reader*, edited by June Nash, 168–74. Malden, MA: Blackwell Publishing.

Borland, Elizabeth, and Barbara Sutton. 2007. "Quotidian Disruption and Women's Activism in Times of Crisis, Argentina 2002–2003." *Gender & Society* 21 (5): 700–22.

Boyer, Dominic. 2013. "Simply the Best: Parody and Political Sincerity in Iceland." *American Anthropologist* 40 (2): 276–87.

Boyer, Dominic. 2011. "Parody and Sincerity in Western Political Culture." Paper presented at the XXIII Conference of the Académie de la Latinité, The Democratic Imaginary in the Era of Globalization, Barcelona, May 2011.

Boyer, Dominic. 2005. "American Stiob: Or, What Late-Socialist Aesthetics of Parody Reveal about Contemporary Political Culture in the West." *Cultural Anthropology* 24 (2): 179–221.

Bradshaw, M. 2004. "The Market, Marx, and Sustainability in a Fishery." *Antipode* 36 (1): 66–85. http://dx.doi.org/10.1111/j.1467-8330.2004.00382.x.

Brettell, C. B. 2007. "Theorizing Migration in Anthropology: The Social Construction of Networks, Identities, Communities and Globalscapes." In *Migration Theory: Talking across Disciplines*, edited by Caroline B. Bretell and James F. Hollifield, 97–136. New York: Routledge.

Brewer, Jennifer. 2011. "Paper Fish and Policy Conflict: Catch Shares and Ecosystem-Based Management in Maine's Groundfishery." *Ecology and Society* 16 (1): 15.

Bromley, D. W. 2009. "Abdicating Responsibility: The Deceits of Fisheries Policy." *Fisheries* (Bethesda, MD) 34 (4): 22.

Brownell, Susan, and Niko Besnier. 2013. "Gender and Sexuality." In *The Handbook of Sociocultural Anthropology*, edited by James G. Carrier and Deborah B. Gewertz, 239–58. London: Bloomsbury.

Bruner, R. F., and S. D. Carr. 2007. *The Panic of 1907: Lessons Learned from the Market's Perfect Storm*. Hoboken, NJ: John Wiley & Sons.

Brydon, Anne. 2006. "The Predicament of Nature: Keiko the Whale and the Cultural Politics of Whaling in Iceland." *Anthropological Quarterly* 79 (2): 225–60. http://dx.doi.org/10.1353/anq.2006.0016.

Buffett, Mary, and David Clark. 1997. *Buffettology: The Previously Unexplained Techniques That Have Made Warren Buffett the World's Most Famous Investor*. New York: Rawson Associates.

Butler, C. 2004. "Fishing for a Pension or for Peanuts?" *Samudra Report* 39:8–14.

Camic, Charles, and Neil Gross. 1998. "Contemporary Developments in Sociological Theory: Current Projects and Conditions of Possibility." *Annual Review of Sociology* 24 (1): 453–76. http://dx.doi.org/10.1146/annurev.soc.24.1.453.

Canarezza, Rita, and Pier Palo Coro. 2010. "Interview with Christian Schön, Director of CIA—Center for Icelandic Art, Reykjavík." In *Little Constellation,*

Contemporary Art in Geo-Cultural Micro Areas and Small States of Europe, edited by Rita Canarezza and Pier Palo Coro, 178–82. Milano: Mousse Publishing.

Carrier, James G. 2013. "Introduction." In *A Handbook of Sociocultural Anthropology*, edited by J. G. Carrier and Deborah B. Gewertz, 1–18. London: Bloomsbury.

Carrier, James G. 2012. "Anthropology after the Crisis." *Focaal* 2012 (64): 115–28. http://dx.doi.org/10.3167/fcl.2012.640110.

Carrier, James G. 1998. "Introduction." In *Virtualism: A New Political Economy*, edited by James Carrier and Daniel Miller, 1–24. Oxford: Berg Publishers.

Carrier, James G., and Daniel Miller, eds. 1998. *Virtualism: a New Political Economy*. Oxford: Berg Publishers.

Carrithers, Michael, Matei Candea, Karen Sykes, Martin Holbraad, and Soumhya Venkatesan. 2010. "Ontology is just another word for culture: Motion tabled at the 2008 Meeting of the Group for Debates in Anthropological Theory, University of Manchester." *Critique of Anthropology* 30 (2): 152–200. http://dx.doi.org/10.1177/030 8275X09364070.

Cartier, D. 2011. *The End of Iceland's Innocence: The Image of Iceland in the Foreign Media during the Financial Crisis*. Ottawa: University of Ottawa Press.

Cassidy, John. 2009. *How Markets Fail: The Logic of Economic Calamities*. New York: Farrar, Straus and Giroux.

Center for Public Education. 2010. "Cutting to the Bone: How the Economic Crisis Affects Schools." http://www.centerforpubliceducation.org/Main-Menu/Public -education/Cutting-to-the-bone-At-a-glance/Cutting-to-the-bone-How-the -economic-crisis-affects-schools.html.

Central Bank of Iceland. 2012. "Exchange Rate" (interactive table). http://www.cb.is /exchange-rate/.

Central Bank of Iceland. 2009. "Monetary Statistics—Lending Categories" (interactive charts). http://sedlabanki.is/?pageid=444&itemid=5a037662–26ea–477d-bda8 -d71a6017cc05.

Chancellor, Edward. 2000. *Devil Take the Hindmost: A History of Financial Speculation*. New York: Plume.

Chomsky, Noam. 1969. *Aspects of the Theory of Syntax*. Cambridge, MA: MIT Press.

Clifford, James, and George E. Marcus, eds. 1986. *Writing Culture*. Berkeley: University of California Press.

Collier, Stephen J. 2012. "Neoliberalism as Big Leviathan, or . . .?" *Social Anthropology* 20 (2): 186–95.

Collini, Stefan. 1999. *English Pasts: Essays in History and Culture*. Oxford: Oxford University Press.

Connolly, William E. 2011. *A World of Becoming*. Durham, NC: Duke University Press.

Consulate General of Iceland. 2006. "Financial Crisis or Economic Opportunity: The Real Story about Iceland" (press release). April 27. http://www.iceland.is /iceland-abroad/us/nyc/news-and-events/financial-crisis-or-economic-opportu nity%E2%80%94the-real-story-about-iceland/6892/.

Copes, P. 1986. "A Critical Review of the Individual Quota as a Device in Fisheries Management." *Land Economics* 62 (3): 278–91. http://dx.doi.org/10.2307/3146392.

Copes, P., and A. Charles. 2004. "Socioeconomics of Individual Transferable Quotas and Community-Based Fishery Management." *Agricultural and Resource Economics* 33 (2): 171–81.

Corgan, Michael T. 2004. "Language as Identity: Icelandic Confronts Globaliza- tion." Paper presented at the Centre for Small State Studies Conference, Reykja- vík, September 16–18.

Costello, C., S. D. Gaines, and J. Lynham. 2008. "Can Catch Shares Prevent Fish- eries' Collapse?" *Science* 321 (5896): 1678–81. http://dx.doi.org/10.1126/science .1159478.

Couldry, Nick. 2010. *Why Voice Matters: Culture and Politics after Neoliberalism.* London: Sage.

Council of Europe. 2001. *Common European Framework of Reference for Languages: Learning, Teaching, Assessment.* Cambridge: Cambridge University Press.

Crosby, Faye. 1976. "A Model of Egoistical Relative Deprivation." *Psychological Review* 83 (2): 85–113. http://dx.doi.org/10.1037/0033-295X.83.2.85.

Danielsson, Jon, and Gylfi Zoega. 2009. *The Collapse of a Country.* Working Paper Series, W09:03. Reykjavík: Institute of Economics Studies, University of Iceland.

Danske Bank. 2006. "Iceland: Geyser Crisis." http://www.mbl.is/media/98/398.pdf.

Davies, James C. 1962. "Toward a Theory of Revolution." *American Sociological Review* 27 (1): 5–19. http://dx.doi.org/10.2307/2089714.

Davies, Jude. 1997. "Anarchy in the UK: Anarchism and Popular Culture in 1990s Britain." In *Twenty-First Century Anarchism: Unorthodox Ideas for a New Mil- lennium,* edited by Jon Purkis and James Bowen, 62–82. London: Continuum International Publishing Group.

Davies, Jude. 1996. "The Future of 'No Future': Punk Rock and Postmodern Theory." *Journal of Popular Culture* 29 (4): 3–25. http://dx.doi.org/10.1111/j.0022-3840.1996 .00397.x.

Davies, William, and Linsey McGoey. 2012. "Rationalities of Ignorance: On Finan- cial Crisis and the Ambivalence of Neo-Liberal Epistemology." *Economy and Society* 41 (1): 64–83. http://dx.doi.org/10.1080/03085147.2011.637331.

de Young, B., R. M. Peterman, A. R. Dobell, E. Pinkerton, Y. Breton, A. T. Charles, M. J. Fogarty, G. R. Munro, and C. Taggart. 1999. "Canadian Marine Fisheries in a Changing and Uncertain World." In *Canadian Special Publication of Fisheries and Aquatic Sciences*, 387–89. Ottowa: National Research Council of Canada.

Dirks, Nicholas B. 1992. "Introduction: Colonialism and Culture." In *Colonialism and Culture*, edited by Nicholas B. Dirks, 1–26. Ann Arbor: University of Michigan Press.

Doane, Molly. 2005. "The Resilience of Nationalism in a Global Era: Megaprojects in Mexico's South." In *Social Movements: An Anthropological Reader*, edited by June Nash, 187–202. Malden, MA: Blackwell Publishing.

Dofradóttir, Andrea G., and Guðbjörg A. Jónsdóttir. 2010. *Matarúthlutanir hjálparstofnana: Könnun á samsetningu hópsins sem þáði matarúthlutun 24. nóvember 2010.* Reykjavík: Social Science Research Institute, University of Iceland.

Doukas, Dimitra. 2003. *Worked Over: The Corporate Sabotage of an American Community.* Ithaca, NY: Cornell University Press.

Dunn, Elizabeth C. 2004. *Privatizing Poland: Baby Food, Big Business, and the Remaking of Labor.* Ithaca, NY: Cornell University Press.

Durkheim, Emile. (1893) 1984. *The Division of Labour in Society.* London: Routledge & Kegan Paul.

Durrenberger, E. Paul. 1996. "Every Icelander a Special Case." In *Images of Contemporary Iceland: Everyday Lives and Global Contexts*, edited by Gísli Pálsson and E. Paul Durrenberger, 171–90. Iowa City: University of Iowa Press.

Durrenberger, E. Paul, and Suzan Erem. 2010. 2nd ed. *Anthropology Unbound: A Field Guide to the 21st Century.* Denver: Paradigm.

Durrenberger, E. Paul, and Suzan Erem. 2007. *Anthropology Unbound: A Field Guide to the 21st Century.* Denver: Paradigm.

Durrenberger, E. Paul, and Gísli Pálsson. 1989a. "Forms of Production and Fishing Expertise." In *The Anthropology of Iceland*, edited by E. Paul Durrenberger and Gísli Pálsson, 3–18. Iowa City: University of Iowa Press.

Durrenberger, E. Paul, and Gísli Pálsson. 1989b. "Introduction." In *The Anthropology of Iceland*, edited by E. Paul Durrenberger and Gísli Pálsson, ix–xxvii. Iowa City: University of Iowa Press.

Dustmann, Christian, Tommaso Frattini, and Caroline Halls. 2009. "Assessing the Fiscal Costs and Benefits of A8 Migration to the UK." Discussion paper at the Center for Research and Analysis of Migration, London, September 18.

Eagleton, Terry. 1991. *Ideology: An Introduction.* London: Verso.

Education International. 2010. "Education and the Global Economic Crisis: Summary of Results of the Follow-up Survey." http://www.eunec.eu/sites/www.eunec.eu/files/event/attachments/report_education_international.pdf.

Edwards, D., A. Scholz, E. E. Tamm, and C. Steinback. 2006. "The Catch-22 of Licensing Policy: Socio-economic Impacts in British Columbia's Commercial

Ocean Fisheries." In *Proceedings of the 2005 North American Association of Fisheries Economists Forum*, edited by U. R. Sumaila and A. D. Marsden, 65–76. Fisheries Centre Research Reports, vol. 14, no. 1. Vancouver: Fisheries Centre, University of British Columbia.

"Eftir höfðinu dansa limirnir" [The limbs dance according to the head]. 2006. Interview with Ármann Thorvaldsson. *Fréttablaðið*, October 25.

Eggertsson, Thráinn. 2005. *Imperfect Institutions: Possibilities and Limits of Reform*. Ann Arbor: University of Michigan Press.

Einarsdóttir, Auður, Guðrún Theodórsdóttir, María Garðarsdóttir, and Sigríður Þorvaldsdóttir. 2009. *Learning Icelandic*. Reykjavík: Mál og Menning.

Einarsson, N. 2012. "From Fishing Rights to Financial Derivatives: Individual Transferable Quotas and the Icelandic Economic Collapse of 2008 / De los derechos de pesca a los derivados financieros: Las cuotas individuales transferibles y el colapso económico de Islandia en 2008." In *European Fisheries at a Tipping Point / La Pesca Europea ante un Cambio Irreversible*, edited by Thomas Højrup and Klaus Schriewer, 204–55. Murcia: Editum.

Einarsson, N. 2011. *Culture, Conflict and Crises in the Icelandic Fisheries: An Anthropological Study of People, Policy and Marine Resources in the North Atlantic Arctic*. Uppsala: University of Uppsala Press.

Ekroth, Power. 2007. "Pissing on the Nordic Miracle." http://artnews.org/texts.php?g_a=index&g_i=5794.

Elíasson, Guðni. 2009. "Vogun vinnur . . . Hvar liggja rætur íslenska fjármálahrunsins?" *Saga* 47 (2): 117–46.

Ellenberger, Íris. 2010. "Markaðsvæðing sjálfsmyndarinnar." *Kistan*, June 15.

Emery, T. J., B. S. Green, C. Gardner, and J. Tisdell. 2012. "Are Input Controls Required in Individual Transferable Quota Fisheries to Address Ecosystem-Based Fisheries Management Objectives?" *Marine Policy* 36:122–31.

Emery, T. J., K. Hartmann, B. S. Green, C. Gardner, and J. Tisdell. Forthcoming. "Fishing for Revenue: How Leasing Quota Can Be Hazardous to Your Health." *ICES Journal of Marine Science*.

Englund, Peter. 1999. "The Swedish Banking Crisis: Roots and Consequences." *Oxford Review of Economic Policy* 15 (3): 80–97. http://dx.doi.org/10.1093/oxrep/15.3.80.

Engqvist, Jonatan Habib, and Karin Englund, eds. 2010. *The Nordic Third World Country? Icelandic Art in Times of Crisis* (catalogue). Östersund: Färgfabriken Norr.

Eriksen, Thomas Hylland. (1995) 2010. *Small Places, Large Issues: An Introduction to Social and Cultural Anthropology*. 3rd ed. London: Pluto Press.

Erlingsdóttir, Rósa. 2007. "Ráðherra líkti íslensku útrásinni við eldgos." *Morgunblaðið*, September 29. http://www.mbl.is/mm/gagnasafn/grein.html?grein_id=1167322.

Evans-Pritchard, Edward Evans. 1940. *The Nuer*. Oxford: Clarendon Press.

Eythorsson, Einar. 2003. "Stakeholders, Courts, and Communities: ITQ's in Icelandic Fisheries, 1991–2001." In *The Commons in the New Millennium: Challenges and Adaptation*, edited by E. Ostrom and N. Dolsak, 129–68. Cambridge, MA: MIT Press.

Eythórsson, Einar. 2000. "A Decade of ITQ-Management in Icelandic Fisheries: Consolidation without Consensus." *Marine Policy* 24 (6): 483–92. http://dx.doi .org/10.1016/S0308-597X(00)00021-X.

Eyþórsson, Einar. 1997. "Coastal Communities and ITQ Management: The Case of Icelandic Fisheries." In *Social Implications of Quota Systems in Fisheries*, edited by Gísli Pálsson and Guðrún Pétursdóttir, 107–20. Copenhagen: Nordic Council of Ministers.

Eythorsson, Einar. 1996. "Coastal Communities and ITQ Management: The Case of Icelandic Fisheries." *Sociologia Ruralis* 36 (2): 212–23. http://dx.doi.org/10.1111/j .1467-9523.1996.tb00017.x.

Exista. 2007. *Annual Report 2007*. Reykjavík: Exista. http://www.euroland.com/omx_ attachments/2008-02/248363-0-is.pdf.

Fabian, Johannes. 1983. *Time and the Other*. New York: Columbia University Press.

Fairclough, Norman. 2000. "Language and Neo-liberalism." *Discourse & Society* 11 (2): 147–48. http://dx.doi.org/10.1177/0957926500011002001.

Feeny, D., Fikret Berkes, Bonnie J. McCay, and James M. Acheson. 1990. "The Tragedy of the Commons: Twenty-Two Years Later." *Human Ecology* 18 (1): 1–19. http:// dx.doi.org/10.1007/BF00889070.

Fine, Elizabeth C., and Jean Haskell Speer. 1992. *Performance, Culture, and Identity*. Westport, CT: Praeger.

Fitzhugh, William W., and Elisabeth I. Ward, eds. 2000. *Vikings: The North Atlantic Saga*. Washington, DC: Smithsonian Institution.

Fix, M., Demetrios G. Papademetriou, Jeanne Batalova, Alejandro Terrazas, Serena Yi-Ying Lin, and Megan Mittelstadt. 2009. *Migration and the Global Recession: A Report Commissioned by the BBC World Service*. Washington, DC: Migration Policy Institute.

Fjármálaeftirlitið. 2003. "Leiðbeinandi tilmæli um aðskilnað reksturs og vörslu og óhæði rekstrarfélaga verðbréfasjóða skv. 15. gr. laga nr. 30/2003, um verðbréfasjóði og fjárfestingarsjóði. nr. 5/2003." http://www.fme.is/log-og-tilmaeli/leidbeinandi -tilmaeli/nr/930.

Fjármálaeftirlitið. 2002. "Leiðbeinandi tilmæli um innra eftirlit og áhættustýringu hjá fjármálafyrirtækjum. nr. 1/2002." http://www.fme.is/log-og-tilmaeli/leidbeinandi -tilmaeli/nr/908.

Flannery, Mark J. 2010. "Iceland's Failed Banks: A Post-Mortem." In Rannsóknarnefnd Alþingis 2010, vol. 9, annex 3. http://www.rna.is/media/skjol/RNAvef Vidauki3Enska.pdf.

Forsætisráðuneytið [Prime Minister's Office]. 2008. *Ímynd Íslands. Styrkur, staða og stefna* [The image of Iceland: Strength, position and direction]. Reykjavík: Prime Ministry. http://www.forsaetisraduneyti.is/media/Skyrslur/Forsaetisr_arsskyrsla_ END2.pdf.

Foucault, Michel. 2010. *The Birth of Biopolitics: Lectures at the Collège de France, 1978–1979*. New York: Picador Press.

Foucault, Michel. 1984a. "Polemics, Politics, and Problematizations: An Interview with Michel Foucault." In *The Foucault Reader*, edited by Paul Rabinow, 381–90. Harmondsworth: Penguin Books.

Foucault, Michel. 1984b. "Truth and Power." In *The Foucault Reader*, edited by Paul Rabinow, 51–75. Harmondsworth: Penguin Books.

Foucault, Michel. 1980. "Two Lectures." In *Power/Knowledge*, edited by Colin Gordon, 78–108. Brighton: Harvester Press.

Fox, Justin. 2009. *The Myth of the Rational Market: A History of Risk, Reward, and Delusion on Wall Street*. New York: Harper Collins.

Freire, Paolo. 1993. *Pedagogy of the Oppressed*. New York: Continuum.

Fridson, Martin S. 1998. *It Was a Very Good Year: Extraordinary Moments in Stock Market History*. New York: John Wiley & Sons.

Galbraith, John K. 1997. *The Great Crash: 1929*. Boston: Mariner.

Galbraith, John K. 1994. *A Short History of Financial Euphoria*. New York: Penguin.

Garðarsdóttir, Ólöf, and Þóroddur Bjarnason. 2010. "Áhrif efnahagsþrenginga á fólksflutninga til og frá landinu." In *Rannsóknir í Félagsvísindum X: Félags- og mannvísindadeild*, edited by Gunnar Þ. Jóhannesson and Helga Björnsdóttir, 559–68. Reykjavík: Félagsvísindastofnun Háskóla Íslands.

Garðarsdóttir, Ólöf, Guðjón Hauksson, and Helga K. Tryggvadóttir. 2009. *Innflytjendur og einstaklingar með erlendan bakgrunn 1996–2008* [Immigrants and persons with foreign background 1996–2008]. Hagtíðindi Statistical Series, vol. 94, no. 4. Reykjavík: Statistics Iceland.

Geertz, Clifford. 1973. *The Interpretation of Cultures*. New York: Basic Books.

George, Susan. 1999. "A Short History of Neoliberalism." Speech presented at the Conference on Economic Sovereignty in a Globalising World, Bangkok, March 24–26. Transnational Institute. http://www.tni.org/article/short-history -neoliberalism.

Gestsson, Þorgrímur, and Þórarinn Hjartarson. 2004. "Saga Mæðrastyrksnefndar Reykjavíkur í 75 ár." Unpublished ms.

Gezelius, Stig S. 2008. "From Catch Quotas to Effort Regulation: Politics and Implementation in the Faeroese Fisheries." In *Making Fisheries Management Work*, edited by S. S. Gezelius and J. Raakjær, 99–129. New York: Springer. http://dx.doi.org/10.1007/978-1-4020-8628-1_4.

Gíslason, Björn 2014. "Háskólamenn óttast valdafólk." *Kjarninn* 1 May. http://kjarninn.is/haskolamenn-hraeddir-vid-valdafolk.

Gibbs, Mark. 2010. "Why ITQs on Target Species Are Inefficient at Achieving Ecosystem-Based Fisheries Management Outcomes." *Marine Policy* 34 (3): 708–9. http://dx.doi.org/10.1016/j.marpol.2009.09.005.

Gibbs, Mark. 2009. "Individual Transferable Quotas and Ecosystem-Based Fisheries Management: It's All in the T." *Fish and Fisheries* 10 (4): 470–4. http://dx.doi.org/10.1111/j.1467-2979.2009.00343.x.

Gielen, Pascal. 2010. *The Murmuring of the Artistic Multitude: Global Art, Memory and Post-Fordism*. Amsterdam: Valiz.

Gielen, Pascal. 2009. "The Biennial: A Post-Institution for Immaterial Labour." *Open* 16: 8–17. http://www.skor.nl/_files/Files/OPEN16_P8-17.pdf.

Gilroy, Paul. 1993. *The Black Atlantic: Modernity and Double Consciousness*. London: Verso.

Ginsburg, Faye D., Lila Abu-Lughod, and Brian Larkin. 2002. "Introduction." In *Media Worlds: Anthropology on New Terrain*, edited by F. D. Ginsburg, L. Abu-Lughod, and B. Larkin, 1–36. Berkeley: University of California Press.

Gísladóttir, Ingibjörg Sólrún. 2010. "Háskaleg og ótímabær samfélagstilraun" [A dangerous and untimely social experiment]. *Tímarit Máls og menningar* 71 (1): 4–16.

Gissurarson, Hannes Hólmsteinn. 2007. Interview with Hannes Hólmsteinn Gissurarson about the *útrás*. *Ísland í dag* (radio broadcast), Stöð2, September 13. Video available at http://www.yourepeat.com/watch/?v=-AHYUehcBrk.

Gissurarson, Hannes Hólmsteinn. 2004. "Miracle on Iceland." *Wall Street Journal*, January 29. http://online.wsj.com/news/articles/SB107533182153814498.

Gledhill, John. 1994. *Power and Its Disguises: Anthropological Perspectives on Politics*. London: Pluto Press.

Gleeson, Janet. 1999. *Millionaire: The Philanderer, Gambler, and Duelist Who Invented Modern Finance*. New York: Simon & Schuster.

Gnarr, Jón. 2012. *Sjóræninginn* [The Pirate]. Reykjavík: Mál og menning.

Gnarr, Jón. 2010. "We Have a Choice." Translation of the mayor's address announcing the city budget for 2011. *Reykjavík Grapevine*, December 10. http://grapevine.is/mag/column-opinion/2010/12/10/jon-gnarr-mayors-budget-address/.

Gnarr, Jón. 2006. *Indíáninn* [The Indian]. Reykjavík: Mál og menning.

Goldgar, Anne. 2007. *Tulipmania: Money, Honor, and Knowledge in the Dutch Golden Age*. Chicago: University of Chicago Press. http://dx.doi.org/10.7208/chicago /9780226301303.001.0001.

Government Offices of Iceland. 2009. "The Policy Declaration of the Government of the Social Democratic Alliance and the Left-Green Movement." http://www .government.is/government/coalition-platform/nr/475.

Graeber, David. 2004. *Fragments of an Anarchist Anthropology*. Chicago: Prickly Paradigm Press.

Grafton, R. Quentin, Ragnar Arnason, Trond Bjørndal, David Campbell, Harry F. Campbell, Colin W. Clark, Robin Connor, Diane P. Dupont, Rögnvaldur Hannesson, Ray Hilborn, and others. 2006. "Incentive-Based Approaches to Sustainable Fisheries." *Canadian Journal of Fisheries and Aquatic Sciences* 63 (3): 699–710. http:// dx.doi.org/10.1139/f05-247.

Gramsci, Antonio. 1971. *Selection from the Prison Notebooks of Antonio Gramsci*. Edited and translated by Quintin Hoare and Geoffrey Nowell Smith. New York: International Publishers.

Grimes, Kimberly. 2005. "Changing Rules of Trade with Global Partnerships: The Fair Trade Movement." In *Social Movements: An Anthropological Reader*, edited by June Nash, 237–48. Malden, MA: Blackwell Publishing.

Grímsson, Ólafur Ragnar. 2006. "Icelandic Ventures." Lecture by President Ólafur Ragnar Grímsson, delivered in a series of lectures presented by the Icelandic Historians' Society, January 10. http://www.forseti.is/media/files/06.01.10.Sagnfrfel.utras .enska.pdf.

Grímsson, Ólafur Ragnar. 2000. "Speech by the President of Iceland, Ólafur Ragnar Grímsson, at the Icelandic American Chamber of Commerce's Lunch, Los Angeles, 5 May 2000." http://www.forseti.is/media/files/00.05.05.Los.Angeles(1).pdf.

Grímsson, Ólafur Ragnar. 1997. "Ávarp." In *Íslenska söguþingið 28.–31. maí 1997*, edited by Guðmundur J. Guðmundsson and Eiríkur K. Björnsson, 15–17. Reykjavík: Sagnfræðistofnun Háskóla Íslands and Sagnfræðingafélag Íslands.

Grönfeldt, Svafa. 2007. "Þekking, kraftur og þrautseigja" [Knowledge, strength, and endurance]. *Morgunblaðið*, "Atvinnulífið 2020," March 18:8.

Guarnizo, Luis E. 2003. "The Economics of Transnational Living." *International Migration Review* 37 (3): 666–99. http://dx.doi.org/10.1111/j.1747-7379.2003.tb00154.x.

Gudeman, Stephen, ed. 2009. *Economic Persuasions*. Oxford: Berghahn.

Guðmundsson, Einar Már. 2009. "A War Cry from the North." *CounterPunch*, February 23. http://www.counterpunch.org/2009/02/23/a-war-cry-from-the-north/.

Guðmundsson, Einar Már. N.d. "The White Book." Translated by Jónas Knútsson. Unpublished manuscript.

Guðmundsson, Friðrik Þór, Kjartan Ólafsson, Valgerður Jóhannsdóttir, and Þorbjörn Broddason. 2010. "Umfjöllun fjölmiðla á Íslandi um banka og fjármálafyrirtæki 2006–2008" [Media coverage in Iceland about banks and financial companies 2006–2008]; prepared for the Working Group on Ethics. In Rannsóknarnefnd Alþingis 2010, vol. 8, annex 1.

Guðnason, Ólafur Teitur. 2004. "Erindi flutt á málfundi Sagnfræðingafélagsins um bókina Forsætisráðherrar Íslands." Reykjavíkur Akademían, September 17.

Guha, Ranajit, ed. 1982. Subaltern Studies. Delhi: Oxford University Press.

Gunnlaugsson, Stefán B., Ögmundur Knútsson, and Jón Þorvaldur. Heiðarsson. 2010. "Áhrif innköllunar aflaheimilda á stöðu íslenskra sjávarútvegsfyrirtækja" [Impact of re-claim of catch quotas on the status of fisheries companies]. In Skýrsla starfhóps um endurskoðun á lögum um stjórn fiskveiða, Annex 4, R09042SJA, May. Akureyri: University of Akureyri Research Institute. http://www.atvinnuvegaraduneyti.is /media/Skyrslur/meginskyrsla_uppsett_lokaeintak.pdf.

Gylfason, Þorvaldur. 2012. "From Collapse to Constitution: The Case of Iceland." CESIFO Working Paper, no. 3770. www.cesifo-group.de/portal/pls/portal/docs /1/1214102.PDF.

Gylfason, Þorvaldur. 2008. "Ætlar linkindin aldrei að líða hjá?" [Will the kid gloves never come off?] Skírnir 182:489–97.

Gylfason, Thorvaldur, Bengt Holmström, Sixten Korkman, Hans Tson Söderström, and Vesa Vihriälä. 2009. Nordics in Global Crisis: Vulnerability and Resilience. Helsinki: Research Institute of the Finnish Economy (ETLA).

Hackman, Michael Z., and Craig E. Johnson. 2009. 5th ed. Leadership: A Communication Perspective. Long Grove, IL: Waveland Press.

Hafrannsóknastofnun [Marine Research Institute]. 2010. "English Summary of the State of Marine Stocks in Icelandic Waters 2009/2010—Prospects for the Quota Year 2010/2011." In Nytjastofnar Sjávar 2009/2010. Aflahorfur Fiskveiðiárið 2010/2011, 167–71. Hafrannsóknir, no. 153. Reykjavík: Hafrannsóknastofnun. http://www.hafro .is/Astand/2010/35-engl-sum.PDF.

Hafstein, Valdimar Tr. 2000. "The Elves' Point of View: Cultural Identity in Contemporary Icelandic Elf-Tradition." Fabula: Zeitschrift für Erzählforschung 41 (1–2): 87–104. http://dx.doi.org/10.1515/fabl.2000.41.1-2.87.

Hagstofa Íslands. 2010. "Hagur fiskveiða og fiskvinnslu 2008" [Profitability in fishing and fish processing 2008; with English summary]. Hagtíðindi Statistical Series, Sjávarútvegur Fisheries 95 (24). https://hagstofa.is/lisalib/getfile.aspx? ItemID=10828.

Hagstrom, Robert. 2005. The Warren Buffett Way. Hoboken, NJ: John Wiley & Sons.

Hákonardóttir, Inga Huld. 2000. "Philanthropy, Politics, Religion, and Women in Iceland before the Modern Social Welfare System, 1895–1935." In *Gender and Vocation: Women, Religion, and Social Change in the Nordic Countries, 1830–1940*, edited by Pirjo Markkola, 177–210. Helsinki: SKS.

Hálfdanarson, Guðmundur. 2003. "Language, Ethnicity and Nationalism: The Case of Iceland." In *Linguistic and Ethnic Plurality, Past and Present*, edited by Guðmundur Hálfdanarson, 193–204. Pisa: Edizioni Plus, Pisa University Press.

Hálfdanarson, Guðmundur. 2000. "Iceland: A Peaceful Secession." *Scandinavian Journal of History* 25 (1–2): 87–100. http://dx.doi.org/10.1080/034687500501156o9.

Hálfdanarson, Guðmundur. 1999. "Hver á sér fegra föðurland': Staða náttúrunnar í íslenskri þjóðarvitund." *Skírnir* 173:304–36.

Hálfdanarson, Guðmundur. 1995. "Íslensk söguendurskoðun." *Saga* 33:62–7.

Hall, Steve. 2012. *Theorizing Crime and Deviance: A New Perspective*. London: Sage.

Hall, Stuart. 1992. "Cultural Studies and Its Theoretical Legacies." In *Cultural Studies*, edited by Lawrence Grossberg, Cary Nelson, and Paula Treichler, 277–94. New York: Routledge.

Halldorsson, Olafur G., and Gylfi Zoega. 2010. *Iceland's Financial Crisis in an International Perspective*. Working Paper Series, W10:02. Reykjavík: Institute of Economic Studies, University of Iceland. http://hhi.hi.is/sites/hhi.hi.is/files /W-series/2010/WP1002.pdf.

Hann, Chris. 2005. "Postsocialist Societies." In *A Handbook of Economic Anthropology*, edited by James G. Carrier, 547–57. Cheltenham: Edward Elgar. http://dx.doi.org/1 0.4337/9781845423469.00053.

Hann, Chris, and Keith Hart, eds. 2009. *Market and Society: The Great Transformation Today*. Cambridge: Cambridge University Press. http://dx.doi.org/10.1017/CBO 9780511581380.

Hannesson, Rögnvaldur. 2004. *The Privatization of the Oceans*. Cambridge, MA: MIT Press.

Hansen, Povl A., and Göran Serin. 1997. "Will Low Technology Products Disappear? The Hidden Innovation Processes in Low Technology Industries." *Technological Forecasting and Social Change* 55 (2): 179–91. http://dx.doi.org/10.1016/S0040-1625 (97)89490-5.

Hardin, G. 1968. "The Tragedy of the Commons." *Science* 162 (3859): 1243–48.

Hardt, Micheal, and Antonio Negri. 2004. *Multitude: War and Democracy in the Age of Empire*. New York: Penguin Press.

Hart, Keith. 2012. "The Roots of the Global Economic Crisis: Guest Editorial." *Anthropology Today* 28 (2): 1–3.

Hartwich, Oliver Marc. 2009. "Neoliberalism: The Genesis of a Political Swearword." Center for Independent Studies (CIS) Occasional Paper 114. http://www.ort.edu.uy/facs/boletininternacionales/contenidos/68/neoliberalism68.pdf.

Harvey, David. 2007. "Neoliberalism as Creative Destruction." *Annals of the American Academy of Political and Social Science* 610 (1): 21–44. http://dx.doi.org/10.1177/0002716206296780.

Harvey, David. 2005. *A Brief History of Neoliberalism.* Oxford: Oxford University Press.

Hassink, R. 2010. "Regional Resilience: A Promising Concept to Explain Differences in Regional Economic Adaptability?" *Cambridge Journal of Regions, Economy and Society* 3 (1): 45–58. http://dx.doi.org/10.1093/cjres/rsp033.

Hebdige, Dick. 1979. *Subculture: The Meaning of Style.* London: Routledge.

Heelas, Paul, and Paul Morris. 1992. *The Values of the Enterprise Culture: The Moral Debate.* London: Routledge.

Helgason, Agnar. 1995. "The Lords of the Sea and the Morality of Exchange: The Social Context of ITQ Management in the Icelandic Fisheries." Master's thesis, Department of Anthropology, University of Iceland.

Helgason, Agnar, and Gísli Pálsson. 1997. "Contested Commodities: The Moral Landscape of Modernist Regimes." *Journal of the Royal Anthropological Institute* 3 (3): 451–71. http://dx.doi.org/10.2307/3034762.

Helgason, Jón Karl. 2006. "Víkingar efnisins: Goðsögnin um útrás Íslendinga verður til." *Lesbók Morgunblaðsins,* November 11:6–7.

Helgason, Þorsteinn. 2008. "Turkräden 1627 i isländska läromedel." Paper delivered at the 26th Nordic History Congress, August 8–12, 2007, Reykjavík.

Henderson, David R. 2008. "German Economic 'Miracle.'" *The Concise Encyclopedia of Economics.* http://www.econlib.org/library/Enc1/GermanEconomicMiracle.html.

Hesmondhalgh, David. 2012. "Defining the Future EU Culture and Media Programmes." Public hearing, European Parliament, Brussels, April 26. http://www.europarl.europa.eu/document/activities/cont/201205/20120507ATT44555/2012050 7ATT44555EN.pdf.

Hesmondhalgh, David, and Sarah Baker. 2011. "A Very Complicated Version of Freedom: Conditions and Experiences of Creative Labour in Three Cultural Industries." *Variant* 41:34–38.

Higgins, Andrew. 2013. "Iceland, Fervent Prosecutor of Bankers, Sees Meager Returns." *New York Times,* February 2.

Ho, Karen. 2009. *Liquidated: An Ethnography of Wall Street.* Durham, NC: Duke University Press.

Holmes, Nigel, and Megan McArdle. 2008. "Iceland's Meltdown: An Economic Morality Play, in 10 Acts." *Atlantic*, December. http://www.theatlantic.com /magazine/archive/2008/12/iceland-s-meltdown/307150/.

hooks, bell. 1994. *Teaching to Transgress: Education as the Practice of Freedom*. New York: Routledge.

Hudson, R. 2010. "Resilient Regions in an Uncertain World: Wishful Thinking or a Practical Reality?" *Cambridge Journal of Regions, Economy and Society* 3 (1): 11–25. http://dx.doi.org/10.1093/cjres/rsp026.

Huijbens, Edward H. 2011. "Nation-Branding, a Critical Evaluation: Assessing the Image Building of Iceland." In *Iceland and Images of the North*, edited by Sumarliði Ísleifsson and Daniel Chartier, 553–82. Sainte-Foy / Reykjavík: Presses de l'Université du Québec / Reykjavíkurakademían.

Huyssen, Andreas. 2001. "Present Pasts: Media, Politics, Amnesi." In *Globalization*, edited by Arjun Appadurai, 57–77. Durham, NC: Duke University Press.

Hymes, Dell. 1971. "On Communicative Competence." In *The Communicative Approach to Language Teaching*, edited by C. J. Brumfit and K. Johnson, 5–26. Oxford: Oxford University Press.

Icelandic Association of Local Authorities. 2008. "Skilgreining grunnþjónustu á sviði fræðslumála." http://www.samband.is/media/skolamal/Grunnthjonusta-a-svidi -fraedslumala.pdf.

"Icelandic Crown Rallies." 2008. Interview with Richard Portes, London Business School. *Europe Today*, CNBC, March 28. http://video.cnbc.com/gallery/?video =696487936.

Illugadóttir, Eygló. 2011. "Efnahagshrunið og skólastarf á Hornafirði: Upplifun stjórnenda" [The economic crisis and education in Hornafjörður]. M.Ed. thesis, University of Iceland.

Ingvarsdóttir, Brynhildur. 1996. "Hvað er á seyði í sagnfræðinni? Erlendar hræringar og íslenskir sagnfræðingar." *Skírnir* 170 (1): 105–43.

International Monetary Fund. 2011. "IMF Completes Fourth Review under the Stand-By Arrangement for Iceland." Press release no. 11/5, January 11. imf.org /external/np/sec/pr/2011/pr1105.htm.

Íslandsbanki Seafood Team. 2010. *Iceland Seafood Market Report: Íslandsbanki Seafood Research*. Reykjavík: Íslandsbanki. http://skjol.islandsbanki.is/servlet/file/store156 /item64129/Seafood%20report%202010%2005%20vef.pdf.

Ísleifsson, Sumarliði. 2011. "Introduction: Imaginations of National Identity and the North." In *Iceland and Images of the North*, edited by Sumarliði Ísleifsson and Daniel Chartier, 3–22. Sainte-Foy / Reykjavík: Presses de l'Université du Québec / Reykjavíkurakademían.

Jacquermin, Frédéric. 2005. "Belgian Barbarians." In *European Cultural Policies 2015: A Report with Scenarios on the Future of Funding for Contemporary Art in Europe*, edited by Raimund Minichbauer and Maria Lind, 50–59. Stockholm / Vienna: International Artists Studio Programme in Sweden / European Institute for Progressive Cultural Policies.

Jasper, James M., and Jane D. Poulsen. 1995. "Recruiting Strangers and Friends: Moral Shocks and Social Networks in Animal Rights and Anti-Nuclear Protests." *Social Problems* 42 (4): 493–512. http://dx.doi.org/10.2307/3097043.

Jóhannesson, Guðni Th. 2012. "Útrásarforsetinn." In *Ísland í aldanna rás 2001–2010*, edited by Björn Þór Sigbjörnsson and Bergsteinn Sigurðsson, 410–3. Reykjavík: JPV.

Jóhannesson, Guðni Th. 2009a. "'Þeir fólar sem frelsi vort svíkja': Lög, ásakanir og dómar um landráð á Íslandi." *Saga* 47 (2): 55–88.

Jóhannesson, Guðni Th. 2009b. *Hrunið: Ísland á barmi gjaldþrots og upplausnar* [The collapse: Iceland on the brink of bankruptcy and dissolution]. Reykjavík: JPV.

Jóhannesson, Guðni Th. 2005. "Umræða um ekkert? Einföld og flókin skoðanaskipti sagnfræðinga um aðferð og afurð, sögur og sagnfræði, skor, skóga og tré." *Kviksaga*, April 5.

Jóhannesson, Guðni Th. 2004. "Hræðilegt og fræðilegt: Umræður um forsætisráðherrabókina." *Fréttabréf Sagnfræðingafélags Íslands* 138:4–5.

Jóhannesson, Sigurður. 2004. "Frelsi á fjármagnsmarkaði eftir 1980." In *Rætur Íslandsbanka: 100 ára fjármálasaga*, edited by Eggert Þór Bernharðsson, 186–97. Reykjavík: Íslandsbanki.

Johnsen, Guðrún. 2014. *Bringing Down the Banking System: Lessons from Iceland*. New York: Palgrave Macmillan.

Jónasson, Jón Torfi. 2008. *Inventing Tomorrow's University: Who Is to Take the Lead?* Bologna: Bononia University Press.

"Jón Gnarr grét á fjölmennum fundi í Þjóðmenningarhúsinu." 2012. Interview with Jón Gnarr. *Harmageddon* (radio broadcast), X-97.7, October 12. Video available at http://www.visir.is/section/MEDIA99&fileid=CLP14313.

"Jón Gnarr vefhetja ársins á NEXPO." 2013. *Morgunblaðið*, February 16. http://www.mbl.is/frettir/taekni/2013/02/16/jon_gnarr_vefhetja_arsins_a_nexpo/.

Jónsdóttir, Sólborg, and Þorbjörg Halldórsdóttir. 2011. *Íslenska fyrir alla, 1–4*. Reykjavík: Hljóðvinnslan.

Jónsdóttir, Vala, Kristín Erla Harðardóttir, and Ragna B. Garðarsdóttir. 2009. *Innflytjendur á Íslandi: Viðhorfskönnun*. Reykjavík: Félagsvísindastofnun Háskóla Íslands.

Jónsson Aðils, Jón. (1915) 1946. *Íslandssaga*. Reykjavík: Ísafoldarprentsmiðja.

Jónsson Aðils, Jón. 1903. *Íslenskt þjóðerni: Alþýðufyrirlestrar*. Reykjavík: Sigurður Kristinsson.

Jónsson, Ásgeir. 2009. *Why Iceland?* New York: McGraw-Hill.

Jónsson, Eiríkur. 2008. "Viðskiptaþingið á Hilton var vel sótt og þar mátti sjá alla þá sem einhverju máli skipta í íslensku viðskiptalífi." *Séð og heyrt* 8 (February): 21–27.

Jónsson, Guðmundur. 2002. "Hagþróun og hagvöxtur á Íslandi 1914–1960." In *Frá kreppu til viðreisnar: Þættir um hagstjórn á Íslandi á árunum 1930–1960*, edited by Jónas H. Haralz, 9–39. Reykjavík: Hið íslenska bókmenntafélag.

Jónsson, Jónas. (1915–1916) 1966. *Íslandssaga: Fyrra hefti*. Reykjavík: Ríkisútgáfa námsbóka.

Jónsson, Örn D., and Rögnvaldur J. Sæmundsson. 2006. "Isolation as a Source of Entrepreneurial Opportunities: Overcoming the Limitations of Isolated Micro-States." In *Developmental Entrepreneurship: Adversity, Risk, and Isolation*, edited by C. Galbraith and C. Stiles, 217–33. International Research in the Business Disciplines, vol. 5. Oxford: Elsevier. http://dx.doi.org/10.1016/S1074-7877(06)05012-4.

Jónsson, Sigurður M. 2009. "Spilaborg eignarhaldsfélaganna fallin." *Viðskiptablaðið*, September 20:22–23.

Jónsson, Stefán. 1967. *Eitt er landið: Um Íslands sögu*. Reykjavík: Ríkisútgáfa námsbóka.

Jonung, Lars. 2008. "Lessons from Financial Liberalisation in Scandinavia." *Comparative Economic Studies* 50 (4): 564–98. http://dx.doi.org/10.1057/ces.2008.34.

Júlíusdóttir, Katrín. 2011. "Culture and Business." http://wayback.vefsafn.is/way back/20110329154336/http://eng.idnadarraduneyti.is/ (select Minister > Speeches).

Júlíusdóttir, Magnfríður, Unnur D. Skaptadóttir, and Anna Karlsdóttir. 2013. "Gendered Migration in Turbulent Times in Iceland." *Norsk Geografisk Tidsskrift—Norwegian Journal of Geography* 67 (5): 266–75. http://dx.doi.org/10.1080/00291951.2013.847483.

Jütte, Robert. 1994. *Poverty and Deviance in Early Modern Europe*. Cambridge: Cambridge University Press.

Kahneman, Daniel, and Amos Tversky. 1982. "Subjective Probability: A Judgment of Representativeness." In *Judgement under Uncertainty: Heuristics and Biases*, edited by D. Kahneman, P. Slovic, and A. Tversky, 32–47. Cambridge: Cambridge University Press. http://dx.doi.org/10.1017/CBO9780511809477.004.

Kalb, Don. 2012. "Thinking of Neoliberalism As If the Crisis Was Actually Happening." *Social Anthropology* 20 (3): 318–30.

Kapferer, B. 2005. "Situations, Crisis, and the Anthropology of the Concrete: The Contribution of Max Gluckman." *Social Analysis* 49 (3): 85–122. http://dx.doi.org/10.3167/015597705780275110.

Karlsdóttir, Anna. 2008. "Not Sure about the Shore! Transformation Effects of Individual Transferable Quotas on Iceland's Fishing Economy and Communities." In *Enclosing the Fisheries: People, Places and Power*, edited by M. Lowe and C. Carothers, 99–119. Bethesda, MD: American Fisheries Society.

Karlsdóttir, Anna. 2009. "Are Living Fish Better than Dead Fillets? The Invisibility and Power of Icelandic Women in Aquaculture and the Fishery Economy." In *Gender, Culture, and Northern Fisheries*, edited by J. Kafarowski, 67–85. Edmonton, Alberta: CCI Press.

Karlsson, Gunnar. 1995. "The Emerge of Nationalism in Iceland." In *Ethnicity and Nation Building in the Nordic World*, edited by S. Tägil., 33–62. Carbondale, IL: Southern Illinois University Press.

Kaupþing. N.d. "*What Is Kaupthinking?*" (video). Reykjavík: Kaupþing. http://www .youtube.com/watch?v=31U54cgf_OQ.

Kirzner, I. M. 1997. "Entrepreneurial Discovery and the Competitive Market Process: An Austrian Approach." *Journal of Economic Literature* 35 (1): 60–85.

Kirzner, I. M. 1973. *Competition and Entrepreneurship*. Chicago: University of Chicago Press.

Kjartansdóttir, Katla. 2011. "The New Viking Wave: Cultural Heritage and Capitalism." In *Iceland and Images of the North*, edited by Sumarliði Ísleifsson and Daniel Chartier, 461–80. Sainte-Foy / Reykjavík: Presses de l'Université du Québec / Reykjavíkurakademían.

Klandermans, Bert, and Sjoerd Goslinga. 1996. "Media Discourse, Movement Publicity, and the Generation of Collective Action Frames: Theoretical and Empirical Exercises in Meaning Construction." In *Comparative Perspectives on Social Movements: Political Opportunities, Mobilizing Structures, and Cultural Framings*, edited by Doug McAdam, John D. McCarthy, and Mayer N. Zald, 312–37. Cambridge Studies in Comparative Politics. Cambridge: Cambridge University Press.

Klein, Naomi. 2007. *The Shock Doctrine: The Rise of Disaster Capitalism*. New York: Picador.

Kline, S. J., and N. Rosenberg. 1986. "An Overview of Innovation." In *The Positive Sum Strategy: Harnessing Technology for Economic Growth*, edited by R. Landau and N. Rosenberg, 275–304. Washington, DC: National Academy Press.

Koser, Khalid. 2007. *International Migration: A Very Short Introduction*. Oxford: Oxford University Press. http://dx.doi.org/10.1093/actrade/9780199298013.001 .0001.

Kristinsdóttir, Erla. 2009. "Kauphöll og sjávarútvegur: Eiga þau samleið?" [The stock market and the fisheries industry: Do they go together?]. MS thesis, School of Business, University of Iceland.

Kristjánsson, Halldór J. 2005. "Viðskipti og menning." *Lesbók Morgunblaðsins*, October 15.

Kristmundsdóttir, Sigríður Dúna. 2004. "Women's Movements and the Contradictory Forces of Globalization." In *Crossing Borders: Re-Mapping Women's Movements at the Turn of the 21st Century*, edited by Hilda Rømer Christense, Beatrice Halsaa, and Aino Saarinen, 323–35. Odense: University Press of Southern Denmark.

Kristmundsdóttir, Sigríður Dúna. 1997. *Doing and Becoming: Women's Movements and Women's Personhood in Iceland 1870–1990*. Reykjavík: Social Science Research Institute, University of Iceland.

Krugman, Paul. 2010. "The Icelandic Post-Crisis Miracle." *New York Times*, June 30.

Lam, M. 2012. "Of Fish and Fishermen: Shifting Societal Baselines to Reduce Environmental Harm in Fisheries." *Ecology and Society* 17 (4): 18. http://dx.doi.org /10.5751/ES-05113-170418.

Landssamtök Lífeyrissjóða [Icelandic Pension Funds Association]. 2012. *Skýrsla úttektarnefndar* [Pension Funds investigative report]. 4 vols. Reykjavík: Landssamtök Lífeyrissjóða. For an English summary of the main conclusions, see http:// ll.is/files/00_2012_Uttektarskyrsla/Bindi_1_Kafli2_engl.pdf.

Latour, B. 2011. "Reflections on Etienne Souriau's *Les differents modes d'existence*." In *The Speculative Turn: Continental Materialism and Realism*, edited by L. R. Bryant, N. Srnicek, and G. Harman, 152–82. Melbourne: re.press.

Latour, B. 2008. "A Textbook Case Revisited: Knowledge as a Mode of Existence." In *The Handbook of Science and Technology Studies*, edited by E. Hackett, O. Amsterdamska, M. Lynch, and J. Wajcman, 83–112. Cambridge, MA: MIT Press.

Lavie, Smadar, and Ted Swedenburg. 1996. "Introduction: Displacement, Diaspora, and Geographies of Identity." In *Displacement, Diaspora, and Geographies of Identity*, edited by Smadar Lavie and Ted Swedenburg, 1–26. Durham, NC: Duke University Press.

Law, J., and M. Lien. 2013. "Slippery: Field Notes in Empirical Ontology." *Social Studies of Science* 43 (3): 363–78.

Laxness, Halldór. 2008. *The Great Weaver from Kashmír*. Translated by Philip Roughton. Brooklyn, NY: Archipelago Books. Originally published as *Vefarinn mikli frá Kasmír* (1927).

Laxness, Halldór. [1944] 1985. "Háheilög mannblót." *Sjómannablaðið Víkingur* 47 (11–12): 37, 39.

Laxness, Halldór. 1972. *Christianity at Glacier*. Translated by Magnus Magnusson. Reykjavík: Helgafell. Originally published as *Kristnihald undir Jökli* (1968).

Laxness, Halldór. 1969. *World Light*. Translated by Magnus Magnusson. Madison: University of Wisconsin Press. Originally published as *Heimsljós* (1937–38).

Laxness, Halldór. 1946. *Independent People*. Translated by J. A. Thompson. New York: Knopf. Originally published as *Sjálfstætt fólk* (1934–35).

Lazar, Sian. 2010. "Schooling and Critical Citizenship: Pedagogies of Political Agency in El Alto, Bolivia." *Anthropology & Education Quarterly* 41 (2): 181–205. http://dx.doi.org/10.1111/j.1548-1492.2010.01077.x.

Lazar, Sian. 2008. *El Alto, Rebel City: Self and Citizenship in Andean Bolivia*. Durham, NC: Duke University Press.

Lazar, Sian. 2007. "'In-betweenness' at the Margins: Collective Organization, Ethnicity, and Political Agency among Bolivian Street Traders." In *Livelihoods at the Margins: Surviving the City*, edited by James Staples, 237–56. Walnut Creek, CA: Left Coast Press.

Leach, Edmund. 1967. "Runaway World." Reith Lecture of the British Broadcasting Corporation. www.bbc.co.uk/programmes/pooh3xy8.

Lévi-Strauss, Claude. 1966. *The Savage Mind*. London: Weidenfeld and Nicolson.

Lévi-Strauss, Claude. 1961. *A World on the Wane*. Translated by John Russell. New York: Criterion Books.

Lewis, Michael. 2011. *Boomerang: Travels in the New Third World*. New York: Norton.

Lewis, Michael. 2010. *The Big Short: Inside the Doomsday Machine*. New York: Norton.

Lewis, Michael. 1989. *Liar's Poker: Rising Through the Wreckage on Wall Street*. New York: Norton.

Lindberg, Carter. 1993. *Beyond Charity: Reformation Initiatives for the Poor*. Minneapolis, MN: Fortress Press.

Loftsdóttir, Kristín. 2012a. "Belonging and the Icelandic Other: Situating Icelandic Identity in a Postcolonial Context." In *Whiteness and Postcolonialism in the Nordic Region: Exceptionalism, Migrant Others and National Identities*, edited by K. Loftsdóttir and L. Jensen, 57–71. Burlington: Ashgate.

Loftsdóttir, Kristín. 2012b. "Colonialism at the Margins: Politics of Difference in Europe as Seen through Two Icelandic Crises." *Identities: Global Studies in Culture and Power* 19 (5): 597–615. http://dx.doi.org/10.1080/1070289X.2012.732543.

Loftsdóttir, Kristín. 2010. "The Loss of Innocence: The Icelandic Financial Crisis and Colonial Past." *Anthropology Today* 26 (6): 9–13. http://dx.doi.org/10.1111/j.1467 -8322.2010.00769.x.

Loftsdóttir, Kristín. 2009. "Kjarnmestafólkið í heimi: Þrástef íslenskrar þjóðernishyggju í gegnum lýðveldisbaráttu, útrás og kreppu." *Ritið* 2–3:113–39.

Loftsdóttir, Kristín. 2007. "Útrás Íslendinga og hnattvæðing hins þjóðlega: Horft til Silvíu Nætur og Magna." *Ritið* 7 (1): 159–76.

Lorey, Isabell. 2011. "Virtuosos of Freedom: On the Implosion of Political Virtuosity and Productive Labour." In *Critique of Creativity: Precarity, Subjectivity, and Resistance in the 'Creative Industries'*, edited by Gerald Raunig, Gene Ray, and Ulf Wuggenig, 79–90. London: MayFly Books.

Lorey, Isabell. 2006. "Governmentality and Self-Precarization: On the Normalization of Cultural Producers." Translated by Lisa Rosenblatt and Dagmar Fink. *Transversal*, January. http://eipcp.net/transversal/1106/lorey/en.

Loucks, Laura. 2005. "The Evolution of the Area 19 Snow Crab Co-Management Agreement: Understanding the Inter-relationship between Transaction Costs, Credible Commitment, and Collective Action." PhD diss., School of Resource and Environmental Management, Simon Fraser University.

Mackey, Eva. 2002. *The House of Difference: Cultural Politics and National Identity in Canada.* Toronto: University of Toronto.

Magna Charta Observatory of Fundamental University Values and Rights. 1988. *Magna Charta Universitatum.* http://www.magna-charta.org/library/userfiles/file /mc_english.pdf.

Magnússon, Sigurður Gylfi. 2010. *Wasteland with Words: A Social History of Iceland.* London: Reaktion Press.

Magnússon, Sigurður Gylfi. 2007. *Sögustríð: Greinar og frásagnir um hugmyndafræði.* Reykjavík: Miðstöð einsögurannsókna, Reykjavíkurakademían.

Magnússon, Sigurður Gylfi. 2006. "'Við' erum frábær!" *Kistan,* January 10.

Mahler, Sarah J., and Patricia R. Pessar. 2006. "Gender Matters: Ethnographers Bring Gender from the Periphery toward the Core of Migration Studies." *International Migration Review* 40 (1): 27–63. http://dx.doi.org/10.1111/j.1747-7379.2006.00002.x.

Malinowski, Bronislaw. 1922. *Argonauts of the Western Pacific.* London: Routledge.

Malinowski, Bronislaw. 1921. "The Primitive Economics of Trobriand Islanders." *Economic Journal* 31 (121): 1–16. http://dx.doi.org/10.2307/2223283.

Mallaby, Sebastian. 2010. *More Money Than God: Hedge Funds and the Making of the New Elite.* London: Penguin.

Mandler, Peter, Sean Lang, and Ted Vallance. 2011. "Debates: Narrative in School History." *Teaching History* 145:22–31.

Marcus, George E. 2008. "The End(s) of Ethnography: Social/Cultural Anthropology's Signature Form of Producing Knowledge in Transition." *Cultural Anthropology* 23 (1): 1–14. http://dx.doi.org/10.1111/j.1548-1360.2008.00001.x.

Martin, Philip. 2009. "Recession and Migration: A New Era for Labor Migration?" *International Migration Review* 43 (3): 671–91. http://dx.doi.org/10.1111/j.1747-7379 .2009.00781.x.

Martin, R. 2012. "Regional Economic Resilience, Hysteresis, and Recessionary Shocks." *Journal of Economic Geography* 12 (1): 1–32. http://dx.doi.org/10.1093/jeg/lbr019.

Masso, Jaan, and Kerly Krillo. 2011. *Labour Markets in the Baltic States during the Crisis 2008–2009: The Effect on Different Labour Market Groups.* Faculty of Economics and Business Administration Working Paper, no. 79. Tartu: University of Tartu. http:// www.mtk.ut.ee/sites/default/files/mtk/RePEc/mtk/febpdf/febawb79.pdf.

Matthíasdóttir, Sigríður. 2004. *Hinn sanni Íslendingur: Þjóðerni, kyngervi og vald á Íslandi 1900–1930.* Reykjavík: Háskólaútgáfan.

Matthíasson, Þórólfur. 2008. "Spinning Out of Control: Iceland in Crisis." *Nordic Journal of Political Economy* 34: 1–19.

Mauss, Marcel. (1925) 1990. *The Gift: The Form and Reason for Exchange in Archaic Societies*. London: Routledge.

McAdam, Doug. 1996. "The Framing Function of Movement Tactics: Strategic Dramaturgy in the American Civil Rights Movement." In *Comparative Perspectives on Social Movements: Political Opportunities, Mobilizing Structures, and Cultural Framings*, edited by Doug McAdam, John D. McCarthy, and Mayer N. Zald, 338–56. Cambridge: Cambridge University Press. http://dx.doi.org/10.1017/CBO9780511803987.017.

McAdam, Doug, John D. McCarthy, and Meyer N. Zald. 1996. "Introduction: Opportunities, Mobilizing Structures, and Framing Processes: Toward a Synthetic, Comparative Perspective on Social Movements." In *Comparative Perspectives on Social Movements: Political Opportunities, Mobilizing Structures, and Cultural Framings*, edited by Doug McAdam, John D. McCarthy, and Mayer N. Zald, 1–20. Cambridge: Cambridge University Press. http://dx.doi.org/10.1017/CBO9780511803987.002.

McCarthy, John D., Jackie Smith, and Meyer N. Zald. 1996. "Accessing Public, Media, Electoral, and Governmental Agendas." In *Comparative Perspectives on Social Movements: Political Opportunities, Mobilizing Structures, and Cultural Framings*, edited by Doug McAdam, John D. McCarthy, and Mayer N. Zald, 291–311. Cambridge: Cambridge University Press. http://dx.doi.org/10.1017/CBO9780511803987.015.

McCarthy, Thomas. 1991. "Introduction." In *The Structural Transformation of the Public Sphere*, edited by Jürgen Habermas, xi–xiv. Boston: MIT Press.

McCay, Bonnie J., Carolyn F. Creed, Alan Christopher Finlayson, Richard Apostle, and Knut Mikalsen. 1995. "Individual Transferable Quotas (ITQs) in Canadian and US Fisheries." *Ocean and Coastal Management* 28 (1–3): 85–115. http://dx.doi.org/10.1016/0964-5691(95)00068-2.

McCloskey, D. N. 1998. *The Rhetoric of Economics*. 2nd ed. Madison: University of Wisconsin Press.

McCloskey, D. N. 1993. "Some Consequences of a Conjective Economics." In *Beyond Economic Man: Feminist Theory and Economics*, edited by Marianne A. Ferber and Julie A. Nelson, 69–93. Chicago: University of Chicago Press.

McCurdy, Earle. 2012. "Nothing 'Modern' in DFO Plan." *The Fisherman* 77 (2): 13.

Mead, Margaret. 1949. *Coming of Age in Samoa: A Psychological Study of Primitive Youth for Western Civilization*. New York: New American Library.

Mead, Margaret. 1930. *Growing Up in New Guinea: A Comparative Study of Primitive Education*. New York.: Morrow.

Menntamálaráðuneyti [Ministry of Education, Science, and Culture]. 2008. *Íslenska fyrir Útlendinga—Grunnnám* [Icelandic for Foreigners—Curriculum]. Reykjavík: Menntamálaráðuneyti.

"Miklu skiptir að Mishkin tók þátt í gerð skýrslu um Ísland" [Very important that Mishkin contributed to the report]. 2006. *Morgunblaðið*, May 11. http://www.mbl.is /vidskipti/frettir/2006/05/11/miklu_skiptir_ad_mishkin_tok_thatt_i_gerd_skyrslu_u/

Milgram, Stanley. 1974. *Obedience to Authority: An Experimental View*. New York: Tavistock.

Mills, David. 2013. "Related Disciplines." In *The Handbook of Sociocultural Anthropology*, edited by James G. Carrier and Deborah B. Gewertz, 570–87. London: Bloomsbury.

Ministry of Fisheries and Agriculture. 2006. *The Fisheries Management Act: Act on Fisheries Management as Subsequently Amended* [Law no. 116, August 10]. Reykjavík: Icelandic Fisheries, Ministry of Fisheries and Agriculture. http://www.fisheries.is /management/fisheries-management/the-fisheries-management-act/.

Ministry of Social Affairs. 2007. "Government Policy on the Integration of Immigrants." Reykjavík: Velferðarráðuneyti. http://eng.velferdarraduneyti.is/media /acrobat-enskar_sidur/stefna_integration_of_immigrants.pdf.

Minnegal, M., and P. Dwyer. 2011. "Appropriating Fish, Appropriating Fishermen: Tradeable Permits, Natural Resources, and Uncertainty." In *Ownership and Appropriation*, edited by V. Strang and M. Busse, 197–215. New York: Berg.

Minsky, H. 2008. *Stabilizing an Unstable Economy*. Yale, CT: Yale University Press.

Mirowski, Philip. 2014. *Never Let a Serious Crisis Go to Waste: How Neoliberalism Survived the Financial Meltdown*. London: Verso.

Mishkin, Frederic S., and Tryggvi Thor Herbertsson. 2006. *Financial Stability in Iceland*. Reykjavík: Iceland Chamber of Commerce.

Mixa, Már Wolfgang. 2009. "Once in Khaki Suits: Socioeconomical Features of the Icelandic Collapse." In *Rannsóknir í Félagsvísindum X*, edited by Ingjaldur Hannibalsson, 435–47. Reykjavík: Háskólaútgáfan.

Mixa, Már W., and Þröstur O. Sigurjónsson. 2010. "Áfram á rauðu ljósi—fjármálahrunið á Íslandi og reynsla Norðurlandanna." *Tímarit um viðskipti og efnahagsmál* 7 (1): 21–40.

Mol, A. 1999. "Ontological Politics: A Word and Some Questions." In *Actor Network Theory and After*, edited by J. Law and J. Hassard, 74–89. Sociological Review Monograph. Malden, MA: Blackwell / Sociological Review.

Moore, H. L. 2004. "Global Anxieties: Concept-Metaphors and Pre-Theoretical Commitments in Anthropology." *Anthropological Theory* 4 (1): 71–88. http://dx.doi .org/10.1177/1463499604040848.

Munro, G. R. 2001. "The Effect of Introducing Individual Harvest Quotas upon Fleet Capacity in the Marine Fisheries of British Columbia." In *Case Studies on the Effects of Transferable Fishing Rights on Fleet Capacity and Concentration of Quota Ownership*, edited by R. Shotton, 208–20. FAO Fisheries Technical Paper 412. Rome: Food and Agriculture Organization of the United Nations.

Münzel, Mark. 2011. "The End." In *The End of Anthropology?* ed. Holger Jebens and Karl-Heinz Kohl, 219–39. Wantage, UK: Sean Kingston Publishing.

Nash, June. 2005. "Introduction: Social Movements and Global Processes." In *Social Movements: An Anthropological Reader*, edited by June Nash, 1–26. Malden, MA: Blackwell.

National Assembly Iceland. 2009. "Þjóðfundur." http://www.thjodfundur2009.is/.

National Research Council. 1999. *Sharing the Fish: Toward a National Policy on Individual Fishing Quotas*. Washington, DC: National Academy Press.

Navaro-Yashin, Yael. 2003. "'Life Is Dead Here': Sensing the Political in 'No Man's Land.'" *Anthropological Theory* 3 (1): 107–25. http://dx.doi.org/10.1177/1463499960300 3001174.

Navaro-Yashin, Yael. 2002. *Faces of the State: Secularism and Public Life in Turkey*. Princeton, NJ: Princeton University Press.

Negri, Toni. 1988. *Revolution Retrieved: Writings on Marx, Keynes, Capitalist Crisis and New Social Subjects (1967–83)*. London: Red Notes.

Nelson, R. R. 1992. "National Innovation Systems: A Retrospective on a Study." *Industrial and Corporate Change*, 1 (2): 347–74.

Niemi, Einar. 1995. "The Finns in Northern Scandinavia and Minority Policy." In *Ethnicity and Nation Building in the Nordic World*, edited by Sven Tägil, 145–78. London: Hurst & Co.

Nikoloyuk, Jordan, and David Adler. 2013. *Valuing Our Fisheries: Breaking Nova Scotia's Commodity Curse*. Halifax: Ecology Action Centre.

Njáls, Harpa. 2003. *Fátækt á Íslandi: Við upphaf nýrrar aldar*. Reykjavík: Háskólaútgáfan.

Njálsdóttir, S. 2012. "Kvenfélagið Gleym mér ei." In *Fólkið, fjöllin, fjörðurinn. Safn til sögu Eyrarsveitar* 2012:9–56. Grundarfjörður: Eyrbyggjar-Hollvinasamtök Grundarfjarðar.

"Nordic Partners kaupa sögufræg hótel í Kaupmannahöfn." 2007. *Viðskiptablaðið*, September 13:1.

Norris, Pippa, Stefaan Walgrave, and Peter Van Aelst. 2005. "Who Demonstrates? Antistate Rebels, Conventional Participants, or Everyone?" *Comparative Politics* 37 (2): 189–205. http://dx.doi.org/10.2307/20072882.

North, Douglass S. 1990. *Institutions, Institutional Change and Economic Performance.* Cambridge: Cambridge University Press. http://dx.doi.org/10.1017/CBO9780511 808678.

Oberschall, Anthony. 1996. "Opportunities and Framing in the Eastern European Revolts of 1989." In *Comparative Perspectives on Social Movements: Political Opportunities, Mobilizing Structures, and Cultural Framings,* edited by Doug McAdam, John D. McCarthy, and Mayer N. Zald, 93–121. Cambridge: Cambridge University Press. http://dx.doi.org/10.1017/CBO9780511803987.006.

Oddsson, Davíð. 2004. "Hannes Hafstein." In *Forsætisráðherrar Íslands. Ráðherrar Íslands og forsætisráðherrar í 100 ár,* edited by Ólafur Teitur Guðnason and Júlíus Hafstein, 19–38. Akureyri: Bókaútgáfan Hólar.

Oddsson, Davíð. 2000. "Ávarp forsætisráðherra við opnun Þjóðmenningarhússins á skírdag 20. apríl 2000." http://www.forsaetisraduneyti.is/radherra/raedur-og -greinar/nr/328.

Oddsson, Guðmundur Ævar. 2010. "Stéttavitund Íslendinga í kjölfar efnahagshruns" [Icelanders' class consciousness in the wake of the economic collapse]. *Íslenska þjóð- félagið* 1 (1): 5–26. http://www.thjodfelagid.is/index.php/Th/article/viewArticle/10.

Óðinsson, Óðinn Gunnar. 1997. "Fagur, fagur fiskur í sjó. Hugmyndir Íslendinga um viðskipti með aflakvóta " [Beautiful, beautiful fish in the sea: Icelanders' ideas about trade in fishing quotas]. MA thesis, Department of Anthropology, University of Iceland. fishernet.is/en/fishing.

OECD [Organisation for Economic Co-operation and Development]. 2011a. *Education at a Glance 2011: OECD Indicators.* http://www.oecd.org/education/skills- beyond-school/48631582.pdf.

OECD. 2011b. *Divided We Stand: Why Inequality Keeps Rising.* http://www.oecd.org /els/soc/49170768.pdf.

OECD. 2010. *Education at a Glance 2010: OECD Indicators.* http://browse.oecdbook shop.org/oecd/pdfs/free/9610071e.pdf.

OECD. 1997. *Towards Sustainable Fisheries: Economic Aspects of the Management of Living Marine Resources.* Paris: OECD.

Ögmundsdóttir, Guðrún, and Haraldur Y. Pétursson. 2007. *Exista hf.: Right Place, Waiting for the Right Time.* http://www.slideshare.net/marmixa/exista-right-place -waiting-for-the-right-time.

Ólafs, Helga, and Małgorzata Zielińska. 2010. "'I Started to Feel Worse When I Understood More': Polish Immigrants and the Icelandic Media." In *Þjóðarspe- gillinn, Rannsóknir í Félagsvísindum XI,* 76–85. Reykjavík: Félagsvísindastofnun Háskóla Íslands.

Ólafsson, Snjólfur. 2007. "Útrás íslenskra fyrirtækja og erlendar fjárfestingar" [The outvading of Icelandic companies and investment]. *Vísbending* 31:2–3.

Ólafsson, Snjólfur, Gylfi Dalmann Aðalsteinsson, and Þórhallur Guðlaugsson. 2007. "Ástæður fyrir örum vexti útrásarfyrirtækjanna" [The reasons for the rapid growth of the outvading companies]. http://ibr.hi.is/sites/ibr.hi.is/files/Snjolfur_thjodar spegill.pdf.

Ólafsson, Stefán. 2008. "Íslenska efnahagsundrið: Frá hagsæld til frjálshyggju og fjármálahruns" [The Icelandic economic miracle: From well-being to neoliberalism and financial meltdown]. *Stjórnmál og stjórnsýsla* 4 (2): 231–56.

Ólafsson, Stefán. 2005. *Örorka og velferð á Íslandi og í öðrum vestrænum löndum.* Reykjavík: Öryrkjabandalag Íslands.

Ólafsson, Stefán. 1999. *Íslenska leiðin: Almannatryggingar og velferð í fjölþjóðlegum samanburði.* Reykjavík: Háskólaútgáfan.

Ólafsson, Stefán. 1993. "Variations within the Scandinavian Model: Iceland in a Scandinavian Comparison." In *Welfare Trends in the Scandinavian Countries,* edited by Erik Jørgen Hansen, Stein Ringen, Hannu Uusitalo, and Robert Erikson, 61–88. Armonk, NY: M. E. Sharpe.

Ólafsson, Stefán, and Karl Sigurðsson. 2000. "Poverty in Iceland." In *Poverty and Low Income in the Nordic Countries,* edited by Björn Gustafsson and Peder J. Pedersen, 101–30. Aldershot: Ashgate.

Olwig, Karen F., and Ninna N. Sørensen. 2002. "Mobile Livelihoods: Making a Living in the World." In *Work and Migration: Life and Livelihoods in a Globalizing World,* edited by Karen F. Olwig and N. N. Sørensen, 1–20. London: Routledge.

Ong, Aihwa. 2006. *Neoliberalism as Exception.* Durham, NC: Duke University Press. http://dx.doi.org/10.1215/9780822387879.

Önnudóttir, Eva Heiða. 2011. "Búsáhaldabyltingin: Pólitískt jafnræði og þátttaka fólks í mótmælum" [The Pots and Pans Revolution: Political equality and protest participation]. In *Þjóðarspegillinn: Rannsóknir í félagsvísindum XII,* edited by Silja Bára Ómarsdóttir, 36–44. Reykjavík: Félagsvísindastofnun Háskóla Íslands.

Opp, Karl-Dieter, and Christiane Gern. 1993. "Dissident Groups, Personal Networks, and Spontaneous Cooperation: The East German Revolution of 1989." *American Sociological Review* 58 (5): 659–80. http://dx.doi.org/10.2307/2096280.

Ortner, Sherry. 1984. "Theory in Anthropology since the Sixties." *Comparative Studies in Society and History* 26 (1): 126–66. http://dx.doi.org/10.1017/S0010417500010811.

Oslund, Karen. 2002. "Imagining Iceland: Narratives of Nature and History in the North Atlantic." *British Journal for the History of Science* 35 (3): 313–34. http://dx.doi .org/10.1017/S000708740200465X.

Ouroussoff, Alexandra. 2010. *Wall Street at War: The Secret Struggle for the Global Economy.* Cambridge: Polity Press.

Pálsson, Gísli. 2007. *Anthropology and the New Genetics.* Cambridge: Cambridge University Press.

Pálsson, Gísli. 1996. "Commodity Fiction and Cod Fishing." *Nordic Journal of Political Economy* 23:75–86.

Pálsson, Gísli. 1991. *Coastal Economies, Cultural Accounts: Human Ecology and Icelandic Discourse.* Manchester: Manchester University Press.

Pálsson, Gísli. 1989. "Language and Society: The Ethnolinguistics of Icelanders." In *The Anthropology of Iceland,* edited by E. Paul Durrenberger and Gísli Pálsson, 121–39. Iowa City: University of Iowa Press.

Pálsson, Gísli, and Paul Durrenberger. 1992. "Individual Differences in Indigenous Discourse." *Journal of Anthropological Research* 48 (4): 301–16.

Pálsson, Gísli, and E. Paul Durrenberger. 1983. "Icelandic Foremen and Skippers: The Structure and Evolution of a Folk Model." *American Ethnologist* 10 (3): 511–28. http://dx.doi.org/10.1525/ae.1983.10.3.02a00070.

Pálsson, Gísli, and Sigurður Örn Guðbjörnsson. 2011. "Make No Bones about It: The Invention of *Homo islandicus.*" *Acta Borealia* 28 (2): 119–41. http://dx.doi.org/10.1080/08003831.2011.626933.

Pálsson, Gísli, and Agnar S. Helgason. 1998. "Cash for Quotas: Disputes over the Legitimacy of an Economic Model of Fishing in Iceland." In *Virtualism: A New Political Economy,* edited by J. Carrier and D. Miller, 117–34. New York: Berg.

Pálsson, Gísli, and Agnar S. Helgason. 1996. "The Politics of Production: Enclosure, Equality, and Efficiency." In *Images of Contemporary Iceland: Everyday Lives and Global Contexts,* edited by Gísli Pálsson and E. Paul Durrenberger, 60–86. Iowa City: University of Iowa Press.

Pálsson, Gísli, and Agnar S. Helgason. 1995. "Figuring Fish and Measuring Men: The Individual Transferable Quota System in the Icelandic Cod Fishery." *Ocean and Coastal Management* 28 (1–3): 117–46. http://dx.doi.org/10.1016/0964-5691(95)00041-0.

"Pabbi minn er ríkari en pabbi þinn." 2008. *DV,* September 2. http://www.dv.is/folk/2008/9/2/pabbi-minn-er-rikari-en-pabbi-thinn/.

Pepper, Mathew J, Tim D. London, Mike L. Dishman, and Jessica L. Lewis. 2010. *Leading Schools during Crisis: What School Administrators Must Know.* Lanham: Rowman and Littlefield Education.

Perez, Carlota. 2002. *Technological Revolutions and Financial Capital: The Dynamics of Bubbles and Golden Ages.* London: Elgar. http://dx.doi.org/10.4337/9781781005323.

Pétursson, Jón Þór. 2004. "Fyrirlestur um forsætisráðherrabókina." *Kistan*, September 23.

Phillipov, Michelle. 2006. "Haunted by the Spirit of '77: Punk Studies and the Persistence of Politics." *Continuum: Journal of Media & Cultural Studies* 20 (3): 383–93. http://dx.doi.org/10.1080/10304310600814326.

Pike, A., S. Dawley, and J. Tomaney. 2010. "Resilience, Adaptation, and Adaptability." *Cambridge Journal of Regions, Economy and Society* 3 (1): 59–70. http://dx.doi.org/10.1093/cjres/rsq001.

Pinkerton, E. 2013. "Alternatives to ITQs in Equity-Efficiency-Effectiveness Trade-Offs: How the Lay-Up System Spread Effort in the BC Halibut Fishery." *Marine Policy* 42:5–13. http://dx.doi.org/10.1016/j.marpol.2013.01.010.

Pinkerton, E. 2009a. "Partnerships in Management." In *A Fishery Manager's Guidebook*, 2nd ed., edited by K. L. Cochrane and S. M. Garcia, 283–300. Oxford: FAO & Wiley-Blackwell. http://dx.doi.org/10.1002/9781444316315.ch11.

Pinkerton, E. 2009b. "Coastal Marine Systems: Conserving Fish and Sustaining Community Livelihoods." In *Principles of Ecosystem Stewardship: Resilience-Based Natural Resource Management in a Changing World*, edited by F. S. Chapin, G. P. Kofinas, and C. Folke, 241–58. New York: Springer-Verlag. http://dx.doi.org/10.1007/978-0-387-73033-2_11.

Pinkerton, E. 1987. "Intercepting the State: Dramatic Assertions of Local Co-management Rights." In *The Question of the Commons: The Culture and Ecology of Communal Resources*, edited by Bonnie McCay and James Acheson, 344–70. Tucson: University of Arizona Press.

Pinkerton, E., and D. Edwards. 2009. "The Elephant in the Room: The Hidden Costs of Leasing Individual Transferable Fishing Quotas." *Marine Policy* 33 (4): 707–13. http://dx.doi.org/10.1016/j.marpol.2009.02.004.

Pinkerton, E., and Martin Weinstein. 1995. *Fisheries That Work: Sustainability Through Community-Based Management*. Vancouver: David Suzuki Foundation. http://davidsuzuki.org/publications/reports/1995/fisheries-that-work/.

Polanyi, Karl. (1944) 1968. *The Great Transformation*. Boston: Beacon Press.

Poppendieck, Janet. 1998. *Sweet Charity? Emergency Food and the End of Entitlement*. New York: Penguin Books.

Portes, Richard, and Fridrik Már Baldursson. 2007. *The Internationalisation of Iceland's Financial Sector*. Reykjavík: Iceland Chamber of Commerce.

Pratt, Mary Louise. 1990. "Women, Literature, and National Brotherhood." In *Women, Culture, and Politics in Latin America: Seminar on Feminism and Culture in Latin America*, edited by E. Bergmann, J. Greenberg, G. Kirkpatrick, F. Masiello, F. A. Miller, M. A. Morello-Frosch, K. Newman, and M. L. Pratt, 48–73. Berkeley: University of California Press.

Preston, Paschal. 2008. *Making the News: Journalism and News Cultures in Europe*. London: Routledge.

PricewaterhouseCoopers. 2012. *Northern Lights: The Nordic Cities of Opportunity*. [Stockholm]: PricewaterhouseCoopers. http://www.pwc.com/gx/en/psrc/global /northern-lights-the-nordic-cities-of-opportunity.jhtml.

PRSA (Public Relations Society of America). 2012. *Public Relations Society of America (PRSA): Member Code of Ethics*. http://www.prsa.org/AboutPRSA/Ethics/Code English/index.html

Raco, M., and E. Street. 2012. "Resilience Planning, Economic Change, and the Politics of Post-Recession Development in London and Hong Kong." *Urban Studies* 49 (5): 1065–87. http://usj.sagepub.com/content/49/5/1065.short.

Rafnsdóttir, G. Linda, Kristinn Tómasson, and Margrét Lilja Guðmundsdóttir. 2005. "Alsjáandi auga tækninnar og líðan kvenna og karla í íslenskum fyrirtækjum" [The eye of technology and the well-being of women and men in Icelandic workplaces]." *Læknablaðið* 91: 821–7.

Ragnarsdóttir, Berglind Hólm, Jón Gunnar Bernburg, and Sigrún Ólafsdóttir. 2013. "The Global Financial Crisis and Individual Distress: The Role of Subjective Comparisons after the Collapse of the Icelandic Economy." *Sociology* 47 (4): 755–75.

Rannsóknarnefnd Alþingis. 2010. *Aðdragandi og orsakir falls íslensku bankanna 2008 og tengdir atburðir* [Antecedents and Causes of the Collapse of the Icelandic Banks in 2008 and Related Events; known in English as *Report of the Special Investigation Commission*]. 9 vols. Edited by Páll Hreinsson, Sigríður Benediktsdóttir, and Tryggvi Gunnarsson. Reykjavík: Alþingi. English summaries available at http://www .rna.is/eldri-nefndir/addragandi-og-orsakir-falls-islensku-bankanna-2008/skyrsla -nefndarinnar/english/.

Ranson, Stewart. 2008. "The Changing Governance of Education." *Educational Management Administration & Leadership* 36 (2): 201–19. http://dx.doi.org/10.1177 /1741143207087773.

Rastrick, Ólafur 2000. "Hús með sál, þjóðarsál. Lesið í sköpun Þjóðmenningarhúss." *Ný saga* 12: 82–88.

Reddy, Deepa. 2005. "At Home in the World: Women's Activism in Hyderabad, India." In *Social Movements: An Anthropological Reader*, edited by June Nash, 304–24. Malden, MA: Blackwell Publishing.

Reich, Robert. 2013. "Political Uses of the 'Free Market' Myth." *Progressive Populist* 19 (18): 11.

Reinhart, Carmen M., and Kenneth S. Rogoff. 2009. *This Time Is Different: Eight Centuries of Financial Folly*. Princeton, NJ: Princeton University Press.

Rice, James G. 2009. "'We Only Help Women with Children Here': Male Clients at an Icelandic Material Aid Charity." *Norma: Nordic Journal for Masculinity Studies* 4 (2): 169–82.

Rice, James G. 2007a. "The Charity Complex: An Ethnography of a Material Aid Agency in Reykjavík, Iceland." PhD diss., Memorial University of Newfoundland.

Rice, James G. 2007b. "Icelandic Charity Donations: Reciprocity Reconsidered." *Ethnology: An International Journal of Cultural and Social Anthropology* 46 (1): 1–20.

Robert, Zoe. 2008. "The Suspect Is a Foreigner." *Iceland Review Online*, April 19. http://icelandreview.com/stuff/views/2008/04/19/suspect-foreigner.

Roepstorff, A. 2000. "The Double Interface of Environmental Knowledge: Fishing for Greenland Halibut." In *Finding Our Sea Legs: Linking Fishery People and Their Knowledge with Science and Management*, edited by L. Felt and B. Neis, 165–88. St. John's: ISER Books.

Rogers, Douglas, and Katherine Verdery. 2013. "Postsocialist Societies: Eastern Europe and the Former Soviet Union." In *The Handbook of Sociocultural Anthropology*, edited by James G. Carrier and Deborah B. Gewertz, 439–55. London: Bloomsbury.

Rolnik, Solnik. 2011. "The Geopolitics of Pimping," translated by Brian Holmes. In *Critique of Creativity: Precarity, Subjectivity, and Resistance in the 'Creative Industries'*, edited by Gerald Raunig, Gene Ray, and Ulf Wuggenig, 23–40. London: MayFly Books.

Rosenberg, Karen. 2008. "Inspired by Vikings and Volcanoes." *New York Times*, June 25. http://www.nytimes.com/2008/07/25/arts/design/25icel.html?_r=1&.

Runciman, Walter Garrison. 1966. *Relative Deprivation and Social Justice*. Berkeley: University of California Press.

Rutherford, Danilyn. 2005. "Nationalism and Millenarianism in West Papua: Institutional Power, Interpretive Practice, and the Pursuit of Christian Truth." In *Social Movements: An Anthropological Reader*, edited by June Nash, 146–68. Malden, MA: Blackwell.

Sabau, Gabriela. 2013. "Small-Scale Fisheries and Alternative Governance Systems." Presentation, Memorial University of Newfoundland.

Sabin, R. 1999. *Punk Rock: So What?* London: Routledge.

Said, Edward. 1978. *Orientalism*. Harmondsworth: Penguin.

Scandinavia House. 2008. "Survey of Contemporary Icelandic Art to Open in NYC. From *Another Shore: Recent Icelandic Art*, May 2–August 15, 2008" (press release).

Schabas, Margaret. 2005. *The Natural Origins of Economics*. Chicago: University of Chicago Press.

Schlager, Edella, and Elinor Ostrom. 1993. "Property Rights Regimes and Coastal Fisheries: An Empirical Analysis." In *The Political Economy of Customs and Culture:*

Informal Solutions to the Commons Problem, edited by T. L. Anderson and R. T. Simmons, 13–41. Lanham, MD: Rowman and Littlefield.

Schott, S. 2004. "New Fishery Management in Atlantic Canada: Communities, Governments and Alternative Targets." In *How Ottawa Spends, 2004–2005: Mandate Change and Continuity in the Paul Martin Era*, edited by G. Bruce Doern, 151–72. How Ottawa Spends Series, no. 5. Montreal: McGill-Queens University Press.

Schram, Arna. 2007. "Spútnik Íslands." *Krónikan* 1 (1): 30–33.

Schumpeter, J. A. (1942) 1976. *Capitalism, Socialism and Democracy*. London: Routledge.

Schumpeter, J. A. 1934. *The Theory of Economic Development*. Cambridge, MA: Harvard University Press.

Schwegler, Tara A. 2009. "The Global Crisis of Economic Meaning." *Anthropology News* 50 (7): 9–12. http://dx.doi.org/10.1111/j.1556-3502.2009.50709.x.

Schwegler, Tara A. 2008. "Take It from the Top (Down)? Rethinking Neoliberalism and Political Hierarchy in Mexico." *American Ethnologist* 35 (4): 682–700. http://dx.doi.org/10.1111/j.1548-1425.2008.00105.x.

Scott, A. D. 1989. "Conceptual Origins of Rights-Based Fishing." In *Rights-Based Fishing*, edited by P. Neher, R. Árnason, and N. Mollett, 11–38. Dordrecht: Kluwer Academic Press. http://dx.doi.org/10.1007/978-94-009-2372-0_2.

Scott, James. 1998. *Seeing Like a State*. New Haven, CT: Yale University Press.

Secor, D. H. 1999. "Specifying Divergent Migrations in the Concept of Stock: The Contingent Hypothesis." *Fisheries Research* 43 (1–3): 13–34. http://dx.doi.org/10.1016/S0165-7836(99)00064-8.

Seðlabanki Íslands [Central Bank of Iceland]. 2000. "Fjármálakerfið: Styrkur og veikleikar" [The financial system: Strengths and weaknesses]. *Peningamál* 2000 (1): 17–31. http://www.sedlabanki.is/lisalib/getfile.aspx?itemid=1235.

"Segja danska fjölmiðla ósanngjarna í garð Íslendinga" [Danish newspapers said to be unfair toward Icelanders]. 2008. Interview with Finn Mortensen, business editor of the Danish newspaper *Berlingske Tidende*. *Viðskiptablaðið*, March 6.

Shafiq, M. Najeeb. 2010. "The Effect of an Economic Crisis on Educational Outcomes: An Economic Framework and Review of the Evidence." *Current Issues in Comparative Education* 12 (2): 5–13. http://devweb.tc.columbia.edu/i/a/document/25569_12_02_Complete_Issue.pdf.

Shields, R. 2003. *The Virtual*. London: Routledge.

Shiller, Robert J. 2001. *Irrational Exuberance*. New York: Broadway Books.

Sholette, Gregory. 2011. *Dark Matter: Art and Politics in the Age of Enterprise Culture*. London: Pluto Press.

Shore, Cris, and Dieter Haller. 2005. "Introduction—Sharp Practice: Anthropology and the Study of Corruption." In *Corruption: Anthropological Perspectives*, edited by Dieter Haller and Cris Shore, 1–26. London: Pluto Press.

Sigfússon, Þór, and Halldór Benjamín Þorgeirsson. 2005. *Útrás íslenskra fyrirtækja til Lundúna*. [Invasion of Icelandic companies into London; with summary in English]. Ritröð Viðskiptaráðs Íslands um íslenskt viðskiptaumhverfi. Reykjavík: Viðskiptaráð Íslands / British-Icelandic Chamber of Commerce. http://www.vi.is /files/567176863Utrasarskyrsla_VI.pdf.

Sigurðardóttir, Jóhanna. 2002. "Fjötrar fátæktar." *Morgunblaðið*, June 29, 31.

Sigurðardóttir, Margrét Sigrún, and Tómas Young. 2011. *Towards Creative Iceland: Building Local, Going Global*. Reykjavík: Consultative Forum of Creative Industries in Iceland. http://www.icelanddesign.is/media/PDF/towardscreativeicelandreport1. pdf.

Sigurðsson, Karl, and Valur Arnarson. 2011. *Erlendir ríkisborgarar á íslenskum vinnumarkaði árin 2006–2009. Veitt atvinnuleyfi, skráning ríkisborgara frá nýjum ríkjum ESB, viðbót um starfsmannaleigur og þjónustusamninga og áætlað vinnuafl og atvinnuleysi*. Reykjavík: Vinnumálastofnun. http://www.vinnumalastofnun.is/files /Erlendir%201r%C3%ADkisborgarar%20%C3%A1%20%C3%ADslenskum%20 vinnumarka%C3%B0i%202006–2009%20II_628248957.pdf.

Sigurgeirsdóttir, Álfrún. 2011. "Polish Labour Workers in the Construction Industry in Reykjavík: Bosses' Perspective." In *Integration or Assimilation? Polish Immigrants in Iceland*, edited by Malgorzata Budyta-Budzyńska, 153–64. Warsaw: Scholar.

Sigurjónsson, Þröstur Olaf, David Schwartzkopf, and Auður Arna Arnardóttir. 2011. "Viðbrögð tengslanets við gagnrýni á fjármálastöðuleika Íslands." *Stjórnmál og stjórnsýsla* 7 (1): 163–86.

Sigurjónsson, Þröstur Olaf, and Már Wolfgang Mixa. 2011. "Learning from the 'Worst Behaved': Iceland's Financial Crisis and Nordic Comparison." *Thunderbird International Business Review* 53 (2): 209–23. http://dx.doi.org/10.1002/tie.20402.

Silbey, Susan S. 2011. "Rotten Apples or a Rotting Barrel." *MIT Faculty Newsletter* 21 (5): n.p. http://web.mit.edu/~ssilbey/www/pdf/Silbey_Ethics_Education _Comments2.pdf.

Simonian, Ligia T.L. 2005. "Political Organization among Indigenous Women of the Brazilian State of Roraima: Constraints and Prospects." In *Social Movements: An Anthropological Reader*, edited by June Nash, 285–303. Malden, MA: Blackwell.

"Sjálfsímynd Dana farin að rispast." 2006. *Viðskiptablaðið*, March 24:12–13.

Sjávarútvegs- og landbúnaðarráðuneytið [Ministry of Fisheries and Agriculture]. 2010. *Skýrsla starfhóps um endurskoðun á lögum um stjórn fiskveiða: Álitamál, greiningar, skýrslur og valkostir við breytingar á stjórn fiskveiða*. Reykjavík:

Sjávarútvegs- og landbúnaðarráðuneytið. http://www.atvinnuvegaraduneyti.is /media/Skyrslur/meginskyrsla_uppsett_lokaeintak.pdf.

Skaptadóttir, Unnur D. 2011. "The Context of Polish Immigration and Integration in Iceland." In *Integration or Assimilation? Polish Immigrants in Iceland*, edited by Malgorzata Budyta-Budzyńska, 18–28. Warsaw: Scholar.

Skaptadóttir, Unnur D. 2010a. "Alþjóðlegir fólksflutningar á tímum efnahagslegs samdráttar." In *Þjóðarspegillinn: Rannsóknir í Félagsvísindum X*, edited by Gunnar Þ. Jóhannesson and Helga Björnsdóttir, 559–68. Reykjavík: Félagsvísindastofnun Háskóla Íslands.

Skaptadóttir, Unnur Dís. 2010b. "Integration and Transnational Practices of Filipinos in Iceland." *E-migrinter*, no. 5:36–45. http://www.mshs.univ-poitiers.fr/migrinter /e-migrinter/201005/e-migrinter2010_05_036.pdf.

Skaptadóttir, Unnur D. 2008. "Að læra íslensku í fjölmenningarlegu samfélagi" [Learning Icelandic in a multicultural society]. *Hrafnaþing* 5: 55–65.

Skaptadóttir, Unnur D. 2007. "Social Changes and Culture in Icelandic Coastal Villages." *Arctic and Antarctic International Journal of Circumpolar Sociocultural Issues* 1 (1): 149–68. http://fishernet.is/images/stories/Skaptadottir_Social_changes_and_ culture.pdf.

Skaptadóttir, Unnur D. 2000. "Women Coping with Change in an Icelandic Fishing Community: A Case Study." *Women's Studies International Forum* 23 (3): 311–21. http://dx.doi.org/10.1016/S0277-5395(00)00089-3.

Skaptadóttir, Unnur D., and Anna Wojtyńska. 2008a. "Labour Migrants Negotiating Places and Engagements." In *Mobility and Place: Enacting Northern European Perspectives*, edited by J. Bærrenholdt and B. Granås, 115–26. Aldershot: Ashgate Publishing.

Skaptadóttir, Unnur D., and Anna Wojtyńska. 2008b. "Gender Migration from Poland to Iceland: Women's Experiences." In *New Subjectivities: Negotiating Citizenship in the Context of Migration and Diversity*, edited by Dorota Golańska and Aleksandra M. Różalska, 81–96. Lodz: University of Lodz Publishing House.

Skocpol, Theda. 1979. *States and Social Revolutions: A Comparative Analysis of France, Russia and China*. Cambridge: Cambridge University Press.

Smith, Heather J., Thomas F. Pettigrew, Gina M. Pippin, and Silvana Bialosiewicz. 2012. "Relative Deprivation: A Theoretical and Meta-Analytic Review." *Personality and Social Psychology Review* 16 (3): 203–32. http://dx.doi.org/10.1177/1088868 311430825.

Smith, Larry, and Dan Riley. 2012. "School Leadership in Times of Crisis." *School Leadership & Management* 32 (1): 57–71. http://dx.doi.org/10.1080/13632434.2011 .614941.

Snow, David A., E. Burke Rochford, Jr., Steven K. Worden, and Robert D. Benford. 1986. "Frame Alignment Processes: Micromobilization, and Movement Participation." *American Sociological Review* 51 (4): 464–81. http://dx.doi.org/10.2307/2095581.

Sobel, R. 1968. *The Great Bull Market: Wall Street in the 1920s.* New York: W.W. Norton & Company.

Soros, George. 2003. *The Alchemy of Finance.* Hoboken, NJ: John Wiley & Sons.

Sparisjóður Keflavíkur [Savings Bank of Keflavík]. 2007. "Útboðslýsing [Prospectus]." September 27.

Special Investigation Commission. 2010. "Executive Summary: Summary of the Report's Main Conclusions." Summary of Rannsóknarnefnd Alþingis 2010, vol. 1, chap. 2. http://www.rna.is/media/skjol/RNAvefKafli2Enska.pdf.

Spyer, Patricia. 2011. "What Ends with the End of Anthropology?" In *The End of Anthropology?* ed. Holger Jebens and Karl-Heinz Kohl, 61–80. Wantage, UK: Sean Kingston Publishing.

St. Martin, K. 2007. "The Difference That Class Makes: Neoliberalization and Non-Capitalism in the Fishing Industry of New England." *Antipode* 39 (3): 527–49. http://dx.doi.org/10.1111/j.1467-8330.2007.00538.x.

Statistics Iceland. 2012. "Population by origin and citizenship. Foreign citizens 1950–2013." http://www.statice.is/?PageID=1174&src=/temp_en/Dialog/varval.asp?ma=MAN04001%26ti=Foreign+citizens+1950%2D2012++++%26path=./Database/mannfjoldi/Rikisfang/%26lang=1%26units=Number.

Stefánsdóttir, Agnes, and Kristín Huld Sigurðardóttir. 2007. "Fornleifar og eftirlíkingar." In *Þriðja íslenska söguþingið 18.–21. maí 2006. Ráðstefnurit*, edited by Benedikt Eyþórsson and Hrafnkell Lárusson, 103–7. Reykjavík: Sagnfræðingafélag Íslands.

Steger, Manfred B., and Ravi Roy. 2010. *Neoliberalism: A Very Short Introduction.* New York: Oxford University Press.

Steinsson, Jón. 2010. "Umsögn um greinargerð Daða Más Kristóferssonar um áhrif fyrningarleiðar á afkomu og rekstur útgerðarfyrirtækja" [Briefing on the memo of Daði Már Kristófersson on the impact of quota re-claim on fish catching companies' economy]. In *Skýrsla starfhóps um endurskoðun á lögum um stjórn fiskveiða: Álitamál, greiningar, skýrslur og valkostir við breytingar á stjórn fiskveiða*, annex 6. Reykjavík: Sjávarútvegs- og landbúnaðarráðuneytið. http://www.liu.is/files/Sk%C3%BDrsla%20starfsh%C3%B3ps%20um%20endursko%C3%B0un%20og%20fylgiskj%C3%B6l_1722083557.pdf.

Stephen, Lynn. 2005. "Gender, Citizenship, and the Politics of Identity." In *Social Movements: An Anthropological Reader*, edited by June Nash, 66–78. Malden, MA: Blackwell.

Stewart, James, and Peter Callagher. 2011. "Quota Concentration in the New Zealand Fishery: Annual Catch Entitlement and the Small Fisher." *Marine Policy* 35 (5): 631–46. http://dx.doi.org/10.1016/j.marpol.2011.02.003.

Stewart, James, Kim Walshe, and Beverley Moodie. 2006. "The Demise of the Small Fisher? A Profile of Exiters from the New Zealand Fishery." *Marine Policy* 30 (4): 328–40. http://dx.doi.org/10.1016/j.marpol.2005.03.006.

Steyerl, Hito. 2012. *The Wretched of the Screen*. Berlin: Sternberg Press.

Stringer, Christina, Glenn Simmons, Daren Coulston, and D. Hugh Whittaker. 2014. "Not in New Zealand's Waters, Surely? Linking Labour Issues to GPNs." *Journal of Economic Geography* 14 (4): 739–58. http://dx.doi.org/10.1093/jeg/lbt027.

Sumaila, U. R. 2010. "A Cautionary Note on Individual Transferable Quotas." *Ecology and Society* 15 (3): 36. http://www.ecologyandsociety.org/vol15/iss3/art36/.

Susser, Ida. 2005. "From the Cosmopolitan to the Personal: Women's Mobilization to Combat HIV/AIDS." In *Social Movements: An Anthropological Reader*, edited by June Nash, 272–84. Malden, MA: Blackwell.

Sylvian, Renée. 2005. "Land, Water, and Truth: San Identity and Global Indigenism." In *Social Movements: An Anthropological Reader*, edited by June Nash, 216–34. Malden, MA: Blackwell.

Symes, D., N. Steins, and J. L. Alegret. 2003. "Experiences with Fisheries Co-Management in Europe." In *The Fisheries Co-Management Experience: Accomplishment, Challenges, and Prospects*, edited by D. C. Wilson, J. R. Nielsen, and P. Degnbol, 119–33. Dordrecht: Kluwer Academic Press. http://dx.doi.org/10.1007/978-94-017-3323-6_8.

Tausig, Mark, and Rudy Fenwick. 1999. "Recession and Well-Being." *Journal of Health and Social Behavior* 40 (1): 1–16. http://dx.doi.org/10.2307/2676375.

Tett, Gillian. 2009. *Fool's Gold: How the Bold Dream of a Small Tribe at J. P. Morgan Was Corrupted by Wall Street Greed and Unleashed a Catastrophe*. New York: Free Press.

"Þjóðarátakið 'Þjóðin býður heim.'" 2010. *Vísir*, June 12. http://www.visir.is/thjodaratakid—thjodin-bydur-heim-/article/201048319853.

Þór, Jón Þ. 2002. *Sjósókn og sjávarfang: Saga sjávarútvegs á Íslandi* [Fishing and marine harvest: History of Icelandic fisheries], vol. 1. Akureyri: Bókaútgáfan Hólar. http://www.atvinnuvegaraduneyti.is/media/pdf-skjal/1_bindi.pdf.

Þórisdóttir, Hulda. 2010. "Afsprengi aðstæðna og fjötruð skynsemi: Aðdragandi og orsakir efnahagshrunsins á Íslandi frá sjónarhóli kenninga og rannsókna í félagslegri sálfræði" [Situational determinants and bounded rationality: Causes and consequences of the Icelandic economic collapse from the viewpoint of social psychology], prepared for the Working Group on Ethics. In *Aðdragandi og orsakir falls íslensku bankanna 2008 og tengdir atburðir*, edited by Páll Hreinsson, Sigríður Benediktsdóttir, and Tryggvi Gunnarsson, vol. 8, annex 2. Reykjavík: Alþingi.

Þorláksson, Helgi. 2007. "Sagnfræðin í heimi menningararfs og minninga." In *Þriðja íslenska söguþingið 18.–21. maí 2006. Ráðstefnurit.* ed. Benedikt Eyþórsson and Hrafnkell Lárusson, 316–26. Reykjavík: Sagnfræðingafélag Íslands.

Thoroddsen, Þorvaldur. 1900. *Lýsing Íslands.* Copenhagen: Copenhagen University.

Tietenberg, T. 2002. "The Tradable Permits Approach to Protecting the Commons: What Have We Learned?" In *The Drama of the Commons*, edited by E. Ostrom, T. Dietz, N. Dolsak, P. C. Stern, S. Stonich, and J. Weber, 197–232. Washington, DC: National Academy Press. http://dx.doi.org/10.2139/ssrn.315500.

Tilly, Chris. 2011. "The Impact of the Economic Crisis on International Migration: A Review." *Work, Employment and Society* 25 (4): 675–92. http://dx.doi.org/10.1177 /0950017011421799.

Togeby, Lise, Jørgen Goul Andersen, Peter Munk Christiansen, Torben Beck Jørgensen, and Signild Vallgårda. 2003. *Power and Democracy in Denmark.* Aarhus: Magtudredningen, c/o Department of Political Science, University of Aarhus.

Traustadóttir, Rannveig, Kristín Björnsdóttir, James Rice, Knútur Birgisson, Karl Ólafsson, and Eiríkur Smith. 2011. *Fátækt og félagslegar aðstæður öryrkjar: Rannsókn unnin í tilefni af Evrópuári gegn fátækt og félagslegri einangrun.* Reykjavík: University of Iceland and Öryrkjabandalag Íslands.

United Nations Development Programme (UNDP). 1990. *The Human Development Report 1990.* New York: UNDP. http://hdr.undp.org/sites/default/files/reports/219 /hdr_1990_en_complete_nostats.pdf.

United Nations Human Rights Committee. 2007. "Erlingur Sveinn Haraldsson and Örn Snævar Sveinsson vs. Iceland." Communication 1306/2004, UN Document CCPR/C/91/D/1306/2004, A/63/40, vol. 2, annex 5 (October 24). http://www .worldcourts.com/hrc/eng/decisions/2007.10.24_Haraldsson_v_Iceland.htm.

Utanríkisráðuneytið [Ministry for Foreign Affairs]. 2009. Áhættumatsskýrsla fyrir Ísland: Hnattrænir, samfélagslegir og hernaðarlegir þættir." http://www.utanrikis raduneyti.is/media/Skyrslur/Skyrsla_um_ahattumat_fyrir_Island_a.pdf.

"Útrás og árangur bankanna." 2007. *Viðskiptablaðið*, December 30:19.

Vaiman, Vlad, Throstur O. Sigurjonsson, and Páll Á. Davídsson. 2011. "Weak Business Culture as an Antecedent of Economic Crisis: The Case of Iceland." *Journal of Business Ethics* 98 (2): 259–72. http://dx.doi.org/10.1007/s10551-010-0546-6.

Valdimarsdóttir, Þórunn. 2013. "Af landamærahéruðum Clio og skáldgyðjanna." *Tímarit Máls og menningar* 74 (2): 58–69.

van Hoof, Luc. 2010. "Co-Management: An Alternative to Enforcement?" *ICES Journal of Marine Science* 67 (2): 395–401. http://dx.doi.org/10.1093/icesjms/fsp239.

van Putten, I., and C. Gardner. 2010. "Lease Quota Fishing in a Changing Rock Lobster Industry." *Marine Policy* 34 (5): 859–67. http://dx.doi.org/10.1016/j.marpol .2010.01.008.

Vertovec, Steven. 2004. "Migrant Transnationalism and Modes of Transformation." *International Migration Review* 38 (3): 970–1001. http://dx.doi.org/10.1111/j.1747 -7379.2004.tb00226.x.

"Við nýjan tón kveður í erlendri umfjöllun" [New tone in foreign media]. 2008. *Fréttablaðið*, March 27.

Viðskiptaráð Íslands . 2007. *90 tillögur að bættri samkeppnishæfni Íslands* [90 suggestions for improved competitiveness of Iceland]. Reykjavík: Viðskiptaráð Íslands.

Viðskiptaráð Íslands . 2006. *Ísland 2015*. Reykjavík: Viðskiptaráð Íslands.

Vincent, Joan, ed. 2002. *The Anthropology of Politics: A Reader in Ethnography, Theory and Critique*. Malden, MA: Blackwell.

Vinnumálastofnun [Directorate of Labour]. 2012. "Mánaðarlegar skýrslur um stöðu á vinnumarkaði" [Monthly reports on the labor market; with unemployment statistics]. http://www.vinnumalastofnun.is/vinnumalastofnun/utgefid-efni-og -talnaefni/manadarlegar-skyrslur-um-stodu-a-vinnumarkadi/.

Volk, Gregory. 2000. "Art on Ice—Icelandic Art." *Art in America* 88 (9): 40–46.

von Hayek, Friedrich A. 1944. *The Road to Serfdom*. London: Routledge.

Wacquant, Löic. 2010. "Crafting the Neoliberal State: Workfare, Prisonfare, and Social Insecurity." *Sociological Forum* 25 (2): 197–220. http://dx.doi.org/10.1111 /j.1573-7861.2010.01173.x.

Wade, Robert, and Silla Sigurgeirsdóttir. 2012. "How to Discredit a Financial Regulator: The Strange Case of Iceland." *Triple Crisis* (blog), March 27. http://triplecrisis. com/the-strange-case-of-iceland/.

Waits, William B. 1993. *Modern Christmas in America: A Cultural History of Gift Giving*. New York: New York University Press.

Wagner, David. 2000. *What's Love Got to Do with It?: A Critical Look at American Charity*. New York: New Press.

Walmsley, Roy. 2011. *World Prison Population List*. 9th ed. London: International Centre for Prison Studies. http://www.prisonstudies.org/sites/prisonstudies.org /files/resources/downloads/wppl_9.pdf.

Walsh, David A. 2013. "Highlights from the 2013 Annual Meeting of the American Historical Association." http://hnn.us/article/149950.

Weaver, Kay, Judy Motion, and Juliet Roper. 2006. "From Propaganda to Discourse (and Back Again): Truth, Power, the Public Interest and Public Relation." In *Public Relations: Critical Debates and Contemporary Practice*, edited by Jacquie L'Etang and Magda Pieczka, 7–22. Mahwah, NJ: Lawrence Erlbaum Associates.

Webmoor, T., and C. L. Witmore. 2008. "Things Are Us! A Commentary on Human/Things Relations under the Banner of a 'Social' Archaeology." *Norwegian Archaeological Review* 41 (1): 53–70. http://dx.doi.org/10.1080/0029365 0701698423.

Whitehead, A. N. 1933. *Adventures of Ideas.* New York: Macmillan.

Wilkinson, Richard, and Kate Pickett. 2007. *The Spirit Level: Why Equality is Better for Everyone.* New York: Penguin.

Wilson, Douglas C., Jesper Raakjaer Nielsen, and Poul Degnbol, eds. 2003. *The Fisheries Co-Management Experience: Accomplishments, Challenges and Prospects.* Dordrecht: Kluwer. http://dx.doi.org/10.1007/978-94-017-3323-6.

Wilson, James, James Acheson, Mark Metcalfe, and Peter Kleban. 1994. "Chaos, Complexity, and Community Management of Fisheries." *Marine Policy* 18 (4): 291–305. http://dx.doi.org/10.1016/0308-597X(94)90044-2.

Wilson, Tamar Diana. 2009. "Economic Crisis and the Decline of Remittances to Mexico." *Anthropological Quarterly* 82 (2): 587–97. http://dx.doi.org/10.1353/anq .0.0068.

Windle, M. J. S., B. Neis, S. Bornstein, M. Binkley, and P. Navarro. 2008. "Fishing Occupational Health and Safety: A Comparison of Regulatory Regimes and Safety Outcomes in Six Countries." *Marine Policy* 32 (4): 701–10. http://dx.doi .org/10.1016/j.marpol.2007.12.003.

Wojtyńska, Anna. 2011. "History and Characteristic of Migration from Poland to Iceland." In *Integration or Assimilation? Polish Immigrants in Iceland,* edited by Malgorzata Budyta-Budzyńska, 175–86. Warsaw: Scholar.

Wojtynska, Anna, Unnur D. Skaptadóttir, and Helga Ólafs. 2011. *The Participation of Immigrants in Civil Society and Labour Market in the Economic Recession.* Research Project Report. Reykjavík: Faculty of Social and Human Sciences, University of Iceland. http://mark.hi.is/sites/mark.hi.is/files/filepicker/17 /wojtynska_skaptadottir_olafs_participation_of_immigrants.pdf.

Wojtyńska, Anna, and Malgorzata Zielińska. 2010. "Polish Migrants in Iceland Facing the Financial Crisis." In *Þjóðarspegillinn: Rannsóknir í félagsvísindum XI,* edited by Gunnar Þ. Jóhannesson and Helga Björnsdóttir, 1–11. Reykjavík: Félagsvísindastofnun, Háskóli Íslands.

Wu, Chin-Tao. 2002. *Privatizing Culture: Corporate Art Interventions since the 1980s.* London: Verso Books.

Yúdice, George. 1999. "The Privatization of Culture." *Social Text* 59 (summer): 17–34.

Yuval-Davis, Nira. 1997. *Gender & Nation.* London: Sage Publications.

Zagorin, Perez. 1973. "Theories of Revolution in Contemporary Historiography." *Political Science Quarterly* 88 (1): 23–52. http://dx.doi.org/10.2307/2148647.

Zald, Mayer N. 1996. "Culture, Ideology, and Strategic Framing." In *Comparative Perspectives on Social Movements: Political Opportunities, Mobilizing Structures, and Cultural Framings*, edited by Doug McAdam, John D. McCarthy, and Mayer N. Zald, 261–74. Cambridge: Cambridge University Press. http://dx.doi.org/10.1017/CBO9780511803987.013.

Zaloom, Caitlin. 2006. *Out of the Pits: Traders and Technology from Chicago to London.* Chicago: University of Chicago Press.

Zimbardo, Philip. 2007. *The Lucifer Effect: Understanding How Good People Turn Evil.* New York: Random House.

individualism, xiv, xxiv, 11, 13; methodological, xxviii, 48
Individual Transferrable Quotas (ITQs), xvi, xvii, xxii, xxvi, 109–10, 126, 130, 218; alternatives to, 119–20; claims about, 111–13; and economic boom and bust, 155–57; and human rights, 152–55; problems with, 113–18; support for, 118–19
industrial sector, 28–29
inequality, economic, 10, 201, 204
innovation, 24–25, 27, 94, 95–96; in banking system, 37–38
Inspired by Iceland (video), 98
intellectuals, role of, 54–57
interest rates, xvii, 37
International Covenant of Civil and Political Rights, 155
International Monetary Fund (IMF), xix, 158
Interpretation of Cultures, The (Geertz), 229
investment banking, 37–39, 45(n3), 46(n13)
Investor AB, 35
Ireland, migration to, 175
Ísland 2015 (Framtíðarhópur Viðskiptaráðs Íslands), 55–56
Íslandsaga (Jónsson, Jónas), 7–8
Íslandsbanki, 37
Íslenskt þjóðerni (Aðils, Jon Jónsson), 7
ITQs. *See* Individual Transferrable Quotas

Jóhannesson, Jón Ásgeir, 3, 13, 17
Jón forseti (trawler), sinking of, 202
Jónsson, Arngrímur, *Brevis Commentarius de Islandia*, 7
Jónsson, Jónas (Jónas from Hrifla), *Íslandsaga*, 7–8
Jónsson, Sigurður, 35
Jónsson, Stefán, 8, 13
Jütte, Robert, 206

Kauphöll Íslands. *See* Icelandic Stock Exchange
Kaupthing Bank, xxiii, xxxvii–xxxviii, xxxix, xlii(n10), 39, 43; and Exista, 35, 36
Keynesian economics, Keynesianism, 44, 230
Kirzner, I. M., 25, 31
Kópavogur, elections in, 80
Kristjánsson, Halldór J., 99

labor, 115; in art, 102–3

labor market: EEA, 176–77; migrants and, 141, 177–78
Laxdæla saga, xxxix
Landsbankiin, xviii, xxiii, 74; IceSave accounts, xxxv, xxxvi
Landssamband íslenskra útvegsmanna (LÍU), 126, 134(n10)
languages, in European Union, 190
Latour, Bruno, 131
Law 81, 189, 190, 199
Laxness, Halldór: works by, xxiv, xxv, xxxiv, xxxv–xxxvi, xxxvii
leadership, school, 164–65, 172–73
leasing, in fisheries, 115, 117
Left-Green Party, xx, xxvi, 50, 158
LennonOno Grant for Peace, 88
Lindberg, Carter, 206
Lippmann, Walter, 222
LÍU. *See* Landssamband íslenskra útvegsmanna
L-List party, 80
loans, xvii, xix, 139, 140, 143; fishing industry, 135(n20), 145; to holding companies, 41–42
lobby exhibitions, 100–102
Lutheran Church, charities, 208, 209
Lýsing Íslands (Thoroddsen), 8

Mæðrastyrksnefnd Reykjavíkur (Mothers' Support Committee of Reykjavík), 202–4, 213; clientele of, 206–7; donations to, 210–11; economic crisis and, 208–10; media and, 205–6, 211–12; seasonal attention to, 207–8
Magnússon, Sigurður Gylfi, 20
maleness, masculinity, of Icelandic identity, 5–6, 8–9, 11, 12
Manic Millennium years, 11, 12, 33, 36, 39
Marcus, George, 232
Marine Research Institute (MRI), 124, 126, 134(n4)
marketing, 100; Iceland's image, 98–99
Matthíason, Pálmi, xxxiv
media, 76, 98; and charities, 203, 205, 210–12; and economic expansion, 10–11; on financial sector, xxiii–xxiv, 52–53
MESC. *See* Ministry of Education, Science, and Culture
migrants, migration, work-related, 175–78. *See also* immigrants

Ministry of Education, Science, and Culture (MESC), 190, 198–99
Ministry of Social Affairs, 195
Ministry of the Interior, Icelandic language curriculum, 189–90
"Miracle on Iceland" (Gissurarson), xxi
Mises, Ludwig von, 222
Mishkin, Frederic (Frederick S.), xxii, 55–57
mobilization: as political opportunity, 73–75; public, 64, 65–73, 75–76
monitoring, of fisheries, 112–13, 117
morality, and banking crash, 48
mortgages, fishing rights as, 156
Mothers' Support Committee of Reykjavík. See Mæðrastyrksnefnd Reykjavíkur
Moussaieff, Dorrit, 209
MRI. See Marine Research Institute
music, nature and, 101

National Centre for Cultural Heritage, 18
National Gallery of Iceland, 100
nationalism, 16, 18, 43, 44, 183; economic expansion and, 9–11, 20; as gendered, 5–6; nature and, 100–101; and neoliberalism, 12–13; Viking, xxiii, xxiv, 4
National Meeting, on social media, xxvii–xxviii
nation branding, 94, 98–99; nature and, 100–101
nature, as master narrative, 100–101, 105(n2)
Negri, Antonio, 201
neoclassical economists, xxv, xxviii
neoliberalism, xiii–xiv, xvi, xx, xxiv, xxv–xxvi, xxxiii–xxxiv, xxxvi, xl, 4, 70, 71, 93–94, 158, 217–19, 222–23, 230, 231; art and, 95–96, 102–3; as banality of evil, xxviii–xxix; as con, 221–25; and fishing industry, 127–28; and nationalism, 12–13; promoting, xxi–xxii
Netherlands, ITQs in, 110, 118
New Zealand, fisheries in, 111, 112, 114, 116–17
Next Best Party, 80
Nordic countries, immigrants from, 177
Nordic Miracle, 96
Nordic Partners, 11–12
Nordic Third World Country? Icelandic Art in Times of Crisis, The (exhibition), 102
Northern Lights: Nordic Cities of Opportunity, 89
Norway, 6, 15, 16

Oddsson, Davíð, xxi, xxxviii, 17, 18, 19, 20, 48, 86
Organisation for Economic Co-operation and Development (OECD), 112, 165, 171; Divided We Stand, 204
organizational culture, of banks, 49–50
Orkuveita Reykjavíkur, 85–86
Ortner, Sherry, 230
Östersund (Sweden), 102
ownership, concentration of, 115

People's Bank of Iceland (Alþýðubanki Íslands), 37
Polayni, Karl, 123
Poles: as fisheries workers, 141, 143, 146; as migrants, 176–79, 181–83
political parties, 43, 218; and financial system, 50–51; financiers and, xxxvi–xxxvii; neoliberal, xxvi, xxvii; as social movements, 80–82. See also various parties by name
politics, politicians, xviii–xx, 17, 76; anarchist, 88, 89–90; art and, 95–97, 100; corruption, xxvii, 70–72; and economic crash, 44–45; election campaigns, 80–81; and financial sector, 50–52; and neoliberalism, xxvi–xxvii; and protests, 73–75
poor, worthy vs. unworthy, 206–7
Þorsteinsson, Þorvaldur, 99–100
Portes, Richard, xxii; on banking system, 56–57
postmodernism, xx, 229–32
Pots and Pans Revolution, xix, 84
poverty, xiv, 138, 204; and material aid charities, 203, 205–6
privatization, xiii, xxi, xl; of banking system, 29–31, 38–39, 43, 51; of fisheries, xvi, 113–14, 153, 159
Progressive Party, xxvii, 51, 218
Promote Iceland (Íslandsstofa), 98, 101–3
property, xxvi; common vs. individual, 129–30, 132, 135(n17); fish stock, 153, 154, 159
Proppé, Óttarr, 83, 88
protests, 63, 152; and economic crises, 64–65; participation in, 67–75; public, xix, 65–66
Proust, Marcel, 123
public: image of, 97–98; mobilization of, 67–76; protests, xix, 63, 64, 65–66; role of, 57–59
Public Image Committee, 97–98